Consumer behaviour

Consumer behaviour

Edited by

Michael Cant
Annekie Brink
Sanjana Brijball

JUTA
AND COMPANY LTD

Consumer Behaviour
First published 2006 by Juta & Co.
Mercury Crescent
Wetton, 7780
Cape Town, South Africa

Reprinted 2006
Reprinted 2007
Reprinted 2008
Reprinted January 2009
Reprinted November 2009

ISBN 978-0-70217-125-3

Typeset in 10/13 Berkley Oldstyle Book and 9/13 Frutiger 45 Light

Project Manager: Sarah O'Neill
Editor: Danya Ristić
Indexer: Jan Schaafsma
Typesetter: MckoreGraphics, 9 Dennelaan, Panorama
Cover designer: Patricia Lynch-Blom
Printed and bound by Mills Litho, Maitland, Cape Town, South Africa

Contents

About the editors

Editors

Prof. Sanjana Brijball Parumasur (Chapters 12 and 15) is Associate Professor: Programme in Human Resources Management in the School of Management Studies, University of KwaZulu-Natal, Westville Campus. She is on the Editorial Board of the International Retail and Marketing Review and reviews manuscripts for the South African Journal of Industrial Psychology. Her publications have predominantly been in the areas of cognitive dissonance and brand loyalty.

Prof. Annekie Brink (Chapters 7, 8, 9 and 16) lectures in the Department of Marketing and Retail Management in the School of Management Sciences at Unisa. She developed the first course in Customer Relationship Management (CRM) offered at a South African University and is co-editor of the first comprehensive CRM textbook in South Africa.

Prof. Mike Cant (Chapters 1 and 10) is Head of the Department of Marketing and Retail Management in the School of Management Sciences at Unisa. He is also the incumbent of the Chair in Retailing, sponsored by MassMart. He is co-editor of the South African journal, the International Retail and Marketing Review, and regularly does consulting for small and medium enterprises.

Contributors

Neels Bothma (Chapter 17) lectures in the Department of Marketing and Retail Management in the School of Management Sciences at Unisa.

Prof. Chris Jooste (Chapter 14) is chair and co-head of the Department of Marketing Management at the University of Johannesburg.

Prof. Pierre Joubert (Chapters 4 and 13) lectures in the Department of Industrial and Organisational Psychology in the School of Management Sciences at Unisa.

Ricardo Machado (Chapter 6) lectures in the Department of Marketing and Retail Management in the School of Management Sciences at Unisa.

Laureane Schoeman (Chapters 3 and 11) lectures in the Department of Marketing Management at the University of Johannesburg.

Prof. Johan Strydom (Chapters 2 and 5) lectures in the Department of Business Management in the School of Management Sciences at Unisa.

Preface

Consumer behaviour is a young discipline; the first textbooks in the field were written only in the 1960s. The marketing concept, which was enunciated in the 1950s, highlighted the importance of the study of consumer behaviour. As stated by Theodore Levitt, the marketing concept embodies 'the view that an industry is a customer–satisfying process, not a goods-producing process. An industry begins with the customer and his needs, not with a patent, a raw material, or a selling skill'. Once it was understood that an organisation can exist only as long as it fulfills its customers' needs and wants, the study of the consumer became an essential part of doing business.

The study of consumer behaviour can be fascinating: not only does it have critical implications for areas such as marketing, public policy and ethics – issues that affect business decisions – it also helps us learn about ourselves; why we buy certain things, why we use them in a certain way and how we get rid of them.

As true believers in the marketing concept, we have tried our best to meet the needs of our consumers – mainly students – of consumer behaviour, by providing a text that is highly readable and that clearly explains the relevant concepts upon which the discipline of consumer behaviour is based.

Most students in consumer behaviour courses aspire to careers in marketing management or advertising. They hope to acquire knowledge and skills that will be useful to them in these careers. The primary purpose of this text is therefore to provide the student with a usable, managerial understanding of consumer behaviour. Many of the fundamental concepts in marketing are based on the practitioner's ability to know people. If we cannot identify their needs, how can we satisfy those needs? The simple premise is that if consumer needs are to drive marketing strategies; a better understanding of these needs should be the foundation for strategy development.

Given the fact that students enjoy seeing how the concepts in consumer behaviour can apply to business practice, a major objective of the book is to provide a very practical orientation. Throughout the text, we present examples – South African ones where possible – that illustrate the objectives of specific marketing activities. By studying these examples and principles on which they are based, students can develop the ability to discern the underlying logic of marketing activities encountered daily. We believe that students can learn best when they see the big picture – when they understand what concepts mean, how they are used in business practice and how they relate to one another.

Consumer primacy is the principle on which the entire field of marketing rests. This principle insists that the consumer should be at the centre of the marketing effort. As Peter Drucker, the well-known management scholar has stated, 'Marketing is the whole business seen from the point of view of its final result, that is, from the customer's point of view'. For any company to be successful, its managers must perceive that 'the consumer is King' or as Pick 'n Pay proclaimed many years ago in its slogan 'The customer is Queen,' because at that time the woman usually did the shopping.

We thank all those who have contributed to Consumer Behaviour, with a special thank you to Ms E M Coetzee.

The Editors

1 Introduction to consumer behaviour

Learning Outcomes

After studying this chapter, you should be able to:

○ define what is meant by customer behaviour

○ explain the three different roles of customers

○ explain the importance of customer behaviour by highlighting the reasons for studying customer behaviour

○ explain and illustrate the applications of customer behaviour

○ discuss the role of customer behaviour in marketing strategy

○ discuss the nature of customer behaviour in terms of the model of customer behaviour.

1.1 Introduction

A basic premise of marketing is that through understanding customers and their purchasing habits, marketers can design an effective offering to help them achieve their objectives. Marketing serves as the link between the customer and the organisation and marketers therefore need to be able to answer basic questions regarding the market, such as who the customers are and why they buy.[1]

Customer behaviour entails the behaviour that customers display in searching for, purchasing, using, evaluating and disposing of products and services that they expect will satisfy their needs.[2] The behaviour of customers plays – and will continue to play – a decisive role in the operations of business organisations all over the world. All businesses that want to be successful in the long term should study customer behaviour – particularly customer *buying* behaviour – in order to understand it as fully as possible. Marketers need to know what their customers need and want. They also need to know how their customers make their decisions about buying and using products.

In this chapter, we focus on what customer behaviour is, the various customer types and their roles, the importance to business management of customer behaviour, the applications of customer behaviour, and the role of customer behaviour in the marketing strategy. We conclude the chapter by presenting the model of customer behaviour that we use in this book.

1.2 Defining customer behaviour

Customer behaviour concerns all the activities and influences that occur before, during and after the purchase itself. Many definitions of this process exist, the most useful one being the one proposed by Hawkins et al.,[4] which defines the study of customer behaviour as 'the study of individuals, groups, or organisations and the processes they use to select, secure, use, and dispose of products, services, experiences, or ideas to satisfy needs and the impacts that these processes have on the consumer and society'. This definition implies that there are indirect influences on consumer decisions, and that the decisions involve more than the buyer and the seller. Furthermore, it implies that when we use the term 'customers', we are referring not only to individual purchasers, but also to families, groups and organisations.

Sheth et al.[5] define customer behaviour as 'the mental and physical activities undertaken by household and business customers that result in decisions and actions to pay for, purchase, and use products and services'. This definition encompasses a variety of activities that people carry out and a number of roles that they play. Illustrated in Figure 1.1, these factors include the types of customers, customer roles, and customers' mental and physical activities. The concept of customer behaviour implied here goes beyond marketers' more traditional focus on consumer behaviour (see below).

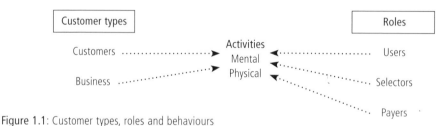

Figure 1.1: Customer types, roles and behaviours

1.2.1 Types of customers[6]

Here we distinguish between consumption by individuals in households and in business. In general, a customer is a person or an organisational unit that plays a role in the completion of a transaction with the marketer or other entity. An organisation's customers may be part of a household or may act as representatives of that organisation. Thus, Sheth et al.'s definition covers the behaviours of customers in both the household and the business markets. Conventionally, the term 'consumer' has referred to household markets only. The corresponding term for the business market has been 'customer'. In this book, we use the term 'customer' to refer to *both* markets.

However, there is a distinction between **consumer** and **business buying behaviour**, in which the latter refers to organisational purchases done for one of the following reasons:

❍ To manufacture other products and services, for example raw materials.
❍ To resell to other organisational buyers or consumers, for example retailers and wholesalers.

◯ To conduct the organisation's operations, for example production of office equipment and stationery.

Unique characteristics of business buying behaviour distinguish it from individual consumer buying, and this type of behaviour is therefore not referred to when the term 'customer behaviour' is used.[7]

The use of the term 'consumer' to refer to the household market is more common in textbooks than in practice. For example, retail stores such as Edgars, Woolworths and Game generally refer to their shoppers as 'customers', not 'consumers'. Similarly, utility companies such as Telkom and Eskom also refer to the people and organisations that use their services as 'customers', as do financial companies such as banks; service companies such as garden services, dry cleaners, etc.; or even personal service providers such as fortune tellers, massage therapists, boutiques, etc. Professional service providers refer to individuals in household markets as 'clients', such as lawyers, estate agents, tax advisors, etc.; and/or by their more context-specific roles, for example doctors call them 'clients', educators call them 'learners' and fund-raisers call them 'donors'. Only manufacturers who do not routinely deal with the end users of a product refer to these household end users as 'consumers', such as Johnson & Johnson and Unilever. To overcome this divergence of terms, we use the term 'customer' all-inclusively.

Given this scenario, it is important that we look at the various roles customers play.

1.2.2 The three roles of customers[8]

Generally, there are three roles which the customer can fulfil in any transaction in the marketplace. These roles include:
1. selecting or choosing a product
2. paying for it
3. using or consuming it.

This implies that a customer can be a selector of a product, or a payer or a user, or all three. The **user** is the person who actually consumes or uses the product, or who receives the benefits of the service. The **payer** or **buyer** is the person who actually finances or pays for the purchase, while the **selector** is the person who participates in the procurement of the product from the marketplace. Each of these roles may be carried out by one person or an organisational unit, such as a department, or by different people or departments.

The roles are more easily clarified by examples. From the household perspective, often both the husband and the wife work, resulting in many households using their housekeepers to do the grocery shopping for the family. The husband and wife pay for the groceries, but they leave the final selection of items and brands up to the housekeeper, who in any case is responsible for the cooking and cleaning chores in the household. From a business perspective, a person, such as a secretary, using a computer system is classified as a user, but he or she may not be the person who actually buys or pays for the computer – it may be bought from departmental funds by a central buying section.

Therefore, we need to consider not only the behaviour of end users, but also that of payers and selectors. As we have seen, the person who pays for the product or service is not always the one who is going to use it, and neither is the person who uses it always the person who selects it. Yet any one of the three customer roles makes a person a customer.

Conflict often arises between these three roles. For example, your parents' (the payers) decision to buy a small car for you (the user) to use at university may be a source of conflict within your family. As they are paying for the car, your parents may have decided that it is financially wise to choose a car that is economical to run, thus making it less of a strain on your student budget, whereas you may prefer to have a flashier car to impress your friends, regardless of its running costs. Similarly, if your employer is paying for your car, cost considerations might lead him or her as the payer to restrict your options as the user.

1.2.3 Mental and physical activities

The definition of customer behaviour refers to both mental and physical activities, as reflected in Figure 1.1 on page 2. **Physical activities** are those actions taken by customers such as visiting a store, discussing the product with a salesperson, comparing information in brochures and buying the product. **Mental activities** take place when customers assess how well products will satisfy their needs, taking into account their knowledge of the brands, their experience with the products, and any other opinions or views they have about the products.

Various individual and group factors influence a customer's decision-making process. These factors also influence the final choice of market offering of the customer.[9] The factors are illustrated in Figure 1.2.

It is clear that there are various factors influencing a customer behaviour, and each customer's decision-making process is unique. Consumer motivation can be described as

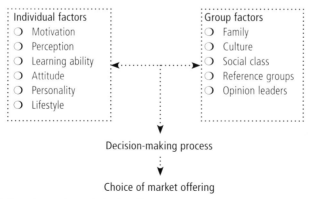

Figure 1.2: Factors influencing customer behaviour[10]

the needs, wants, drives, and desires of an **individual** that lead him or her toward the purchase of products or ideas. According to the American Marketing Association (AMA), these motivations can be physiological, psychological or environmentally driven.[11] More simply put, **motivation** is the driving force within individuals that pushes them to action. **Perception** in turn refers to the entire process through which an individual becomes aware of his or her environment and interprets it in such a way that it will fit into his or her frame of reference.

Learning can be used by marketers who want customers to learn about their particular product. **Learning** describes the process by which individuals acquire the purchase and consumption knowledge, as well as the experience, that they apply to future-related behaviour. **Customer attitude** can be defined as the learned predisposition to behave in a consistently favourable or unfavourable way toward market-related objects, events or situations. **Personality** and **lifestyle** are also individual factors. The former refers to a customer's psychological characteristics that both determine and reflect how he or she responds to his or her environment, while the latter refers to the customer's way of living.[12]

Group factors which influence customer behaviour include family, which consists of the customer's nuclear family, that is, husband, wife and children, and extended family, which includes grandparents and other relatives.[13] **Culture**, according to the AMA, refers to the 'institutionalised ways or modes of appropriate behaviour. It is the modal or distinctive patterns of behaviour of a people including implicit cultural beliefs, norms, values, and premises that govern conduct. It includes shared superstitions, myths, folkways, mores, and behaviour patterns that are rewarded or punished'.[14]

A customer's **social class** is a useful indication of the type of product that the customers would buy. A social class is a group of customers that enjoy more or less the same prestige and status in society. Another group influencing variable is the **customer reference group**, which involves one or more people that the customer uses as his or her basis for comparison or 'point of reference' in forming responses and performing behaviours. When the reference group consists of only one person who influences the customer's purchasing decisions, that person is called an '**opinion leader**'.[15]

As customer behaviour is influenced by, and in turn influences, the abovementioned factors, which all form a critical part of our everyday existence, the importance of our understanding thereof becomes clear.

1.3 The importance of customer behaviour

The relevance and importance of studying customer behaviour is aptly summarised by Schiffman and Kanuk,[16] who state that the study of customer behaviour is 'the study of how individuals and businesses make decisions to spend their available resources (time, money, effort) on consumption-related items. It includes the study of what they buy, why they buy it, when they buy it, where they buy it, how often they buy it, and how often they use it'.

It is becoming apparent that, increasingly, businesses are growing aware of and recognising the importance of understanding customer behaviour and the vital role it plays in their success. Now more than ever, owing to the increase in competition, as well as the effects of numerous internal and external forces, understanding their customers will play a cardinal role in the success and survival of organisations.[17]

By learning more about how customers behave, organisations gain a better understanding of why customers buy what they buy or, more generally, why they respond to marketing stimuli as they do. An understanding of this behaviour makes it possible for organisations to develop marketing communications, such as advertisements, brochures, etc., that are focused on the way customers react.

> If a business sells cameras, it needs to know what types of cameras customers buy (e.g. 35 mm instant video digital); what brand (e.g. Olympic, Kodak, Minolta, Sony); why they buy these cameras (e.g. for professional reasons, for entertainment, for household use); where they buy them (e.g. department store, speciality store, discount store, supermarket); how often they use them (e.g. daily, weekly, occasionally, only on holiday); and how often they buy them (e.g. once in a lifetime, yearly, irregularly).

Organisations must deliver long-term customer value if they are to survive and thrive. They can achieve this only if they retain customers by satisfying the customers' needs, adopting the marketing concept, and becoming focused on the customer. These are the basic three reasons for understanding customer behaviour, and they are illustrated in Figure 1.3.

Figure 1.3: The reasons for understanding customer behaviour[18]

We now discuss these concepts briefly.[19]

1.3.1 Customer satisfaction and customer retention

The cost of organising and recruiting new customers is far greater than the cost associated with keeping existing customers. There has been a growth in customer loyalty schemes in the past few years as businesses have recognised the advantages of retaining customers.[20] Understanding customer behaviour, therefore, is intricately linked to understanding the needs and wants of customers. Any profit-oriented organisation must satisfy the needs and wants of its customers. Today, it is no longer sufficient for a business to simply satisfy a customer during a single transaction, rather, it must try to retain the customer for life, that is, achieve customer retention.

Thus the focus of marketing has shifted from the short-term transactional view of customers to seeing customers as a long-term income stream. Organisations that meet or exceed customers' expectations of service, quality, price and delivery achieve such lucrative relationships.[21]

Companies have to make money if they are to survive, and they can achieve this only if they satisfy their customers. Businesses are supported by society because they serve society's members by catering to their needs and, thus, satisfying them. Should enough customers be unhappy with a business's product or service, they will stop buying from that business. Moreover, society at large will turn against the business and penalise it by refusing to deal with it – to the point that it goes out of business.[22]

The realisation that long-term survival is possible only if customer satisfaction is achieved has led companies and their employees to change the ways in which they treat customers. Employees are told that customer satisfaction is the bottom line – if these needs are not satisfied, the long-term survival and success of the company may come under pressure. It is becoming increasingly clear that the key to business success is in building relationships between brands and customers that will last a lifetime, that is, in retaining customers. Marketers who believe in relationship marketing are making it company policy to interact with customers on a regular basis and encourage them to maintain a bond with the company over a long period of time.[23]

1.3.2 The marketing concept[24]

Marketing maturity tends to be a gradual development process and, usually, firms that have reached full marketing orientation have done so by evolving through secondary and timely steps of development.[25] Four competing orientations have strongly influenced business marketing activities over the years. We now explore these orientations.

Production orientation
In the nineteenth and most of the twentieth century, the primary purpose of business was production. Production managers were key to organisations and the understanding of customer requirements was of secondary importance.[26] Production orientation therefore focused on the internal capabilities of the business rather than on the desires and needs of the marketplace. Such an orientation meant that management assessed its resources and asked questions such as 'What can we do best?', 'What can our engineers design?' and 'What is easy to produce, given our equipment?' In the case of a service organisation, managers asked, 'What services are most convenient for the business to offer?' and 'Where do our talents lie?'

Ford motor company's classic statement 'You can have any colour you want, as long as it is black!' is a prime example of a production orientation.[27] The major shortcoming lay in the fact that the orientation did not consider whether the goods and services that the business produced met the needs of the marketplace.

Sales orientation

It was simply not enough to produce goods as efficiently as possible in an increasingly competitive environment. Demand needed to be created through the art of persuasion using sales techniques.[28] A sales orientation was based on the premise that people would buy more products and services if aggressive sales techniques were used, and that high sales resulted in high profits. Not only were sales to the final buyer emphasised, but intermediaries were also encouraged to 'push' (promote) a manufacturer's products more aggressively. To sales-oriented businesses, marketing simply meant selling.

The major shortcoming of a sales orientation was a lack of understanding of the needs and wants of the marketplace. Sales-oriented companies often found that, despite the quality of their products and their sales force, they could not convince people to buy products or services that they neither wanted nor needed.

Marketing orientation

Where the selling concept focused on the needs of the sellers, and on existing products, the marketing concept focused on the needs of the buyers. The marketing concept was based on the premise that a marketer should make what it could sell, and not sell what it could make.[29] Companies that had progressed to perceiving the satisfaction of customer needs as their top priority exhibited a marketing orientation. Through focusing on the satisfaction of customer needs and wants, companies could ensure that profits from an increase in sales followed.[30]

It was only after World War II that a change in management's approach to the market occurred. The production plants producing war material could now be used to satisfy the demand for all sorts of products for normal consumption. Because of the widening gap between the producer and the customer, management needed reliable information on how best to satisfy customer needs. A change from sales-oriented management to marketing-oriented management resulted in an emphasis not only on the sales message and the price but also on the quality of products, the packaging, the methods of distribution and the necessity of providing information through advertising. Customers also developed more sophisticated needs and were financially in a better position to satisfy them. There was a large variety of competing products from which they could choose. This led management to realise the importance of the marketing function. Production could begin only after management had obtained market information on what customers wanted, how much they were willing to pay, and how they could best be reached by means of advertisements, sales promotion methods, publicity and personal selling.

A marketing orientation, which is the foundation of contemporary marketing philosophy, is therefore based on an understanding that a sale depends not on an aggressive sales force but rather on customers' decisions to buy a product. What a business thinks it produces is not of primary importance to its success. Instead, what customers think they are buying – that is, **perceived value** – defines a business. Perceived value also determines a business's products and its potential to prosper. To marketing-oriented firms, marketing means building long-term relationships with customers. This orientation has led to what is commonly called the **'pure marketing concept'**.

The marketing concept can be regarded as an ethical code or philosophy according to which the marketing task is performed. It serves as a guideline for management decision-making about an organisation's entire activities.

The essence of the marketing concept lies in three principles:

1. **Consumer orientation**: This principle holds that all marketing actions should be aimed at satisfying consumer needs, demands and preferences. However, this should be carefully balanced with organisational resources. Customer needs therefore should not be satisfied to the extent that the organisation no longer makes a profit.

2. **Profit orientation**: The marketing concept views customer orientation as a means of achieving the goals of the business.[31] In the free-market system, achieving profitability is vital, as maximising profitability is the primary objective of a business and can be achieved only with due consideration of customer needs. This overriding objective is usually expressed in quantitative terms. For example, a business can aim at attaining a rate of return on total assets of 25% on investment, and can regard this figure as the maximum profitability that can be achieved in a specific time and under specific conditions.

3. **Organisational integration**: This is also known as a 'systems orientation', in which the organisation (or system) is seen as an integrated whole or a group of units that work together to achieve a joint objective.[32] This is an important principle of the marketing concept and entails all departments in the business working together to achieve the successful marketing of the business's market offering – that is, its products or services. All the divisions in the marketing department also direct their activities and decisions towards achieving a situation in which the target market prefers the business's market offering to that of the competitors. This implies that all business activities should be targeted towards the satisfaction of customer needs and wants.[33]

Societal marketing orientation

Societal marketing orientation questions whether the pure marketing concept as it stands is adequate in an age of environmental problems, resource shortages, rapid population growth, worldwide economic problems and neglected social services. It also asks if the company that senses, serves and satisfies individual wants is always doing what is best for customers and society in the long run. According to the societal marketing concept, the pure marketing concept overlooks possible conflicts between customer short-term wants and customer long-term welfare.

These concerns and conflicts have led to the societal marketing concept. This concept requires marketers to balance these three considerations in setting their marketing policies: **company profits**, **customer wants** and **society's interests**. Businesses often demonstrate social responsibility through sponsoring community projects and employee programmes like health programmes and care centres for babies, and through abstaining from any action that is in conflict with society's current norms and moral and ethical standards.[34]

Today, marketers are looking a little further and aim to forge long-term relationships with certain groups – customers, shareholders, and so on. This process is called 'relationship marketing', and we discuss it in Chapter 16.

1.3.3 Customer focus[35]

Organisations that focus on the needs of customers ensure that the needs of the society as a whole are served better. By listening to customers, and paying attention to how they behave, organisations are in a more suitable position to meet their customers' needs.

Customers express their support for a company by buying, and continuing to buy, its products. Generally, this loyalty depends on the perceived value of the products to the customer. A product will therefore sell well only if it meets the customers' needs, and the customers exercise their 'choice' by patronising the marketer that they believe responds best to those needs.

How this knowledge of customers is applied is highly relevant and valuable to a business, and we discuss this application in the next section.

1.4 The applications of knowledge of customer behaviour[36]

Customer behaviour plays an important role in aspects such as marketing strategy, social marketing and the process of marketers becoming better informed individuals. We now explore each of these aspects.

1.4.1 Marketing strategy

Any marketing strategy, along with the tactics used in its implementation, is based on explicit and implicit beliefs about customer behaviour. Decisions based on assumptions and sound theory, as well as on the results of pertinent and relevant market research, are more likely to be successful than would be decisions based on intuition alone. Therefore, a company that knows a great deal about the behaviour of its customers has a significant advantage over its competitors. Understanding the behaviour of customers can reduce the marketers' chances of making the wrong decision, as in the example below.

> BIC Corp introduced a small $5 bottle of perfume to be sold in supermarkets and drugstore chains where it had tremendous distribution strength. The perfume was to be easy and convenient to buy and use. However, as one expert said in examining the $11 million loss project: 'Fragrance is an emotional sell, not convenience or utility. The BIC package wasn't feminine. It looked like a cigarette lighter.'[37]

Figure 1.4: The marketing strategy process[38]

Customer behaviour therefore affects the strategic situation and strategy selection of the organisation. The marketing strategy process is depicted in Figure 1.4.

We intend this book to help you to obtain a practical understanding of customer behaviour. We base this intention on the belief that in order to be a more effective marketing manager, it is essential for you to understand the behaviour of customers.

1.4.2 Social marketing[39]

Social marketing is the application of marketing strategies and tactics to alter, influence or create organisational behaviours that have a positive effect on the targeted individuals and/or society as a whole. In the past, this type of marketing has been used in various ways:
○ To create awareness about specific social issues, such as the harmful effects of drugs, alcohol and smoking.
○ To increase the percentage of children receiving vaccinations.
○ To encourage environmentally sound behaviour, such as recycling.
○ To reduce behaviours potentially leading to Aids infection.
○ To enhance support of charities, and many other important causes.

Just as an effective marketing strategy is based on a sound knowledge of customer behaviour, a successful social marketing strategy requires a sound understanding of the behaviour of those targeted by the strategy. Consider the following example:

Tobacco companies spend almost $5 billion a year on advertising and promotions in the United States. While they claim they do not target children, children are exposed to many of the ads and appear to be influenced by them. The federal government, many state governments, the Centers for Disease Control and Prevention, and other organizations have prepared public service ads, brochures, and school programs designed to discourage kids from smoking. Smoking rates among teenagers were 35 percent lower in communities where the campaign was shown than in similar communities without the campaign.

Because researchers familiarised themselves with the behaviour of teenagers, they were in a position to stress the negative social consequences rather than the health issue.

1.4.3 Becoming better-informed individuals

By knowing how customers behave, we can increase our understanding of ourselves and our environment. Organisations all over the world are spending millions of rands firstly to gain an understanding of customers, and secondly to try to influence society as a whole, and certain groups of people in particular, to buy their products. This occurs in advertisements, product packaging, product features, sales themes and store environments. It also occurs in the content of many television shows, and in the products used in movies – such as the cars used in the James Bond movies.

Given this situation, it is important that customers understand the strategies and tactics that companies are using to influence them in order for them to make properly informed decisions about what they buy instead of being unwitting 'victims'. Similarly, as potential marketers ourselves we should all understand the customer behaviour on which these strategies and tactics are based, so that we can set appropriate limits on them when necessary.

Because virtually all the applications of customer behaviour focus on the development, regulation or effects of marketing strategy, we now examine marketing strategy in more detail.

1.5 The role of customer behaviour in marketing strategy[40]

As we have seen, companies fight for the patronage of customers. Even though their products may be virtually the same, organisations try to use their understanding of customers' buying motives to offer these customers better value. In this way, each organisation attempts to differentiate itself from its competitors, based on some benefit that its products or operations offer to its customers. In order for this benefit to be meaningful, the customer must perceive it to be meaningful. This involves the concept of customer value.

We can define **customer value** as the difference between all the benefits derived from a product and all the costs of acquiring those benefits. For example, owning a laptop computer can provide you with a number of benefits, including efficiency, flexibility, image, status and even social acceptance. However, to secure these benefits, you must pay for the computer, insurance and security, and you must risk theft and damage that results from computer viruses. The difference between the total benefits and the total costs makes up customer value.

This can be applied to all products on the market. Fundamentally, a company tries to convince its customers that they will receive superior value from its products. We deal with customer value further in Chapter 2.

In order to offer superior value to its customers, a company should react more effectively and appropriately to their needs, either real or anticipated, than does its competitors. As Figure 1.5 on the next page indicates, an understanding of customer behaviour is the basis for formulating a marketing strategy that allows the company

Figure 1.5: Marketing strategy and customer behaviour

to react better to customer needs. The reaction of customers to the chosen marketing strategy will determine the organisation's success or failure.

Marketing strategy, as described in Figure 1.5, is fairly straightforward. We work from the bottom upwards. The strategy begins by analysing the market that the organisation is considering entering. This requires a detailed analysis of the organisation's capabilities, the strengths and weaknesses of competitors, the economic and technological forces affecting the market, and the current and potential customers in the market. Based on this analysis, the organisation identifies homogeneous groups or segments – individuals, companies, etc. – on which to focus in a process known as '**market segmentation**'. The segments are described in terms of demographic, psychographic and geographic aspects. One or more of these segments is selected as the target market, based on the organisation's capabilities relative to those of the competition.

The next step is to formulate the actual marketing strategy aimed at penetrating the selected segment(s). As we have seen, the main aim of such a strategy is to provide the customer with more value than the competitors can do, and in the process making a profit for the company. A company formulates its marketing strategy in terms of the **marketing mix**, which involves combining the 4 Ps, namely, the **product** features, the **prices** to be charged, the **promotion** of the product and making it available to customers in the **place** where they want it, that is, distributing the product in such a way that customers receive superior value. This combination is described as the '**total product**'.

The way the product is offered makes the customers form an image of the product.

This image is manifested in the sales of the product that result, which is the customers' way of expressing their satisfaction (high sales) or dissatisfaction (low sales) with the product that the company is offering. Marketers try to create satisfied customers rather than mere sales because satisfied customers are more profitable in the long run – they come back and buy more. The impact on the customer is the payment of money, a changed or confirmed opinion, and need satisfaction, among others. Even for society as a whole this has an impact, as the cumulative effect of the marketing process affects economic growth, pollution, social problems and social benefits.

It should be clear that whatever the reactions of customers, the company needs to analyse these reactions and take the necessary corrective steps to ensure that their product begins to sell successfully. Failure to do this will result in the collapse of the company. Customers change their minds and behaviour all the time; companies should identify these changes and adapt their marketing strategy to accommodate those that the company regards as significant.

1.6 The components of market analysis

Market analysis requires a thorough understanding of the customers, the organisation's capabilities, the capabilities of current and future competitors, the consumption process of potential customers, and the environment in which these elements interact.

1.6.1 The customers

As we have seen, in order for a company to be able to anticipate and react to the needs and wants of its customers, it must understand their behaviour. Market research forms the basis for gaining such an understanding. Customer value analysis is one form of research that companies can conduct. This entails the use of a customer information database to enable the organisation to project the future of customers on the basis of their purchase histories.[41] This is a complex process which must be carried out properly if it is to be successful. Specifically, marketers need to understand the behavioural principles that guide consumption behaviours – principles which we cover in depth in this book.

1.6.2 The organisation

An organisation can be defined as a 'consciously coordinated social unit, composed of two or more people, that functions on a relatively continuous basis to achieve a common goal or set of goals'.[42] And organisational behaviour in turn investigates the impact that individuals, groups and structure have on behaviour within organisations.

Part of an organisation's success depends on its understanding of its capabilities. A company must be fully cognisant of its ability to meet customer needs – if it does not, it may overextend itself or misdirect its efforts. This requires an objective evaluation of finances, managerial skills, production capabilities, technological sophistication, marketing skills, and so on. Only if marketers know where they are, and what their strengths and weaknesses are, will they be able to take decisions about the company's future actions. A company that overestimates its strengths may find itself in serious difficulties. For example, a company that does well in the industrial market might experience problems if it enters the household market without having acquired the necessary knowledge of that market.

1.6.3 The competitors

We can define competition as a type of relationship in which two or more firms are trying to achieve the same goals and penetrate the same markets with broadly similar product offers.[43] Owing to improved technology, globalisation and the speed with which developments are taking place, a drastic increase in competition in the market has occurred where organisations compete not only on a local or national scale but also on a global scale. Moreover, the differences between competitors are shrinking in terms of product quality, and it is therefore much more difficult for companies consistently to do a better job of meeting customer needs than the competition without a thorough understanding of the competition's capabilities and strategies, as well as the behaviour of customers. This means that a company must understand its competitors *as well as it understand itself*.

1.6.4 The environment

The marketing environment comprises all the variables that directly or indirectly influence marketing activities.[44] The environment in which a company operates affects not only the company itself but also its customers and competitors. For example, concern about the ozone layer and safety has led many companies seeking to change the ingredients they use in their products. Pressure from organisations such as Greenpeace have an effect on companies' operations, for example the banning of the use of thin plastic bags by the South African government from 2003 onwards.

It is therefore obvious that organisations cannot develop a sound marketing strategy without anticipating the conditions under which that strategy will be implemented. Failure to do so, and to make provision for eventualities, can result in the failure of the marketing strategy.

1.7 Market segmentation[45]

Essentially, a market segment is part of a larger market, and is made up of individuals or groups with similar needs and wants. These people form a homogeneous group that is large enough for the company to supply with goods and/or services and make a profit.

Arguably, the most important marketing decision a company makes is the selection of one or more market segments on which to focus. Selecting the wrong market segment can have serious consequences. Since a market segment has unique needs, the company that develops a total product focused solely on the needs of that segment should be able to meet the segment's needs better than a company whose product or service attempts to meet the needs of the total market or a wide number of segments.[46]

For a market segment to be attractive to a company, it must be large enough in either numbers or turnover to be served profitably. Historically, the smaller the segment, the more it cost to serve it, for example a tailor-made suit cost more than a mass-produced suit. However, more and more companies find it profitable to focus on niche, or smaller, markets when developing their products.

To ensure its continuity and growth, an organisation is dependent on, among others, customers and the satisfaction of their needs. Although such satisfaction is not a goal in itself, it enables the organisation to achieve its goals. Therefore, the greater the need satisfaction customers can derive from an organisation's products, the easier it becomes for the organisation to achieve its goals. To achieve maximum customer satisfaction, marketers thus divide the different markets into fairly homogeneous subsets of customers in the process that is referred to as 'market segmentation'. Each segment of the market, it is assumed, will have similar needs, and will respond in a similar way to the market offering and strategy. We can divide the market for hotels, for example, into the following subsegments: business travellers, sports participants, conference delegates, tourists, local travellers, overseas travellers, etc. Each of these segments has different characteristics and needs with regard to the accommodation, facilities and services that it requires. It follows that no single hotel can cater for every unique need of all these market segments.[47]

The organisation must decide next which market segment's (or segments') needs it can satisfy best. The Protea Hof hotel in Pretoria, situated in the city centre, for example, decided to cater primarily for the needs of business travellers, and has therefore developed its product offering around their needs. The process of making this decision is referred to as **'market targeting'**.[48]

Once it has chosen the target market segment, the organisation must decide how to compete effectively in this market. It must decide on the competitive advantage that it will aim to achieve. This is known as **'positioning'**. The Protea Hof hotel can decide to compete on the basis of a lower price (in comparison to its competitors) or of ambience and prestige, which would be reflected by the quality of the interior of the hotel, the professional service of its employees and the availability of facilities and services required by business travellers, such as internet access, fax machines, photocopiers, secretarial services and chauffeurs. Alternately, its management may decide to compete on the basis of the hotel's superior location and accessibility to most government departments situated in Pretoria.

Market segmentation offers the following benefits to marketers:[49]

❍ It forces marketers to *focus on customer needs*. In a segmented market, the marketer can fully appreciate the differences in customer needs and respond accordingly. A greater degree of customer satisfaction can be achieved if the market offering is developed around customer needs, demands and preferences.

❍ Segmentation leads to the *identification of new marketing opportunities* if research reveals a previously unexplored segment. Without proper segmentation, such a market segment may remain untapped for years.
❍ Market segmentation *provides guidelines* for the development of separate market offerings and strategies for the various market segments.
❍ Segmentation can facilitate the *appropriate allocation of marketing resources*. A large, growing market segment may be allocated a greater proportion of the marketing budget, while a shrinking one may be scaled down or eventually abandoned if it becomes unattractive.

However, market segmentation also has the following disadvantages, which marketers must consider:
❍ The development and marketing of separate models and market offerings is extremely *expensive*. One standardised model is much cheaper to manufacture and to market.
❍ *Limited market coverage* is achieved, since marketing strategies would be directed at specific market segments only.
❍ Excessive differentiation of the basic product may eventually lead to a proliferation of models and variations, and finally to *cannibalisation*, that is, when one product takes away market share from another product developed by the same enterprise.

Market segmentation must enhance customer satisfaction and the profitability of share-holders. For example, to divide the market for small delivery vehicles into segments like Western Cape farmers and KwaZulu-Natal farmers would make little marketing or business sense. In this case, geographic location is irrelevant, since the requirements of the farmers remain the same regardless of location. However, geographic location would be highly effective as a means of segmenting the market for insecticides, since farmers in the Western Cape and KwaZulu-Natal have to deal with different types of pests.
For market segmentation to be effective, it must meet the following criteria:
❍ It must be **measurable**. The size, buying power, potential profit and profile of the segment must be measurable. Failing this, a company would find it extremely difficult to compare one segment with others, or to properly assess its appeal.
❍ It must be **large enough**. Pursuing a market segment that is too small is not profitable. A segment must be the largest homogeneous group of people worth exploiting with a tailored market offering and marketing strategy. Although South Africa contains a large variety of cultures, some of them, such as the Chinese community, may be so small that they do not warrant special attention by marketers.
❍ It must be **accessible**. Marketers must be able to reach the market segment with their market offering and strategy. How is it possible, for example, to reach rural people if they cannot read or do not have a radio to listen to? Such a segment

is largely inaccessible to marketers who use print or the radio to advertise their products.

○ It must be **actionable**. A company must be able to develop separate market offerings for different market segments. Smaller enterprises are often unable to do this, even if they realise that there are distinct differences between various segments.

○ It must be **differentiable**. Different market segments must exhibit heterogeneous needs. In other words, people in different segments must have different needs, demands and desires. People in the same segment, by contrast, must exhibit similar characteristics and needs. Marketers should also be able to distinguish the segments from each other with ease.

Once marketing management is satisfied that a specific segment conforms to these conditions, it can consider the segment as a possible target market. It can use different variables to segment a market. These variables can generally be classified according to geographic, demographic, psychographic and behaviouristic bases, which we discuss in more detail in Chapter 11.

1.8 Marketing strategy[50]

A company needs to formulate a marketing strategy for each target market that it has selected. It needs to select the market segments using the criterion of its ability to offer superior value to them.

In order to do this, the company must arrange the four Ps – product, price, distribution and communication elements – in such a way that it best satisfies the needs of the market as well as its objectives. As we have seen, the combination of the four Ps is called the 'marketing mix'. It is this combination that meets customer needs and provides customer value. We now briefly discuss each component.

1.8.1 The product

A company fulfils a dual purpose as a business entity through, on the one hand, existing to satisfy customer needs and, on the other hand, existing to make a profit.

In a narrow sense, a product is a set of basic attributes, or qualities, assembled in an identifiable form. In a broader sense, a product is a set of tangible and intangible attributes which may include packaging, colour, price, quality and brand, as well as the seller's services and reputation. In essence, when they buy a product, customers are buying much more than a set of attributes – they are buying 'want satisfaction' in the form of the benefits they expect to receive from the product.[51] For example, customers do not buy 8 mm drill bits, they buy the ability to create 8 mm holes. In the recent past, courier companies lost much of their overnight letter delivery business to fax machines and e-mail because these could meet the same customer needs faster, cheaper or more conveniently.

Meeting the needs of customers better than the competition's capability to do so is not an easy task. Neither is it always economically viable for a company to make specialised products for a few customers. More often, it is less expensive to manufacture one version of a product than a number of versions. Marketers must balance the benefits of customisation against a wide range of product options.

1.8.2 Promotion (marketing communications)

Promotion, or marketing communications, in whatever form is a company's attempt to influence potential customers. Specifically, it is the element in an organisation's marketing mix that serves to inform, persuade and remind the market of a product and/or the organisation selling it in the hope of influencing the recipients' feelings, beliefs or behaviour.[52]

There are five forms of marketing communications:
1. Personal selling.
2. Advertising.
3. Sales promotion.
4. Public relations.
5. Publicity.

To communicate effectively with the target market, the marketing communications strategy requires answers to these questions:[53]

With whom do we want to communicate?
Generally, messages are aimed at customers, but they can also be aimed at channel members or those who influence the target market. It is important to decide who within the target market should receive the marketing message. In the case of a child's toy, for example, should the communications be aimed at the children or the parents, or both?

What effect do we want our communication to have on the target audience?
The ultimate aim is usually to increase sales, but initially it may be to create awareness of a company's products.

What message should we convey to the target market?
This includes the words, pictures and symbols that a company should use to capture attention and produce the desired effect. The company's understanding of the culture and norms of the target market will affect the way in which it formulates the message.

What means and media should we use to reach the target audience?
This refers to the different forms of marketing communication available to management. Should the company use personal selling or rely on the package to provide the necessary information? Should it advertise in the mass media or use direct mail? Which

one of the mass media should it use? Having decided on the form of the message, the company should evaluate the finer details of the media for suitability.

When should we communicate with the target audience?

Marketers must decide when they want to advertise – in the morning, in the afternoon, at the beginning of the month or at the end of the month. Answering these questions requires a knowledge of the decision-making process used by the target market for this product.

1.8.3 Price

Price is the amount of money and/or other items with utility needed to acquire a product. Customers can buy ownership of a product or, for many products, limited usage rights, that is, they can rent or lease the product. It is sometimes assumed that lower prices for the same product will result in more sales than will higher prices. But this may not always be the case, as price is often used as a measure of *quality*. Customers might see a product priced 'too low' as having low quality. Owning expensive items also provides information about the owner. Apart from anything else, it indicates that the owner can afford the items. This is a desirable feature to some customers. Therefore, to set a price the company needs to have a thorough understanding of the symbolic role that price plays for the product and target market in question.

'It is important to note that the price of a product is not the same as the cost of the product to the customer. The cost to a customer is everything the customer must surrender in order to receive the benefits of owning/using the product.'[54] One of the ways that organisations try to provide customer value is to reduce the non-price costs of owning or operating a product for example, travel expenses or inconvenience. If successful, the total cost to the customer decreases while the revenue to the marketer stays the same or even increases.

1.8.4 Place (distribution)

Distribution's role within the marketing mix is to get the product to its target market, that is, to the place where the customer buys the product. If the product is not available where the customer wants it, the company will likely not survive. Only rarely will customers go to a lot of trouble to get hold of a particular brand. Even before a product is ready for the market, management must decide on the methods and routes it will use to get it there. This entails establishing strategies for the product's distribution channels and physical distribution. Obviously, accurate channel decisions require a sound knowledge of the places where target customers shop for the product they want.

1.9 Customer decisons[55]

As shown in Figure 1.4 (on page 11), the customer decision-making process takes place between the market strategy – as implemented in the marketing mix – and the outcomes. In other words, the outcomes of the organisation's marketing strategy depend on its interaction with the customer decision-making process. For a business to succeed, customers must believe that the product being offered can satisfy their need. Furthermore, they must be aware of it being offered and of its capabilities, they must decide that it is the best available solution, they must buy it, and they must be satisfied with the results of the purchase.

1.10 Outcomes[56]

In this section, we deal with organisational, individual and societal outcomes.

1.10.1 Organisational outcomes

You need to address the following factors in considering organisational outcomes:

Product position
This is the way that customers define the product's important attributes. Put differently, it is the place the product occupies in the customers' minds relative to competing products.[57] The positioning of an organisation's product is seen as the most basic outcome of its marketing strategy. In order to secure loyal customers, the organisation must persuade customers to see its product as a value offering that is identifiable by its brand. Most organisations aim for a specific product position that they want their brands to have, and they measure this position continually. In a market where brands are important, an organisation with a strong brand has a better chance of achieving customer loyalty.

Sales
Sales produce the revenue necessary for organisations to stay in business, and they act as a method used by companies to measure the success of their selected marketing strategies and programmes.

Customer satisfaction
It is a known fact in business that it is less expensive to keep existing customers than to find new customers. To keep existing customers requires that they be satisfied with the products they have bought and used. Organisations are concerned not only with the threat of losing existing customers through dissatisfaction, but also with the fact that dissatisfied customers will share their experience with other, potential customers, leading to a wider network of dissatisfaction.

1.10.2 Individual outcomes

You need to address the following factor in considering individual outcomes of customer behaviour:

Need satisfaction
The outcome an individual requires differs from that of an organisation. Two key processes are involved: the **actual need fulfilment** and the **perceived need fulfilment**.

For many customers, fulfilling one need affects their ability to fulfil others, because of financial or time constraints. For example, if people spend their money on gambling, they will have less money to buy food and clothes for their children.

1.10.3 Societal outcomes[58]

You need to address the following factors in considering societal outcomes:

Economic outcomes
The cumulative impact of customers' buying decisions, including the decision not to buy, is the major factor that defines the state of a given country's economy. By spending and not saving, or vice versa, customers impact on the economic growth of a country as well as on the capital available in the country for investment.

Physical environment outcomes
The types of products a society uses can impact on the environment through pollution – for example using plastic containers, using gases that destroy the earth's ozone layer, and so on – and the availability, or scarcity, of natural resources.

1.11 The nature of customer behaviour[59]

Figure 1.6 (on page 23) is the model of customer behaviour that we use as the basis for the following discussion. This model is *conceptual*, and it reflects our beliefs about the general nature of customer behaviour. *Based on mental concept*

> Individuals develop self-concepts, and subsequent lifestyles, based on a variety of internal (mainly psychological and physical) and external (mainly sociological and demographic) influences. These self-concepts and lifestyles produce needs and desires, many of which can only be satisfied by buying something. As individuals encounter particular situations, the customer decision-making process is activated, i.e. they decide to buy something. This process and the experiences and acquisitions it produces in turn influence the customers' self-concepts and lifestyles by affecting their internal and external characteristics.

This model, while simple, is both conceptually sound and intuitively appealing. Each of us has a view of ourselves (self-concept), and we try to live in a particular manner given our resources (lifestyle). Our view of ourselves and the way we try to live are determined by internal factors (such as our personality, values, emotions and memory) and external factors (such as our culture, age, friends, family and subculture). Our view of ourselves and the way we try to live results in desires and needs that we bring to the many situations we encounter daily. Many of these situations will cause us to decide to buy something. Our decision (and even the process of making it) will cause learning and may affect many other internal and external factors that will change or reinforce our present self-concept and lifestyle.[60]

We explore each of the factors shown in Figure 1.6 in detail in the chapters that follow. In the rest of this section we give a brief overview of the concepts present in the model to help you to form an overall picture of customer behaviour.

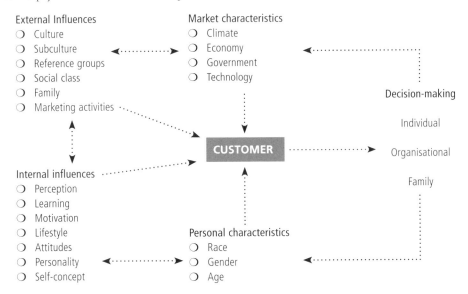

Figure 1.6: An overall model of customer behaviour

1.11.1 External influences

These influences are also referred to as the 'social' and 'group factors' influencing customer behaviour. As you can see in Figure 1.6, they include culture and subculture (which we discuss in Chapter 4); social class and reference groups (see Chapter 5); family (see Chapter 13); and marketing activities, namely, market segmentation (see Chapter 11), customer loyalty (see Chapter 15), relationship-based buying (see Chapter 16) and e-commerce (see Chapter 17). Dividing the factors that influence customers into categories is rather arbitrary. For example, learning is regarded as an internal influence, despite the fact that much learning involves interaction with other individuals. In other words, learning could also be considered as part of group factors. In Figure 1.6 the two-directional arrows indicate that each set of influences interacts with the other.

1.11.2 Internal influences

These influences are also known as the 'psychological forces' that influence customer behaviour. Internal influences begin with perception – the process by which individuals receive and assign meaning to stimuli, followed by learning – changes in the content or structure of long-term memory (see Chapter 7), motivation – the reason for a behaviour (see Chapter 8), personality – an individual's characteristic response tendencies in similar situations (see Chapter 10), and attitudes – strong, relatively uncontrolled feelings that affect our behaviour (see Chapter 9).

1.11.3 Market characteristics

Customers live in a physical place. Products and services are produced, transported, stored and used in a physical space. Moreover, they affect the physical qualities of the place where they are produced and used. The physical characteristics of the marketplace, such as climate, and other market characteristics, such as the economy, government and technology (see Chapter 3), all influence customer behaviour.

1.11.4 Personal characteristics

These are the characteristics that customers possess as individuals. They include the biological and physiological features that a person is born with, such as their gender and race, and those that develop as the person grows, such as their age (see Chapter 6).

The external influences, internal influences, market characteristics and personal characteristics exert a force on an individual's self-concept and lifestyle.

1.11.5 The customer (with his or her self-concept and lifestyle)

As a result of the interaction of all the abovementioned variables, individuals develop a self-concept that is reflected in a lifestyle. The **self-concept** is the totality of an individual's thoughts and feelings about himself or herself (see Chapter 10). **Lifestyle**, quite simply, is how each of us lives. It includes the products we buy, how we use them, what we think about them and how we feel about them. It is the manifestation of our self-concept – the total image we have of ourselves as a result of the culture in which we live and the situations and experiences that make up our daily existence (see Chapter 8). It is the sum of our past decisions and future plans.

Our lifestyles are determined by both conscious and unconscious decisions. Often, we make choices knowing the impact they will have on our lifestyle, but generally we are unaware of the extent to which our decisions are influenced by our current or desired lifestyle. The model of customer behaviour above shows that customers' self-concepts and lifestyles produce needs and desires that interact with the situations in which they find themselves to trigger the customer decision-making process, that is, the decision to buy.

Most customer decisions involve little effort or thought on the part of the customer. They are what we call '**low-involvement decisions**'. Feelings and emotions are as important in many customer decisions as logical analysis or physical product attributes. Nonetheless, most customer purchases involve at least a small amount of decision-making, and most are influenced by the buyer's current and desired lifestyle.

1.11.6 The customer decision-making process[61]

Customers' decisions result from perceived problems ('I'm hungry') and opportunities ('That looks like good value for money'). Customer problems arise in specific situations, and the nature of the situation influences the resulting customer behaviour. We distinguish between individual decision-making (see Chapter 12), organisational buying (see Chapter 14) and family decision-making (see Chapter 13).

As Figure 1.6 indicates, a customer's needs/desires may trigger the different levels of his or her decision-making process. It is important to remember, as explained above, that for most purchases, customers devote little effort to this process, and emotions and feelings often have as much or more influence on the outcome as do facts and product features. Despite this, the results have important effects on the individual customer, the organisation and society.

1.12 Summary

Making the correct marketing decisions requires a thorough understanding of customer behaviour. A good knowledge of customer behaviour provides marketers with a sound basis from which to make decisions regarding forthcoming marketing strategies, including product positioning, market segmentation, market targeting, the development of new products, and so on.

The aim of the customer behaviour model is to provide you with a framework from which you can study customer behaviour. The model shows the major factors, both internal and internal, that exert an influence on the customer decision-making process. The combination of these influences is reflected in the lifestyles of customers as well as in their choice of products and services.

Endnote references

1. Strydom, J. 2004. *Introduction to Marketing*. 3rd ed. Cape Town: Juta.
2. Schiffman, L.G. and Kanuk, L.L. 2004. *Consumer Behaviour*. 8th ed. New Jersey: Pearson Prentice-Hall.

3. Strydom, op. cit.
4. Hawkins, D.I., Best, R.J. and Coney, K.A. 1998. *Consumer Behavior: Building Marketing Strategy.* 7th ed. Boston: McGraw-Hill, p. 7.
5. Sheth, J.N., Mittal, B. and Newman, B.I. 1999. *Customer Behavior: Consumer Behavior and Beyond.* Orlando: Dryden, p. 5.
6. Taken largely from ibid., pp. 5–6.
7. Strydom, op. cit.
8. Ibid., pp. 6–7.
9. Strydom, op. cit.
10. Ibid.
11. American Marketing Association (AMA). 2005. Dictionary of Terms. Available on the internet from: www.marketingpower.com (accessed 25 July 2005).
12. Strydom, op. cit.
13. Ibid.
14. AMA, op. cit.
15. Strydom, op. cit.
16. Schiffman, L.G. and Kanuk, L.L. 1997. *Consumer Behaviour.* 6th ed. Upper Saddle River: Prentice-Hall, pp. 6–7.
17. Sheth et al., op. cit., p. 9.
18. Adapted from Sheth et al., op. cit., pp. 5–6.
19. Taken largely from ibid., pp. 11–15.
20. Wilson, R.M.S. and Gilligan, C. 2005. *Strategic Marketing Management: Planning, Implementation and Control.* 3rd ed. Italy: Elsevier.
21. Lancaster, G. and Reynolds, P. 2005. *Management of Marketing.* UK: Elsevier.
22. Ibid., pp. 11–12.
23. Solomon, M.R. 1996. *Consumer Behavior: Buying, Having and Being.* 3rd ed. Upper Saddle River: Prentice-Hall, p. 11.
24. Taken largely from Cant, M.C., Strydom, J.W. and Jooste, C.J. 1999. *Essentials of Marketing.* Cape Town: Juta, pp. 9–16.
25. Strydom, op. cit.
26. Lancaster and Reynolds, op. cit.
27. Ibid.
28. Ibid.
29. Shiffman and Kanuk, op. cit.
30. Lancaster and Reynolds, op. cit.
31. Strydom, op. cit.
32. Ibid.
33. Ibid.
34. Ibid.
35. Taken largely from Sheth et al., op. cit., pp. 14–15.
36. Taken largely from Hawkins et al., op. cit., pp. 9–10.
37. Ibid., p. 10.
38. Wilson and Gilligan, op. cit.
39. Taken from Hawkins et al., op. cit.
40. Taken largely from ibid., pp. 11–15.
41. Strydom, op. cit.
42. Robbins, S.P. 2003. *Organizational Behavior.* 10th ed. USA: Prentice-Hall.
43. Wilson and Gilligan, op. cit.
44. Strydom, op. cit.

45. Kotler, P. and Armstrong, G. 1993. *Marketing: An Introduction*. 3rd ed. Upper Saddle River: Prentice-Hall, p. 190.
46. Adapted from Hawkins et al., op. cit., pp. 16–18.
47. Taken from Cant et al., op. cit., pp. 166–8.
48. Ibid., p. 166.
49. Ibid., pp. 167–8.
50. Based on Hawkins et al., op. cit., pp. 18–20.
51. Etzel, M.J., Walker, B.J. and Stanton, W.J. 1997. *Marketing*. 11th ed. New York: McGraw-Hill, p. 193.
52. Ibid.
53. Hawkins et al., op. cit., p. 19.
54. Ibid., p. 20.
55. Ibid., p. 21.
56. Kotler and Armstrong, op. cit., p. 205.
57. Ibid.
58. Based largely on Hawkins et al., op. cit., p. 25.
59. Ibid., pp. 26–30.
60. Hawkins et al., op. cit., p. 26.
61. Ibid.

2 Creating market value for consumers

Learning Outcomes

After studying this chapter, you should be able to:

○ define the concept of value

○ discuss the components of market value

○ explain 'value bundling' as it is applied to a product or service

○ demonstrate how value is added to the product or service bought by the consumer

○ develop a way to measure customer value.

2.1 Introduction

In Chapter 1 we pointed out that an organisation should offer superior value to its customers to differentiate itself from its competitors.

In this chapter we look at the concept of value in general, and more specifically at the market value that a consumer has of a product or service. We then examine value bundling of products and services and the way in which the marketer can use it. We consider the viewpoint of the business, we discuss the measurement of value and we explain the techniques for measuring it. Lastly, we assess the marketing implications of value creation.

2.2 The definition of value

Broadly, we can describe value as the beliefs that a community shares and that provide guidelines for how community members should think, act and feel in a given situation.[1] Value is closely tied in with customer culture, which we deal with in Chapter 4.

Looking at value in a narrower (marketing) sense, we refer to it as the 'market value'. We can determine the **market value** of any product or service by what it can do to solve a problem for a consumer. If you have a transportation problem and you buy a bicycle for R500, the problem-solving ability of the product is the fact that it can take you, with some effort on your part, from point A to point B.

The official definition of market value is that it 'is the potential of a product or service to satisfy a customer's wants and needs'.[2]

2.3 The market value of a product or service[3]

This usually consists of a universal or a personal value, or both. **Universal values** satisfy the basic *needs* of the customer – we can call these values the 'bottom line values' that every customer expects from a product or service. In practice, they consist of hunger, thirst, safety, and so on.

Personal values are more diverse and vary from consumer to consumer. They satisfy the *wants* of the customer, which are usually of a more personal nature. Personal values can be either group specific, for example values that are adhered to by a group of consumers, which we may call the 'target market'; or they may be individual specific – implying that the product or service must be presented in such a manner that the individual customer can have customised enjoyment of it. Group specific personal values are the basis for segmentation strategies, while individual specific personal values form the basis for one-on-one marketing and relationship marketing strategies. The entire concept of market value is depicted in Figure 2.1.

Figure 2.1: Components of market value

We can also pinpoint three customer roles, namely, the user of the product or service, the payer for the product or service, and the buyer of the product or service. The **user** of the product is the person who uses the product. For example, a baby is the user of powdered formula, while the mother or the father is the **buyer** and **payer** of the product.

The above discussion is summarised in the matrix of values and customer roles in Table 2.1.

Table 2.1: The matrix of values and customer roles[4]

	User	Payer	Buyer
Universal values	Performance value	Price value	Service value
Personal values: Group specific	Social value	Credit value	Convenience value
Personal values: Individual specific	Emotional value	Financing value	Personalisation value

We now discuss the matrix in more detail.

2.3.1 Market values sought by users

Universal value – performance

The universal value sought by the user is what the product or service can do for him or her. For example, we buy food to obtain nutrition and energy. And you buy a cell phone in order to communicate freely and with convenience with your family and friends. You expect the phone to function effectively, that is, that the communication with the receiver will be clear. This is one of the crucial values that mobile phone operators are looking for and, for a long time, it was the ultimate way in which they distinguished themselves. Even today, we find advertisements implying that Vodacom's reception is better than the other cell phone operators and vice versa.

Personal values – social and emotional

The personal values that come into play when we obtain a product or service are also important. Referring to the cell phone example above, we can say that social and emotional values play a significant role in the acquisition process. Social values influence the consumer to buy a cell phone that is congruent with the norms and standards of their friends – it influences the type of phone that they buy. Some cell phone users believe that only a certain brand of cell phone will do, thus they buy the Nokia 9300, for example. The recently introduced 3 G cell phone – the Blackberry – also imposes on certain social values to the users.

Other market choices are based on the ability to satisfy emotions, that is, the emotional value. Some consumers buy a certain type of car because of its emotional value – a Mercedes Benz has emotional value as it tells the world that the owner has 'arrived' (made a success of themselves).

The 'WaBenzi' is an example of consumers who buy cars for their emotional value:[5]

The Wabenzi is an East African description of wealthy people, especially those that are rich enough to own expensive foreign cars such as Mercedes Benz. The word is from the Swahili (wa = people + Mercedes Benz (the German luxury car company nowadays called Daimler Chrysler.) The term 'Wabenzi' describes those people that made it to the top. One of the status symbols that tells the world that you have arrived is a luxury car. They can be seen as an example of a group of consumers who buys expensive cars such as Mercedes Benz for the emotional value.

In summary, many consumers acquire emotional value when they spend money on an *experience*, for example a boat cruise to the Eastern Caribbean or an air ticket to exotic places such as Phuket, Zanzibar or Dubai. The consumer creates the emotional value through **experiential consumption**. South Africa wants more tourists to visit the country – this can be created by generating emotional value for the tourists, who will then tell other, potential tourists about the country.

2.3.2 Market values sought by payers

Universal value – price

The universal value of paying for a product is the price value of the product that the consumer is obtaining. The payer looks for the utility that he or she can obtain for paying a certain price for a product. The question is how reasonable or affordable is the price in the context of what he or she is obtaining? Currently, South African retailers are struggling with an extended period of deflation, which leaves them little option of increasing prices of products. What can they do? They must increase the price value equation of the product. The result, for instance, is better quality clothing at the same price, or even better quality clothing at a lower price.

Personal values – credit and financing

By using credit and financing the consumer will be able to pay for a product or service. In this way, the consumer can delay paying for a product for a certain period, while obtaining the necessary financing is another, more personalised, form of using credit to obtain value for the customer.

Credit value, for instance, is created when the customer pays by credit card. The seller, in this instance the retailer, accepts the credit card as full payment while the consumer or payer has between 30 and 45 days, interest free, in which to make a consolidating payment. Credit value is created for a qualified group of customers, as not all South African consumers have access to credit cards or are eligible for receiving credit.

Financing value is created when the payer is offered terms of payment to make the payment more affordable. A typical example is in the motor vehicle sector, in which a structured payment system (for example hire-purchase agreement) is used. For example, a motorcar manufacturer can allow a customer to purchase (and drive) a car in May of 2006 and pay the first instalment for it in September of the same year.

2.3.3 Market values sought by buyers

Universal value – service

For the buyer of a product or service, the universal value that they seek is service value. The service value is measured according to the following three elements:

1. The **pre-purchase advice and assistance** of the salespeople. Using the car example above, how knowledgeable was the car salesperson and what assistance did he or she provide the buyer in obtaining finance to help conduct the transaction?
2. The **post-purchase advice and assistance** of the salespeople or of other people involved, for example the service station from which the buyer obtains petrol. Customers also expect prompt and reliable repairs and maintenance service. In South Africa, this is an area where there is difference in service levels – there is a saying that 'there are no poor quality cars manufactured today in South Africa, only poor quality service provided by some of the manufacturers and their officially accredited service stations'.

3. The **freedom from risk** of a miss-purchase. According to the local press and various internet articles, this is one of the problems encountered by many South African consumers, as the following example illustrates.

THE WORST 4 X 4 X FAR[6]

A consumer will experience post-purchase satisfaction and the feeling that they received value if they believe that after sales service will also include reimbursement for or replacements of faulty products. A dissatisfied consumer who feels that their freedom from risk of a miss-purchase has been jeopardised may go to great lengths to obtain compensation for the damages that they felt they suffered.

In 2000, Jaco van der Merwe bought an Isuzu 4 X 4 bakkie from a Delta dealer. A year after purchasing the bakkie, Mr van der Merwe and his family went on holiday in Namibia. While driving on a gravel road, the bakkie's chassis bent. Van der Merwe felt that the bent chassis was a manufacturing error and he therefore approached the dealership upon his return to South Africa. Delta replied that the bent chassis was due to reckless driving and overloading by the buyer.

Van der Merwe asked a private firm recommended by the SABS to inspect the bakkie. They found that the bent chassis was due to an inconsistency in the steel structure. Van der Merwe again approached Delta, which continued to deny responsibility and claimed the chassis was manufactured within specifications.

The buyer felt that he was being taken advantage of and retaliated by sending e-mails to several people in which he explained his version of the story and the dissatisfaction he felt after dealing with Delta. The words 'Worst 4 X 4 far' were also displayed on the bakkie, which he exhibited in public places. Four years after the incident Delta took Van der Merwe to court, arguing that the statements were defamatory and amounted to a 'smear campaign' against them. The court eventually made a final ruling in favour of the buyer.

Another example is that of a Land Rover customer who received no compensation or reimbursement from Land Rover after his car was damaged while in the care of the organisation. He put up a website entitled 'Worst 4 X 4' that has about 1 500 visitors a month.

There is great economic risk involved when buying a product such as a car, which is a high involvement decision-making product. It is therefore important that the consumer feels that they have freedom from the risk of a miss-purchase and that after-purchase service should lead to their feeling that they received value for money. This influences consumers' brand loyalty and positive word of mouth communication. Both car manufacturers incurred direct costs – for example legal costs – that go beyond the initial cost of replacing the cars. Furthermore, there is the amount of bad publicity that surely must have tarnished both manufacturers' reputations.

As we have seen, customers seek freedom from risks. Value is added when they feel comfortable that they can easily return the product and obtain a refund or an exchange.

Personal values – convenience and personalisation

In order to buy a product or service, customers usually must make some effort in the form of time and money. The savings that they could enjoy in this context is the convenience value. The retailer creates such value for the buyer, for instance, by making the product easy to buy – the retailer could provide sufficient parking space, stay open 24 hours a day, and have knowledgeable salespeople to guide the buyer's decision.

The buyer also wants to conclude the transaction in a personalised or individualised manner. The personalisation value is created for the buyer by means of customisation and interpersonal relations. Customisation is created, for instance, when the buyer is assured by Pick 'n Pay that their internet purchase of groceries will be delivered to their home between 10:00 and 12:00 on a Saturday morning. By being able to receive their groceries in this way, the buyer has customisation value and can plan their other activities for the day on this basis.

Personalisation refers to the way in which a transaction is handled. If you buy a product in an environment that is pleasant, and you have an effective interaction with salespeople or after-salespeople, then positive personalisation has taken place, which adds value for you as the customer.

Some buyers prefer to buy from a store where there is interpersonalisation, that is, where he or she is greeted by name and where there is a socialisation ritual. A personal banker, for example, provides interpersonalisation value in his or her dealings with a high net-worth client by visiting the client at their office and generating a cordial, one-on-one business relationship with the client.

2.4 The value bundling of products or services[7]

The different types of products and services generate various value bundles. We now look at the categories of non-durable goods and durable goods, and services.

2.4.1 Non-durable goods

Non-durable goods or products such as groceries offer a bundle of up to all six of the values we discussed above. This is represented in Table 2.2 on the next page.

2.4.2 Durable goods

For durable products all six of the values also play a role. Table 2.3 on the next page summarises the values for a durable product such as a Harley Davidson motorbike.

Table 2.2: Matrix of values and customer roles for non-durable products such as groceries

	User	Payer	Buyer
Universal values	Performance value = energy and nutrition	Price value = especially for families with a number of dependants to feed	Service value = applicable if the customer eats at a restaurant
Personal values: Group specific	Social value = social class association of food, e.g. maize meal for poor people, caviar for rich people	Credit value = relevant because a number of buyers pay by credit card	Convenience value = especially home delivery of fast food products
Personal values: Individual specific	Emotional value = childhood associations, e.g. Black Cat peanut butter and syrup sandwiches	Financing value = not as relevant as groceries are paid for by cash or credit card	Personalisation value = applicable when eating out; the interpersonal behaviour of the waiter and the person handling the reservation

Table 2.3: Matrix of values and consumer roles of a durable product such as a Harley Davidson motorbike

	User	Payer	Buyer
Universal values	Performance value = safety and reliability of the bike, also repair and maintenance service	Price value = is the bike worth its price and is the price affordable?	Service value = obtaining excellent knowledgeable service from the salesperson creates value
Personal values: Group specific	Social value = social statement, as with the Harley Davidson brand and the corresponding image	Credit value = how available is credit to buy the bike?	Convenience value = created by time and place utility, i.e. having the salesperson brings the bike to the home for a demonstration
Personal values: Individual specific	Emotional value = deep attachment to the bike, such as giving it a name	Financing value = hire purchase was the traditional way to create value while today it is substituted by leasing the bike	Personalisation value = generated by creating convenience values, e.g. the salesperson opening a bottle of champagne when the consumer buys the bike

2.4.3 Services

The six values are also applicable to services used by the consumer. See Table 2.4 in this regard.

Table 2.4: Matrix of values and consumer roles for a service such as using an airline

	User	Payer	Buyer
Universal values	Performance value = safety record and reliability of airline	Price value = the cost of the air ticket	Service value = ease of making a reservation
Personal values: Group specific	Social value = the class that the consumer flies, e.g. economy class and business class	Credit value = relevant because a number of buyers pay by credit card	Convenience value = the consumer can buy the ticket and pay for it online
Personal values: Individual specific	Emotional value = fear of flying in some passengers, or excitement in others	Financing value = relevant as it is usually a large amount to pay and also important as a form of medical insurance	Personalisation value = occurs when the airline can cater for the consumer's specific food requirements, e.g. low-sodium food

We have examined the market value, which is focused on the values that the customer wants. It is also necessary for us to consider the value concept from the point of view of the organisation. We now determine how the organisation can measure whether it is creating value for the customer.

2.5 The organisation's perspective of measuring value

The concept of adding value for the consumer is widely discussed in the literature on consumer behaviour. It is important that you note that the measurement conducted by organisations has evolved over the years. There was a move away from the measurement of **customer satisfaction**, which is the older paradigm, towards the measurement of **customer value**, which is the newer paradigm. Nevertheless, the customer value paradigm contains many of the elements of the older paradigm, which focused on how to satisfy customers who were using the organisation's products or services. Most customer metrics in the past used the older paradigm and research was done solely on the organisation's own customers and not on the customers of the competition.

By contrast, the more recent approach focuses on how customers choose among competing organisations. Organisations must now ask themselves the following:
○ What are the key buying factors that customers value when they choose between our organisation and the competitors?
○ How do customers rate our performance versus that of the competitors?

By identifying the best competitor on each key buying factor, the organisation gets a good idea of the unique value proposition that each competitor has. There is often a major difference between the ways in which the organisation and the consumer see the value proposition.

The best way to accurately determine whether value has been added for the customer is to quantify it in what is called the **'value metrics process'**. This entails finding out the different values that consumers expect from a product or service, that is, creating a benchmark, developing a strategy to deliver the value to the consumer, and measuring whether the consumer's expectations were met or exceeded. The process is schematically depicted in Figure 2.2.

Determine what value the customer expects from a
product or service

⋮
▼

Prepare a strategy to deliver value

⋮
▼

Measure how well value was delivered

⋮
▼

Investigate any deviations and adapt strategy
accordingly

Figure 2.2: The measurement of value

2.5.1 Determining the expected value

The first step is to determine a baseline of the expected consumer values. The most basic way to do this is to conduct a **consumer satisfaction index** (CSI). This measurement is done with an ordinary questionnaire. Answers to questions such as 'What are your feelings about the new car that you have bought?' could indicate to the motorcar manufacturer what the consumer expected from the product, and could be quantified into a quantitative CSI score. This is a typical example of measurement in the customer satisfaction paradigm.

The organisation needs to build on the CSI using the concept of **consumer value management** (CVM). CVM focuses more specifically on the value component.[8] The **value component** measures the consumer satisfaction relative to the price paid for the product or service, and is called the customer's **'perceived value'**. Moreover, CVM measures the value perceptions of the competitors' consumers, hence the customer value paradigm approach.

By using CVM, the organisation is able to determine the following:

❍ The **key buying factors** (also called the 'key performance indicators') that consumers favour when they choose between the organisation's product and that of the competitors. This could involve delivery time, the product's quality, etc.

❍ How the **organisation rates against its competitors** in the key buying factor arena. Is the organisation delivering the product consistently more quickly than competitors?

❍ What the relative importance is of these components to **delivering consumer value**. If the consumer rates delivery time as 50% of the value added, then the organisation should infer that it should pay particular attention to this aspect.

2.5.2 Formulating a strategy for delivering value to the consumer

The second step is to prepare a strategy to deliver the value to the consumer. The starting point is to convince the organisation's personnel, including top management, of the benefit of CVM. Once convinced, the organisation must generate and implement action plans to deliver value to the consumer. If the organisation has discovered that on-time delivery is important to their customers, for example, then it needs to devise an action plan to ensure that delivery takes place on time or even prior to the stipulated time.

2.5.3 Measuring value delivery

The third step is value measurement, which again can be done through CVM. However, another measurement instrument is the **balanced scorecard** (BSC). This is an instrument that evaluates the performance of an organisation not only by concentrating on financial issues, but also by including non-financial measures such as consumer satisfaction, employee satisfaction and innovation.[9] In a study, it was found that the BSC can be used as an instrument to measure the long-term value creation process in an organisation. It can also be focused more specifically on the consumer. In doing this, the organisation must align its core consumer outcome measures – namely, consumer satisfaction, consumer loyalty, consumer retention, consumer acquisition and consumer profitability – with consumer expectations.[10] These core measures are depicted in Figure 2.3.

Figure 2.3: Core consumer outcome measures

Figure 2.3 illustrates these aspects:

- ○ The **market share** shows the proportion of the business that the organisation has in a certain market. This proportion may be in the form of rands spent, units sold, etc.
- ○ **Consumer acquisition** measures the rate at which the organisation attracts new consumers.
- ○ **Consumer retention** tracks the rate at which the organisation retains ongoing relationships with consumers.
- ○ **Consumer satisfaction** measures the satisfaction level of consumers against the set performance criteria.
- ○ **Consumer profitability** measures the net profit of a consumer after deducting the expenses to support the consumer.

2.5.4 Investigating deviations and adapting the strategy

In the last step, the organisation must determine if there are any deviations, that is, if anything is going wrong, and correct them, which starts a new cycle of research to assess whether the organisation is delivering what the consumer expects.

2.6 Marketing implications of the concept of value

Value has been described as the only way that an organisation can differentiate itself consistently from its competitors. Day states this succinctly: 'The only way that a business can succeed is to deliver superior consumer value'.[11] In order to deliver superior value to the consumer, the organisation must become *market driven*. This implies that the organisation must understand its consumer and be able to adapt to changes in the environment that influence the consumer, thus retaining him or her. This ties in with another current concept, namely, the idea of **value-based marketing**, which is defined as 'the way in which the organisation designs and manufactures useful products that it delivers on time while maintaining a more than satisfactory level of service for an extended period'.[12] To deliver superior value, it is therefore necessary for the organisation to understand consumer behaviour.

Case study

HOW MUCH VALUE ARE YOU GETTING WHEN YOU BUY A SOUTH AFRICAN CAR?

The Competitions Commission announced in 2005 that they were investigating all the major car manufacturers in South Africa for anti-competitive behaviour inter alia fixing dealer discounts. In effect this means that dealers are restrained by the manufacturer to use indiscriminate discounting measures to lure customers to the dealership. Toyota paid an administrative fee of R12 million to the Commission and it would seem that it will now be the turn of the other manufacturers to do some explaining about their pricing structures.

Observers[13] are not sure of the so-called 'anti-competitive behaviour' of the South African manufacturers – the real reason for the behaviour is for the high price that consumers pay. Some of the other reasons supplied for the high car prices are:

○ The role of government. The car allowance tax scheme allows customers to make full use of the car allowance, which may be higher than what they really need. Also, there are the import duties that are payable on importing cars (currently 38%, but this will be reduced to 20% in 2012).

○ The role of banks. Banks contribute to the high costs by the kickbacks that they give to the motor dealers. When you buy a car on instalment sale or lease, and you finance it through the motor dealer and its bank, the bank gives the dealer a commission.

The question is: Are South African manufacturers and importers charging too much? Let us look at two examples:

1. The UK price of the Chrysler Crossfire is (rand equivalent) 290 400 excluding tax. In South Africa, the same car costs R356 000 excluding tax. The cars are imported from the USA. Logistics could be a reason for the price difference.

2. The Mercedes Benz C180 Kompressor, made in South Africa, costs R204 680 excluding tax. In the UK, the same car, still manufactured in SA, costs R214 000 excluding tax.

Another commentator[14] states that complex economic factors are at work and that prices of cars in real terms have dropped. Buyers are getting more car for their Rand, in the sense that they acquire new technology, such as airbags and ABS braking, at the same price as the old model.

It would seem that the price differences are not so great, but the fact remains that the consumer does not have all the information to make a factual comparison. As long as the South African customer struggles to make an informed decision the debate about expensive cars and high prices will be prevalent.

2.7 Summary

In this chapter we discussed the concept of value creation for the consumer. We described value in both a broad and narrow context. For the purposes of this book, we use the narrower definition of market value. Furthermore, we broke down the market value into universal and personal values, with the personal values split between group specific and individual specific values. We used a matrix depicting market values and consumer roles to illustrate the specific values that are important for a consumer.

We explored how value bundling occurs for certain products and services, and we examined the steps in the measurement of value, referring to CVM. We also indicated the use of BSC in value measurement. Lastly, we considered the marketing implications of the value concept, stressing the importance of organisations being market driven, and discussing the links with value-based marketing.

Questions for self-assessment

To assess your progress, answer these questions:
1. Define the concept of value.
2. Describe the different components of market value.
3. Discuss the value bundling that occurs when a consumer wants to buy a new house.
4. Discuss the steps in the process of value measurement.
5. Explain how an organisation can use the BSC in value measurement.
6. Why does an organisation need to take cognisance of the value concept?
7. With reference to the case study above, answer the following questions:
   a. Identify the universal values that a user, payer and buyer are looking for in a car.
   b. Write down the individual specific values that a customer will be looking for when buying a car.
   c. What are the perceived values that a South African customer has when buying an expensive car today?

Endnote references

1. Wells, W.D. and Prensky, D. 1996. *Consumer Behavior*. New York: Wiley.
2. Sheth, J.N., Mittal, B. and Newman, B.T. 1999. *Customer Behavior: Consumer Behaviour and Beyond*. Orlando: Dryden, p. 58.
3. Based on ibid., pp. 58–80.
4. Ibid., p. 61.
5. Champkin, J. 1984. The WaBenzi. New International List. Available on the internet from: www.newint.org/org/issue139/wabenzi.htm (accessed 10 June 2005).
6. Van Velden – Duffey Attorneys. Law of Delict. Available on the internet from: www.vvd.co.za/law_of_delict.htm; and The Supreme Court of Appeal of South Africa. May 2004. *Delta Motor Corporation* v *Delta Motor Corporation*. Media summary of judgement delivered in the Supreme Court of Appeal and *The Consumer Technology Magazine*. Nightmare on online street. Available on the internet from: www.gadget.co.za/pebble.asp?relid=265&t=83.
7. Loosely based on Sheth, et al., op. cit., pp. 77–80.
8. Daniels, S. 2000. Customer value management. *Work Study*, 49(2), 68.
9. Sim, K.L. and Koh, H.C. 2001. Balanced scorecard: A rising trend in strategic performance measurement. *Measuring Business Excellence*, 5(2), 19–24.
10. Du Plessis, P.J., Jooste, C.J. and Strydom, J.W. 2001. *Applied Strategic Marketing*. Sandown: Heinemann.
11. Day, G. 2002. Staying close, but not too close, to the customer. Available on the internet from: http://knowledge.wharton.upenn.edu/articles.cfm?catid=4&articleid=112 (accessed 2 April 2005).
12. Walters, D. and Lancaster, G. 1999. Value-based marketing and its usefulness to customers. *Management Decision*, 37(9), 697.
13. Oxley, J. 2005. Available on the internet from: www.fincne24.com/articles/default/display_article.asp?ArticleID=1369-1372_1525147 (accessed 11 May 2005).
14. Flynn, A. 28 January 2005. Available on the internet from: www.sadirectory.co.uk/index2.php?option=content&ask-view&id=28&pop=1&p (accessed 8 June 2005).

3 Market characteristics

Learning Outcomes

After studying this chapter, you should be able to:

○ explain the composition of the South African population in terms of age, gender, living area, education and literacy, the labour market, unemployment and migrant work

○ use the information about this population in marketing decision-making

○ describe the composition of South African households in terms of housing, access to electricity, health care, refuse removal, sanitation, the possession of a telephone and their monthly household income

○ use the information about these households in marketing decision-making

○ explain the influence of the physical, economical, governmental, societal and technological factors on consumer behaviour

○ use this information in marketing decision-making

○ describe the various market-related trends that have evolved over the past few years and explain how these trends influence consumer behaviour.

3.1 Introduction

In Chapter 2 we saw that, as consumers, we live in a physical place where products are produced, transported, stored and used. The physical environment also affects the physical qualities of this marketplace. Furthermore, there are numerous market characteristics that influence this environment and therefore the way in which consumers live. From Figure 1.4 in Chapter 1 (page 11), it is clear that market characteristics include a country's climate, the economy, government and technology – all of which we deal with in this chapter. We also address some additional factors that in recent years have had an immense effect on consumer behaviour. Some of these factors relate to consumers' demographical composition (with particular reference to the South African consumer) as well as to certain societal changes occurring daily that influence how consumers purchase.

We examine market characteristics because they influence consumer behaviour. They influence what consumers need, how consumers behave, who will be involved in the purchase decision and how that decision will be made. As a result, a clear understanding of all these aspects enables marketers to blend the marketing mix instruments into suitable offerings, that is, products and services, thereby satisfying an individual's or a household's needs.

3.2 Market characteristics and the influence on consumer behaviour

In this section, we highlight how particular market characteristics influence consumer behaviour in the South African context.

3.2.1 Demographical characteristics of the South African population

Demography is the study of people's vital statistics, such as our age, race or ethnicity, and location. These characteristics are strongly related to consumer buyer behaviour and are accurate predictors of how the target market will respond to a specific marketing mix. Since we explore demography in more detail in later chapters, here we focus on the current demographical composition of the South African consumer.[1] The characteristics of the South African population are best described in the 2001 Census Report published by Statistics SA, which divides the findings into the two broad categories of individuals and households in this country.

Individuals

We now briefly consider the various aspects of the findings on individuals as provided by the 2001 Census Report:

- ○ **Population**: The size of the South African population in 2001 was estimated at 44.8 million people. This indicates an increase of 4.2 million since the first census that followed the democratic elections of April 1994.[2]
- ○ **Age distribution of the population**: The age distribution resembles the structure of a developing rather than a developed country, with proportionately more young people than older people.
- ○ **Physical distribution of the population**: A high percentage of the population – approximately 53% – are living in urban areas, while approximately 47% are living in non-urban areas and are primarily African.

    Influence on consumer behaviour: The diverse and growing population, its age and the high urbanisation rate we described above have a direct impact on the type of products and services consumers want and need. This situation influences the type of message marketers convey, as well as the price they charge for the product or service that the company offers. Marketers can use these aspects to segment the local market (a process we discuss further in Chapter 11).
- ○ **Education and literacy levels**: Formal education in South Africa is presently reaching the vast majority of children between the ages of 7 and 15 years. The

ability to read in at least one language continues to vary with age, population group, gender, and urban and non-urban place of residence. The highest proportion of non-readers is found among African women aged 20 years and older, living in non-urban areas.

Influence on consumer behaviour: This literacy rate and level of education has a direct impact on the **integrated marketing communication** (IMC) mix that marketers use to promote their products and services to current and potential consumers. For example, in regions where literacy rates and levels of education are low, road-shows that *demonstrate* products and services are more effective than the traditional promotional methods that rely on consumers being able to read.

○ **Labour market**: In 2001 an estimated 24.3 million people in South Africa were between the ages of 15 and 65 years, and 18.8 million of these people were classified as being unemployed or not economically active. From October 1995 to October 1999, the number of employed people increased from 9.6 million to 10.4 million.

○ **Unemployment**: There is a complex relationship between education and unemployment.[3] The lowest unemployment rate is found among those with tertiary education. The unemployment rates among those with education up to matriculation are higher.

○ **Formal and informal sectors**: The formal sector employment rate significantly outweighs the informal sector employment rate.

○ **Migrant work**: Migrant work is more common for African people than it is for those of other population groups. A migrant worker is a person who is absent from home for more than a month each year to work or to seek work.

Influence on consumer behaviour: The composition of the South African labour market, the high unemployment rate and the migrant worker status of the African people influence the blend of products and services that local companies provide. For example, the high unemployment rate results in poverty, and the consumers affected can afford only the basic products and services to satisfy their physiological needs of food, clothing and shelter. This phenomenon results in a declining market for luxury goods and services, such as cars, entertainment, and so on.

Households

We now briefly consider the various aspects of the findings on households', as provided by the 2001 Census Report:

○ **Housing**: Approximately 69.9% of the South African population is living in formal housing, and approximately 30.1% in informal dwellings. A large proportion of the latter live in formal and informal squatter camp dwellings.

○ **Water sources**: A large proportion of South African households have access to clean water, and the proportion of households obtaining water from rivers, streams and dams is continually declining.

Influence on consumer behaviour: Although there is a decrease in this state of informal housing and in the number of households accessing water from rivers, streams and dams, there is still a proportion of the population that cannot satisfy their basic needs for shelter and water. Marketers may well be able to provide such people with affordable products that could help their situation, for example a simple, cheap and effective method of filtering water.

○ **Energy sources**: Since 1995 there has been a gradual increase in the use of electricity for lighting, and a gradual decrease in the use of paraffin and candles. More than 50% of South African households mainly rely on electricity for cooking. Proportionally fewer households are using wood to cook.

○ **Telephones**: The proportion of households with a telephone in the dwelling, or with a mobile or cellular telephone, has increased immensely.

Influence on consumer behaviour: The current increase in access to electricity and telephones provides local marketers with the opportunity to sell more electronic products, such as electric stoves, microwave ovens, VCR and DVD players, and DStv access equipment. This has an additional impact on local marketers as they have to educate consumers on how to use this new and sometimes foreign-made equipment.

○ **Health care**: There has been a gradual increase in the use of public health care facilities in recent years and a gradual decrease in the use of private facilities.

Influence on consumer behaviour: The increase in the access to sanitation and health care facilities we describe above indicates that there is a change in the way people make decisions regarding their health care. They consider more decision criteria, evaluate more alternatives and carry out enhanced post-purchase evaluation. Marketers may even find opportunities for developing new alternative products and services here.

○ **Household income**: This income is given in the monthly figures issued in the Living Standards Measurement (LSM), published by the South African Advertising Research Foundation (SAARF). This survey allocates the South African population into ten universal groups based on their standard of living, ranging from group 10, which has the highest living standard with a monthly income of approximately R13 406, to group 1, which has the lowest monthly income of approximately R748.[5] (See Chapter 6 for a detailed discussion of the LSM.)

Influence on consumer behaviour: The current state of housing and access to water, sanitation, electricity and health care facilities, along with the low household income of the majority of South African households, are all indications of the socio-economic conditions that this population faces. As we have seen, a large proportion cannot satisfy their basic physiological needs. Marketers may well be able not only to sell appropriate products to this group, but also to help raise their standard of living in the process.

3.2.2 Economic factors influencing consumer behaviour

The economic conditions prevailing in a country act as the starting point of an assessment of opportunities and threats in the marketplace. The economic areas of greatest concern to most marketers are the conditions of inflation and the impact of interest rates and currency fluctuations on prices and consumer demand.[6]

The cumulative impact of consumers' purchase decisions, including the decision to forgo consumption – in other words, not to buy – is a major determinant of the state of a given country's economy. Consumers' decisions of whether to buy or save affect economic growth, the availability and cost of capital, employment levels and so forth. The types of products and brands that they purchase influence the balance of payments, industry growth rates and wage levels. Decisions made in one society, such as in particularly wealthy societies like the United States, Western Europe and Japan, have a major impact on the economic health of various other countries. A recession in the United States, or a strong shift toward purchasing American-made products only, would have profound negative consequences on the economics of many other countries.[7]

South Africa is a *developing* country, but it is also regarded as the economic power-house of sub-Saharan Africa. In South Africa there is a wide dispersion of income and a relatively low inflation rate compared to other developing countries. SAARF's universal LSM shows a skew distribution of monthly household income among the ten universal groups.[8] It also indicates that a massive redistribution of resources has been taking place in South Africa since the first democratic elections held in 1994.

Inflation means a general rise in prices without a corresponding increase in wages, which results in decreasing buying power. In light of inflation, it is important for South African marketers to realise that as buying power decreases, consumers will not pay more for a product than the subjective value they place on it.

Another factor that can influence the economic condition of a country is the occurrence of a recession. Marketers need to be aware that during a recession consumers switch to buying basics rather than luxuries, and they generally become more price sensitive.[9] This calls for a dramatic change in pricing structures and promotional activities.

3.2.3 Governmental factors influencing consumer behaviour

Every aspect of the marketing mix is subject to laws and restrictions. It is the duty of marketing managers or their legal assistants to understand these laws and to conform to them. Failure to comply with regulations can have major consequences for a firm. Sometimes, just sensing trends and taking corrective action before a government agency acts can help a company to avoid legal action. However, the challenge is not simply to keep the marketing department 'out of trouble', but to help them to devise creative programmes that can assist them in accomplishing their marketing objectives.[10]

Business needs government regulation to protect innovators of technology, to promote the interests of society in general, to protect one business from another, and to protect consumers. In turn, government needs business because the marketplace generates taxes that support public efforts to educate our youth, to protect our shores, and so on.

Legislation affecting marketing activities can be divided into three main categories:
1. **Promoting competition** – such as the bill that prohibits restrictive trading practices like price collusion.
2. **Limiting competition** – such as the laws providing Telkom and the Post Office with legal protection against competition.
3. **Protecting consumer rights** – such as the proposed Consumer Affairs Act.

In South Africa, marketers have recently had to deal with a deluge of new legislation at both central government and provincial government levels. Examples include:
○ Privacy and data protection (still under investigation: Issue Paper 24, Project 124).
○ Tobacco Products Control Act, 1993.
○ The Competition Act, 1998.
○ The Electronic Communications Act, 2002.

Today, the South African government is trying to create informed and well-educated consumers. Therefore, marketers should encourage consumers to exercise their rights and make better informed buying decisions.

A major consideration for marketers is the legislation passed in response to pressure created by consumers, for example in response to those who have conducted business unethically. This has resulted in many organised formal structures to protect consumers' rights. Eight basic rights for consumers have been identified:
1. The right to basic needs.
2. The right to safety.
3. The right to be informed.
4. The right to choose.
5. The right to be heard.
6. The right to redress.
7. The right to consumer education.
8. The right to a healthy environment.

This movement is known as '**consumerism**' and is receiving immense attention in today's marketplace.

3.2.4 Physical conditions influencing consumer behaviour

Marketers need to be aware of the threats and opportunities associated with the physical environment. Today, there are two aspects playing an increasingly important role in terms of the physical environment: climate and environmental deterioration. These aspects influence consumer behaviour on a daily basis.

South Africa has a primarily temperate and pleasant **climate** and is regarded as one of the most attractive tourism destinations in the world. The country has it all – natural beauty, a year-round sunny climate, abundant wildlife, beautiful beaches and superb facilities for sport and business.[11]

The climate also determines the kinds of crops that farmers grow here, and has an immediate influence on food consumption, use of clothing, housing patterns and the geographical distribution of the population itself. Thus we can say that climate affects all the basic needs and wants of South African consumers: food, clothing and shelter. Logically, marketers need to pay attention to the influence of climate on the population, and must provide goods and services accordingly.

The **deterioration of the natural environment** is a major global concern. In many cities, air and water pollution have reached dangerous levels. There is great concern about 'greenhouse gases' in the atmosphere due to the burning of fossil fuels, about the depletion of the ozone layer owing to certain chemicals, and about increasing water shortages.[12]

This deterioration has resulted not only in consumer demand for environmentally friendly, sound products but also in government regulations affecting product design and manufacture.

Increasing the number of 'green products' requires challenging consumers' loyalty habits, overcoming consumer scepticism about the motives behind the introduction of such products and their quality, and changing consumer attitudes about the role they themselves play in environmental protection. The hope is that companies will adopt practices to protect the natural environment. Great opportunities await companies and marketers who can create solutions that promise to reconcile prosperity with environmental protection.

3.2.5 Societal factors influencing consumer behaviour

Social change is perhaps the most difficult external variable for marketing managers to forecast, influence or integrate into marketing plans. Social factors include our attitudes, values and lifestyles. These factors influence the products and services that we buy and use; the prices we are prepared to pay for those products and services; the effectiveness of specific promotions; and how, where and when we make our purchases.[13]

Purchasing power is directed *towards* certain goods and services and away from others according to people's tastes and preferences. Society shapes the beliefs, values and norms that largely define such tastes and preferences. Consciously and unconsciously, people absorb a worldview that defines their relationships with themselves, with others, with organisations, with society as a whole, with nature and with the universe.

The world as we know it has also undergone numerous societal changes in recent years, and we explore some of these developing trends in section 3.3.

3.2.6 Technological factors influencing consumer behaviour

Few environmental factors have such a pervasive influence on consumers as do technological developments. The rate at which these developments are commercialised is increasing exponentially. New scientific knowledge, research results, inventions and innovations that often lead to new products and services arise on a regular basis, for example e-commerce, electronic banking, shopping and accessing information on the internet, cellular telephone technology such as WAP and Bluetooth, and satellite technology such as DStv and video conferencing. The internet is a hypertext system that allows computer users to send and receive text, graphics, video and sound to or from anywhere in the world. It has a particularly significant impact on local consumer markets and marketing practices in general.

These technological advances affect consumer behaviour in South Africa in several ways, such as:

○ the way people access information about the marketplace and the alternatives it offers has been permanently altered
○ the way marketers communicate with their consumers has taken on a more electronic form
○ the ways consumers' purchase processes are increasingly changing to take place via the internet and using credit card technology
○ the way consumers can now purchase anything from everywhere in the world at any time, thereby increasing competition for South African companies.

Marketers need to come to terms with this rapidly changing situation if they intend to achieve success.

3.3 Developing trends that influence consumer behaviour

We now examine four marketing responses to some of the abovementioned market characteristics.[14]

3.3.1 Green marketing

Owing to our growing concern for the environment, marketers have begun to establish a different approach to marketing. This approach, called 'green marketing', focuses on the environment and generally involves:

○ developing products whose production, use or disposal is less harmful to the environment than the traditional versions of the products
○ developing products that have a positive impact on the environment
○ linking the purchase of a product to an environmental organisation or event.

As a result, many firms are improving their products and processes in relation to the environment and to the advertising of these improvements.

Sustainability: The key to green packaging paradigm[15]

Brand owners, designers, packaging technicians and waste management consultants – all driven by consumer insights – are creating a new, environmentally friendly packaging paradigm that is sustainable and relevant. This means that the conventional, long-lasting linear approach to packaging is on its way out.

Economics aside, green legislators, pressure groups and concerned citizens are putting environmental issues on commercial agendas everywhere, and the packaging industry must meet the challenge of creating responsible packaging that attracts, protects and dispenses in an environmentally friendly manner. Packaging design trends will be driven by consumers, who have the power to boycott; by government, which has the power to legislate; and by designers, who understand the importance of delivering sustainable packaging that meets legislative requirements and brand imperatives.

Where possible, nature's own packaging provides the optimum solution, for example the banana skin. It is easy to handle, opens easily, protects the product, has a built-in sell-by date and is biodegradable. So why package it in plastic? Where it is not possible to eliminate packaging, environmental guidelines call for the minimal approach. Look at cereal boxes and potato-chip packets – although they are designed to reach maximum shelf impact, they are only filled half the space within the box. Can't we save?

There is an international trend towards 'dejunking' design, with brands embracing simpler ideas and concepts, which has seen the emergence of trendy cosmetics and lotions being packaged without the frills and wastage. This is evident in the increasing popularity of brands such as The Body Shop. Furthermore, the use of reusable, consumable and returnable packaging is becoming increasingly popular. Questions are also being raised about recyclable material packaging, which has been proclaimed as an environmentally friendly alternative.

3.3.2 Cause-related marketing

The term 'cause marketing' is sometimes used interchangeably with 'social marketing' to refer to the application of marketing principles and tactics, and to advance a cause such as a charity, an ideology or an activity. Social marketing differs from traditional marketing in the intangible and abstract nature of the 'product' and in the absence of a profit motive. At one extreme, such as a health-related campaign, there are potential *direct* benefits to the individual. However, in general, the benefits to the individual are *indirect*, for example a better society in which to live. Often, the benefit is purely or primarily emotional. Marketers encourage individuals to change their beliefs or behaviours, or purchase a product or service, because 'it is the right thing to do' and they will 'feel good' or 'be a better person' as a result.

Cause-related marketing ties a company and its products to an issue or cause with the goal of improving sales or the corporate image while providing benefits to the cause. Companies associate with causes to create long-term relationships with their consumers, and to build corporate and brand equity that should eventually lead to increased sales. The foundation of cause-related marketing is marketing to consumers' values. By addressing issues such as breast cancer, Aids or pollution, cause-related marketing relates to actions that consumers can take to help solve these problems.

Deep branding, the millennium marketing tool[16]

A new concept in Corporate Social Responsibility (CSR) has been introduced. It is called 'deep branding' and it combines Corporate Social Investment (CSI) with marketing to help boost corporate reputation and the brand image, and, more importantly, to improve the return on CSI investments.

Globally, consumers have become much more aware of the work and impact of corporations, and therefore expect much more accountability and social responsibility from them. Today, a corporation needs to focus not only on what it does, but more importantly on what *good* it does in order to win the support of the consumer. Consumers want to know how the manufacturer treats workers, what impact factories and products have on the environment, and whether it is investing sufficiently in the communities supporting its brands.

Deep branding begins with a shared corporate vision, dedicated financial resources and understanding between the CSI and marketing division. By allocating percentages from both CSI and marketing budgets to spread the good word regarding the actions of the organisation, relationships between the organisation and its consumers will deepen.

3.3.3 Marketing to gay and lesbian consumers

Society in general is shifting from valuing uniformity to valuing diversity: **diversity** in terms of ethnicity, religious beliefs and race. One of the largest groups to begin to gain public acceptance has been the gay and lesbian community.

Like heterosexual consumers, gay consumers are members of ethnic groups, live in various regions of the country and belong to occupational categories and age groups. These and a host of other factors influence their behaviour and, in most instances, play a much larger role in their consumption process than does their sexual orientation.

Any firm that desires to capture the loyalty of the gay community must ask itself a number of questions when approaching this market:

❍ Must we modify the product in any way to meet the needs of this market?
❍ Should we advertise in gay-oriented media using our standard ads?

Gay lifestyle gets wrapped up[17]

❍ The gay and lesbian community now has a magazine that caters to its lifestyle, with the launch of *Wrapped* magazine by Brave Publishing. This magazine not only entertains, it also addresses important issues facing this community. *Wrapped* is positioned as a quality read for gays and lesbians, and their families and friends.

❍ Radio 2000 launched a weekly two-hour radio show, *The Tuesday Night Show*, that is aimed primarily at the gay and lesbian community.

❍ The annual Gay Pride March through the streets of Johannesburg offers a unique chance for marketers to reach the 'Pink' community. Research done both locally and internationally has proven that this market generally falls into the higher LSM groups, has on average a high annual income and a larger disposable income. Moreover, this market is not only brand conscious, but extremely receptive to brands that are seen as supporting social diversity and freedom of expression.

○ Should we advertise in gay media using ads with gay themes?
○ To what extent should we be involved in gay community activities?
○ Should our major media ads include ads with gay themes?

While the exact dimensions of the gay market remains unclear and a lack of sound data reduces the willingness of many firms to target this group, many others have concluded that it represents a significantly attractive market to pursue.

3.3.4 Gender-based marketing

Until recently, the prevailing stereotype of a motorcar purchase involved a man making the purchase alone. If he was accompanied by his wife or a girlfriend, she simply offered suggestions concerning colour and interior features. Today, more and more women influence such purchases and are becoming predominant buyers of various models.

Gender roles have undergone massive changes over the past few years. Increasingly, women are participating in the working world. Moreover, their effort to balance this role with that of mother and/or wife is matched by men's effort to balance their work with being a father and/or a husband. Indeed, in many cases, the traditional situation of the woman staying at home to look after the family has been replaced by the situation of the man fulfilling this role. We find a pattern typical of a changing value: growing acceptance of the change, but not for *all* aspects of it, and substantial resistance to the new behaviours coming from the more traditional groups or those who stand to lose as the new value is accepted. While men and women express strong preferences for the modern lifestyle as a general concept, most recognise that it comes at a cost, and their attitudes and behaviours toward specific aspects of that lifestyle remain conservative.

Today, women have a variety of role options and display a range of attitudes concerning their gender. Some relevant marketing implications relate to:
○ market segmentation
○ product strategy
○ marketing communications
○ retail strategy.

This trend is receiving increased attention, and companies that do not conform to it are likely feeling the pressure.

It's only a matter of time[18]

More women today are expressing a need to 'own' or reclaim their time. South African women have to juggle their traditional identities with new contemporary roles as mothers, career women, housekeepers, girlfriends, wives, daughters and singletons, while also trying to find time for the community, the gym, religion and a good night out. For marketers looking for ways to grow their brands and businesses, products and services that SAVE time, TAKE time and facilitate a little ME time are those that women are reaching out for.

3.4 Marketing implications

South African marketers must know the characteristics of their market. Having obtained all the relevant information from every relevant source, marketers can use this information to plan a marketing campaign. Then, based on their knowledge of the diverse composition of the South African population, local marketers need to develop unique marketing methods to reach their consumers. These marketing methods will be different from the traditional methods, for example to reach consumers in the rural areas where the literacy rate is relatively low, marketers can make use of road-shows, bus advertising and taxi radio advertising.

3.5 Summary

The knowledge and insight that they gain from the various marketing characteristics will empower South African marketers to develop marketing strategies that will best fit their intended target markets. It is critical that they stay abreast of what is happening in the consumers' environments. They must consider factors relating to the demography of the consumer, prevailing economic conditions, governmental legislation protecting consumers, the influence of the physical environment, and the societal and technological factors influencing consumer behaviour. By understanding this behaviour clearly, marketers will be able to blend the marketing mix instruments to suit the consumers' needs.

Questions for self-assessment

To assess your progress, answer these questions:
1. List all possible variables that can make a contribution to the composition of the South African population profile.
2. Describe the variables that you can use to investigate the composition of South African households.
3. Discuss some of the major current trends that are influencing consumer behaviour. How will this knowledge influence your role as a marketing manager.
4. With reference to the case study on the next page and the chapter as a whole, answer the following questions:
   a. How will genetically modified food and biotechnology influence the South African consumer in terms of their demographic composition?
   b. Which market characteristics will be influenced by biotechnology?
   c. How do you think genetically modified food and biotechnology will influence consumer behaviour?
   d. As a marketer, how would you market genetically modified foods and/or biotechnological products to consumers?

Case study

BIOTECHNOLOGY AND BEYOND[19]

The world as we know it is changing rapidly. There is a concept that has been receiving attention recently which will cause dramatic changes in the way consumers behave in the future – it is called **'biotechnology'**.

Proponents believe the gains that currently accrue mainly to biotech companies and 'big business' farmers will spread as consumers receive more nutritious foods and farmers in the developing world produce better crops. Detractors say that genetic engineering is a Pandora's box, and that we are releasing uncontrollable forces into our environment and food supply. Recently, in Mexico, birthplace of corn and storehouse of its genetic diversity, researchers reported that local varieties had been contaminated by modified genes – even though Mexico has banned the planting of engineered corn. Some scientists question the findings of the report, but others see them as evidence of risks.

Biotechnology is still in its infancy, but we are now able to have strawberries throughout the year by combining the frost gene of fish with the fruit, thereby making it frost resistant.

The following are some other possible developments:

○ Combining a scorpion gene with corn to harvest corn that has not been attacked by insects.
○ Combining firefly genes and tobacco to develop glow-in-the-dark cigarettes.
○ Growing mustard plants that mine gold.

This is just a brief look at where the world is going. All of these aspects will have a dramatic effect on consumer behaviour. Are you willing to purchase maize that has been 'grown' with scorpion genes, or strawberries with fish genes? How do you change your perception as a consumer? How will these developments change your needs and wants? Where will it end?

Endnote references

1. Lamb, C.W., Hair, J.F., McDaniel, C., Boshoff, C. and Terblanché, N.S. 2004. *Marketing.* 2nd ed. Cape Town: Oxford University Press.
2. Achieving better life for all. Progress between Census 1996 and Census 2001. Report 03-02-16. Available on the internet from: www.statssa.gov.za (accessed 12 August 2005).
3. Ibid.
4. Ibid.
5. Ibid.
6. Lamb et al., op. cit.
7. Hawkins, D.I., Best, R.J. and Coney, A. 2004. *Consumer Behaviour: Building Marketing Strategy.* 9th ed. New York: McGraw-Hill/Irwin.
8. Available on the internet from: www.saarf.co.za (accessed 12 August 2005).

9.   Lamb et al., op. cit.
10. Lamb et al., op. cit.
11. Available on the internet from: www.southafrica.net.
12. Hawkins et al., op. cit.
13. Hawkins et al., op. cit.
14. Hawkins et al., op. cit.
15. Enterprise IG. 2003. Sustainability: The key to green packaging paradigm. Available on the internet from: www.biz-community.co.za (accessed 12 August 2005).
16. 2004. Deep branding, the millennium marketing tool. Available on the internet from: www.biz-community.co.za (accessed 12 August 2005).
17. 2004. Gay lifestyle gets wrapped up in gloss. Available on the internet from: www.bizcommunity.co.za (accessed 12 August 2005).
18. Added Value. 2005. It's only a matter of time. Available on the internet from: www.biz-community.co.za (accessed 7 August 2005).
19. Loosely based on information obtained at a seminar presented by Wolfgang Grulke, Future World. May 2002. Pretoria: Sheraton Hotel.

4 Culture and subculture

Learning Outcomes

After studying this chapter, you should be able to:

❍ define culture and subculture

❍ explain how culture is acquired

❍ apply measurements of culture and subculture in analysing consumer markets

❍ outline South African core values

❍ apply means-end chain analysis in understanding consumer markets

❍ position brands based on values

❍ use acquired knowledge of values in segmenting consumer markets.

4.1 Introduction

The study of culture is a challenging undertaking because its primary focus is on the broadest component of social behaviour in an entire society. In this chapter, we explore the basic concept and dynamic nature of culture, as well as the role that customs and beliefs, needs, learning, language, symbols and rituals play in culture. We give particular attention to the role that values play as an underlying influence on consumer behaviour. Throughout this discussion, we emphasise the role that culture plays in influencing consumer behaviour. We also briefly discuss the core South African values and the measurement of culture.

4.2 The nature of culture

Given the broad and pervasive nature of culture, its study generally requires a detailed examination of the character of a total society, including such abstract elements as values, attitudes, ideas, personality types, language, laws, religions, politics, customs and work patterns, and material elements such as books, computers, tools, buildings, music, art, specific products and other artefacts that give a society its distinctive quality. In a sense, culture is a society's personality.[1] For this reason, it is not easy to define its boundaries.

Culture is difficult to define in short, simple terms. It seems there are as many definitions of culture as there are anthropologists and social scientists, each defining it to suit his or her understanding and interpretation.

To some, the term refers to finesse in self-comportment. According to this view, 'A cultured person is one who behaves in a becoming way according to his society's standard of behaviour, a gentleman, a well brought up lady, one that is so holistically educated that he is at home with any given subject of discussion in art, music, literature, politics etc., who has cultivated taste for what society judges admirable and worthy of the human spirit.' To others, culture refers to masquerades, traditional dances, festivals, traditional marriage ceremonies, etc. In this instance, fierce arguments in defence of polygamy, violence in masquerades, extraordinary spending in the burial of the dead, and so on are expressed in the name of culture.

Culture is also seen as a selective human-made way of responding to experience, or a behavioural pattern, which means that culture influences or affects motives, brand comprehension, attitudes and consumers' intention to use.[2] From a consumer behaviour perspective, culture can be defined as the sum total of learned beliefs, values and customs that serve to direct the consumer behaviour of members of a particular society.[3]

We can make the following observations from these definitions:

❍ Culture, as a 'complex whole', is a system of interdependent components.
❍ Culture is not only a narrow view of people's activities, it extends to include all the activities that characterise the behaviour of particular communities of people – the way they eat, how they talk, their appearance and their general behavioural patterns.

4.2.1 Customs, beliefs and values

Customs are overt modes of behaviour that constitute culturally approved or acceptable ways of behaving in specific situations.[4] Customs consist of daily or routine behaviour. While beliefs and values are *guides* for behaviour, customs are usual and acceptable *ways* of behaving. In South Africa, for example, it is customary not to be totally naked in public. In Japan, by contrast, groups of men and women may take steam baths together, naked, without being perceived as improper. At the other extreme, women in some African countries are not even allowed to reveal their faces. Significantly, the things that some countries view as moral may in fact be regarded as highly immoral by the standards of other countries. For example, the law that once banned interracial marriages in South Africa was named the 'Immorality Act', even though in most civilised countries this law, and any degree of explicit racial prejudice, would itself be considered highly immoral.

Beliefs consist of the great number of thought or expressed statements that reflect a person's particular knowledge and assessment of something.[5] **Values** are also beliefs. However, values differ from beliefs in that each one must meet the following criteria:

❍ They are relatively few in number.
❍ They serve as a guide for culturally appropriate behaviour.
❍ They are enduring, or difficult to change.
❍ They are not tied to specific objects or situations.
❍ They are widely accepted by the members of a society.

The impact of culture is so natural and automatic that we usually take for granted its influence on our behaviour. Often, it is only when we are exposed to people with different cultural values or customs that we become aware of how culture has moulded our own behaviour. While most South African citizens are born in South Africa, some retain a pride in, and an identification with, the language and customs of their ancestors. This identification shows itself in consumer behaviour. When it comes to such behaviour, we can see ancestral pride most strongly in the consumption of ethnic foods, in travel to the 'homeland' and in the buying of cultural artefacts.

Marketers always try to identify cultural shifts in order to discover products that consumers might want. For example, the cultural shift towards greater concern about health and fitness has created a huge industry for exercise equipment and clothing, low fat and more natural foods, and health and fitness services. Also, the shift toward informality has resulted in a greater demand for casual clothing and simpler home furnishings. And our increased desire for leisure time has resulted in our increased demand for convenience products and services, such as microwave ovens and fast food.

4.2.2 Needs and culture

Culture exists to satisfy the needs of people in a society. It offers order, direction and guidance in all phases of human problem-solving by providing tried and trusted methods of satisfying physiological, personal and social needs. Similarly, culture also defines what is considered to be suitable dress for specific occasions, such as what to wear around the house, to school, to work, to church, at a restaurant or a movie, etc.

We continue to follow cultural beliefs, values and customs as long as they give us satisfaction. In a cultural context, when we no longer find a product acceptable because its related value or custom does not adequately satisfy our needs, it must be modified.

4.2.3 Learning and culture

At an early age, we begin to acquire from our social environment a set of beliefs, values and customs that make up our culture. For children, the process of playing with toys reinforces the learning of these acceptable values and customs. As children play, they act out, or rehearse, important cultural lessons and situations.

There are three distinct forms of learning:
1. **Formal learning**, in which adults and older siblings teach a young family member 'how to behave'.

2. **Informal learning**, in which a child learns primarily by imitating the behaviour of selected others.
3. **Technical learning**, in which teachers instruct children in an educational environment as to what, how and why they should do certain things.

Advertising proves a strong influence on all three forms of learning. It primarily influences informal learning by providing models, and the repetition of advertising messages creates and reinforces cultural beliefs and values.

4.2.4 Language, symbols and rituals

Language
Members of a society must be able to communicate with each other through a common language. Without this, shared meaning could not exist and true communication would not take place. Fundamentally, the symbolic nature of human language sets it apart from all other animal communication.

Symbols
A symbol is anything that stands for something else, for example a cross symbolises Christianity while a star and a crescent symbolises Islam. Symbols may have several, even contradictory, meanings. Marketers use symbols to convey desired product images or characteristics. Price and channels of distribution are also significant symbols of marketers and marketers' products. The type of store where a product is sold is also an important symbol of quality.

Ritual
Rook[7] defines a ritual as a type of symbolic activity consisting of a series of steps occurring in a fixed sequence and repeated over time. Rituals extend over the human life cycle, and can be public or private. A ritual is often formal and scripted, such as the way proper conduct is prescribed. Rituals are important to marketers because they tend to be linked to ritual artefacts or products that are associated with, or somehow improve, performance of that ritual.

4.3 The dynamic nature of culture

As culture continually evolves, marketers must carefully monitor the socio-cultural environment in order to market an existing product more effectively or to develop promising new products. This is not easy; many factors are likely to produce cultural changes in a given society. The changing nature of culture means that marketers have to consistently reconsider:
○ why consumers are now doing what they are doing
○ who the buyers and users of their products are

○ when consumers do their shopping
○ how and where the media can reach consumers
○ the new product and service that may be emerging.

4.3.1 Enculturation and acculturation

Enculturation is the learning of our *own* culture, while **acculturation** is the learning of a *new* or *foreign* culture. The South African consumer market exists at various levels of sophistication and acculturation. The process of acculturation results in the growth of a cosmopolitan urban community, with different ethic groups experiencing constant interaction. This results in the development of subcultures, for example the dynamic growth in township cultures characterised by unique belief systems, dress codes and language patterns. The ongoing process of acculturation also ensures that lifestyles and consumption patterns change – a fact that marketers need to monitor continuously.

4.4 Subculture

We can define subculture as a distinct cultural group that exists as an identifiable segment within a larger, more complex society.[8] Subcultures include nationalities, religions, language groups, racial groups and geographic regions. Many subcultures make up important market segments, and marketers often design products and marketing programmes tailored to these subcultures' needs.

Different perspectives on the diversity in South African culture exist. The 'rainbow nation' metaphor suggests strength and richness in diversity. The 'salad bowl' metaphor, by contrast, suggests that although ethnic groups will interact as a whole (through the whole mix of salad) and contain some elements of the whole (through the dressing), each group will maintain its own significant traits (each vegetable is different from the others). Another perspective suggests that, in the long run, there will be fewer differences between ethnic groups; instead, one mainstream culture that incorporates elements from each will result. This 'melting pot' view suggests that marketers should run integrated promotions aimed at all groups, while the 'salad bowl' approach suggests that each group should be approached separately.

Subculture is often categorised on the basis of demographics. Thus, for example, we have the 'teenage' subculture and the 'older affluent' subculture. While part of the overall culture, these groups often have distinguishing characteristics. Values tend to be associated with age groups because people within an age group have shared experiences. For example, it is believed that people old enough to have experienced the Great Depression during the 1930s were more frugal in later years because of that experience.

Geographic region – that is, rural, villages, towns, peri-urban and metropolitan – is a significant subcultural consumer group. In South Africa, various toiletry, food and grocery consumption patterns are evident in the more rural provinces of Limpopo and the Eastern Cape as compared to the more urbanised provinces of Gauteng and the Western Cape.

Other examples of important South African subcultural groups are language communities – Afrikaans, English, Sotho, Xhosa, Zulu, etc., racial population groups – Asian, African, coloured and white, and religions – various denominations.

4.5 Cultural values and society

In order for a particular belief, value or practice to be considered a cultural characteristic, a significant portion of the society must share it. Various social institutions transmit the elements of culture and make sharing of culture a reality:

○ **Family** is the primary agent for enculturation, and from a marketer's point of view it teaches consumer-related values and skills.
○ **Educational institutions** impart basic learning skills, history, patriotism, citizenship and technical training.
○ **Houses of worship** provide religious consciousness, spiritual guidance and moral training.
○ The **mass media** are the often overlooked transmitters of culture. They disseminate information about products, ideas and causes. We have daily exposure to advertising, and through advertisements we receive cultural information.

The distinction between individualistic and collectivist societies is crucial to the cross-cultural understanding of consumer behavior.[9] This dimension has been identified as one of the major aspects of culture and is perhaps one of the most significant ways in which societies differ. The complexity of the dimension has been indicated in studies of motivation, affect, cognition, self-concept and social behavior.[10]

Generally speaking, this dimension refers to the relationship we perceive between our selves and the group to which we belong. **Individualism** is defined as *emotional independence* from 'groups, organisations, and other collectivities.'[11] Compared to people in collectivist cultures, people in individualistic societies tend to be more self-centred and self-enhanced; less willing to sacrifice for their in-groups; less loyal and emotionally attached to in-groups; and less concerned with their in-group needs, goals, norms, interests, integrity and consequences. They tend to consider the individual self as the basic unit and a source of life identity, purpose and goals.[12] By contrast, those in **collectivist** cultures value their group membership, respect group processes and decisions, and expect other in-group members to look after or protect them in case of need or crisis. For them, keeping good and harmonious relationships inside their in-group is a priority, and avoiding loss of face is important.[13] Their identity is based on the strong and cohesive in-groups to which they belong. In collectivist cultures, cooperation is high within in-groups, but is unlikely when the other person belongs to an out-group. By way of comparison, people in individualist cultures are good at forming new in-groups and getting along with those from out-groups.

4.5.1 Social values

Values are a complex area of discussion. Before we discuss the particular instruments that measure values, we need to look in some detail at what exactly values are.

Values are the deep-seated motivations instilled from culture. People feel them more deeply than opinions, which can be easily influenced by current debates, and hold values far more strongly and change them less easily than they would change their attitudes.

Values exist mainly at the individual level, but when one is substantially shared throughout a society, it becomes a **cultural value**. Knowledge of the socio-cultural sector in terms of cultural values is crucial to marketing, because cultural values influence the behaviours of most individuals in consumption situations. As cultural values shift, so will consumers' motives for buying products, and so the firm that fails to recognise this will overlook opportunities for new products.

Values are widely viewed as the outcomes of culture and ethnicity of a society,[14] and have underlying multi-dimensions. Thus, we can regard certain types of values as more important to consumers in one country's market than to those in another country's market owing to differences in culture and socio-economic conditions. Evidently, certain values affect more significantly consumers' attitudes and purchase decisions in specific country markets.

As markets become more modern and affluent, with increased exposure to other material-oriented cultures, consumers may want the goods that they see are being consumed in other cultures. This trend suggests that consumer values shape motivations to purchase particular products or brands by prioritising consumer needs and influencing consumers' product evaluation and consumption decisions.

In his seminal work, *The Nature of Human Values*, Rokeach makes a fundamental distinction between **terminal values**, that is, beliefs about desired *end-states* such as freedom, comfortable life and mature love, and **instrumental values**, that is, beliefs about desired *modes of action*, such as being independent, ambitious or honest.[15] Rokeach also suggests that human values serve psychological functions that are similar to the functions underlying attitudes. Thus, it is likely that the psychological function of an individual's attitude is matched by the psychological function of his or her human values and, consequently, each psychological function spans the breadth of the value-attitude-behaviour system. Human values are distinct from attitudes, because attitudes refer to specific mental or physical objects – a person, thing or issue – whereas human values have no object of reference. Nevertheless, human values guide object evaluation and attitude formation by motivating individuals to seek out objects that will satisfy or fulfil their values.

Consumer behaviour studies[16],[17] have therefore investigated how human values influence the psychological functions of attitudes. That is, like attitudes, human values can serve expressive, instrumental, knowledge and social-adjustive psychological functions. The motivation underpinning the instrumental function is our desire to feel that we can competently and effectively control and manipulate our environment. As such, an object's benefits to an individual holding an instrumental function are the object's intrinsic qualities, its means to an end and its ability to control the environment. In contrast, the motivation for the expressive function of the value-attitude-behaviour system is the need for self-expression in general, and the need for self-consistency and social-adjustment/approval in particular. In this case, the object's benefit is its use as a vehicle for self-expression.

Consumer researchers often investigate how the psychological function that an individual's attitude serves affects his or her ability to be persuaded by advertisements that focus on the product's tangible attributes and utility versus those that focus on its intangible, symbolic attributes. For instance, individuals who value a comfortable life may seek out, and in turn have positive attitudes towards, objects that bring about a comfortable life, such as luxury cars, large boats, large homes, etc.

If an individual buys a luxury car to express his or her human values and make his or her real self closer to the ideal self, then simply owning the car would be enough to expand the self-image. By contrast, the car's non-use would be unsatisfactory for an individual who purchased it for the utility of getting from point A to point B. Individuals who place greater ultimate weight on states of existence and less on 'actions' – in other words, who favour terminal over instrumental values – should seek out those objects in the environment that can bring about the states of existence. Thus, individuals who favour terminal over instrumental values should have a predisposition to attend to a product's symbolic meanings when evaluating a product. Individuals who favour instrumental values over terminal values should place greater emphasis on the product's utilitarian meaning.

The findings suggest that consumers may relate to products essentially in two ways. On the one hand, the crucial concerns of consumers are the product's intrinsic qualities, its means to an end and its ability to control the environment, each of which serves their need for an efficient and effective manipulation of the environment. On the other hand, the issue for consumers is how the product can be used as a vehicle for self-expression and can serve social-adjustive and/or self-consistency needs. Moreover, during product evaluation and selection, consumers in the former mode would weigh up the product's utilitarian and tangible attributes in an attribute-by-attribute, or piecemeal, judgement, whereas, in the latter mode, consumers would evaluate the symbolism/image of the product in an affective, intuitive and holistic judgement.

Thus, marketing managers could develop these promotional materials:

○ **'Instrumental' advertisements**:
  – promote the utilitarian and tangible benefits of the product
  – present information in a detailed, point-by-point list, which should facilitate a piecemeal judgement
  – illustrate what the product 'does' or what consumers can do with the product, which should encourage consumers to use their instrumental values as criteria with which to judge the product
  – imply how using the product will enable more efficient and effective manipulation of the environment.

○ 'Terminal' advertisements:
  – promote the symbolism/image of the product by using metaphors, or by illustrating the kinds of people and social groups who use the product, etc.
  – encourage consumers to consider their intuition and emotional response, which should facilitate an affective judgement
  – portray states of 'being' or ultimate goals, which should encourage consumers to use their terminal values as criteria with which to judge the product
  – imply how using the product will enable self-expression in general, and social approval and self-consistency in particular.

The most effective and persuasive instrumental and terminal adverts would match the promotional strategy to each consumer's way of relating to a given product. Whether consumers relate to products in an instrumental or expressive way would depend on the type of product, that is, tools would probably be more instrumental and clothes more expressive, but the results of the present studies also suggest that some consumers have a predisposition to relate to products in a particular way. This means that given that human values are non-object-specific and instead guide object evaluation and attitude formation, individuals' relative preference for instrumental or terminal values would leave them more likely to have instrumental or expressive product attitudes, respectively. As such, individuals who favour instrumental over terminal values would tend to have instrumental attitudes towards a range of products. Likewise, individuals who favour terminal to instrumental values would tend to have expressive attitudes towards many products.

Zetterberg[18] concludes that values are the fundamental force that drives markets. They indicate how people wish to live and they can be expressed in the marketplace. They have diagnostic qualities within a socio-cultural framework, especially for longer-term planning. In addition, marketers must understand them in order to devise effective marketing tactics and strategies.[19] Values are particularly important in media selection, in order for marketers to obtain the optimum results from promotion and to maintain brand loyalty.

Consumers may choose particular products and brands not only because these provide the functional or performance benefits they expect, but also because they can use the product to express their personality, social status or affiliation (symbolic purposes), or to fulfil their internal psychological needs, such as the need for change or newness (emotional purposes).

4.5.2 Personal values

Personal values are shown as the underlying determinant of consumer attitudes and consumption behaviour. Homer and Kahle refer to several studies on values behaviours to support the linkage of values, attitude and behaviour, demonstrating that individual value differences are related to significant differences in a variety of attitudinal and behavioural outcomes with respect to, for example, motorcar purchase, mass media subscription and cigarette smoking.[20] Lerena draws attention to the increased emphasis placed on personal values by marketing theorists.[21] By knowing about values, marketers understand why consumers behave in certain ways and can predict the media and products that consumers will use.

Hence, we can view personal values as one of the most influential factors that affect the type of needs consumers try to satisfy through purchase and consumption behaviours.[22] In other words, consumers' needs and desires are shaped by their values, which in turn are influenced by the society to which they belong.

4.5.3 The value concept in marketing

In marketing, the value concept refers to people and to objects. A brand will be a strong brand if people's values match the values of the brand. 'Branding' means adding values to products, and advertising is an important instrument for achieving this.

Values play an important role in consumer behaviour because they influence choice. They provide consumers with standards for making comparisons between alternatives. Values offer an opportunity to differentiate brands by going beyond attributes and benefits or the deliverance of higher level consequences to consumers. Adding values creates association networks that distinguish the brand from the competitive brands in the category and thus can help build strong positions for brands.

A conceptually appealing strategic tool is the **value structure map** (VSM), which describes how a particular group of subjects tends to perceive or think about a specific product or brand. A VSM links the product's attributes and benefits to values. Attributes can be concrete or abstract; benefits can be the functional or psychosocial consequences of the product's attributes. VSMs provide a structure of people's associations with a brand at the three levels: attributes, benefits and values. They show how the types of associations that people make between specific attributes of a product are connected to subsequent benefits and values. This connection, developed by Gutman,[23] is presented as the means-end chain model.

Gutman formulated the idea as follows: Means are objects (products) or activities in which people engage; ends are valued states of being such as happiness, security and accomplishment. A **means-end chain** is a model that seeks to explain how the choice of a product or service facilitates the achievement of desired end-states. The model consists of elements that represent the major consumer processes that link values to behaviour. Rokeach's distinction of instrumental and terminal values compares with the means and ends.

The technique Gutman used to develop means-end chains is **laddering**: an in-depth, one-on-one interviewing technique that facilitates the development of an understanding of how consumers translate the attributes of products into meaningful associations with respect to the self. The length and content of a means-end chain depend on the content and organisation of the semantic knowledge structures that consumers have learned through experiences. When product attributes are not connected to values, the means-end chains are short. The end level of a means-end chain reflects the extent to which consumers feel that the product or brand attribute is personally relevant or valuable to their self-concepts.

4.6 South African core values

According to Nyasani, African, Asian and European minds are products of unique 'cultural edifices' and 'cultural streams' that resulted from environmental conditioning and long-standing cultural traditions.[24] In the African cultural stream are psychological and moral characteristics pertaining to African identity, personality and dignity. Makgoba goes further by arguing that peoples of African descent are linked by shared values that are fundamental features of African identify and culture, including hospitality, friendliness or consensus, a common framework seeking principle, ubuntu (see shortly below), and the emphasis on community rather than on the individual.[25] These features typically underpin the variations of African culture and identity everywhere.

Mbiti believes that the individual has little latitude for self-determination outside the context of the traditional African family and community.[26] Whatever happens to the individual happens to the whole group, and whatever happens to the whole group happens to the individual. According to Shutte, the Xhosa proverb *umuntu ngumuntu ngabantu* (a person is a person through persons) refers to a notion that is common to all African languages and traditional cultures.[27] He mentions that in European philosophy of whatever kind, the self is always envisaged as something 'inside' a person, or at least as a kind of container of mental properties and powers. In African thought, by contrast, it is seen as 'outside', in the natural and social environment, subsisting in relationship to what is other. Self and world are united and intermingle in a web of reciprocal relations.

Identification of core values in South Africa is an extremely difficult task for several reasons. According to Corder, South Africa is a highly diverse country consisting of a variety of subcultures, each of which interprets and responds to society's basic beliefs and values in its own, specific way.[28] Moreover, rapid technological change has occurred in this country, which in itself makes it difficult to monitor changes in cultural values.

The Sociomonitor is an investigation of the values of South African adults that are relevant to decision-makers.[29] The value groups identified can be used in the segmentation of consumer markets. A major advantage of segmentation based on values is that it identifies groups of people in terms that are the *causes* of behaviour, rather than descriptions of behaviour. Benefit and value segmentation have this in common, which is not surprising, as the benefits consumers look for in products are expressions of values. Benefits often resemble the 'desirable end-states' of Rokeach's terminal values, e.g. a comfortable life, family security and mature love. Values would tend to be all embracing, while benefits are more product related.

De Vulpian originally developed the technique that is used by Sociomonitor to measure values, and that is similar in concept to the procedure devised by Yankelovich in the United States.[30, 31] The power of Sociomonitor is that it explains and describes the link between consumer values or psychographics, consumer motivations and the image or positioning of products and brands. It is a valid, reliable and scientific reflection of South African society, as the 183 psychographic measures are analysed using multi-variate statistics to create a psychographic tool for users of the model. Brand users are plotted among these in order to investigate how a brand is psychographically positioned and whether it is well differentiated.

Sociomonitor is applied to users of brands and competitor brands, segments, target markets, and any other consumers that marketers may want to analyse, to give them insight into the consumers' psychographics, who the consumers are, how they spend their time, why they behave as they do, and how to communicate more effectively with them. Table 4.2 on page 67 summarises a number of South African core values based on the Sociomonitor survey.

Young & Rubicam, an international advertising agency, developed a model of behaviour following Maslow's theory that certain goals, motivations and values are universal.[33,34] The primary objective of this approach was to describe various internal inputs that are related through choice to alternative external outcomes, as shown in Figure 4.2.

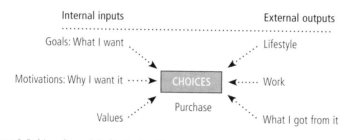

Figure 4.2: Young & Rubicam's model of behaviour[35]

The model postulates seven value typologies, each with characteristic goals, motivations and values. These typologies were further grouped, in line with Maslow's theory, into three types: need-driven, outer-directed and inner-directed, as shown in Table 4.3 on page 68.

4.7 The measurement of culture

We now explore the various methods that are employed to measure culture.

4.7.1 Content analysis

Content analysis focuses on the content of verbal, written and pictorial communications. It is a relatively objective way of determining social and cultural changes within a specific society. It is useful to marketers and policy makers interested in comparing the claims that competitors in a specific industry make in their advertising.

Table 4.2: A summary of South African core values[32]

Value groups	Incidence	Value
Innovatives	24% of urban white population	Individualistic Open to change Status through ownership
Responsibles	25% of urban white population	Traditional values Collectivism Reluctance to accept change Family and national identity Respect for authority
Brandeds	25% of urban white population	Materialistic and status conscious Desire to flaunt their possessions
Self-motivateds	26% of urban white population	Emancipation Racial harmony Blurring of gender roles
Conservatives	36% of urban black population	Religious Family-oriented Sense of national identity Concern for the community Tending towards collectivism
Progressives	31% of urban black population	Individualistic and self-centred Physical health focus Self-improvement focus Antagonistic to authority Seek sensation and novelty Value system typical of individualism
Laggers	33% of urban black population	Value system oriented to the present Aggressive and violent, yet aimless Conspicuous consumption Individualistic, extrovert and outer-directed
Self-gratifiers	33% of urban population	Above average propensity for taking risks Seek out new sensations Live for the moment Conspicuous consumption
Traditionals	32% of urban population	Conformity to rigid norms and morals Religious Home activities
Emancipateds	35% of urban population	Loyalty to family and country High degree of self-interest Focus on looking good, being healthy and improving oneself Blurring of sexual roles Emancipation of women Focus on harmony between races

Table 4.3: Value typologies of the Young & Rubicam model[36]

Type and characteristic	Goal	Motivation	Value
NEED-DRIVEN Resigned Struggling	Survival Improvement	Given up Escape from hardship	Subsistence Hope and luck
MORE OUTER-DIRECTED Mainstreamers Aspirers Succeeders	Security Success Control	Conformity Family responsibility Envy Achievement	Social Status Recognition
MORE INNER-DIRECTED Transitionals Reformers	Self-identity Social betterment	Rebellion Social conscience	Self-satisfaction Social altruism

4.7.2 Consumer fieldwork

Here researchers are likely to select a small sample of people from a particular society and carefully observe their behaviour. Field observation has certain of distinct characteristics:

❍ It takes place within a natural environment.
❍ It is performed sometimes without the subjects' awareness.
❍ It focuses on observation of behaviour.

Instead of simply *observing* behaviour, researchers sometimes take on a participant-observer role, and become active members of the environment they are studying.

Marketers frequently employ other forms of fieldwork, that is, depth interviews and focus group sessions, to obtain an initial view of an emerging social or cultural change. In the relatively informal atmosphere of focus group discussions, consumers are more likely to reveal attitudes or behave in a way that may signal a shift in values that, in turn, may affect the market acceptance of a product or service in the long run.

4.7.3 Social values measurement

Anthropologists have traditionally observed behaviour and inferred dominant or underlying values, but recently there has been a gradual shift to directly *measuring* values. Researchers use value measurement instruments to ask people how they feel about such basic personal and social concepts as freedom, comfort, national security and peace. A variety of popular value instruments have been used in research: the Rokeach Value Survey, the Swarz Value Scale, List of Values (LOV) and Values and Lifestyles 2 (VALS 2).

Lifestyle research for marketing aims to group people according to their value systems as expressed by their lifestyle. In the early days of consumer behaviour research, there was great interest in explaining consumer choices based on psychological personality measurements. Lifestyle research grew out of this. Working with AIO variables – attitudes, interests and opinions – researchers identified segments such as 'the happy housewife' and the 'price conscious shopper'. This work had limited success in explaining consumer choices, particularly at brand level, and the segments did not seem to be stable over time. In the late 1970s and early 1980s, researchers began to work with more general values in an attempt to identify variables that could explain consumer behaviour while also being relatively stable over time.

4.8 Summary

We live in the age of information and globalisation, when information technologies are breaking down traditional barriers in time and space. However, converging technologies and disappearing income differences across countries will not necessarily lead to homogenisation of consumer behaviours. Instead, as the world economy is becoming more and more cross-cultural, consumer behaviour might become more *heterogeneous* because of newly exposed cultural differences. This makes it increasingly important for marketers to understand the values of national cultures and their impact on consumer behaviour. In the context of international marketing, cross-cultural value orientations can profoundly affect the way products are consumed in a culture. Thus, knowledge and understanding of cultural values are essential to successful international marketing efforts. It is hoped that marketers would benefit from gaining an insight into the way in which cross-cultural values are related to specific consumer behaviours.

The study of culture is the study of all aspects of a society that give it its distinctive character and personality. The impact of culture is so natural and ingrained that we rarely note its influence on our behaviour. Culture is dynamic, and gradually and continually evolves to meet the needs of society. Beliefs, values and customs are acquired through formal learning, informal learning and technical training. Advertising enhances formal learning by reinforcing desired modes of behaviour and expectations; it enhances informal learning by providing models for behaviour.

Culture is communicated to members of society through a common language and through commonly shared symbols. Marketers are able to promote tangible and intangible products and product concepts to consumers because of our minds' ability to absorb and process symbolic communication. Three pervasive social institutions transmit the elements of culture: the family, the religious institution and the school. Marketers employ various measurement techniques to study culture, and have identified a wide range of South African core values.

Every group or society has a culture, and cultural influences on buying behaviour may vary greatly from country to country. Failure to adjust to these differences can result in ineffective marketing. International marketers must understand the culture in each international market and adapt their marketing strategies accordingly.

Questions for self-assessment

To assess your progress, answer these questions:

1. Distinguish between beliefs, values and customs. Illustrate how the clothing a person wears at different times or for different occasions is influenced by customs.

2. A marketer of a yoghurt brand is considering targeting 8–16-year-olds by positioning her company's product as a healthy, nutritious snack food. How can she use an understanding of the three forms of cultural learning in developing an effective strategy to target the intended market?

3. A marketer of pure fruit juice is planning a promotional campaign to encourage the drinking of his company's brand of juice in situations where many consumers normally drink carbonated soft drinks. Using a means-end chain analysis, identify relevant product attributes, consequences and values for pure fruit juices as an alternative to soft drinks. What are the implications of these values for an advertising campaign designed to increase the consumption of pure fruit juice?

4. For each of the products and activities listed below:
   a. Identify the core values most relevant to their purchase and use.
   b. Determine whether these values encourage or discourage use or ownership.
   c. Determine whether these core values are shifting and, if so, in what direction.
   Products and activities:
   - gambling or gaming in a casino
   - donating blood
   - a television set
   - toothpaste
   - carbonated soft drinks
   - beer
   - cell phones
   - fat-free foods.

5. Read the case study above, and then answer the following questions:
   a. How are the beliefs, values and customs of the various cultural groups different/similar?
   b. What different symbols are used to convey messages within the different magazines?
   c. Are the predominant executional elements of the advertisements different?

Endnote references

1. Hofstede, G. 1991. *Cultures and Organizations: Software of the Mind*. New York: McGraw-Hill.
2. Schiffman, L.G. and Kanuk, L.L. 2000. *Consumer Behaviour*. 7th ed. Upper Saddle River: Prentice-Hall.
3. Ibid.
4. Ibid.
5. Ibid.

6. Ibid.
7. Rook, D.W. 1985. The ritual dimension of consumer behaviour. *Journal of Consumer Research*, December, 251–64.
8. Schiffman and Kanuk, op. cit.
9. Maheswaran, D. and Shavitt, S. 2000. Issues and new directions in global consumer psychology. *Journal of Consumer Psychology*, 9(2), 59–66.
10. Shkodriani, G.M. and Gibbons, J.L. 1995. Individualism and collectivism among university students in Mexico and the United States. *The Journal of Social Psychology*, 135(6), 765–73.
11. Hofstede, G. 1980. *Culture's Consequence: International Differences in Work-related Values*. Boston: Sage.
12. Kagitcibasi, C. 1990. Family and socialization in cross-cultural perspective: A model of change, Berman, J., Cross-cultural Perspectives: Nebraska Symposium on Motivation, 1989, University of Nebraska Press, Lincoln, NE.
13. Wong, N.Y. and Ahuvia, A.C. 1998. Personal taste and family face: Luxury consumption in Confucian and Western societies. *Psychology & Marketing*, 15(5), 423–41.
14. Phinney, J.S. 1992. The multi-group ethnic identity measure: A new scale for use with diverse groups. *Journal of Adolescent Research*, 7, 156–76.
15. Rokeach, M. 1973. *The Nature of Human Values*. New York: Free Press, Macmillan.
16. Maio, G.R. and Olson, J.M. 1994. Value-attitude-behavior relations: The moderating role of attitude functions. *British Journal of Social Psychology*, 33, 301–12.
17. Mellema, A. and Bassili, J.N. 1995. On the relationship between attitudes and values: Exploring the moderating effects of self-monitoring and self-monitoring schematicity. *Personality and Social Psychology Bulletin*, 21(9), 885–92.
18. Zetterberg, H.L. 1996. The study of values. In R. Swedberg and E. Uddhammar (eds), *Sociological Endeavour: Selected Writings*. Stockholm: City University Press, pp. 191–219.
19. Browne, K. 1998. Window into consumers' psyche. *Finance and Technology Weekly*, 14 August, p. 30.
20. Homer, P. and Kahle, L.R. 1988. A structural equation test of the value-attitude-behavior hierarchy. *Journal of Personality and Social Psychology*, 54, 638–46.
21. Lerena, S. 1999. Getting to an emotional outcome. In Proceedings of the Twenty-First Southern African Marketing Research Convention (SAMRA). Johannesburg: SAMRA, pp. 217–25.
22. Tse, D.K., Belk, R.W. and Zhou, N. 1989. Becoming a consumer society: A longitudinal and cross-cultural content analysis of print advertisements from Hong Kong, People's Republic of China, and Taiwan. *Journal of Consumer Research*, 15, 457–72.
23. Reynolds, J.T. and Gutman, J. 1988. Laddering theory, method, analysis, and interpretation. *Journal of Advertising Research*, 18(1), 11–30.
24. Nyasani, J.M. 1997. *The African Psyche*. Nairobi: University of Nairobi and Theological Printing Press.
25. Makgoba, M.W. 1997. *MOKOKO, the Makgoba Affair: A Reflection on Transformation*. Florida Hills: Vivlia.
26. Mbiti, J.S. 1969. *African Religions and Philosophy*. New York: Praeger.
27. Shutte, A. 1993. *Philosophy for Africa*. Rondebosch: University of Cape Town Press.
28. Corder, C.K. 2001. The identification of a multi-ethnic South African typology. Unpublished DPhil thesis, University of Pretoria, Pretoria.
29. Market Research Africa (MRA). 1995. Subscribers' Manual for the White Sociomonitor 1995. Johannesburg: MRA.
30. De Vulpian, A. 1980. Social change and its implications for policy making in France. In Proceedings of Social Change Analysis as a Tool for Strategic Marketing and Decision Making. Barcelona: European Society for Opinion and Marketing Research, pp. 9–40.

31. Yankelovich, D. 1981. *New Rules: Searching for Self-fulfilment in a World Turned Upside Down.* New York: Random House.
32. Corder, op. cit.
33. Young & Rubicam. 1988. Cross-cultural consumer characterisation (4Cs). *Y & R Consumer Insight*, 3(3), 1–14.
34. Maslow, A.H. 1954. *Motivation and Personality.* New York: Harper.
35. Young & Rubicam, op. cit., p. 5.
36. Young & Rubicam, op. cit., p. 7.

5 Reference groups and social class

Learning Outcomes

After studying this chapter, you should be able to:

○ describe a reference group

○ differentiate between the different types of reference groups in South African society

○ assess the use of reference groups as a way to segment the market and to describe consumer behaviour

○ define the phenomenon of social class

○ justify the use of social class as a way to segment the market and to reflect on the role that social class plays in South African society

○ explain how the changes in the social class structure will influence the marketing of products and services in South Africa.

5.1 Introduction

In this chapter, we focus on the next two group factors that influence consumer behaviour, namely, reference groups and social class. Our conclusion highlights certain developments in the evolution of the social class structure of South African consumers.

5.2 Reference groups

As consumers, we are involved with other people on a daily basis. The social interaction that occurs influences our behaviour in specific ways. Some people volunteer to donate blood even though they are scared of the sight of it. This is the result of the influences at play when a person forms part of a group, such as students living in a student residence (and explains why blood-donation drives on university campuses are usually so successful). **Reference groups** form part of group dynamics and can be defined as any person or group that serves as a point of comparison or reference for an individual consumer in forming certain values, attitudes and behaviour patterns.[1]

In all reference groups there are distinctive norms of behaviour, and each member of the group is expected to conform to these norms – if they do not, sanctions may be applied to them.

The more involved the person is with the group, the more likely is it that his or her purchasing behaviour will correlate with that of the other members. The consumer draws upon the groups' frame of reference or value system to guide his or her decision-making in the marketplace. There is usually a strong relationship between reference group influence and the choice of speciality or luxury products and a weak relationship in the case of necessities such as convenience products like milk and bread.

With young black consumers, there is a need for group support, with a small percentage of youths being individualists. The main influences on the black consumer's buying behaviour in South Africa are family members, peer group pressure and, in particular, role models. **Role models** are usually successful people whom others admire for what they have attained in life. South African role models include Patrice Motsepe – mining magnate and CEO of ARMgold, Tokyo Sexwale – CEO of Mvelaphanda (the Venda word for 'progress') and presenter of the local adaptation of the TV programme *The Apprentice*, and Cyril Ramaphosa – the non-executive chairman of Johnnic and MTN Group Limited.

We now consider the different types of reference groups that we find in South Africa.

5.2.1 Types of reference groups

There are several types of reference groups in our country, which we now discuss in detail.

Formal and informal reference groups

Each formal reference group has a clearly defined structure and membership, such as the people who work with you or the soccer club that you play for. Membership may have an impact on behavioural processes such as having drinks at the local club after a soccer match.

Informal reference groups also have significant interaction, but they have no formal rules that you would need to adhere to, as in the case of formal reference groups. Examples of informal reference groups are families, friends and peer groups, which exert a great influence on our buying decisions. Some families have preferences that they pass on from generation to generation, such as preferring to drive a particular make of car, living in a particular neighbourhood or supporting a particular soccer club.

Primary and secondary reference groups

Primary reference groups have face-to-face interaction while secondary reference groups do not. A primary reference group would be the pupils in a class at school, who have daily contact with each other. A secondary reference group could be a group of people who live in another country, but who still exert an influence on your buying behaviour. For example, the Manchester United Supporters Club in the United Kingdom may be a secondary reference group for South African fans of the 'Red Devils'. (See, for instance, the unofficial website of South African supporters of the Manchester United football club, called the SA Reds, at www.manutd.co.za.)

Membership and non-membership reference groups

We tend to be members of a certain group and model our behaviour on others in the group. Members of a church congregation may model their behaviour on that of the parson and his family. Non-members do not have any membership, but may still model their behaviour on members of this group. You may not be a member of the church, but you could still be influenced by members' behaviour to use money sparingly and to support others who may be less privileged.

Aspirational reference groups and dissociative groups

Aspirational reference groups are groups that people aspire to belong to. For example, you may want to belong to the group of politicians who sit in parliament and make decisions about the future of South Africa, and earn a substantial salary.

Dissociative reference groups are groups that you avoid and reject. For example, you may have strong objections to smoking and you would then reject people belonging to a group of smokers. Some people reject youth gangs who take drugs and are involved in criminal behaviour, and they teach their children not to associate with gangsters.

5.2.2 Use of reference groups in marketing

Marketers try to determine the shared values and beliefs of the various reference groups, and to align their marketing with these values and beliefs. In general, consumers associate with certain reference groups for the following three reasons:[4]

1. **Information (informational influence)**: Reference groups transmit valuable information, for example about the use of a product or service such as a third generation cellular phone, or about how to search the internet to gather information needed to complete an assignment.
2. **Reward and punishment (normative or utilitarian influence)**: When consumers fulfil the expectations of a particular group, they may receive a reward or be sanctioned. For example, if you collect donations and canvass votes for a political party you may eventually be elected to the local city council. By contrast, a person might be expelled from his or her position as town councillor for not paying a municipal account.
3. **Aspiration (identification influence; value-expressive reference groups)**: A person's aspiration to belong to a certain reference group may enhance their self-concept. For example, by being a supporter and wearing a Bafana Bafana shirt, you would be aspiring to be associated with the South African soccer team.

5.2.3 Determinants of reference group influence

Some of the determinants of reference group influences are as follows:
- Group influence is strongest when a product or brand is visible to the group. For example, a dress is visible in terms of product category and style, but the brand of the dress is less obvious. Reference group influence affects only those aspects of the product that are visible to the group.
- Reference group influence is higher the less of a necessity an item is. Thus, reference groups have a strong influence on the ownership of products such as designer clothes, but much less influence on necessities such as refrigerators.
- The more commitment a person feels to a group, the more he or she will conform to its norms. For example, we are much more likely to consider group expectations when we are dressing to go to dinner with a group we would like to join than we would do with a group that is not important to us.
- The more relevant a particular activity is to the group's functioning, the stronger the pressure to conform to the group norms concerning that activity. For example, style of dress may be important to a social group that frequently eats dinner together at trendy restaurants, and unimportant to a reference group that meets for tennis at the local community centre courts.

5.2.4 Reference groups and advertising

Marketers often position their products in a way that plays on people's desire to join groups. They promote goods by subtly inducing the prospective consumer to identify with the person in the advertisement who is using the product. This identification may be based on admiration – for example, of a good cricket player, on aspiration – for example, to be a celebrity, on empathy – for example, with a person or situation, or on recognition of a person. The prospective consumer thinks, 'If he or she uses it, it must be good. If I use it, I'll be like him or her.'

5.3 Social class

A social class is a group of people in a country who are considered equal in status or community esteem, who socialise together on a regular basis formally and informally, and who share behaviour patterns.[5]

Social classes have distinctive behaviour patterns that are a function of occupation, income and education. In a study done in 1997 on the leisure and recreational activities of American consumers, it was found that different social classes pursue markedly different leisure and recreational activities, which highlights the value of using social class to influence consumer behaviour.[6]

Every country has a different social class structure. The USA has a class structure that distinguishes between an upper, middle and lower class.[7] The structure is diamond-shaped, meaning that a small part of the population is classified as the upper class, the middle class is the largest part of the population, and a relatively small number of people are in the lower class. By contrast, South Africa has a Gini coefficient that is one of the largest in the world. A Gini coefficient represents the gap in income between the richest and poorest people in the country. This is the result of the social engineering policies of the pre-1994 government, which favoured the white population group and seriously disadvantaged people of colour in almost every sphere of life. South Africa therefore represents a social structure that is fairly triangle-shaped, with a limited number of people in the upper class, more in the middle class, and the majority in the lower class. Figure 5.1 illustrates the American and the South African cases.

Figure 5.1: Social class structure in the USA and South Africa

A strong middle class is essential for a vigorous democratic society because it guarantees political stability for the country in the long run. Usually, the middle classes are those people that have the most to lose from radical political change. Over the past ten years, many of the previously disadvantaged people in South Africa have moved into the middle and upper social classes. There is massive interest currently on the emerging black middle class in South Africa. This ever increasing group is contrasted with the 'ordinary' black working class, and distinctive changes in consumption patterns between these two groups are identified. Even in the traditional townships there are different consumption patterns between these groups. A modern shebeen, for example, will have a separate drinking lounge where the more affluent middle class consumer will be encountered, while the working class consumers will be enjoying themselves in another area. The social structure of the middle income and working class black consumer is also reflected in the areas in which they choose to live. In the townships there are upmarket areas, middle of the road areas and poverty stricken 'shanty towns'.

One of the most important ways in which South African social classes are described is by using the **Living Standards Measure** (LSM), which is the most universally applied method of segmenting the South African consumer market. The LSM is based on the standard of living of the population. The South African population is currently divided into ten LSMs, with LSM 1 being the lowest and LSM 10 being the highest. In the past, the division was of eight LSMs. The criteria used to measure the standard of living of the population include access to flush toilets, microwave ovens, retail credit cards, fridges/freezers, TV sets and hot running water.[8] We examine the LSM further in Chapter 6, and the details of all the categories are laid out in Table 6.2.

Social class strongly influences customer lifestyles and in general is a good indicator of the type of product that a customer would be interested in buying. Moreover, people buy products to demonstrate their membership of a particular social class and to help them to advance their social standing in society. In a study done in the Gauteng province of South Africa on the newly emerging middle class and its activities, lifestyles and status providing products, the following five products were identified as giving status to the respondents: a car, a music centre/radio, a suit/clothing, education and a television set.[9] Cell phones were also mentioned as a status symbol.

5.3.1 The marketing implications of social class

People buy products that communicate their status in society. Marketers should therefore position their store and products in such a way that they reinforce the messages suited to particular individuals and groups. The most important single implication of social class is the valid assumption that people at the same social level tend to exhibit similar behaviour, especially in the clothing and cars they buy, and in their leisure pursuits and media preferences.

The types of shops at which South African consumers buy certain products, especially clothing, reflect differences in social class. Consumers at a more sophisticated level, and thus of a higher social class, buy clothing with value for money in mind. Less privileged consumers buy from stores which sell clothes that they are more likely to be able to afford, and which are within easier access, such as Mr Price, because of their low incomes and their lack of access to shopping malls. Lower class home executives tend to do their shopping in the central business district (CBD). The traditional 'discount store' originally appealed primarily to the middle class, whose members had both the confidence and the motivation to shop in such outlets. However, this varies according to the product type, for example as people move to higher social classes, their purchases of clothing at discount stores tend to decrease. Generally, higher social classes are less inclined to shop at discount stores than are the lower social classes, especially if they are buying products with a higher social risk.

To a large extent, a person's social class also determines their media usage. Education generally is the best predictor of media usage. Better educated individuals have different media usage patterns than have less well-educated ones, and these differences cannot be attributed to differences in the amount of free time available to the two groups. Better educated people spend more time reading magazines and books, listening to the radio and going to the cinema, and they spend less time watching television than the less well educated. In addition to its effect on the time spent on various mass media, education level also influences the content of what people take in through the media. The better educated read more news, non-fiction books and editorial material in newspapers. They also listen to classical and 'background' music on the radio, while the less educated listen more to the 'top 20' radio stations.

In the next section, we deal with a model developed by the Bureau of Market Research

(BMR) at Unisa that uses level of education and income as criteria for tracking changes in South African society.

5.4 Changes in South African class structure[10]

Market researchers have developed a large number of market segmentation tools and strategies during the past decades, including the abovementioned LSM and lifestage segmentation, that companies, market research agencies and researchers in South Africa use on a daily basis. The BMR did a study on the changes occurring in the social environment of South Africa and reported certain dramatic changes in our social class structure. They developed a matrix using two sets of variables, namely, living standard and level of education. For the former, they used the old LSM categories 1 to 8 and grouped them into three categories, namely, high living standard (LSMs 7 and 8), middle living standard (LSMs 4–6) and low living standard (LSMs 1–3). They combined this with the latter, which they had split into three broad categories, namely, low education (no education to Grade 7), middle education (Grade 8 to Grade 12) and high education (post-matric).

The BMR developed their matrix with the use of figures from the 1998 and 2003A AMPS surveys, as shown in Table 5.1.

Table 5.1: The BMR segmentation matrix using 1998 and 2003A AMPS data

	1998	2003	1998	2003	1998	2003
High living standard	164 154	174 310	3 369 102	4 205 433	1 535 257	1 652 429
Middle living standard	3 559 469	3 637 253	7 697 213	11 427 498	752 075	795 080
Low living standard	5 525 141	4 243 055	3 016 234	3 462 224	102 974	75 845
	Low education		Middle education		High education	

It appears from the table that on a national basis significant changes in the economic demographics occurred during the period 1998 to 2003. The indication is that during this period there were large increases in consumers who moved into the middle living standard–middle education grouping (from 7.6 million to 11.4 million), as well as consumers moving into the high living standard–middle education grouping. At the same time, the number of consumers in the low living standard–low education category showed a significant decrease.

We now explore a breakdown of the figures into race groups and geographic area.

5.4.1 Changes in the social structure of the South African race groups

Looking at Table 5.1's results by race grouping, we see that the demographics of the African population in South Africa are changing dramatically. Some of the most interesting developments are as follows:

○ The number of Africans with a combination of high level education and high living standard increased by 107% from 1998 to 2003. This rapid growth can be ascribed to improved success in using tertiary education institutions to obtain tertiary qualifications and the resultant access to higher income employment and entrepreneurial opportunities. The role of employment equity, black advancement and black economic empowerment (BEE) legislation, policies and programmes also played a role in this increase.

○ There was a rapid growth in the number of Africans who obtained matric and earn a medium living standard. This group of people increased by 55% during the period 1998 to 2003, and is expected to keep on growing. The principal driver of these changing demographics is greater access of the broader African population to schooling and the fairly rapid urbanisation of the African population bringing children to urban schools.

○ There was a decline in the number of Africans with low education and low living standards. The primary driver of this phenomenon is also greater access to education and urbanisation, as we noted above.

During the period 1998 to 2003 there has been a decline in the number of Asians with a low education, and a simultaneous growth in the segments of Asians with a medium and high level of education. In this period the number of Asians experiencing higher living standards increased by 15%. The most rapid growth was in the segment of Asians experiencing a medium living standard and medium education (25.4% growth) and those with a medium education and a high living standard (19.8% growth).

With regard to the coloured population, over the period 1998 to 2003 it was found that there has been 12.8% growth of coloured people in the high living standard–high education segment. It appears that the extent to which the African population have benefited from labour market segmentation, BEE and black advancement programmes was significantly greater than that experienced by the coloured population. Rapid growth is also evident in the grouping medium living standard–medium education segment of coloureds. The main reasons for these changing demographics are higher school enrolment figures and resultant higher levels of matric completion, urbanisation, the growing Western Cape economy and the subsequent opportunities for employment and entrepreneurial opportunities.

The demographics of the white population also saw drastic changes over this period. These changes include the following:

○ A stagnation and eventual decline of the number of whites with a high education and a high living standard. Some of the reasons for this occurrence are the high level of emigration of highly skilled affluent whites, the negative popula-

tion growth rate, and the harmful impact of labour market segmentation, black advancement and BEE legislation, policies and programmes.
○ Some growth – about 6% – in the medium education–medium living standard and in the medium education–high living standard segments was driven by higher levels of entrepreneurship among members of the white population.

5.4.2 Changes in the social structure of the South African provinces

We now examine the social structure changes according to province.

Eastern Cape
It appears that the number of consumers in the Eastern Cape experiencing low living standards decreased by 5% during the period 1998 to 2003. Moreover, the number of people with high living standards showed an increase. The changes suggest that although there is a clear decrease in the segment low living standard-low education, the growth in the high living standard segments and the high education segments are lower than expected.

Free State
Some of the changes in the Free State were as follows:
○ A 22% decrease in the number of consumers with a low level of education during the given period.
○ A 31% increase in the number of consumers with a medium level of education.
○ A 30% increase in the number of people enjoying a high living standard.

Gauteng
This province shows a profile of a rapidly developing province in both living standards and education for the given period. Some of the findings are as follows:
○ The number of consumers experiencing a high living standard increased by 21% and is expected to keep on growing.
○ The number of people with some or all high school education increased by 23% and is expected to keep on growing.
○ The number of people with a medium living standard–medium education increased by 20% and is expected to grow even further.

However, there are certain problem areas for this province:
○ High levels of emigration of highly skilled people.
○ The negative impact of high levels of capital intensification on job creation.
○ The large number of lower skilled people not directly benefiting from the positive effects of economic growth, that is, not finding jobs or having success as entrepreneurs.

KwaZulu-Natal

KwaZulu-Natal has been successful with regard to the number of its consumers obtaining a medium level of education and attaining a medium living standard. The indication is that the number of consumers with a medium level of education increased by 43% during the given period, and is expected to continue growing. The number of people with a medium living standard increased by 43%, and is expected to continue growing. There are also serious challenges that are preventing more consumers from becoming upwardly mobile, namely:

○ The high HIV prevalence rate and the increasing number of Aids-related deaths.
○ The high levels of unemployment.
○ The migration of highly skilled people to Gauteng and the Western Cape, and the emigration of highly skilled people.
○ A skewed distribution of income.

Limpopo

The Limpopo province is bucking the positive trend with respect to the move to a higher living standard, although there are hefty gains in the number of people completing higher education. This could be attributed to the following three problems:

○ High unemployment rates, even for consumers with higher educational qualifications.
○ The miss-match between the high level of skills on offer with the expectations of prospective employees.
○ The low levels of formal sector entrepreneurship.
○ The negative impact of HIV/Aids.

Mpumalanga

Mpumalanga shows a growing number of its population moving into the higher education and higher living standards segments. For example, the total number of people in this province in the medium education band increased by 40% and is expected to continue to grow over the medium term. The number of people in the high education band grew by 11%, while the number of people in the high living standard band grew by 37%.

Northern Cape

The Northern Cape encountered the fairly rapid growth of 43% in the number of people with a medium level of education, which is expected to show high growth over the medium term. This province does not have enough access to residential tertiary education institutions, however, and is losing its highly educated people to the Western Cape and to Gauteng. The number of people with a high living standard increased from 183 594 in 1998 to 240 859 in 2003, and is expected to grow to about 306 379 in 2008.

North West
The number of people in this province with a tertiary education qualification also improved from about 114 455 in 1998 to 178 572 in 2003, and is expected to increase to 237 871 by 2008. One of the main reasons of the growing increase in the number of tertiary qualified people is the presence of a few higher education institutions in this province, for example the University of the Northwest. There is a clear correlation between the number of people obtaining higher educational qualifications and improvements in living standards. It appears that the number of people experiencing a high living standard, and who have higher education qualifications, increased dramatically, namely, by 113%. There is a concurrent decline of 47% in the number of people in the low living standard–low education category. Furthermore, the medium living standard–medium education category increased by 92% during this period.

Western Cape
A high percentage of people in the Western Cape already enjoyed a high living standard by 1998. This number increased to 1 408 634 in 2003, and is expected to increase to about 1 760 061 in 2008.

This province also experienced significant improvements in the number of people with higher educational qualifications, namely, from 362 623 in 1998 to 454 092 in 2003, which is expected to increase further to 564 135 in 2008. This improvement can be partly ascribed by the various higher educational institutions in this province, including the University of Cape Town and the University of Stellenbosch, and the migration of skilled people to this province.

In summary, we can say that it appears that the South African population as a whole experienced significant improvements in living standards and education during the period 1998 to 2003, and it is expected that such improvements will continue for the foreseeable future. Having mentioned some of the positive developments with regard to living standards and education, we also need to emphasise the following challenges in the progress towards further improvements in the areas of education and living standards:

○ The impact of HIV/Aids on the life expectancies of the highly educated and the concurrent negative influence of this pandemic on general living standards.

○ The continuing skills flight from South Africa.

○ The problem of economic growth that does not engender job creation that could also improve living standards.

○ The quality and labour market relevance of tertiary education in South Africa.

○ The inability of urban metropolitan areas to cope with a rapidly urbanising population, resulting in poor service delivery.

Case study

NEW GENERATION OF TEENAGERS IN SOUTH AFRICA IGNORES RACE BUT LOVES MONEY![11]

A new social structure is developing in South Africa that focuses more on money than race. In research undertaken by UCT's Unilever Institute of Strategic Marketing, a new breed of self-assured urban youth has been identified that was colour-blind with regard to race and more interested in the colour of money.

The study shows that urban youth was the most integrated in South Africa and that friendships are now based on shared interests such as music and fashion. The group is highly interested in money and the designer brands that it can buy – cutting edge clothing brands are significant in the development of a new South African identity. Brand names such as Diesel, Polo and Moscow jeans say a lot more about a teenager today than in the past. Many of the urban youth look to South African celebrities as role models, believing that money brings power and freedom.

Teenagers are an important market for South African marketers – they spend R25 billion each year and have R20 billion spent on them. Research has shown that 90% of product requests by children to their parents are for brand name products.

5.5 Summary

In this chapter, we discussed two of the group factors influencing consumer behaviour, namely, reference groups and social class. For consumers, the value of reference groups lies in these groups' information, possible rewards and identification. In our examination of social class and its influence on consumer behaviour, we referred to the use of the LSM in describing social class in South Africa. Finally, we consider some of the changes occurring in the South African class structure.

Questions for self-assessment

To assess your progress, answer these questions:

1. Define reference groups and explain their place in the realm of consumer behaviour.
2. Differentiate between the different reference groupings that we discuss in this chapter. Is it possible to belong to more than one reference group at the same time?
3. Explain why customers try to belong to particular reference groups.
4. Explain the use of social class as a way of determining consumer behaviour.
5. Assess the trends in the South African social class structure and indicate the influence of these trends on consumer behaviour patterns in South Africa.

6. With reference to the case study, answer the following questions:
   a. Assume that you are the marketing manager of a new branded range of clothing aimed at teenagers in South Africa. State how you will use social class as a method of defining the target market for this range of products. Is social class the only way in which marketers can describe the target market?
   b. If marketers use reference groups in the branded clothing sector for teenagers, will this help them to sell more of the product?
   c. Write an essay on the trends in teenage consumer behaviour identified in the case study.

Endnote references

1. Schiffman, L.G., Bednall, D., Watson, J. and Kanuk, L.L. 1997. *Consumer Behaviour.* Sydney: Prentice-Hall.
2. Peter, J.P. and Olsen, J.C. 2002. *Consumer Behavior and Marketing Strategy.* 6th ed. Boston: Irwin McGraw-Hill.
3. Hawkins, D.I., Best, R.J. and Coney, K.A. 2001. *Consumer Behavior.* 8th ed. Boston: Irwin McGraw-Hill, pp. 232–3.
4. Trocchia, P.J. and Swinder, J. 2000. A phenomenological investigation of Internet usage among older individuals. *Journal of Consumer Marketing,* 17(7), 605–16.
5. Lamb, C.W., Joseph, J.H. and McDaniel, C. 2002. *Marketing.* 6th ed. Cincinnati: South-Western.
6. Sivadas, E. 1997. A preliminary examination of the continuing significance of social class to marketing: A geodemographic replication. *Journal of Consumer Marketing,* 14(6), 463–79.
7. Lamb et al., op cit.
8. Haupt, P. 2002. The SAARF Living Standards Measure (LSM): Separating myth from reality. Available on the internet from: www.saarf.co.za/lsm-article.htm (accessed 10 April 2003).
9. Ungerer, L.M. 1999. Activities, lifestyles and status products of the newly-emerging middle class in Gauteng. Report 262, Bureau of Market Research. Pretoria: Unisa, pp. 30–44.
10. Van Aardt, C. 2005. Class-based population segmentation model for South Africa, 1998 to 2003. Report 344, Bureau of Market Research. Pretoria: Unisa.
11. Power, M. New generation of teenagers in South Africa ignores race but loves money! *Sunday Times,* 19 June 2005, p. 10.

6 Personal characteristics

Learning Outcomes

After studying this chapter, you should be able to:

○ differentiate between and discuss the three different customer roles

○ discuss the influence of race and gender and age on customer behaviour.

6.1 Introduction

When we consider how to market to a customer, we need to ask two basic questions: 'Who is the customer?' and 'Why do they buy?' In this chapter we discuss the influence of the customer's personal characteristics on marketing, an aspect that is closely related to the first question. We look at the personal characteristics that customers have no direct control over, namely, race, gender and age. These characteristics are part of the personal context of customers that shape and drive the needs and wants that they will seek to fulfil in the marketplace.[1] We address each of these aspects in detail. Another personal characteristic that influences behaviour is personality. We deal with this in Chapter 10.

Age, race and gender are termed 'personal characteristics'[2] in that each customer possesses these characteristics as an individual. Furthermore, since they are not *unique* to the individual, they are also termed **'group traits'**, because they belong to, are shared by and help to describe groups of people. These traits allow marketers to analyse markets and investigate customers at a group or segment level. They can also investigate differences between groups of customers that have different traits, for example young men as opposed to older women.

Personal characteristics influence customer behaviour in distinct ways. Table 6.1 summarises some of these influences with regard to the three customer roles of user, payer and buyer. (We clearly defined and discussed these three roles in Chapter 2.) Remember that each of the roles does not necessarily need to be carried out by the same person or organisational unit.[3]

Table 6.1: Personal characteristics and the three customer roles[4]

Characteristic	User	Payer	Buyer
Race	For personal care items, customers seek products that are compatible with their skin and hair needs Ethnic tastes in food, clothing, and homes differ Some minority groups seek social values as compensation	Economic means are unevenly distributed across races and ethnic groups Race-based discrimination in credit limits affordability for some customers	Many customers prefer ethnic stores and suppliers Race and ethnic group influence the preferred modes of interaction with vendors
Gender	Many products and services are gender specific, owing to either physiology or culture In some cultures, women might use emotional products more	Gender roles may be the basis for allocating the payer role	Gender roles may be the basis for allocating the buyer role Where gender roles include women in the workplace, women might seek convenience and time saving in shopping. In some cultures, men are still learning shopping skills
Age	Product/service usage in many categories is contingent on age Social and emotional values are more important for youth Product/service needs are influenced by the physical limitations related to aging (such as inability to lift heavy weights or read fine print)	Age influences the amount of financial resources The payer's role is more separate from the user's among youth (dependent on parents) and the elderly (dependent on government for income)	Elderly buyers need more service and convenience Word-of-mouth communication about shopping is highest among youth Older buyers (in both businesses and households) prefer to buy based on the relationship with the seller

6.2 Race

The issue of race has been prevalent in marketing for many years, and will continue to be so, because it is a trait that marketers can use to establish subcultures. Marketers segment the market and investigate if behaviours vary across race. In South Africa in the past, race was often used as a segmenting variable, but increasingly its validity is being questioned, as we shall see.

Race can be defined the *genetic* heritage group into which a person is born. Common racial groups in South Africa are black, white, Indian and coloured. A related concept is **ethnic identity**, which is the *ethnic* heritage into which a person is born,[5] for example the different tribes in South Africa. In the United Kingdom, ethnic identity includes Welsh, Scots, British and Irish origins.

We seek to make it clear that race is a variable that marketers can use if it helps them to establish groups whose needs and values differ. Ethnic segments may have their own culture, language, religion and distinct requirements. In this case, it may not always be appropriate to target them with general products or services, or merely change advertisements in some superficial way for them.[6] If different skin has different moisture content, for example, then the formulation of cosmetics for each skin type should be different, and it would not be enough for the marketer of the cosmetic simply to suggest to the consumer how to use the existing product ranges that may not cater for these specific characteristics.

This raises the sensitive issue of whether targeting ethnic segments is racist. Our position is that if the ethnic segments differ in their needs and values then they should be treated differently by marketers. This does not mean that any segment is discriminated against; instead, it means that their differences are noted and catered for. A criticism of many South African marketers is that race is still being used without it being a genuinely valid variable in terms of differences in consumers' needs, wants or behaviour. Too many marketers use it because it is easy, instead of checking to see if it really does define differences between customer groups.

Easy Waves product development[7]

In developing a hair product for its target market, Easy Waves had to consider the characteristics of the hair itself. Their target market was urban black females aged 18–35 in the higher income groups who wanted to have hair products that reflected their upmarket image. As the result of extensive research, Easy Waves noted that black hair has these characteristics:

○ It is fragile and dry.

○ It tends to grow at an angle against the scalp, resulting in a very curly strand of hair.

○ The style at the time for black customers in South Africa was the curly perm, which often dried the scalp and made the hair even more fragile.

The company subsequently developed a line of moisturiser gels, sprays, conditioners and shampoos that catered for these needs.

6.2.1 Race and products

The Easy Waves example above makes the point that marketers must ascertain if there are valid differences between the needs and wants of the different racial groups, and, if so, they should respond to these differences. In the fields of cosmetics and similar products, the products appropriate for white customers are often inappropriate for black customers. Many major companies have taken this into account and are now competing aggressively for success in this market. Brands such as Black Like Me and Dark and Lovely have been established to suit this market's needs.

Other marketers have targeted the unique social needs of the different races. Greeting card manufacturers design cards featuring black characters and sayings, dolls are offered in different racial versions, and services are designed to cater for specific racial categories that have different customers. The burial services market is a case in point.

New hairstyle trends[8]

South African women are following the American trend of wearing their hair in natural styles. This emerging niche is the second largest group behind relaxer users. Dark and Lovely, a brand owned by Carson products, created a line of products called Dark and Lovely Naturally for this niche.

The line was specially created for natural styles – braids, locks, twists, waves and short crops. The products aimed at the niche for women of colour with natural hairstyles address the hair-care problems they face: dryness, manageability and style maintenance. These styles were chosen because of convenience, low maintenance, a desire for healthier hair and a personal expression of culture and heritage.

6.2.2 Race and marketing communications

One of the common mistakes that marketers make when communicating with ethnic groups is to assume that the members are the same as other cultural groups, except for superficial differences.[9] Failure to recognise possible differences between groups often produces advertisements, targeted at black customers, for example, that simply place the standard advert in black media or that replace white actors with black actors, without changing the script, the language or the setting. However, marketers must explore the needs, wants and actual differences of their markets to see if there are valid differences – not all messages targeted at ethnic groups need to differ significantly from those targeted at other groups.

Sometimes advertisers can change only the race of the actors in the adverts to indicate that the product is appropriate for the needs of a specific ethnic group. This would work when the product, the advertising appeal and the appropriate language are the same for one ethnic group as for another. Castle beer, for example, has developed different executions of its 'The Friendship Brew' positioning that reflect the interests of different race groups in South Africa, but which have the same message delivery and advertising appeal, that is, 'Castle is the friendship brew'.

6.2.3 The Living Standards Measurement

As we have seen in preceding chapters, a tool has been developed by SAARF to aid marketers in South Africa with regard to the issue of race, namely, the Living Standards Measurement (LSM).[11] It measures social class, or living standards, regardless of race and without using income as a variable to segment the market. The LSM uses wealth, access and geography as major indicators with which to segment the South African market. Since it is often used for the selection of appropriate media, its construction involves neither media-related variables nor personal attributes such as race. It cuts across race and other outmoded techniques of categorising people, and instead groups people according to their living standard by using the abovementioned variables as well as degree of urbanisation and ownership of assets and major appliances.[12]

The latest version of the tool, available since 2001, is called the 'new SAARF Universal LSM'. The variables[13] it uses have been adjusted to take into account the new realities of South Africa, and they give a better indication of the financial status of the respondent.

There are 29 variables, as follows:[14]

1. water and electricity
2. fridge/freezer
3. microwave oven
4. flush toilet
5. no domestic in household
6. VCR
7. vacuum cleaner/floor polish
8. no cell phone in household
9. traditional hut
10. washing machine
11. PC in home
12. electric stove
13. TV
14. tumble dryer
15. home telephone
16. less than two radio sets in household
17. hi-fi/music centre
18. rural outside Gauteng/W Cape
19. built-in kitchen sink
20. home security service
21. deep freezer
22. water in home/on plot
23. M-Net/DSTV subscription
24. dishwasher
25. electricity
26. sewing machine
27. Gauteng
28. Western Cape
29. motor vehicle in household

These variables divide the South African population into ten LSM groups. The characteristics of each group are shown in Table 6.2.

Table 6.2: Descriptions of the LSM groups

LSM 1 (10.5%)	
Demographics	**Media**
Female	Radio below but strongest medium
16–24, 50+ years old	African Language Services (ALS)
Up to some primary education	**General**
Rural	Minimal access to services
Traditional hut	Minimal ownership of durables, except radio
R777 per month income	Activities: Gardening
LSM 2 (14%)	
Demographics	**Media**
16–24 years old	Radio: ALS
Up to primary school complete	**General**
Rural	Water on plot
R885 per month	Minimal ownership of durables, except radio and stove
	Activities: Gardening
LSM 3 (14.3%)	
Demographics	**Media**
16–49 years old	Radio: ALS, Radio Bop
Up to some high school education	TV: SABC 1
Rural	Outdoor
R1 107 per month income	
General	
Electricity, water on plot	Minimal ownership of durables, except radio set and stove
Activities: Minimal	

LSM 4 (13.8%)	
Demographics	**Media**
16–34 years old	Radio: ALS, Radio Bop, Metro FM, YFM
Schooling up to some high school	TV: SABC 1, 2, 3, Bop TV
Urban	Outdoor
R1 523 per month income	
General	
Electricity, water on plot, flush toilet	TV set, hi-fi/radio set, stove, fridge
Activities: Stokvel meetings, lottery tickets	

LSM 5 (12.5%)	
Demographics	**Media**
16–34 years old	Radio: ALS, Radio Bop, Metro fm, KAYAfm, Yfm
Some high school to matric, urban	TV: SABC 1, 2, 3, Bop TV, e.tv
R2 205 per month income	Weekly newspaper, magazines
	Outdoor
General	
Electricity, water, flush toilet	Activities: exercising, painting interior of house, stokvel meeting, buys music, lottery tickets
TV set, hi-fi radio/radio set, stove, fridge	

LSM 6 (12.6%)	
Demographics	**Media**
16–34 years old	Wide range of commercial/community radio
Up to post-matric, not university, urban	TV: SABC 1, 2, 3, e.tv
R3 557 per month income	Daily/weekly newspapers, magazines
	Cinema and outdoor
General	
Electricity, hot running water, flush toilet	Owner of a number of durables plus cell phone
Activities: exercising, painting interior of house, stokvel meeting, buys music, lottery tickets	

LSM 7 (6.05%)	
Demographics	Media
Male	Wide range of commercial/community radio
35+ years old	TV: SABC 1, 2, 3, e.tv, M-Net
Matric and higher	Daily/weekly newspapers, magazines
Urban	Accessed internet once in last four weeks
R5 509 per month	Cinema and outdoor
General	
Full access to services	Participation in all activities
Increased ownership of durables plus motor vehicle	

LSM 8 (5.8%)	
Demographics	Media
35+ years old	Wide range of commercial/community radio
Matric and higher	TV: SABC 1, 2, 3, e.tv, M-Net, DSTV
Urban	Daily/weekly newspapers, magazines
R7 428 per month income	Accessed internet once in last four weeks
	Cinema and outdoor
General	
Full access to all services	Full ownership of all durables, including PC and satellite dish
Increased participation in activities	

LSM 9 (5.4%)	
Demographics	Media
Male	Wide range of commercial/community radio
35+ years old	TV: SABC 2, 3, e.tv, M-Net, DSTV
Matric and higher	Daily/weekly newspapers, magazines
Urban	Accessed internet once in last four weeks
R9 861 per month income	Cinema and outdoor
General	

Full access to services	Full ownership of durables including PC and satellite dish
Increased participation in activities, excluding stokvel meetings	
LSM 10 (5.1%)	
Demographics	Media
35+ years old	Wide range of commercial/community radio
Matric and higher	TV: SABC 1, 2, 3, e.tv, M-Net, DSTV
Urban	Daily/weekly newspapers, magazines
R13 788 per month income	Accessed internet once in last four weeks
	Cinema and outdoor
General	
Full access to services	Full ownership of durables including PC and satellite dish
Increased participation in activities, excluding stokvel meetings	

The LSM system has become the most widely used marketing research tool in South Africa, and it is a unique method of segmenting the market. The index differentiates the market more accurately than any single demographic variable, and it has broad applications across a variety of media/product groups. More importantly, its greatest benefit is that it is simple to use, and although the breakdown of each LSM according to race can be done, race itself is not used as a variable in determining the composition of the LSMs.

6.3 Gender

The terms 'sex' and 'gender' are used interchangeably to refer to whether a person is biologically male or female.[15] This trait usually remains constant throughout an individual's life, and it is of great importance to marketers because it influences the customers' values and preferences, as shown in Table 6.3 on the next page. The table highlights some basic differences between the sexes in terms of certain product categories. These differences are carried through into shopping behaviour.

A recent study that compared loyalty patterns of men and women found significant differences. Men were more loyal to domestic or local retailers than women. Women were more responsive to international retailers, and were a more attractive market for the retailers entering a country. Women would be especially attracted to a retailer who was entering a culture where women tend to make the majority of shopping and buying decisions across a wide variety of product categories.[16]

Table 6.3: Differences between men and women

Consumption category	Men	Women
Food	Single men 25–34 years old spend more of food budget away from home than women (65% v 55%)	Buy fresh vegetables because they eat more healthily. Diet foods and drinks more popular
Clothing	Predominantly white, blue, black, brown, grey. Men use women's styles as indicators of women's motivations and moods	Certain fabrics almost exclusively used by women (e.g. chiffon). Bright, full spectrum of colours used; wider style range
Housing	More concerned with construction of house, heating/cooling system, kind of building material used	More concerned with functional features such as closet space, size of kitchen, proximity to playground
Home decorating	Focus on den or TV room (for parties or to watch sports)	Focus on kitchen and living room
Weddings	Reception key event. Concerned with reception hall, good food and socialising during reception	Ceremony itself is key event. Wedding dress very important, as well as location, flowers, decorations and music

'**Gender identity**' refers to traits of *femininity* – expressive traits like tenderness and compassion – and *masculinity* – instrumental traits like aggression and dominance. These traits embody opposite ends of a continuum, in which individuals have varying levels of each trait.[17]

Gender roles can be described as 'the behaviors considered appropriate for males and females in a given society'. In America, especially, the concept of gender roles has undergone a major shift: behaviour previously considered appropriate primarily for men is now acceptable for women too. Gender roles are **ascribed roles** and therefore are based on 'an attribute over which the individual has little or no control'. This is contrasted by **achievement roles**, which are based on the performance criteria over which the individual has some degree of control. Logically, individuals can choose their achievement roles but cannot determine their gender roles.[18]

Even though it is common to find products that are exclusively or strongly associated with either men or women, such as hair spray and hair dryers for women and ties and cigars for men, for many of these products the 'sex role' link has either diminished or disappeared altogether. An interesting example is men's fragrances: even though men are increasingly wearing fragrances, an estimated 30% of fragrances produced for men are worn by women.[19]

6.3.1 The changing role of women

There has been a shift in values from the 'traditional women', portrayed as wives running the house and taking care of the babies, to a more modern perception of a woman's role in society. There is a growing acceptance of part of this change, but not all aspects of it, and substantial resistance has occurred from more traditional groups, or those who stand to lose if the new values are accepted.[20]

Marketers were initially interested in women because, traditionally, they bought many of the products used for household consumption. This interest is now intensifying because of the changing role of women.[21] Significantly, in the USA the female population is growing faster than the male population, because the life expectancy for females is higher than for males. This general trend is also reflected in South Africa. In addition to longevity, there is the fact that today many more women are attending universities and developing their own professional careers. These factors underline the increasing importance of female roles.

Working women spend less time shopping than those who do not work, and they accomplish 'time economy' by being loyal to certain brands and stores. Moreover, working women are more likely to shop during evening hours and on weekends, as well as buying through direct-mail catalogues.[22]

In one research study, it was found that women account for 30% of students at top-level business schools. This figure is expected to increase worldwide as women overcome problems that may have prevented them from studying further, such as lack of role models, work/life balance issues, lack of finance and inadequate encouragement from employers. In South Africa, the percentage of women taking MBA programmes is steadily increasing. The impact of women in the workplace became evident earlier in the USA, because it was more egalitarian and less traditional than other economies. In South Africa the process has lagged behind the American trend, but the movement of women into corporate life is gathering strength.

US statistics on the role of women in business[23]

The futurist Faith Popcorn used the following statistics to support her conclusion that women will dominate business over the next two decades:

- ○ Women buy, or influence the buying of, 80% of consumer goods. This includes 54% of electronic goods and 75% of over-the-counter medicines. Women also influence 80% of all health care decisions.
- ○ Women buy 50% of motor vehicles and influence 80% of vehicle sales. They also buy 50% of personal computers, while 48% of stock exchange investors are women.
- ○ In 22.7% of households where the men and women both work, the women earn more than the men.
- ○ Twice as many women as men start businesses. Businesses owned or managed by women earn US$3.6 trillion each year and they have 27.5 million employees – more than all the Fortune 500 companies put together.

Car marketers adapt to the changing role of women[24]

Women represent about half of the buyers of cars in the USA, and they exert an influence on about 80% of all new car sales. Marketers are responding to this by targeting women in their advertisements, and they are training their dealerships on how to better market to the female customer. Special training courses and videos are used to train dealer staff on how to attract and work with female customers. Special events and promotions are being targeted at women, financing programmes have been streamlined to make financing for women easier, and even car designs have been adapted. For example, doors and other car parts are made to open more easily, and features such as child seats are now integrated into the car design.

A **role** specifies what someone is expected to do in a given position in a particular social context. This definition highlights the concern of marketers with the gender roles of women as buying agents for their families. Generally, marketers and advertisers have portrayed women in limited, stereotypical roles. Women were shown as the buyers of low-unit price items and as career housewives or homemakers, and not as serious, career-oriented professionals. Today, these stereotypes are changing as a result of the increasing number of women in the workplace and in managerial and executive positions throughout the public and private sectors of the economy.

Women are increasingly oriented towards self-realisation, self-expression and personal fulfilment. The changing role of women is reflected in the influence of women on the buying of major durables, such as cars. In South Africa, there are more than two million black households headed by women.[25] It has been found that in South African black families, the women play a prominent part in buying decisions, especially for food, clothing, footwear and pharmaceutical and medical products.

These statistics show that South African women are a powerful economic force:
○ Women made up 34% of employees in 1990, 40% in 1999 and 50% in 2001.
○ Women made up 39% of graduates, and this figure is expected to increase. In 2002, there were 100 000 more women students than men.
○ Women made up 19% of management in 1990, and 28% in 1999.
○ Table 6.4 gives the figures for women in business in South Africa.

Table 6.4: Women in business in South Africa

	1998–1999	2000	2001
Small businesses	32%	34%	35%
Medium-sized businesses	23%	28%	40%
Large businesses	–	24%	32%
Corporations	15%	18%	25%

There are some marketing implications of this changing role. Even though neither the women's nor the men's markets are homogeneous, there are at least four significant female market segments:[26]

1. **Traditional housewife**: Generally, this refers to a married woman who prefers to stay at home, and is home- and family-centred. She strives to please her husband and/or children, and seeks satisfaction and meaning from these tasks as well as from volunteer activities. She experiences strong pressure to work outside the home and is well aware of the forgone income opportunity.

2. **Trapped housewife**: This woman is married and prefers to work, but stays at home to look after the young children as a result of a lack of outside opportunities or family pressure. She seeks satisfaction and meaning outside the home and does not enjoy doing most household chores. She tends to have mixed feelings about her current situation.

3. **Trapped working woman**: This woman is either married or single and works, but she would prefer to stay at home. She does not strive for satisfaction or meaning from her work, and is frustrated by a lack of time. She feels conflict about her role and resents missed opportunities for caring for her family and doing volunteer activities. However, she is proud of her financial contribution to the household.

4. **Career working woman**: This woman is married or single and prefers to work. She derives satisfaction or meaning from her employment rather than, or in addition to, home and family activities. She experiences some conflict over her role if young children are involved, but generally she is content. However, she feels pressed for time.

Although these classifications are oversimplified, they signify the diverse nature of the adult female population. Significantly, this diversity is declining, but the segments are still sizeable and each has different needs and communication requirements.[27]

6.3.2 The changing role of men

The concept of the 'new man' emerged in the literature at the end of the 1980s.[28] Traditionally, men were less involved in family shopping or childrearing, but recently this has changed partly as a result of the increased female participation in the workplace, and partly because of the changing role expectations of men as a result of the drive towards equality of the sexes. This changed role is being reflected in adverts, in which the 'caring, sharing man' is featuring more often.

The issue as to whether the 'new man' actually exists is still being debated, but what is clear is that as women's roles change, so the role of men will change too.[29] Men are now more knowledgeable about household goods, and women are buying more durable products, but there are still some activities that have a high masculine bias, such as watching sport and drinking beer.

The new man?[30]

Simon Silvester has found that when a woman leads a car focus group, the men in the group talk about safety features and leg-room. By contrast, when a man leads the discussion, they say, 'I just want something I can accelerate at traffic lights.' Sylvester concludes: 'A lot of men are going in for this New Man image, but deep down inside they are all the same.'

In summary, women are now an economic 'powerhouse'.[31] In the USA, they make over 85% of customer purchases and influence over 95% of total goods and services. They represent over 50% of the buyers of traditionally male categories of goods such as cars, consumer electronics and personal computers. These trends are also reflected in South Africa. Marketers need to respond to this, taking the role of women into account and avoiding stereotypical thinking in their marketing campaigns. Furthermore, American women are in the majority as users of the internet and do the most online shopping. Marketers who want to succeed must take into account these new marketplace realities.

The internet also holds different appeal for men and women. Women tend to surf the Web for reference materials, online books, medical information, cooking ideas, government information and chatting. Men tend to focus on exploration, discovery, identifying free software and investments. Contrary to what is stated above, this reinforces the notion that men are 'hunters' and women are 'nurturers'.[32]

Gay power a profitable niche in South Africa[33]

The gay market is being recognised more and more as a separate but profitable niche in its own right. Cape Town has capitalised on the growth of gay tourism and the large disposable income that the gay community freely spends. It is estimated that there are 100 000 gays living in the city and that 24 000 gay foreigners visited the city in 1999, a number that is thought to have increased sharply in the following years. Gay travellers spend more than 'straights', and they are the ideal DINK (double income, no kids) couples because they have no kids and are usually professional people with high incomes.

Cape Town has a well-known nudist beach at Sandy Bay that appeals to the gay market and there are 15 guest houses that cater exclusively for gays or are gay-friendly. The Cape Town gay festivals and parties that the city sponsors generate an estimated R20–50 million a year, as thousands of tourists of all sexual persuasions flock in. And the biggest gay festival, Sydney's Mardi Gras, generates about R630 million for the city each year, so the numbers are impressive in terms of catering to this free-spending niche.

6.4 Age

Age is one of the most important variables that affects customer behaviour. Many marketers are acutely focused on analysing trends affecting particular age groups, because it is easier for them to make accurate predictions of the future age composition of the population than of other demographic variables such as income or occupation.[34]

This allows them to identify potential marketing opportunities well in advance, and facilitates marketing planning.

6.4.1 Defining age

There are various meanings of the word 'age', and marketers must understand exactly what they refer to when they discuss the concept.[35] **Chronological age** refers to the length of time (usually years) that has passed since a person's birth. **Biological ageing** refers to changes taking place in the human functional capacity over time. It usually correlates with chronological age, and can be affected by diet, lifestyle and health habits. **Psychological ageing** refers to the changes in people's self-perceptions and cognitions, that is, the way people view themselves and others.

Marketers must be clear about the type of age or ageing that they have in mind, because it will influence their marketing decisions. Frequently, for example, there is a large gap between a person's chronological age and their psychological age – they may be 60 years old, but they feel and act as if they are 40.

6.4.2 Importance of age to marketers

There are three major reasons for studying age and its impact on marketing:[36]
1. The **things that a person needs or wants** change as their age changes. Think back to what you thought you needed when you were a child and compare this to what you think you need now.
2. Age helps marketers to calculate the **lifetime value** of a customer. This concept refers to the value of goods and services a customer could buy from one company over their lifetime. This is a highly important concept as it forms the corner-stone of the current emphasis of many organisations on loyalty programmes and customer relationship management initiatives. We deal with this further in Chapter 16.
3. Changes in the **age composition of a population** correlate with significant shifts in values and demand. The 'greying' of the population in Western countries, with corresponding shifts in demand for products and services such as health care, medicine and security is a case in point. This is in sharp contrast to South Africa, where 48.7% of the black population was under the age of 20 in 1995.[37] Given the large percentage that black people represent in terms of the total population, this means that the youth market should emerge as the major market segment in the country, although the older market has greater spending power.

6.4.3 Age subcultures

Marketers can divide the population into cultures by using **cohort analysis**, which is the process of describing and explaining the attitudes, behaviours and values of an age group.[38] Marketers can also use it to predict an age group's future attitudes, values and behaviours. This process divides the population up into generations, or **age cohorts**, which are groups of people who experience a common social, political, historical and economic environment.[39] Interestingly, each generation behaves differently from the preceding one, as it passes through the generational categories.

Seniors

There are three main factors that drive the growth of the senior sector: the declining birth rate in developed countries, the aging of the massive Baby Boomer segment, and improved medical diagnoses and treatment.[40]

The American market can be divided into four generations or age cohorts.[41] The Pre-Depression generation is called the 'mature market' (the Great Depression started in October 1929). This generation will increase in numbers over the next ten years (in line with the ageing population). This is a result of healthier lifestyles and improved health care, which has resulted in longer life expectations. This cohort has tremendous economic clout in the USA, and product categories such as exercise facilities, cruises and tourism, cosmetic surgery and education are targeting this generation as a result.

While it would appear that older consumers are without substantial financial resources, in poor health and have plenty of free time, this is not necessarily the case. In 2001, 31% of men and 20% of women aged between 65 were employed, as were 19% of men and 12% of women aged between 70 and 74. In addition, many senior citizens are involved in the daily care of grandchildren and volunteer work. The annual discretionary income of this group amounts to 50% of the discretionary income in the USA. They are also major consumers of luxury products such as cars, alcohol, vacations and financial products. Americans over 65 now control more than 70% of the economy.[42]

These are certain values that marketers should consider when marketing to older customers:[43]

○ **Autonomy**: Seniors want to lead active lives and be self-sufficient.
○ **Connectedness**: Seniors value the bonds with family and friends.
○ **Altruism**: Seniors feel that they would like to give back to the world and help others.
○ **Personal growth**: Seniors are still interested in trying new activities and experiences, and developing their potential.

Many of these people think of themselves as younger than their actual age. As we have seen, the perceived age represents the age that a person feels, and it often differs from the chronological age, which is the actual number of years they have lived. As a result, marketers who market to this segment use people in adverts that are a bit younger than this market. Marketers also stress product benefits instead of age appropriateness because many of these customers do not identify with products directed at their age.

Marketers sometimes segment the elderly in terms of motivations and quality of life orientations. They then divide these consumers into 'new age elderly' and 'traditional/

stereotypical elderly' categories. The new age elderly are 'individuals who feel, think, and do according to a cognitive age that is younger than their chronological age'.[44]

Table 6.5 shows a comparison of some of the factors defining these subgroups.

Table 6.5: Comparison of the new age and traditional elderly categories[45]

New age elderly	Traditional elderly
Perceive themselves to be different in outlook from other people their age	Perceive other people their age to have the same outlook
See age as a state of mind	See age as a physical state
See themselves as younger than their chronological age	See themselves as near their chronological age
Feel younger, think younger and 'do' younger	Tend to feel, think and do things that they feel match their chronological age
Have greater self-confidence when it comes to making consumer decisions	Have the normal range of self-confidence when it comes to making consumer decisions
Are especially knowledgeable and alert consumers	Have low-to-average consumer capabilities
Are selectively innovative	Are not innovative
Seek new experiences and personal challenges	Seek stability and a secure routine
Feel financially secure	Are somewhat concerned about financial security

The elderly are by no means a homogeneous subcultural group, and gerontologists suggest that they are more diverse in interests, opinions and actions than other segments of the adult population. It has been proven time and time again that age is not necessarily a major factor in determining how older consumers respond to marketing activities.[46]

In terms of packaging, marketers must take into account the failing strength and dexterity of seniors. This group finds many packages awkward and hard to handle or open, for example pull-tabs and zip-lock packages.

Baby Boomers

This refers to the generation born after the Second World War, which saw a boom in the birth of babies that lasted through to the mid-1960s. This generation is almost twice the size of the previous two generations combined. It also comprises about 50% of people in professional and managerial occupations, more than half of whom have at least a college degree.[49] Because of its size, it is the mass market in the USA, and as it ages, marketers are going to have to change their approaches to deal with a maturing market.

The age range of this generation is mid-thirties to mid-fifties, which is characterised by family and home orientations.[50] Other characteristics of this generation include high

Gerentographics[47]

Gerentographics divides the mature into categories based on physical health, mental outlook and social condition such as losing a spouse or partner. This idea can be used to divide the senior market further into four subsegments:

Healthy indulgers	This group have experienced the fewest events related to ageing, such as retirement or widowhood, and are most likely to behave like younger customers. Their main focus is on enjoying life	They are looking for independent living and are good customers for discretionary services such as home cleaning and answering machines, as well as high-tech home appliances, cruises and group travel
Healthy hermits	This group reacts to life events like the death of a spouse by becoming withdrawn. They resent that they are expected to behave like old people	They emphasise conformity. They want to know that their appearance is socially acceptable, and tend to be comfortable with well-known brands. They like do-it-yourself applications
Ailing outgoers	This group maintain positive self-esteem despite adverse life events. They accept limitations but are still determined to get the most out of life	They have health problems that may require a special diet, and promotions will aim at bringing these people into restaurants that are seen as catering to their needs. They are a key market for retirement homes and assisted living
Frail recluses	This group have adjusted their lifestyles to accept old age, but have chosen to cope with negative events by becoming spiritually stronger	They like to stay in the house where they raised their families. They are good candidates for remodelling, and also for emergency-response systems. They like high levels of personal service, especially in financial services

How old am I?[48]

Senior customers perceive themselves to be younger than their actual age across four age dimensions:
1. 'Feel' age – how old they feel (perceived age).
2. 'Look' age – how old they look.
3. 'Do' age – how active they are in terms of activities favoured by their age group.
4. 'Interest' age – how similar their interests are to those of other specific age groups.

Research in the USA has highlighted the differences between actual age, cognitive age and ideal age or the age people *wish to be*. Younger people want to feel older or more mature than their actual age. After 30, however, the cognitive and ideal ages drop below chronological age. This is compounded by the emphasis on youth and youth-related products in advertisements. For the mid-20s group, the three measures are fairly level.

education levels, high incomes and dual-career households. This causes enormous pressures on time, as this generation struggles to cope simultaneously with family and career responsibilities. Their concerns include expenses for education, weddings and retirement.

Marketing to this age category is particularly appealing to marketers as:[51]

○ it comprises the single largest distinctive age category alive today
○ members frequently make important consumer purchase decisions
○ it contains small subsegments of trend setting consumers known as 'yuppies' (young upwardly mobile professionals), who influence consumer tastes in the other age segments of society.

Baby Boomers tend not to like the idea of growing old. This is evident in the increase of health club memberships and the boom in vitamin and health supplement sales. These consumers try very hard to look and feel young, and will pay whatever is necessary to do so. For example, 30–35-year-olds are the largest market for plastic surgery, while the majority of cosmetic dentistry patients are 40–49-years-old.[52]

Baby Boomers are motivated, consumption-oriented individuals. They enjoy buying for themselves, for their homes and for others. Yuppies are the most sought after subgroup of boomers, even though they constitute only 5% of the population. Generally, they are financially well off and have enviable careers, but as they are now maturing, their focus is shifting. Yuppies are thinking less about status products and more about travelling, physical fitness and planning for a second career as more enriching experiences.[53]

Levi's adapt to Baby Boomers[54]

In the early 1980s, Levi's, producer of denim jeans, was the world's largest clothing manufacturer, yet by the late 1980s, sales were dropping dramatically. One of their strategic responses was to develop roomier khaki and chino trousers, which fit the baby boomers' middle-age spread better than jeans. Dockers, by Levi's, became one of the company's strongest brands. Also helping this trend was the buying of Dockers by young males who needed a 'dressier' pair of trousers than jeans. Upscale designers like Tommy Hilfiger and Geoffrey Beene have added elastic waistbands to trousers to adapt to baby-boomer requirements.

Generation X

The generation born between the mid-60s and the mid-70s is called 'Generation X'. While the Baby Boomers grew up in the USA with a strong economy, Generation X have grown up in difficult economic times, and they struggled to find meaningful jobs, and career placement and advancement. As a result, they are disillusioned and less materialistic than the Boomers. Their outlook is reflected in consumption patterns of products such as rap and hard rock music – by bands such as Pearl Jam and Coolio.[55] Generation X'ers have often been referred to as the 'MTV generation', for whom it is more important to enjoy a life that provides freedom and flexibility.[56] In fashion, it is reflected in the 'grunge' look and the increase in the use of accessories such as earrings and tattoos. The stereotypical perception of this generation is that they are slackers who do not have much drive, yet this is not actually the case. The generation has found success and achievement through technology, where many have their own computers and use them daily, and are heavy users of internet services.

Job satisfaction is extremely important for Generation X'ers. They reject the values of older co-workers who may neglect their families in order to secure higher salaries and career advancement, because many of them observed their parents (often Baby Boomers) being retrenched after many years of loyalty to an employer. It has often been said that 'while Baby Boomers live to work, Generation X'ers work to live'. They are not particularly interested in working for one company for their whole lives. And unlike their parents, Generation X'ers are in no rush to marry, start a family or work excessive hours to earn high salaries.[57]

This means that marketers can use global brands for this generation.[58] Marketers have noticed that there are many people in the generation around the world who act in the same ways and who have similar educational and income backgrounds. These common characteristics provide cross-national marketing opportunities for products such as Coke, McDonald's, Levi's 'baggies', Nike, Doc Martens and MTV.

Generation X and the media[59]

In spite of the hip-hop culture and younger outlook, this generation is a serious set of customers. In 1992, then-president George Bush refused an invitation to appear on MTV, which was the most popular television station for American youth at the time. He described it as a teeny-bopper network. In contrast to this, the then-candidate Bill Clinton appeared on the network extensively, using it to discuss his political platform and holding question-and-answer sessions. Needless to say, it resulted in Clinton winning many of the 'younger' votes – and the election.

Today, this group is important also because its members are moving into the time of life when they buy durable products such as cars, houses and other high-priced items.

Although Generation X'ers are not necessarily materialistic, they pride themselves on their sophistication and purchase good quality brands, but not necessarily designer labels. They want to be recognised as a group in their own right, and marketers should target communication at their sense of style in music, fashion and language. One key element is that marketers need to appear to be sincere, as X'ers are not necessarily opposed to adverts (like Generation Y'ers, see further below), only to insincerity.[60]

An interesting phenomenon of this generation is that they tend to leave home later than previous generations.[61] Many live at home until well into their 30s or until they marry, in order to save money or have more discretionary income. They feel less pressure to settle down and often delay marriage. This leads to a segment with a low total income resulting from difficulties in obtaining meaningful work but with a high dispos-able income.

A number of other factors characterise Generation X.[62] For example, X'ers are preoc-cupied with possessions and shopping. This was the first generation to be exposed to malls from an early age, and its members spend more time in malls than anywhere else except home or school. In the USA, moreover, they were exposed to an average of 20 000 television commercials a year, as a result of the heavy incidence of television watching. Average household viewing in the USA grew from about five hours a day in 1960 to just over seven hours a day in 1992. This heavy exposure to television has meant that they are highly customer-oriented and 'driven to shop'. In turn, this has affected their attitudes to marketing and promotions. They have been labelled as 'media knowledgeable' and the most customer-wise generation yet.

Product categories and Generation X[63]

The Generation X market segment is a key segment for music, movies, budget travel, bars and alcohol, fast food, clothing, jeans, athletic shoes and cosmetics. They are in the market for PCs, CD-ROMs, online services and video games.

Because of their exposure to television and adverts, Generation X customers are cynical about obvious marketing techniques.[64] They react positively to marketing campaigns that they see as clever or that are in tune with their values and attitudes. To reach these customers, marketers should consider using media such as popular or alternative radio stations, television stations such as MTV and music-related magazines. Messages should also be displayed at concerts, sporting events and popular vacation spots, and marketers can target sales promotions to this age group through music promotions and movie tie-ins.

Generation Y

The most recent generation, called 'Generation Y', comprises the children of the Boomers born between 1977 and 1994.[65] Its members have grown up in an era char-acterised by instantaneous global communication, fragmented media and a powerful focus on materialism. The teenagers of today are probably going to be, or are already, the most sophisticated and seasoned customers yet.

Also known as 'echo boomers' and the 'millennium generation', Generation Y'ers can be further divided into three subsegments:
1. Adults of 19 to 24.
2. Teens of 13 to 18.
3. Children of 8 to 12.

The members are described as pragmatic, savvy, socially and environmentally aware, and open to new experiences. They have moved some of their TV viewing time to the internet and are less likely to read the newspaper, compared to their parents. Moreover, they do not trust the stores that their parents shop in.[66]

The traditional marketing approaches that succeeded in reaching the older generation worked less well with regard to Generation X, and will be even less effective for Generation Y.[67] This generation has an increased influence on household spending, and has developed sophisticated decision-making skills as a result of having to shop for themselves because of parents who both work or are divorced. They are fussy about where they spend their money and tend to shop extensively for sales and good value.

> Generation Y is even more pragmatic than the other generations ever were, and has a no-nonsense alarm that goes off fast. Its members walk in and usually make up their minds fairly quickly about whether it's 'that' or 'not that', and whether they want it or not. They know a lot of advertising is based on lies and hype.[68]

An important aspect of selling to this market segment is that the customers will carry through brand loyalties into adulthood. One study found, for example, that about half of female teenagers had developed brand loyalties to cosmetics by the time they were 18 years old.[69]

Marketers wishing to connect with teens need to ensure that their campaigns and messages incorporate symbols, issues, language, images and media that are appropriate and relatable, for example music and sport are extremely important to teens worldwide, so popular music and sports personalities often appear in adverts for this market. PepsiCo has used singer Britney Spears to reinforce its image that it is the premier soft drink for the young generation.[70]

> **Retailer uses CD-ALOG to target teens[71]**
>
> Macy's, a well-known US retailer, is sending a CD-ROM to about half-a-million teenagers across the US. The disc is packaged in a mini-catalogue, in case the customers favour print. It comes with a $5 gift card to spur them into action. When it is popped into their computer drive, they will be treated to pop tunes and videos of teens wearing the latest fashions available at Macy's. Clicking on a picture will reveal a clothing brand and price, which can be added to a 'wish list'. The teen cannot order online, and so must actually visit the store. Macy's is keeping costs down by using music acts who are willing to trade the exposure for licensing fees. Macy's is also hoping that the CD will help update its image among teens.

The portrayal of multiple ethnic and racial groups in adverts is common, and urban African-American teenagers and hip hop cultural icons are frequently style leaders for this generation. The breaking down of cultural and ethnic boundaries is aided by the increased ownership, and use of computers and the internet. This means that trends in beauty and fashion can go global much more quickly than before, and can reflect customer fashion from anywhere in the world.[72]

In South Africa, the impact of Generation Y is even more important than in the USA.[73] Generation Y customers make up about 64% of the local population and spend R2 billion a year. Their profile is described as follows:

- ○ Nguni languages speakers – 45%.
- ○ Majority are female – 52%.
- ○ Live in Gauteng, KwaZulu-Natal and the Western and Eastern Cape – 65%.
- ○ Have matric – 20%.

South Africa marketers must be careful not to categorise all the people in this market as 'youth', since the group consists of school pupils, university students and young working adults. The drive to create a 'normal' society in South Africa means that global brands, which represent normality, are powerful attractions for this age group.

Demographic shifts in South Africa[74]

Recent research in South Africa indicates that a drop in fertility rates caused the country's population growth to slow down to less than 1.5% a year in the late 1990s. The research suggests that South Africa was poised for a demographic transition that preceded a rapid growth phase in developed countries. It noted that the education system, for example, could possibly concentrate more on quality than on quantity. South Africa created an embedded human capital measured in completed school years improving from 48 million in 1990 to 230 million in 1996. Although Aids would have an impact, this could augur well [predict good things] for the future of this generation of school leavers.

Generation Y'ers, Generation X'ers and Baby Boomers differ in their purchasing behaviour, attitudes toward brands and behaviour toward advertisements.[75] The main differences in these groups are illustrated in Table 6.6.

Table 6.6: Comparison of selected age cohorts across marketing-related issues[76]

Themes	Generation Y	Generation X	Baby Boomers
Purchasing behaviour	Savvy, pragmatic	Materialistic	Narcissistic
Coming of age technology	Computer in every home	Microwave in every home	TV in every home
Price-quality attitude	Value-oriented: weighing price–quality relationships	Price-oriented: concerned about the cost of individual items	Conspicuous consumption: buying for indulgence
Attitude toward brands	Embracing brand	Against branding	Loyal to a brand
Behaviour toward advertisements	Rebel against hype	Rebel against hype	Respond to image-building hype

Case study

SHOULD COLOUR BE PUT BACK INTO RESEARCH?

A recent debate by members of the Advertising Media Association of South Africa discussed the removal of references to race from SAARF's annual All Media Products Survey (AMPS). Below is a summary of the main arguments presented by panellists and members of the audience.

Reasons for *removing* race data from AMPS:

○ It does not fit in with the new non-racial society in South Africa. Marketers should be looking at how they position their communication in the new South Africa, which is seeking to remove the racial tags of the past.

○ Many marketers no longer use racial data for target marketing, realising that all black people are not the same and all white people are not the same.

○ Some less diligent members of the industry use the data as a crude shorthand for measuring markets that are, in fact, multi-dimensional and multi-faceted. They should instead be formulating a closer understanding of their target markets and the subtle differences within these.

○ The decision was taken by the Foundation's board members, and all industry members were given an opportunity to debate the issue. It is an indictment of people now raising their voices against the move that they did not avail themselves of the opportunity to do so earlier.

○ The Foundation helped to prop up the apartheid notion of the superiority of one race over another, and the organisation should be moving away from its old ways of doing things.

○ Racism will not disappear in South Africa as long as racial differences are emphasised.

○ Marketers should look at similarities between people rather than at what divides them. 'A 35-year-old black man from Sandton is likely to want many of the same things a 35-year-old white man from Sandton wants.'

○ Marketers should be looking for alternative tools to gain an understanding of what really 'makes the market tick'.

○ Race is not an effective discrimination. Marketers should rather be scrutinising value systems – for example the values between different ethic groups within a race vary considerably.

Reasons for *putting back* the race data:

○ It is inappropriate to remove it as the nation grapples with what it means to be South African. 'We are just avoiding the bigger issue of what it means to be rooted in the consciousness of South Africa.'

- Few brands can be viewed as being exclusively bought by blacks, such as Lifebuoy, Mageu No 1, Black Like Me. Many other brands are also bought by black people, and marketers need to know which ones within certain categories – like Nike, Adidas and Reebok among sport shoes – are being favoured by whom. 'We need some kind of dissection. People from Soweto might prefer Nike to Reebok and we need to know that.'
- It provides a tool for understanding the intricacies of the emerging black market. 'For a total picture of the consumer, we need to understand all variables' – such as whether someone who lives in Sandton has relatives living in Soweto.
- If it becomes invisible, the black market, already being written off by many advertisers and marketers, will be written off further by the industry.
- Until the ad and media industries are fully transformed, there has to be a focus on race to ensure continuing change.
- The industry needs to be able to track the progress in transforming society. 'This country hasn't changed – it is changing. And we need to be able to measure that change in order to fine tune our marketing.'
- If race is excluded from the survey, marketers will try to find other ways to isolate race data, which might be less accurate. 'For example, they will look at the readership of *The Sowetan* newspaper and make the assumption that all readers are black.'
- Race data is included in similar surveys in most places in the world.

6.5 Summary

In this chapter we studied the personal characteristics of customers that influence their behaviour. These include age, gender and race. The make-up of South African society in term of these three characteristics is unique, yet the general trends in terms of marketers adapting their marketing activities to take into account the differences among these three parameters are universal. Our discussion emphasised that marketers must take care with stereotypes, which are often outdated and are not representative of the realities in South Africa today. Moreover, marketers must determine how specific subcultural members interact to influence purchase decisions, because consumers can be members of several subcultural groups simultaneously.

Questions for self-assessment

To assess your progress, answer these questions:
1. Define and give examples of the personal characteristics of customers.
2. Explain how marketers should take race into account in terms of designing the product and marketing communication aspects of the marketing mix.
3. Briefly explain, in about half a page, what the LSM is.

4. Discuss the changing role of women and how marketers should take this into account.
5. Explain the different meanings that can be associated with the word 'age'.
6. Discuss three reasons why marketers should study age and its impact on marketing.
7. Explain the action marketers should take if they want to connect well with Generation Y customers in South Africa.
8. Examine the arguments for and against the use of race in market research given in the case study above, and try to come to a balanced conclusion about the issue.

Endnote references

1. Kotler, P. 2000. *Marketing Management: The Millennium Edition*. Upper Saddle River: Prentice-Hall.
2. Sheth, J.N., Mittal, B. and Newman, B.I. 1999. *Customer Behavior: Consumer Behavior and Beyond*. Orlando: Dryden, p. 203.
3. Ibid.
4. Adapted from ibid.
5. These definitions come from ibid., p. 209.
6. Evans, M.J., Moutinho, L. and Van Raaij, W.F. 1996. *Applied Consumer Behaviour*. Harrow: Addison-Wesley.
7. Adapted from Cant, M.C. and Machado, R. (eds). 1998. *Marketing Success Stories*. 3rd ed. Johannesburg: International Thomson Publishing.
8. Looking lovely naturally. *Pretoria News*, 12 December 2000, p. 11.
9. Hawkins, D.I., Best, R.J. and Coney, K.A. 1998. *Consumer Behavior: Building Marketing Strategy*. 7th ed. Boston: McGraw-Hill, p. 146.
10. Adapted from Mabote, R. 2001. Beer/women ... and bad marketing. *Journal of Marketing*, 7(2), 29.
11. Haupt, P., Smit, P. and Ncube, M. 2002. Industry PowerPoint presentation on the SAARF Universal LSM. University of Pretoria, April.
12. Living Standards Measure. Available on the internet from: www.saarf.co.za/lsms.htm.
13. Haupt et al., op. cit.
14. Strydom, J.W. 2004. *Introduction to Marketing*. 3rd ed. Cape Town: Juta.
15. Hawkins et al., op. cit.
16. Straughan, R.D. and Albers-Miller, N.D. 2001. An international investigation of cultural and demographic effects of domestic retail loyalty. *International Marketing Review*, 18(5), 521–41.
17. Hawkins et al., op. cit.
18. Ibid.
19. Schiffman, L.G. and Kanuk, L.L. 2004. *Consumer Behavior*. 5th ed. New Jersey: Pearson Prentice-Hall.
20. Hawkins et al., op. cit.
21. Engel, J.F., Blackwell, R.D. and Miniard, P.W. 1993. *Consumer Behavior*. Orlando: Dryden, pp. 187–97.
22. Schiffman and Kanuk, op. cit.
23. Adapted from Snapping up the MBAs. Women in Business Survey, *Finance Week*, 24 May 2002, p. 37.
24. Adapted from Sheth et al., op. cit., pp. 220-3, and Engel et al., op. cit., pp. 194–5.

25. Adapted from Brink, A. 1997. The marketing perception of grocery store retailers belonging to black business associations in Gauteng. Unpublished DCom thesis, University of South Africa, Pretoria.
26. Hawkins et al., op. cit.
27. Ibid.
28. Evans et al., op. cit.
29. Ibid.
30. Adapted from Engel et al., op. cit., p. 199.
31. Learned, A. The six costliest mistakes you can make in marketing to women. Available on the internet from: www.marketingprof.com/print,asp?source=perspect.learnedI.asp.
32. Schiffman and Kanuk, op. cit.
33. Lovell, J. 2001. Cape's pink promotion pesters the pious. Available on the internet from: www. news24.com (accessed 3 April).
34. Mowen, J.C. and Minor, M. 1998. *Consumer Behavior*. 5th ed. Upper Saddle River: Prentice-Hall.
35. Sheth et al., op. cit.
36. Ibid., pp. 224–5.
37. Brink, op. cit.
38. Hawkins et al., op. cit.
39. Ibid.
40. Schiffman and Kanuk, op. cit.
41. Solomon, M. 1999. *Consumer Behavior*. 4th ed. Upper Saddle River: Prentice-Hall, pp. 483–7.
42. Schiffman and Kanuk, op. cit.
43. Ibid.
44. Ibid.
45. Schiffman and Sherman in Schiffman and Kanuk, op. cit.
46. Schiffman and Kanuk, op. cit.
47. Adapted from Solomon, op. cit., p. 486, and Hawkins et al., op. cit., p. 174.
48. Schiffman, L.G., Bednall, D., Watson, J. and Kanuk, L.L. 1997. *Consumer Behaviour*. Sydney: Prentice-Hall, p. 427.
49. Schiffman and Kanuk, op. cit.
50. Hawkins et al., op. cit.
51. Schiffman and Kanuk, op. cit.
52. Ibid.
53. Ibid.
54. Mowen and Minor, op. cit., p. 593.
55. Hoyer, W.D. and Maclnnis, D.J. 1997. *Consumer Behavior*. Boston: Houghton Mifflin.
56. Schiffman and Kanuk, op. cit.
57. Ibid.
58. Hawkins et al., op. cit.
59. Hoyer and MacInnis, op. cit., p. 356.
60. Schiffman and Kanuk, op. cit.
61. Ibid.
62. Roberts, J.A. and Manolis, C. 2000. Baby boomers and busters: An exploratory investigation of attitudes toward marketing, advertising and consumerism. *Journal of Consumer Marketing*, 17(6), 481–97.
63. Adapted from Hoyer and Maclnnis, op. cit., p. 355.
64. Ibid.
65. Schiffman and Kanuk, op. cit.
66. Ibid.

67. Hawkins et al., op. cit.
68. Ibid.
69. Hoyer and MacInnis, op. cit.
70. Kaduc, D. 2002. Has Coke lost its fizz *Time*, 15 April, p. 43.
71. Manners, T. (ed.). 2001. Macy's targets teens with CD-ALOG. Cool News. Available on the internet from: www.reveries.com (accessed 2 August).
72. Omelia, J. 1998. Understanding generation Y: A look at the next wave of US consumers. Available on the internet from: www.dindarticles.com (accessed December X).
73. This section is adapted from Taylor, A. 2001. Youth marketing needs to be spot on. *Sunday Times*.
74. Owen, K. 2002. Quality education the only hope. *Business Day*, 27 May, p. 9.
75. Schiffman and Kanuk, op. cit..
76. Noble and Noble in Schiffman and Kanuk, op. cit.

7 Customer perception and learning

Learning Outcomes

After studying this chapter, you should be able to:

○ explain the nature of perception

○ illustrate the implications of the perceptual process

○ highlight the marketing implications of perception

○ explain the nature of learning

○ explain the elements of learning

○ illustrate the marketing implications of the various learning theories.

7.1 Introduction

We live in a world that is overflowing with sensations. Wherever we turn, we are bombarded with colours, sounds and odours. We are never far from advertisements, product packages, billboards, and radio and television commercials, all clamouring for our attention. Each of us copes with this bombardment by paying attention to some messages and 'tuning out', or ignoring, others. The messages we pay attention to often end up being rather different from what the marketers intended, as each of us puts our own meanings on them by adapting them to fit in with our unique experiences, biases and desires. What we have learned, therefore, will determine how we perceive the surrounding world. Marketers are particularly interested in how customers sense external information, how they select and attend to various sources of information, and how they interpret and give meaning to this information.

In this chapter we investigate what it means for customers to be perceivers and learners. We look at the nature of perception and the perceptual process, exploring how customers 'defend' themselves against incoming stimuli, that is, messages that impact on our consciousness, and what marketers can do to overcome these perceptual defence mechanisms. We explain how learning occurs and how customers learn to respond to their environment. We highlight the fact that customer behaviour is largely learned behaviour, and that the way in which customers learn is of immense importance to marketers, who want customers to learn about their particular products or services.

7.2 The customer as perceiver

7.2.1 The nature of perception

Perception is the process by which people select, organise and interpret stimuli to the five senses of sight, sound, smell, touch and taste. In other words, it is the way that buyers interpret or give meaning to the world around them.[1] Therefore, we can say that the **process of perception** involves being exposed to a stimulus, paying attention to it and then interpreting its meaning in order to respond to it. Like computers, people undergo stages of information processing in which stimuli are inputted and stored. Unlike computers, we do not passively process whatever information happens to be present. In the first place, perception is *selective*, that is, we notice only a small number of the stimuli in our environment; and of these, we attend to an even smaller number. Secondly, each of us interprets the stimuli *subjectively*, that is, according to our unique personalities, biases and needs. Thirdly, perception is based on each of our *personal experiences*. Evidently, the second and third factors are connected, as a person's nature and their experiences together make up what they are.

Perception is selective
Although we are exposed to a huge quantity of information, we attend to only a relatively small percentage, which we pass on to the central processing part of our brains for interpretation. This selectivity is called '**perceptual defence**', and it means that as individuals we are not passive recipients of marketing messages. Rather, customers largely determine the messages they will notice as well as the meaning they will assign to the messages. Clearly, marketers face a challenging task when communicating with customers.

Perception is subjective
Subjective factors always play a role in perception. In other words, we see and hear what we are interested in because of what we are, what we believe in, what our values are, and so on.

Perception is based on the individual's frame of reference
The individual's act of perceiving is based on his or her experience.[2] This experience has built up a relatively stable cognitive organisation in the individual that determines the meaning of a particular perception. We add to or take away from these sensations as we assign meaning to them based on our experience. For example, a woman who shops for the first time in a store and who finds that its employees are extremely unfriendly will probably avoid the store in future because of her newly formed perception of it. Experience of the store has moulded her perception of it.

The perceptual process influences marketers' ability to reach customers in a crowded marketplace. Look at the way in which people respond to advertising messages or other marketing information. First, they differ in their ability to 'pick up' the messages via sensations. Once a message has been received, its effectiveness hinges on the customer's interest in paying attention to it. Customers are often in a state of sensory overload, exposed to far more marketing stimuli than they are capable of processing. To further complicate matters for marketers, when people *do* pay attention to marketing information, the meaning they see may be quite different from what the marketer intended.[3]

We now consider this perceptual process more closely.

7.2.2 The perceptual process

The perceptual process consists of four stages, namely, exposure, attention, interpretation and memory (or recall), as shown in Figure 7.1.

Figure 7.1: Stages in information processing[4]

Exposure

Exposure is the degree to which people notice a stimulus that is within range of their sensory receptors. The individual need not receive the stimulus for exposure to have occurred. For example, you have been exposed to a TV commercial if it was aired while you were in the room, even if you were talking to a friend at the time and did not notice the commercial. Because customers do not all watch the same TV programmes or read the same magazines, it is the marketer's responsibility to place the company's messages where targeted customers will be exposed to them.

Most of the stimuli to which an individual is exposed are 'self-selected', that is, we mentally tune out messages we do not want to hear or see, and we deliberately ignore messages in which we have no interest.[5] Customers therefore seek out some adverts, some shelf displays, some salespeople or sources of information, while they avoid others, depending on their needs and interests. For example, if customers think a particular store is too expensive, they would not enter it, even if it displayed adverts for huge savings.

Because customers are being exposed to so many advertising stimuli, marketers are becoming increasingly creative in their attempts to gain exposure for their products.[6] One of their solutions is to put adverts in unconventional places, where there will be less competition, such as on the backs of shopping trolleys, on walls in sports stadiums, at the beginning of movies, and even in rest rooms, where the marketer has a 'captive audience'. The proper approach in media planning, therefore, would be to determine which media customers in the target market are most frequently exposed to, and then to place the advertisement in these media.

Exposure to a message means only that it has been seen or heard. There is no guarantee that the individual will pay attention to it.

Attention

Attention refers to the extent to which the processing activity is devoted to a particular stimulus.[7] As you know from sitting through both interesting and boring lectures, this allocation can vary according to the recipient – that is, your mental state at the time, and the characteristics of the stimulus – that is, the lecture itself. Of course, attention always occurs in the context of a situation. Therefore, we can say that attention is determined by the individual, the stimulus and the situation:

○ **The individual**: Customers are more likely to be aware of stimuli that relate to their current needs. Interest or need seems to be the primary individual characteristic that influences attention.[8] Interest is a reflection of overall lifestyle as well as a result of long-term goals and plans, such as becoming a lawyer, and short-term needs, such as satisfying hunger. For example, a customer who rarely notices car adverts will become highly aware of them when he or she is in the market for a new car. The receiver's mindset therefore plays a crucial role in paying attention to a stimulus. Initially, a person's attention is attracted by the stimulus characteristics of, for example, contrast. Beyond this initial reaction, however, a person's further processing of a stimulus advert or display depends on the personal interest the featured product or service arouses in him or her. Thus, people will pay attention only to those messages that are in line with their personality, experience and attitudes, and their image of themselves and their social and cultural environment.[9]

○ **The stimulus**: The characteristics of the stimulus itself also play an important role in determining what gets noticed and what gets ignored.[10] Marketers need to understand these factors so that they can apply them to their messages and packages to boost their chances of cutting through the clutter of a multitude of stimuli and commanding the customer's attention. In general, stimuli that differ from others around them are more likely to be noticed. This contrast can be created in several ways:

    – *Size and intensity*: Larger stimuli are more likely to be noticed than smaller ones.[11] A full-page advert is more likely to be noticed than one of half a page. Insertion frequency, that is, the number of times the same advert appears in the same issue of a magazine, has an impact similar to advert size. The intensity, such as the loudness and brightness, of a stimulus operates in much the same way. For example, marketers address the problem of clutter on a supermarket shelf with attractive package design, point-of-purchase display materials and eye-level shelf displays.[12] Every aspect of the package – the name, shape, colour, label, etc. – must provide sufficient sensory stimulation to be noted and remembered.

- *Colour*: This is a powerful way of drawing attention to a product or giving it a distinct identity. Most car rental companies use a consistent colour scheme for their rental counters, staff uniforms, fleet of shuttle buses, stationery and almost anything else that is physical, except the rental cars themselves. However, while colour can increase attention and readership, if not used properly it can also distract from the message and the ability of the audience to effectively process the message.
- *Position*: Stimuli that appear in places we are more likely to look stand a better chance of being noticed. Objects placed near the centre of the visual field are more likely to be noticed than those near the edge of the field. This is a primary reason for consumer goods manufacturers competing fiercely for eye-level space in supermarkets. Similarly, adverts on the right-hand page of a magazine or newspaper receive more attention than those on the left.[13]
- *Isolation*: This is the process of separating a stimulus object from other objects. The use of 'white space', that is, placing a brief message in the centre of an otherwise blank or white advert, is based on this principle, as is surrounding a key part of a radio commercial with a brief moment of silence.[14]

○ **The situation**: In perceiving a stimulus with a given set of characteristics, customers will also be influenced by the context of the stimulus, namely, the situation. The factors involved here include stimuli in the environment other than the central, focal stimulus, such as the advert or package, and temporary characteristics of the individual that are induced by the environment, such as time pressures or a crowded store. For example, a waiter in a restaurant treats customers with politeness but not friendliness. He might be thought of as unfriendly in a low- to mid-price, mass-market restaurant such as the Spur, but if he treats customers in the same way in an up-market restaurant they may well consider him as being respectful. The clearest illustrations of the effect of the situation on the perception of marketing stimuli are **blind-taste test studies** such as studies of beer taste. In these tests, customers pick the brand they think is their usual or favourite brand, even when the brand names have been switched. The taste perceptions are influenced by the context that the brand name provides.

Interpretation

Once a customer has been exposed to a marketing message, and has attended to it, they still need to interpret it in the way intended by the marketer. The third stage of the perception process therefore is interpretation, which is the meaning that people assign to sensory stimuli. Just as we differ in terms of the stimuli that we perceive, the eventual meanings we assign to these stimuli vary as well. Two people can see or hear the same event, but their interpretations of it can be completely different.[15]

Individuals tend to interpret information according to their existing beliefs, attitudes and general disposition, and experiences, in other words, the subjective qualities and frame of reference we refer to earlier.[16] A brand name can communicate expectations about product attributes and can influence customers' perceptions of product performance.[17] Marketers therefore rely heavily on signs and symbols in marketing messages, and sometimes turn to a field of study known as '**semiotics**', which examines the correspondence between signs and symbols and the perceived meaning that customers assign to them. For example, the use of a pine tree symbol on some cleaning products conveys an association of freshness and cleanliness, while the protective hands of the Sanlam logo provide an association of trust.

Thus we can say that interpretation is selective. Selective interpretation acts as a screen or filter through which information must flow – from the communicator (the marketer) to the receiver (the customer).[18] This screen or filter enables the customer to ignore some bits of information included in a marketing message, to change the meaning of other bits or to focus their attention on certain aspects of the message. Selective interpretation may be due to mis-indexing the message or distorting the meaning of the message:[19]

◯ **Mis-indexing**: This refers to the way people tend to classify or categorise the meaning of the message. The reason for mis-indexing lies in the message construction, and it often occurs in the following situations:

  – *A novel or amusing situation*: When the situation, for example the advertisement itself, is novel or amusing then frequently the situation itself is the message, with the result that the advertised product is forgotten.

  – *An inappropriate attention seeking device*: When the attention seeking device is inappropriate, the device itself becomes the message, with the result that the advert is more likely to stimulate thoughts about the subject from which attention was 'borrowed'.

  – *'Me-too-ism'*: Marketers confuse the customer by copying each other's competitive promotion programmes, types of packaging or colour schemes.

    To avoid mis-indexing, the message must form an integrated whole, combining elements and symbols such as the heading, the slogan, the illustration, the body copy, the typeface, the billboard design, the package, etc. The consistent and repetitive use of certain stimuli – frequently by means of special effects, sounds and images – to illustrate the customer's experience of the product during actual use, brands, slogans and typefaces are aids in tying in the message with the product or service being advertised.

◯ **Distorting**: Either purposefully or subconsciously, customers distort the message to fit in with their likes, dislikes, prejudices and attitudes. The message can be distorted by levelling or by sharpening:

  – *Levelling*: This means that individuals ignore an important bit of information or point in the marketing message, or they simplify the message, perhaps by removing dissonant elements, so that it becomes more acceptable. For example, warnings against the dangers of smoking, which by law have to be included on advertising and packaging of cigarettes, are likely to be 'screened out' by habitual smokers.

  – *Sharpening*: This means that the customer reads additional information into the message, by adding new elements to make it fit in with predispositions and value systems.[20] For example, some people are interested in diet, nutrition and health, and may therefore be unusually sensitive to information, including adverts, about fresh vegetables, fruit and vitamins. They may tend to add new dimensions to some of this information to support their beliefs and practices.

Recall (or memory)

The last stage of the perceptual process is recall. Customers do not remember all the information they see, hear or read, even after attending to it and interpreting it. Advertisers try to make sure that information will be retained in the customer's memory so that it will be available when the customer is considering buying something. Customers tend to forget the marketing message when they are actually making the purchase, that is, at the point of purchase, even if they have perceived it correctly. To avoid this, marketers use point-of-purchase promotions to remind the customer of their messages and products. In this regard, marketers should be aware of the following three important factors that affect recall:[21]

1. **The positive-sleeper effect**: A customer may not be convinced by an advertising message, but may still react in the desired way – by buying the product. This is may be the result of highly effective point-of-purchase promotion.
2. **The boomerang effect**: In much the same way, the boomerang effect may result in customers reversing their decision to buy one product and taking the directly opposite course of action by buying another, competing product. This may be because the competing product is well positioned on the shelf, or because it is being promoted effectively by a point-of-purchase promotion.
3. **Overcrowded file space**: Recall may be extremely difficult if the 'file spaces' in the customers' minds are overcrowded with information, causing them to mis-index the message. In such a situation, they become confused, and may end up buying the competing product. Therefore, the marketing message should be as simple and direct as possible, in order not to contribute to the confusion. Marketers must reinforce the potential customer's initial, tentative acceptance of a message through reminder advertising.

7.2.3 Perception and marketing

An understanding of perception is an essential guide to marketing. We now look at a number of areas in which such an understanding is particularly useful.

Retail strategy[22]

Retailers often use exposure effectively. Store interiors are designed with the intention of separating goods that are bought frequently, such as canned foods, fresh fruits or vegetables and meats, from those that are bought less often, so that the average customer will travel through more of the store. This increases the customers' total exposure to goods in the store. High margin items, that is, items on which the retailer makes a larger profit, are often placed in high traffic areas to capitalise on increased exposure.

Shelf position and amount of shelf space influence which items and brands are allocated attention by customers. Point-of-purchase displays also attract attention to sale and high margin items. Stores are designed with highly visible shelves and overhead signs to make locating items as easy as possible. Stores provide reference prices to increase customers' ability to accurately interpret price information. Unit price information by brand may be displayed on a separate sign in ascending or descending order to help the customers to compare prices.

In-store information cues comprise brands, layout, point-of-purchase displays, and so on. The total mix of these cues, of what the outside of the store looks like and of advertising combine to form the image or opinion that customers have of the store.

Brand image[23]

The image of a product that the customer has in their mind, that is, how it is positioned, is probably more important to its ultimate success than its actual characteristics. Marketers try to position their brands so that the brands are perceived by customers to fit a distinctive (otherwise unoccupied) niche in the marketplace by stressing the product's attributes that they claim will fulfil the customers' needs better than competing brands.

A survey conducted by Markinor on brand awareness illustrates customer perception of brands.[24] The top brands rated by customers were Coca-Cola, Telkom, Eskom, Checkers and SA Breweries, in that order. The most admired companies were Coca-Cola, Telkom, Eskom, SA Breweries and Standard Bank, in that order. Winners in the other categories were: new companies – Vodacom; retailers – Edgars; cars – Toyota; cell phones – Nokia; fast food outlets – Kentucky Fried Chicken; and petrol brands – BP.

Price as a quality cue[25]

Since customers often rely on price as an indicator of product quality, marketers emphasise the high price of some products to underscore their claims of quality. Rombouts coffee, with its individual filters, was originally introduced as a high priced coffee that was 'worth the difference' in cost because of its superior flavour and taste.

Case study

LONG LIFE MILK

Many people in the world drink milk out of a box every day. Long life milk manufactured by Parmalat SA is specially processed without any preservatives. The milk has been heated until the bacteria causing spoilage are destroyed, and it can last for five to six months without refrigeration if its aseptic container is unopened. Shelf-stable milk is particularly

IIII➡

popular in areas where refrigerator space in homes and stores tends to be more limited or even non-existent. The milk does require refrigeration after opening, but until then, it can be stored on dry goods shelves for up to six months. There are many advantages to customers – it saves refrigerator space, and they can stock extra milk in their pantries so that they don't have to run to the store at midnight having just discovered that they are out of milk.

When Parmalat first introduced this product, it was expected that customer acceptance would be immediate and high. The product concept sounded great in theory. However, the actual products sales were extremely low. Somehow, customers just could not understand the concept of fresh milk in a dry goods box. They seemed to have trouble believing that the milk was not spoiled or unsafe. Some even felt that the name 'Parmalat' sounded too much like baby formulas such as Similac.

This is an example of a situation in which customers' perceptions and learning are at odds with the new product concept. In some rural areas, medical doctors have found that customers perceive the concept of 'long life' to be pasteurised milk that can be given to newborn babies, thus ensuring 'long life' for their children.

Source: Sheth et al. 1999:297

7.3 Customer learning

7.3.1 The nature of learning

All aspects of the individual – perception, needs, motives and attitudes – are either directly or indirectly determined and influenced by the ability of the customer *to learn*. In addition, the external determinants or group factors that affect customer behaviour – the family, culture, social class and reference groups – greatly influence the individual as he or she learns and experiences in these contexts and situations. To a large extent, the learning experiences determine the products that customers will buy and, more importantly, why they prefer a particular product. Any facet of people's behaviour is therefore dependent on what they learn and remember about objects and situations. In other words, the whole decision-making process is dependent on past learning situations.[26]

From a marketing perspective, learning is the process by which individuals acquire the buying and consumption knowledge and experience they apply to future-related behaviour.[27] This definition means that the process of learning continually evolves and changes as a result of newly acquired knowledge or experience. Both such knowledge and experience serve as feedback to the individual. Consequently, all the individual's future behaviour is based on this knowledge or experience.

Put simply, learning is a change in the content of long-term memory. As humans, we learn because what we learn helps us to respond better to our environment. A child that accidentally touches a hot electric light bulb learns not to touch anything resembling that object. Similarly, a customer who is trapped into buying a sub-standard product from a mail-order firm on non-returnable terms of purchase, for example, learns not to buy anything from that firm again.[28] As customers we face a marketplace environment of a multitude of product and service choices, and we learn to adapt and respond to this environment.

We now consider the elements of learning, in other words, how individuals learn.

7.3.2 The elements of learning

All individuals learn, but not every individual learns the same things, nor do they learn at the same speed or in the same way. The basic elements of learning, stimulus, response and reinforcement, shown in Figure 7.2, are found in all learning, but there are differences in their use and application.[29]

Figure 7.2: The elements of learning

Stimulus

The first requirement of learning is a stimulus, which is something that stimulates the learner's interest. Marketers can stimulate customers using **physical** things such as products, brands and size, or **intangibles** such as service, quality and satisfaction. Once customers have perceived a stimulus, they must be motivated to seek the object before learning occurs. Motivation thus acts as a spur to learning, with motives serving as stimuli to learning. The stronger the motivation, the quicker customers learn. For example, someone who is keen to become a good tennis player is motivated to learn all they can about tennis. They will look for information about the prices and quality of tennis rackets if they 'learn' that a good racket is vital to playing a good game.

Response

Motives stimulate learning, while the cues are the stimuli that give direction to the motives. The advert is the cue or stimulus that suggests a specific way to satisfy a particular motive. This may cause a customer to respond. A response is any action, reaction or state of mind resulting from a particular stimulus or cue. The same response to a stimulus may occur several times before we can say that the response has been learned. Marketers who provide consistent cues, or advertising messages, to customers may not always succeed in stimulating them to buy, even if they are motivated to do so. Instead, these marketers may succeed in creating a favourable image of their products in the customers' minds. Cues provide some direction, but there are many cues competing for the customers' attention. Which response they will make depends heavily on reinforcement.

Reinforcement

Reinforcement increases the likelihood that a particular response will occur in the future as the result of specific cues or stimuli. Reinforcement, or reward, is the satisfaction resulting from successful behaviour that triggers human memory of how the satisfaction was obtained. It can also be viewed as an inducement, that is, the probability that a given response to a specific stimulus will reoccur, given the same stimuli and situation. This means that reinforcement is the 'thing' that causes the individual to relate the response to the stimulus correctly, resulting in repetitive behaviour that establishes future behaviour. For example, a woman whose friends often ask her to serve a certain brand of coffee (stimulus) when they visit her and comment on its flavour may learn to prefer that brand of coffee (response) herself. Two important aspects of reinforcement are repetition and participation:

1. **Repetition**: To increase reinforcement, the same action should be performed several times.[30] The concept of repetition in learning has many applications in retail merchandising. In the area of store layout, for example, shoppers learn where the goods are by developing an in-store travel pattern that they repeat each time they visit the store. Over time, these shoppers become extremely comfortable and more efficient with their in-store behaviour, and any changes in store layout will force them to relearn the store and the new locations of the items on their shopping list – a process not likely to be greeted with enthusiasm.

2. **Participation**: Participation can help reinforcement. An active role in any activity generally results in the acquisition of more knowledge about that activity. Free samples, trial-size products and demonstrations are participation devices that marketers use in guiding the customers' learning processes towards products. If customers can see a product, feel it, smell it, taste it and/or hear it, they are bound to learn more about it. The retailer must therefore encourage customers to get involved in the merchandise and the buying process.

Having considered these basic principles, we now discuss some well-known theories or models of how learning occurs, which are also known as the 'mechanisms' of learning.

7.3.3 Theories of learning

The behavioural theories with the greatest relevance to marketing are classical conditioning, instrumental conditioning and cognitive learning.

Classical conditioning

This is the process in which a person learns an association between two stimuli because of their constant appearance as a pair.[31] Owing to such constant contiguity or pairing, customers tend to attribute to the previously unknown stimulus (a product or service) whatever they think or feel about the other paired stimulus. Two ideas presented together are considered together, providing there is something to connect them in the individual's mind.

It is the possibility of a *reward* that connects the objects or ideas. Pavlov's work with the conditioning of dogs is well known in this area. By ringing a bell every time the dogs ate, he taught the dogs to associate the ringing of the bell with food, so that eventually he was able to get dogs to salivate simply by ringing the bell. In this way, two unrelated ideas are related by having each idea associated with a reward.

Marketers often rely on conditioned responses to reach customers. Most reminder advertising falls into this category. In all kinds of selling, some reward is associated with the marketers' products in an attempt to persuade the customer to buy. Habitual buying is another form of conditioned response. Customers can be conditioned to favour products, brands, stores, prices and services.

Marketers put this principle to use when they pair their brand with a likeable celebrity. The celebrity's personality, by classical conditioning, rubs off onto the product itself. For example, CK perfume is seen as 'youthful' because of the teenage models used in the brand's advertising. Moreover, products are packaged to look a certain way – expensive or inexpensive, fancy or simple, special or everyday. The way the waiters dress, the typeface on the menu and even the appearance of paper napkins in a restaurant are designed to classically condition the perceived quality of the restaurant and its food.

Instrumental conditioning

Also known as 'operant conditioning', this type of conditioning occurs as the individual learns to perform behaviours that produce positive outcomes and to avoid those that yield negative outcomes.[32] Whereas responses in classical conditioning are involuntary and fairly simple, those in instrumental conditioning are made to achieve a goal, and can be more complex. The customer may learn the desired behaviour over a period of time, as their intermediate actions are rewarded in a process called **'shaping'**. For example, the owner of a new store may award prizes to shoppers just for coming in, hoping that over time they will continue to do so and eventually will buy something.

While classical conditioning involves the close pairing of two stimuli, instrumental learning occurs as a result of a reward received following the desired behaviour. Learning takes place over a period of time, during which other behaviours are attempted and abandoned because they are not reinforced. Over time, customers come to associate with people who reward them and to choose products that make them feel good or that satisfy some need.

Instrumental conditioning is widely used by marketers.[33] The most common application is to provide products with consistent quality so that the use of the product to meet a customer need is reinforced. Other applications include a simple 'thank you' after someone buys something, giving large discounts, giving samples to encourage product trial and making follow-up telephone calls. A popular technique known as **'frequency marketing'** reinforces regular buyers by giving them prizes with values that increase along with the amount bought. This instrumental learning strategy was pioneered by the airline industry, which introduced 'frequent flyer' programmes in the early 1980s to reward loyal customers.

Cognitive theory

In contrast to the abovementioned behavioural theories of learning, cognitive learning approaches stress the importance of *internal mental processes.*

Not all learning takes place as a result of repeated trials – a considerable amount of learning takes place as the result of customer thinking and problem-solving. The cognitive theory views people as problem-solvers who actively use information from the world around them to master their environment. Supporters of this viewpoint also stress the role of creativity and insight in the learning process. Unlike the theory of conditioning, the cognitive theory holds that problem-solving involves mental processing, and it emphasises the role of motivation and mental manipulation in arriving at a desired response. It is concerned with how individuals think and how they learn. It is therefore necessary to know how the mind functions.

These three types of cognitive learning are important to marketers:[34]

1. **Iconic rote learning**: This involves learning the association between two or more concepts in the absence of conditioning. For example, you may see an advert that states, 'Ketaprofen is a headache remedy', and you could associate the new concept of 'Ketaprofen' with the existing concept of 'headache remedy'. There is neither an unconditioned stimulus nor a direct reward involved. Through iconic rote learning, customers may form beliefs about the attributes of products without being aware of the source of the information. When the need arises, they may buy the product based on those beliefs.

2. **Vicarious learning or modelling**: It is not necessary for customers to directly experience a reward or punishment to learn. Instead, we can observe the outcomes of others' behaviours and adjust our own behaviour accordingly. When buying a suit, for example, a new employee may deliberately observe the styles worn by others at work or by role models in other environments, including adverts. Throughout the course of our lives we observe people using products and behaving in a wide variety of situations. Most of the time we pay limited attention to these behaviours. However, over time, we learn that certain behaviours – and, of course, products – are appropriate in some situations, while others are not. Many promotional strategies are centred around endorsements by celebrity athletes, film stars and music idols for this reason.

3. **Reasoning**: In reasoning, individuals engage in creative thinking to restructure and recombine existing and new information to form new associations and concepts. In problem-solving, the customer who is faced with a market-related problem is capable of thinking logically to arrive at a solution. The reward may come by solving the problem or from the satisfaction that results from solving the problem. A customer who is new to a city uses problem-solving to decide on which grocery store to shop at. By a process of trial and error, they find a satisfactory store. The customer uses insight to make the connection that a known solution to a problem can be applied to a different problem.

Case study

XEROX COPIERS

It was 1980, and industrial buyers were not buying Xerox Corporation's new 8200 office copier. Xerox's management was stunned, because it was the first time that customers had balked at one of its products. Meanwhile, the market share of Japanese competitors was rapidly increasing. Why were Xerox's customers rejecting the 8200? A technological masterpiece, the copier boasted the three most advanced features demanded by business: collating, enlarging and reducing capabilities. In the lab, the copier worked perfectly. It was reliable, it contained an onboard computer and it produced excellent copies.

Xerox instituted a crash programme to find out why the 8200 copier was a market failure. The project manager brought in cognitive scientists, anthropologists and the repair personnel who were closest to the product's users. The problem quickly became apparent – people found the copier too complicated to use. As the project manager commented, 'No one paid attention to the human interface – to the user.' People had to wade through buttons and visual 'noise' and the manual to find out how to use all the features, including the most frequently used ones, simply to copy a page or two. Customers who had used the 8200 copier hated it.

As a result of this analysis, the 8200 copier was totally redesigned. Clear graphic displays and touch-screen menus were created that quickly and easily guided users through the machine's operations. By paying attention to its customers and their needs, Xerox was able to redesign and relaunch its copier – and this time it succeeded in the marketplace.

Source: Mowen, J. C. & Minor, M. 1998. *Consumer Behavior*

7.4 Summary

In this chapter we dealt with customer perception in a discussion that includes the nature of perception, the perceptual process and the marketing implications of customer perception. We also considered customer learning, which entails the elements of learning and the most relevant learning theories. We also assessed the marketing implications of these concepts and theories.

Questions for self-assessment

To assess your progress, answer these questions:
1. Explain the nature of perception by referring to the three important elements of perception.
2. What is the significance of selective exposure for marketing?
3. Explain the role of the individual, the stimulus and the situation in attention.
4. How can marketers create contrast so that customers will notice the stimulus?
5. Explain the importance of situational factors in perception.

6. What are the marketing implications of selective interpretation?
7. Why is it important for marketers to understand customer recall?
8. Illustrate the usefulness of perception in a marketing strategy.
9. In the case study on Parmalat milk, how did the principles of perception affect the customers' perceptions of the milk?
10. Explain the nature of learning.
11. Explain the elements of learning.
12. Explain the marketing implications of the learning theories we discuss.
13. Refer to the case study on Xerox copiers and explain how the company should have taken into account the principles of customer learning in designing the new office copier.

Endnote references

1. Solomon, M.R. and Stuart, E.W. 1997. *Marketing: Real People, Real Choices*. Upper Saddle River: Prentice-Hall.
2. Chisnall, P.M. 1995. *Consumer Behaviour*. London: McGraw-Hill.
3. Brink, A. 1998. The marketing perception of grocery store retailers belonging to black business associations in Gauteng. Unpublished DCom thesis, University of South Africa, Pretoria, p. 104.
4. Based on Hawkins, D.I., Best, R.J. and Coney, K.A. 2001. *Consumer Behavior: Building Marketing Strategy*. 8th ed. Boston: Irwin McGraw-Hill, pp. 284–304.
5. Botha, J.A.R., Brink, A., Machado, R. and Rudansky, S. 1997. *Consumer-oriented Marketing Communication*. Pretoria: Unisa, pp. 53–64.
6. Solomon and Stuart, op. cit.
7. Solomon, M.R. 1999. *Consumer Behavior: Buying, Having and Being*. Upper Saddle River: Prentice-Hall.
8. Hawkins et al., op. cit.
9. Botha et al., op. cit.
10. Solomon, op. cit.
11. Hawkins et al., op. cit.
12. Sheth, J.N., Mittal, B. and Newman, B.I. 1999. *Customer Behavior: Consumer Behavior and Beyond*. Orlando: Dryden.
13. Solomon, op. cit.
14. Hawkins et al., op. cit.
15. Solomon and Stuart, op. cit.
16. Chisnall, op. cit.
17. Solomon and Stuart, op. cit.
18. Botha et al., op. cit.
19. Ibid., p. 60.
20. Chisnall, op. cit.
21. Botha et al., op. cit.
22. Hawkins et al., op. cit., pp. 305–7.
23. Schiffman, L.G., Bednall, D., Watson, J. and Kanuk, L.L. 1997. *Consumer Behaviour*. Sydney: Prentice-Hall, pp. 177–8.
24. Available on the internet from: www.markinor.co.za
25. Sheth et al., op. cit.
26. Botha et al., op. cit.

27. Schiffman et al., op. cit.
28. Sheth et al., op. cit.
29. Based on Botha et al., op. cit., pp. 83–6.
30. Brink, A., Cant, M.C., Machado, R. and Theron, D.P. 2000. *Customer Behaviour*. Pretoria: Unisa.
31. Botha et al., op. cit., pp. 86–7.
32. Solomon, op. cit.
33. Hawkins et al., op. cit.
34. Ibid., pp. 330–2.

8 Customer motivation

After studying this chapter, you should be able to:

○ describe the nature of motivation

○ explain the different classifications of motives and illustrate how marketers can use these different types of motives in their marketing messages

○ illustrate the use of psychographics

○ explain motivational research.

8.1 Introduction

To understand motivation is to understand why customers do what they do. Why do some people choose to bungy jump off a bridge or go white-water rafting, while others spend their leisure time playing chess or gardening? Be it to quench our thirst, ease boredom or attain a deep spiritual experience, for example, we do everything for a reason, even if we cannot give the precise reason. If we turn our attention to marketing, people usually are not fully aware of the forces that drive them towards some products and away from others. Often, these choices are influenced by the person's values, that is, their priorities, and their beliefs about the world.

Marketing students are taught right from the start that the goal of marketing is to *satisfy customers' needs*. In other words, the basic philosophy of marketing rests on the premise that customers' needs are the starting point from which all other business activities should logically be planned. However, this insight is useless unless we can discover what these needs are and why they exist. Because customers experience many and different kinds of needs, an appreciation of the nature of needs offers marketers a valuable approach to the study of motivational influences in buying behaviour.

In this chapter, we examine the motivation process and need arousal, highlighting the fact that motivation links needs and objectives. We look at the classification of motives, and examine psychographics. In conclusion, we briefly discuss motivational research.

8.2 The nature of motivation

8.2.1 Needs, motives and objectives

Motivation occurs when a customer wants to satisfy a need that has arisen. We can there-fore say that motivation is what moves people, and that it is the driving force for all human behaviour.[1] The term 'need' refers to something physical or psychological that the body must have in order to function and develop. Every individual has needs; some are innate, others are acquired.[2] **Innate needs** are physiological and help to sustain biological life, such as the need for food, water, air and shelter. **Acquired needs** are those we learn in response to our culture or environment, such as the need for affection, prestige and learning.

In marketing, a need by itself is not enough: the customer must also want *to do something* about it. When someone wants to satisfy a need, we call what they experience 'motivation'. Clearly, there is a close relationship between needs and motives. As the driving force within individuals that impels them to action, motivation is produced by a state of tension that exists as the result of an unfulfilled need. Individuals try to behave in such a way that they fulfil their needs and thus relieve themselves of the stress they feel. The specific goals they select and the patterns of action they undertake to achieve their goals are the result of individual thinking and learning. Figure 8.1 shows the relationship between needs, motives and objectives (or behaviour).

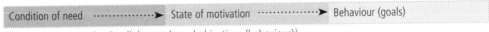

Condition of need   ·············➤   State of motivation   ·············➤   Behaviour (goals)

Figure 8.1: How motivation links needs and objectives (behaviour)[3]

For any given need, there are various appropriate goals. The goals chosen by individuals depend on those individuals' personal experiences, physical capacities, and prevailing cultural norms and values, and upon the goals' accessibility in the physical and social environment. The person's perception of their own self also influences the specific goals they select. We often perceive the products we own, would like to own or would not like to own in terms of how closely they reflect or are congruent with our self-image. Thus, a man who sees himself as young and fashionable may drive a Ferrari, while a woman who sees herself as rich and conservative may drive a Mercedes Benz. People often choose the types of houses they live in, the cars they drive, the clothes they wear, the foods they eat, and so on because symbolically these things reflect their individual self-images, while they satisfy specific needs.[4]

Everyone must satisfy **basic** needs such as hunger and thirst. But the way two hungry people go about this can be very different: one person wants a hamburger and soft drink, while the other wants organically grown food and filtered water. Other needs are **utilitarian**, that is, the person wants to achieve some functional or practical benefit, as when a customer looks for long-lasting torch batteries. Needs may also be **hedonistic**, involving pleasant emotional responses or fantasies, as when customers choose greeting cards that show they 'care enough to send the very best'.[5]

We now look at the arousal of needs.

8.2.2 Need arousal

Need arousal begins with the presence of a stimulus that causes the recognition of a need. For example, you could feel the need for a CD player because you dislike the sound quality of your tape player (the actual state) and because you realise that a CD player would provide a much clearer, cleaner sound (the desired state).[6] The arousal of specific needs at a specific point in time may be caused by internal stimuli found in the individual's physiological condition, or emotional or cognitive processes, or by external stimuli in the environment – all of which imply that there are various types of arousal.[7]

Physiological arousal

The stimulus that causes the recognition of a need may come from inside the customer – feeling hungry is an example of internal stimuli that can result in the recognition of a need such as to eat and to travel. Most of these physiological cues are involuntary; however, they arouse related needs that cause uncomfortable tensions until they are satisfied.

Emotional arousal

Sometimes, thinking or daydreaming results in the arousal or stimulation of latent (unconscious) needs. People who are bored, or frustrated in their attempts to achieve their goals, often engage in daydreaming, in which they imagine themselves in all sorts of desirable situations. For example, a young man who wants to play soccer profession-ally may identify with an important soccer player and use the products he endorses in adverts.

Cognitive arousal

Cognitive awareness of a need may be triggered by a stimulus in the environment. For example, a remark made by a friend or a news report may trigger thoughts in a person that will result in a cognitive awareness of needs. An advert by Telkom reporting low long-distance call rates can arouse a cognitive need in a person to speak to a friend in another country.

Environmental arousal

The needs activated at a specific time are often determined by specific cues in the envi-ronment. Without these cues, the needs would remain dormant, that is, they would not be aroused. For example, the smell of food may arouse the 'need' for food. Adverts often produce a psychological imbalance in the viewer's mind. For example, a keen tennis player sees a professional tennis star playing with a new type of racket and immediately feels unsatisfied with their own racket. The tension they experience disappears only when they buy themselves the racket that the professional used.

Once a need is aroused, it produces a drive state.[8] A **drive** is an affective state in which a person experiences emotions and physiological arousal. When we experience a drive state, we engage in goal-directed behaviour, that is, we act in ways that will relieve our need state. In the customer context, examples are searching for information, talking to other customers about a product, shopping for the best bargain, and buying products and services.

Customer decision-making is activated when the customer recognises that a problem exists, and problem recognition occurs when the customer's actual state of being differs from a desired state of being. Thus problem recognition and need activation are essentially synonymous concepts, they are the same; and goal-directed behaviour and the search for information are closely related. In each case, the customer engages in a series of behaviours to fulfil a need or solve a problem.[9] Following the automatic or chosen behaviour, the final outcome will be the experience of a new state and, possibly, a sense of satisfaction. This outcome, if positive, feeds back to calm the drive. If the new state is not satisfactory, the feedback recycles the process; in other words, it starts the process all over again.

Some people seek more arousal than others. These customers also take more risks in their activities in general and in their buying behaviour. They tend to adopt new products and switch brands just to try out a different brand. Moreover, they look for more information about products and get bored when exposed to repetitive advertising. Arousal seekers are also users of a greater assortment of options within the same product category, such as fast food.[10]

We have never been able to count how many needs people actually have. To overcome the problem of a virtually infinite number of possible needs, psychologists and researchers have suggested various categories or general groupings of needs, as we now explore.

8.3 The classification of motives (needs)

There are three particularly useful approaches to understanding and classifying customer motivation. The first approach, Maslow's motive hierarchy, is a macro or overall theory designed to account for most human behaviour in general terms. The second approach, based on McGuire's psychological motives, uses a fairly detailed set of motives to account for a limited range of customer behaviours. The third, the economic and emotional classification, distinguishes between rational and emotional (or non-rational) motives.

8.3.1 Maslow's hierarchy of needs

Maslow was one of the first psychologists to try to identify specific human motives and classify them in a general scheme. Maslow's hierarchy is based on three premises, or basic ideas:[11]

1. All humans adopt a set of motives through genetic endowment and social interaction.

2. Some motives are more basic than others.
3. The most basic motives need to be satisfied to a minimum level before other, more advanced motives come into play.

Maslow formulated a hierarchy of needs in which levels of motives are specified, as shown in Figure 8.2. A hierarchical approach implies that the order of development is fixed, that is, one level must be attained before the next, higher level is activated. Marketers have adopted this universal approach to motivation because it indirectly specifies certain types of product benefits that people might be looking for, depending on the different stages in their development and their environmental conditions.

Upper-level needs

SELF-ACTUALISATION
Self-fulfilment, enriching experiences

EGO NEEDS
Prestige, status, accomplishment

BELONGING
Love, friendship, acceptance by others

SAFETY
Security, shelter, protection

PHYSIOLOGICAL NEEDS
Water, sleep, food

Lower-level needs

Figure 8.2: Needs in the Maslow hierarchy[12]

Physiological needs
These needs or motives are necessary for a person's biological functioning and survival, such as the need for food, water, sleep and shelter. They are the most prominent motives of all, and human behaviour will be primarily directed at the satisfaction of these needs for as long as they are not satisfied. The customer whose main preoccupation is obtaining enough food to live on is not likely to have the inclination or the money to devote to other products – for instance, they would not be interested in buying a life assurance policy or a hang-glider. Some southern African countries such as Zimbabwe are caught up in famine at the moment (2002), so many of the people in these countries are struggling for survival – hence physiological needs are prominent.

The need for safety

Once people have managed to satisfy their physiological needs at least partially, the next level in the hierarchy emerges and the former level becomes less important. People now become aware of the need for protection against both physical and psychological dangers.[13] Some car manufacture companies, for example, consistently promote safety and durability as attractive design features of their products, as in the case of Mercedes Benz and Volvo.

The need to belong

This need relates to the fundamental need for love and affiliation. The affiliation need finds expression in the buying of gifts and participating in in-group activities, such as sports and other cultural pursuits. As we have seen in Chapter 2, emotional needs play a significant role in the decisions that customers make about many types of products. The social motives of belonging and love are evident when customers want to buy products that are regarded highly by others, so that their use brings the customers who buy them peer approval from other people who use the products, thus producing a sense of belonging.[14]

The need for esteem (ego needs)

We can divide the need for esteem into two subgroups: the first is concerned with self-respect and self-esteem, and the second with the need for respect and approval by others.[15] By acquiring objects (products) of various kinds, and by demanding an ever-widening range of services, customers in modern society try to express their needs for power and prestige. Many people buy antiques because of their symbolic value, even when their functional value is doubtful. Moreover, customers' self-images tend to be developed and confirmed by the material possessions they acquire. We drive a car that, in our judgement, reflects who we are; we visit stores where we are treated with respect; and so on.

The need for self-actualisation

When the foregoing needs have been satisfied, or when they can be satisfied without much effort, people will search for opportunities to realise their potential in full, to become all that they are capable of becoming. This self-actualisation motive is the basis of people's engagement, for example, in self-improvement activities, such as taking a course or pursuing a skill until they are perfect at it, such as a competitive sport.

   At each level of Maslow's hierarchy, different priorities exist in terms of the product benefits a customer is looking for. Ideally, individuals progress up the hierarchy until their dominant motivation is a focus on 'ultimate' goals, such as justice and beauty. Unfortunately, this state is difficult to achieve, at least on a regular basis. Most of us have to be satisfied with attaining this state occasionally, in peak experiences.

   Table 8.1 on the next page gives examples of product appeals tailored to each level.

Table 8.1: Maslow's hierarchy and marketing strategies[16]

Level of hierarchy	Relevant products	Example
Self-actualisation needs	Hobbies, travel, education	Appeal: 'Be all you can be', 'Amstel, for the connoisseur'
Ego needs	Cars, furniture, credit cards, stores, country clubs, liquors	Appeal: 'When it's time to be noticed, wear a Seiko quartz watch'
Belonging needs	Clothing, grooming products, drinks	Appeal: 'You're part of the Pepsi generation'
Safety needs	Insurance, alarm systems, retirement investments	Appeal: 'You're in good hands with the Perm'
Physiological needs	Medicines, staple items, generics	Appeal: 'It's the right thing to eat – Quaker Oat Bran'

The hierarchy provides a useful framework for marketers to segment the market, and it helps with product positioning:

○ **Segmentation applications**: The needs hierarchy is often used as the basis for market segmentation (see Chapter 11), as specific advertising appeals are directed to individuals on one or more need levels. For example, soft drink advertisements directed at teenagers may stress a social appeal by showing a group of young people sharing good times as well as the product.

○ **Positioning applications**: Another way to use the hierarchy is for positioning products, that is, deciding how the product is to be perceived by prospective customers.[17] The key to positioning is to find a niche that is not occupied by a competing brand. This application relies on the notion that no need is ever fully satisfied, it usually *continues* to be motivating to a certain extent. For example, most manufacturers of luxury cars use status appeals – 'Impress your friends', self-actualisation appeals – 'You deserve the very best', or social appeals – 'The whole family can ride in luxurious comfort'. To find a unique position among its luxury competitors, Mercedes Benz has used a safety appeal by showing pictures of Mercedes that have overturned or been badly damaged, yet whose passengers have been unhurt.

8.3.2 McGuire's psychological motives

McGuire has developed a motive classification system that is more specific than Maslow's. The most useful of his motives to marketing are shown in Tables 8.2 and 8.3 on the following pages. McGuire's classification consists of two categories: internal and external motives.

McGuire's internal motives

Table 8.2: McGuire's internal non-social motives[18]

Consistency:	The need for internal equilibrium or balance
Causation:	The need to determine who or what causes the things that happen to us
Categorisation:	The need to establish categories or mental partitions that provide frames of reference
Cues:	The need for observable cues or symbols that enable us to infer what we feel and know
Independence:	The need for a feeling or self-governance or self-control
Novelty:	The need for variety and difference

The motives are as follows:

◯ **The need for consistency**: This is the need for internal equilibrium or balance. One of our basic desires is to have all facets or parts of our selves consistent with each other. These facets include attitudes, behaviours, opinions, self-images and the view others have of us. To marketers, this clarifies the need for a consistent marketing mix. Marketers should not price a product that is positioned as a luxury product – with an elegant design, expensive packaging, limited distribution and adverts that stress exclusiveness – the same as or below the price of an average product. This inconsistency could cause customers to reject it.

◯ **The need to attribute causation**: This set of motives deals with our need to determine who or what causes the things that happen to us.[19] The need to attribute cause has led to an area of research known as '**attribution theory**'. This approach to understanding the reasons for customers assigning particular meanings to the behaviours of others has been used primarily for analysing customer reactions to promotional messages in terms of credibility. Customers tend to discount the advice given by a shop assistant or advert, because both are obviously trying to sell the particular product. However, the same advice given by a friend would likely be seen as an attempt to be helpful and might therefore be accepted. This is why marketers use a credible spokesperson in advertisements.

◯ **The need to categorise**: We need to establish categories or mental partitions that provide us with frames of reference that allow us to process large quantities of information. Marketers often categorise prices so that different prices connote different categories of goods. Cars over R100 000 and cars under R100 000 may produce two different meanings because of information categorised on the basis of price level. Many stores price items at R9.95, R19.95, R49.95, etc. in order to avoid their products being categorised in the over-R10.00, -R20.00 and -R50.00 groups.

◯ **The need for cues**: These motives reflect our needs for observable cues or symbols that enable us to infer what we feel and know. Clothing, for example, plays an important role in presenting the subtle meaning of a desired image and customer lifestyle. Thus, the clothing of consultants should convey the correct image of the business.

○ **The need for independence**: This refers to the need for a feeling of self-governance or self-control. Marketers have responded to this motive by providing products that suggest that you 'do your own thing' and 'be your own person'.

○ **The need for novelty**: We often seek variety and differences simply out of a need for novelty. Marketers refer to the outcome of this motive as 'variety-seeking behaviour'. This may be a prime reason for brand switching and some so-called 'impulse buying'. The travel industry, for example, segments the holiday market in part by promoting 'adventure' holidays or 'relaxing' holidays to groups, depending on their likely need for novelty.

McGuire's external motives

Table 8.3: McGuire's external non-social motives[20]

Self-expression:	The need to express self-identity to others
Ego defence:	The need to defend or protect our identities or egos
Assertion:	The need to increase self-esteem
Reinforcement:	The need to act in such a way that others will reward us
Affiliation:	The need to develop mutually satisfying relationships with others
Modelling:	The need to base behaviour on that of others

Self-expression, assertion and reinforcement motives seem to be similar – all refer to achievement, gaining esteem, receiving admiration and expressing our identity. Therefore, they are similar to Maslow's ego motive, while the affiliation motive is the same as Maslow's belonging motive. Modelling is a major means by which children learn to become customers/consumers. The tendency to model explains some of the conformity that occurs within reference groups. Marketers utilise this motive by showing desirable types of individuals using their brands, for example tennis player Anna Kournikova appears in an advert wearing a Rolex watch.

8.3.3 Economic and emotional classification

Customers are not always motivated by psychological needs in their decision-making.[21] When customers buy products, they are also concerned about such aspects as economy, quality, performance, suitability and reliability. They can satisfy these economic motives by applying economic criteria in decision-making. Customers often disagree on the relative importance of the criteria, which differ from one customer to another, from one buying situation to another and from one product to another. They are shown in Table 8.4 on the next page.

Table 8.4: Economic criteria in customer decision-making

Cost criteria	Performance criteria
price	durability
repairs	efficiency
installation	economy
operating costs	materials
cost of extras	dependability

The economic motives are rational in nature and marketers often express them in quantifiable terms, for example 'Buy now and save R10', or, in less specific terms, 'Suit your family ... suit your pocket', as in some car adverts. It is interesting to note that in the latter example, the emotional appeal of affiliation with the family and the economic appeal of 'You can afford it' are combined in a single sentence.

The emotional motives in customer decision-making include all the social and ego motives of Maslow and McGuire. While the economic motives are considered to be completely rational, customers do not necessarily act in a non-rational manner when they allow their emotions to influence their buying decision. The satisfaction of emotional needs is not a non-rational act. Moreover, it is almost impossible for us to make any decision on a purely rational basis, as emotional motives invariably influence our customer decision. Nevertheless, people are usually reluctant to *admit* that their buying behaviour is influenced by emotional motives. For example, someone who buys a BMW will not readily concede that the underlying motive was their need for recognition (an ego motive). Frequently, they will rationalise their decision by saying that in fact the reason for buying the car is its durability (an economic motive).

Marketers often use two divergent approaches in advertising. The heading and copy of the advert may be rational and therefore appeal to economic motives, while the illustration tends to suggest satisfaction of emotional motives. Some adverts are purely rational, but there are many that are totally emotional. Appeals to emotional motives are strongly persuasive. Marketers therefore should consider the characteristics of their product and review their particular situation before they decide on a particular mix of appeals in a marketing message.

An important facet of motivation is psychographics, which we now consider.

8.4 Psychographics

Psychographics are characteristics of individuals that describe them in terms of their psychological and behavioural make-up – how people occupy themselves (behaviour) and the psychological factors that underlie this activity pattern. They are a manifestation of, and they define, an individual's underlying motivations. For example, a person's need to seek affiliation of peer approval may make them engage in going to the theatre or playing golf. Theatre-going or playing golf thus becomes part of their psychographics. In turn, the psychographic drives customer behaviour towards doing whatever is needed to implement it; thus it becomes motivational.[22]

8.4.1 Psychographics and lifestyle

Psychographic research is research that attempts to assess customers on the basis of psychological dimensions as opposed to purely demographic dimensions.[23] A person's motivations determine their behaviour as well as their lifestyle.

Consider a team of marketers who want to target a student population. They identify their ideal customer as 'a 21-year-old senior business management student living on a large university campus whose parents earn between R100 000 and R500 000 per year'. You may know many people who fit this description. Do you think they are all the same? Would they all be likely to share common interests and buy the same products? Probably not, since their lifestyles are likely to differ considerably. In other words, customers may share the same demographic characteristics and still be very different people. Hence, retailers need to find a way to 'breathe life' into demographic data to identify, understand and target customer segments that will share a set of preferences for their products and services.

The term 'psychographics' is often used interchangeably with 'lifestyle' to denote the separation of customers into categories based on differences in choices of consumption activities and product usage. There are many psychographic variables that marketers can use to segment customers, but they all share the underlying principle of going beyond superficial characteristics to an understanding of customers' motivations for buying and using products. **Demographics** allow us to describe *who* buys, while **psychographics** allow us to understand *why* they buy. This is largely based on the values of the customer concerned.

8.4.2 Values determine lifestyle

Our lifestyle *expresses* the goals we live for,[24] while values *are* the goals we live for. Our values are related to customer activities, for example people who value a sense of belonging particularly like group activities. Those who value fun and enjoyment particularly like skiing, dancing, hiking and camping, and they often consume a lot of alcohol. People who value a warm relationship with others tend to give gifts to others for no obvious reason. A person's set of values plays an extremely important role in consumption activities, that is, people buy many products and services because they believe that these will help them to attain a value-related goal.[25]

8.4.3 Psychographic profiles

Marketing Research Africa's Sociomonitor Value Groups Survey is the most authoritative psychographic profile of its kind in South Africa.[26] In order to create the value groups, respondents answered an extensive battery of psychographic statements. Their answers were then grouped and scored, giving every single respondent a different score and position on the 'social map', depending on their answers. These scores were analysed statistically and the value groups – broad groups of customers with similar values, attitudes and motivations (psychographics) – resulted. Ten groups have been identified from the latest all-adults database, which are shown in Table 4.2 in Chapter 4 (page 66).

8.4.4 The uses of psychographics

We can use psychographics in a variety of ways, most notably in market segmentation.[27] They allow marketers to go beyond the simple demographic or product usage descriptions. Sometimes, marketers create their strategies with a typical customer in mind. However, the stereotype may not be correct, because the actual customer may not match these assumptions. For example, certain marketers of a facial cream for women were surprised to find their key market was composed of older, widowed women rather than the younger, more sociable women to whom they were pitching their appeals.

Psychographic information can guide marketers in emphasising features of the product that fit in with a person's lifestyle. Products targeted at people whose lifestyle profiles show a high need to be around other people may focus on the product's ability to help meet this social need.

Furthermore, psychographic information can offer useful input in advertising, that is, specifically communicating something about the product. The advertiser obtains a much richer mental image of the target customer than that obtained through statistics, and this insight improves the advertiser's ability to 'talk' to that customer. For example, it was found that heavy beer drinkers tended to feel that life's pleasures were few and far between. Commercials were developed using a theme that told these drinkers, 'You only go around once, so reach for all the gusto you can'.

Understanding how a product fits or does not fit into customers' lifestyles allows marketers to identify new product opportunities, design media strategies and create environments that are the most consistent and harmonious with these consumption patterns.

8.5 Motivational research

Motivational research is directed at discovering the reasons, that is, the motives, for a person's behaviour. It is conducted to find out the conscious or unconscious reasons that motivate people to buy or not to buy a particular product or service, to patronise or avoid a store, or to accept or reject a marketing communication.[28] Two techniques, namely, depth interviews and projective techniques, are frequently used in marketing studies.[29]

8.5.1 Depth interviews

These are interviews with individual customers designed to determine deep-seated or repressed motives that could not be brought out by structured questions. Customers are encouraged to talk freely in an unstructured interview, and their responses are interpreted carefully to reveal their motives and potential buying inhibitions.

A related feature of the depth interview is the **focus group interview**, in which 8 to 12 customers are brought together under the direction of a moderator to discuss issues that may reveal their deep-seated needs or unconscious motives. Focus groups are likely to stimulate discussion because of the context, and they may bring out thoughts and motives that individual depth interviews will not. Depth and focus group interviews in several studies have provided useful findings:

- Customers want a sense of freedom and power when they get behind the wheel of a car. They use the surge of acceleration to free themselves of the mundane aspects of life. If marketers want to advertise petrol, they should go along with this feeling and talk about 'the tiger in your tank'.
- Men dislike air travel because of 'posthumous guilt' – they are afraid that they will die in a crash, thus turning their wives into widows. To combat this anticipation, airlines should advertise how quickly they can return businessmen home to their loved ones.
- Eating sweets is a source of guilt because of childhood associations with reward and punishment. Any attempt to market sweets to adults should emphasise the fact that they deserve the rewards associated with the consumption of the sweets.

8.5.2 Projective techniques

These techniques are designed to determine motives that are difficult to express or identify. Researchers cannot ask customers direct questions because customers may not always be aware of their motives for buying and thus will be unable to answer. Instead, they give customers a situation, a cartoon or a set of words, and ask them to respond. Customers project their feelings and concerns about products onto this less threatening or involving situation.

In one experiment, for example, researchers tried to discover why women were reluctant to buy instant coffee when it was first introduced in 1940. The researchers drew up two identical shopping lists, with the exception that one included regular coffee and the other instant coffee. They asked the women to project the type of woman most likely to have developed each list. The 'housewife' who included instant coffee in the list was characterised as lazy and a poor planner. These findings demonstrated that many women had a deep-seated fear of buying products like instant coffee, or instant cake mixes, because of a concern that their husbands would feel they were avoiding their role of homemaker. As a result of the study, marketers advertised instant coffee in a family setting portraying the husband's approval. The psychoanalytic approach may not be empirical, but motivational researchers were the first to argue that customers are complex and difficult to understand, and are driven by powerful forces of which they are largely unaware.

Motivational research provides marketers with a basic orientation for new product categories, and enables them to explore customer reactions to ideas and advertising at an early stage so that they can avoid costly errors.[30] Furthermore, motivational research provides marketers with basic cues for more structured, quantitative marketing research studies – studies that can be conducted on larger, more representative samples of customers. It continues to be a useful tool for many marketers who want to know the genuine reasons underlying customer behaviour. However, it is no longer considered the only method for uncovering human motivation, but rather one of a variety of research techniques available to the customer researcher. Despite some shortcomings, motivational research has proved to be of great value to marketers concerned with developing new ideas and new advertising appeals.

Case study

PRACTICALITY OR APPEARANCE?

Mr and Mrs Green and their two children live in a middle-class, suburban neighbourhood in Cape Town. They both work, and use the bus to get to their jobs. As a result, they are a one-car family. They buy a new car about every three years, and have owned three different Toyotas in the past ten years. They are no longer satisfied with the economy or styling of their current model, however, and are in the market for a new car. As a result, they recognise a need.

The status communicated by a car is not very important to them. They see substantial financial and performance risks in buying, so they are highly involved in the buying decision. They place more importance on economy, performance and comfort, in that order. They use their car primarily on weekends and for shopping needs, and it has served them well according to these benefit criteria. Their teenage daughter has mentioned on more than one occasion that Toyota has a stodgy image and that the family should consider getting a sportier, more up-to-date-looking car.

8.6 Summary

In this chapter, we dealt with customer motivation, a discussion that included a description of the motivation process that revolves around needs, motives and objectives, and the different ways of need arousal. We examined the different ways in which motives can be classified in order to be useful to marketing. We also explored psychographics, which is a facet of motivation. We concluded with a discussion of motivational research.

Questions for self-assessment

To assess your progress, answer these questions:
1. Explain the nature of motivation and its significance to marketing.
2. How can a marketer use Maslow's hierarchy of needs (or motives)?
3. Explain McGuire's and the economic and emotional classification of motives and highlight the marketing implications.
4. Illustrate the use of psychographics in marketing.
5. Explain depth interviews and projective techniques used in motivational research and indicate how the findings can be of use to marketers.
6. With reference to the case study, answer the following questions:
   a. Mr and Mrs Green have identified a need for a new car. How does the motivation process apply in their particular case?
   b. How would you classify the motives of Mr and Mrs Green and their teenage daughter in terms of Maslow's hierarchy of needs, McGuire's motives and the economic and emotional classification of motives?
   c. With Mr and Mrs Green in mind, how should marketers take psychographics into account in their marketing strategies?

Endnote references

1. Sheth, J.N., Mittal, B. and Newman, B.I. 1999. *Customer Behavior: Consumer Behavior and Beyond.* Orlando: Dryden.
2. Botha, J.A.R., Brink, A., Machado, R. and Rudansky, S. 1997. *Consumer-oriented Marketing Communication.* Pretoria: Unisa.
3. Based on Chisnall, P.M. 1995. *Consumer Behaviour.* London: McGraw-Hill, p. 40, and Botha et al., op. cit., p. 65.
4. Schiffman, L.G., Bednall, D., Watson, J. and Kanuk, L.L. 1997. *Consumer Behaviour.* Sydney: Prentice-Hall.
5. Solomon, M.R. 1999. *Consumer Behavior: Buying, Having and Being.* Upper Saddle River: Prentice-Hall, p. 104.
6. Mowen, M.J. and Minor, M. 1998. *Consumer Behavior.* Upper Saddle River: Prentice-Hall.
7. Based on Schiffman et al., op. cit., pp. 79–80, and Mowen and Minor, op. cit., p. 161.
8. Mowen and Minor, op. cit.
9. Assael, H. 1992. *Consumer Behavior and Marketing Action.* Boston: PWS-Kent.
10. Sheth et al., op. cit.
11. Botha et al., op. cit., pp. 66–72.
12. Based on Botha et al., op. cit., p. 67.
13. Chisnall, op. cit.
14. Sheth et al., op. cit.
15. Botha et al., op. cit.
16. Adapted from Solomon, op. cit., p. 111.
17. Schiffman et al., op. cit., pp. 105–7.
18. Adapted from Hawkins, D.I., Best, R.J. and Coney, K.A. 2001. *Consumer Behavior: Building Marketing Strategy.* Boston: Irwin McGraw-Hill, pp. 363–6.
19. Ibid., p. 363.

20. Based on Botha et al., op. cit., p. 68.
21. Botha et al., op. cit.
22. Sheth et al., op. cit., p. 362.
23. Hawkins et al., op. cit.
24. Ibid., p. 364.
25. Solomon, op. cit.
26. Strydom, J.W., Cant, M.C. and Jooste, C.J. 2000. *Marketing Management*. Cape Town: Juta.
27. Solomon, op. cit.
28. Sheth et al., op. cit.
29. Assael, op. cit., pp. 287–90.
30. Schiffman et al., op. cit., pp. 108–10.

9 Customer attitudes

Learning Outcomes

After studying this chapter, you should be able to:

○ explain the nature of attitudes

○ explain the ABC model of attitude and illustrate its implications

○ describe the functions of attitudes

○ explain and illustrate how attitudes are formed

○ illustrate how marketers can bring about attitude change.

9.1 Introduction

Attitudes influence everyone's lives, and they affect the ways in which individuals judge and react towards other people, objects and events. While people often use the word 'attitudes' in conversation, probably only a few can define precisely what this popular term means. The frequency with which it is used suggests that attitudes play a highly important role in our personal and professional lives. So much of life is affected by the attitudes – favourable or otherwise – that we hold that some deeper understanding of their nature and effects is necessary.

In the context of customer behaviour, using attitudes can be extremely productive. For example, there has been rapid growth in the sale of bath, body and cosmetic products made from natural ingredients throughout the world. This trend seems to be linked to the currently popular attitude that 'natural' things are good, and 'synthetic' things are bad. Yet, in reality, the positive attitude favouring natural things is not based on any systematic evidence that natural cosmetic products are any *safer* or *better*.

Attitude research enables marketers to:

○ answer many marketing questions, such as whether customers will accept a product

○ gauge why a retailer's target audience has not reacted more favourably to its new promotional theme

○ learn how target customers are likely to react to a proposed change in a product's packaging.

In this chapter, we examine the nature of customer attitudes. We consider the components and functions of attitudes, and we discuss the formation of attitude and attitude change.

9.2 The nature of customer attitudes

An attitude describes a person's relatively consistent evaluations, feelings and tendencies towards an object or an idea. People in a market can be enthusiastic, positive, indifferent, negative or hostile about a product. Attitude in marketing terms can thus be defined as 'a learned predisposition to behave in a consistently favourable or unfavourable way toward market-related objects, events or situations'.[1] Thus, for marketers, an attitude is the way we think, feel and act towards some aspect of the commercial environment, such as a retail store, a television programme or a product.

The important facets of this definition are as follows:

○ **Attitudes are learned**: We form attitudes relevant to buying behaviour as a result of direct experience with the product, information acquired from others and exposure to mass media, such as advertising in newspapers, on television, etc. Therefore, we can say that attitudes are learned.

○ **Attitudes tend to be consistent**: An important property of an attitude is that it is relatively consistent with the behaviour that it reflects. However, attitudes are not necessarily permanent – they can and do change. Normally, we expect customer attitudes to correspond to behaviour. For example, if a customer likes full-cream milk, we expect them to buy it. Similarly, if a customer is not particularly fond of full-cream milk, we expect them not to buy it. Thus, when customers are free to act as they wish, we expect that their actions will be consistent with their attitudes.

9.2.1 Attitudes as a combination of interrelated beliefs and values

It is important for marketers to recognise that attitudes are different from personal values and beliefs. Our **beliefs** are what we think or believe about the things that make up the world we live in. For example, we may believe that Shell Oil is a major manufacturer of oil and petrol. Our **attitudes** are a more enduring combination of interrelated beliefs that describe, evaluate and direct our action in respect of a particular object or situation. Thus, our attitude towards Shell would comprise additional beliefs, our feelings about the company and our behavioural response tendencies towards it. **Values** are not tied to any specific situation or object, but are part of the setting of the standards for guiding our behaviour and influencing beliefs and attitudes. We have a large number of beliefs, a smaller number of attitudes and even fewer values.[2]

9.3 The ABC model of attitude

According to the ABC model of attitude, the individual's attitude has three components: affect (feelings), behaviour (actions) and cognition (beliefs). Table 9.1 summarises these.

Table 9.1: Attitude components and manifestations[3]

Initiator	Component	Component manifestation	Attitude
Stimuli: Products, situations, retail stores advertisements	Affective	Emotions or feelings about specific attributes or overall object	Overall orientation toward project
	Behavioural (Conative)	Behavioural intentions with respect to specific attributes or overall object	
	Cognitive	Beliefs about specific attributes or overall object	

Depending on the nature of the product, one of these three components – feelings, actions or beliefs – will be the dominant influence in creating a person's attitude toward a product.[4]

9.3.1 The cognitive component

The cognitive component consists of a customer's beliefs about an object, that is, their knowledge about it. For most attitude objects, we have a number of beliefs. For example, we may believe that Coke is popular with younger people, contains caffeine, is competitively priced and is made by a large company. The total configuration of beliefs about this brand of soft drink represents the cognitive component of an attitude toward Coke. It is important for marketers to note that beliefs need not be correct or true – they only need to exist.

Cognition is more critical for important or complex products such as computer systems, which require us to process objective or technical information before we can come to a decision.

A customer's beliefs about a brand are the characteristics they ascribe to it. There are two types of beliefs: informational and evaluative. **Informational beliefs** are associated with product *attributes*, such as the number of calories it contains, the vitamin content, etc. **Evaluative beliefs** are associated with product *benefits*, such as economy, flavour, and so on.

Benefits are a basis for:

○ defining opportunity – 'Is there a segment emphasising nutrition? What is its size?'
○ positioning a new product – 'Can we introduce a new beverage to appeal to this segment?'
○ developing advertising strategy – 'What symbols, ideas and messages will communicate nutrition to the whole family?'[5]

Through market research, marketers develop a vocabulary of product attributes and customer benefits similar to the vocabulary developed for a beverage, as illustrated in Table 9.2.

Table 9.2: The vocabulary of brand beliefs for a beverage product[6]

Product attributes	Product benefits
Calorie content	Good at mealtimes
Vitamin content	Refreshing
Natural ingredients	Good for the whole family
Sweetness	Gives a lift
Bitterness	Thirst-quenching
After-taste	Restores energy
Carbonation	Nutritional

These vocabularies are usually based on the results of a series of in-depth interviews with customers. Once marketers establish such a vocabulary, they include it in a questionnaire and conduct a customer survey in which respondents are asked to rate brands using the vocabulary. A study of soft drinks may thus involve asking customers to rate various brands on the criteria listed in Table 9.2.

9.3.2 The affective component

The affective component involves our feelings and emotions towards an object. This evaluation may be simply a vague, general feeling developed without cognitive information or beliefs about the object or product.[7] It may also be the result of certain evaluations of the product's performance on each of several attributes. Thus, the statement 'Coffee X is overpriced' implies a negative affective reaction to a specific aspect of the product that, in combination with feelings about other attributes, will determine the overall reaction to this brand of coffee.

Affect is usually most important for products that we use to say something about ourselves, such as perfume. Since products, like other objects that we react to, are evaluated in the context of a specific situation, a customer's affective reaction to a product may change as the situation changes. For example, a customer may believe that a particular soft drink has caffeine in it, and that caffeine will keep them awake. These beliefs may cause a positive affective response when the customer needs to stay awake to study for an examination, and a negative response when they want to drink something late in the evening that will not keep them awake later.

9.3.3 The behavioural component

This component represents the outcome of the cognitive and affective components – to buy or not to buy? What a customer does about their knowledge of and feelings towards a product is most important to a company. The behavioural component is manifested in both intention to buy and actual buying. The customer may have positive information about a product and may like it, but may not actually buy it for a variety of reasons. Habit in respect of another brand may be strong, there may be other brands that the customer likes better or the preferred brand may be unaffordable.

Our behaviour often determines our attitudes to commonly bought items such as chewing gum, with regard to which we tend to form an attitude based on how the product tastes or performs.

9.3.4 Component consistency

The cognitive, affective and behaviour components of attitudes tend to be consistent. This means that a change in one attitude component tends to produce related changes in the others. This tendency is the basis of much marketing strategy – brand ratings on specific attributes such as taste, price, nutrition and the package are closely related to overall evaluation of the brand.[8] We consider the following example.

> A friend tells a loyal user of a hair conditioner that it makes her hair greasy. This information is inconsistent with the user's beliefs. If the user accepts the new information, her feelings towards the brand will become increasingly negative and she will be less likely to buy the product again. Alternatively, she could question how valid her friend's opinion is and maintain a positive brand attitude in accordance with her prior beliefs. However, a positive evaluation may not lead to someone buying something. Even if a customer evaluated the Mercedes Benz positively, they might not buy it because it is out of their price range.

Marketers are ultimately concerned with influencing behaviour. However, it is often difficult for them to influence behaviour directly. Generally, they are unable directly to cause customers to buy, use or recommend products. However, customers will often listen to salespeople, attend to adverts or examine marketers' packages. Therefore, marketers can indirectly influence behaviour by providing information, music or other stimuli that influence a customer's belief or feeling about the product, if the three components are indeed consistent with each other.[9]

We now consider how attitudes fulfil important functions in helping customers to adjust to difficult situations, express their values, organise their knowledge and defend their egos in threatening situations. Unless marketers know the function served by a particular attitude, they are in a poor position to understand or influence it.

9.4 The functions of attitudes

The following major functions that attitudes perform can be grouped according to their motivational basis.[10]

9.4.1 The utilitarian function

The utilitarian function of attitudes refers to the idea that people express feelings to maximise the rewards and minimise the punishments they receive from others. In this sense, attitudes guide behaviour to gain positive reinforcers and avoid punishers. Put simply, we are nice to people who are nice to us, and we avoid people who are unpleasant. From a marketing point of view, we develop positive attitudes towards those products that have satisfied us, and we form negative attitudes towards those that fail to satisfy. In this way, our attitudes become guides to behaviour that will satisfy our needs. For example, a salesperson might learn that making positive comments to a customer, that is, expressing favourable attitudes, is more likely to result in a sale, that is, this becomes a positive reinforcer. Similarly, someone might express a positive attitude towards a particular opera singer like Pavarotti to gain the approval of someone known to love Pavarotti's music.

9.4.2 The ego-defensive function

The function of ego-defensive attitudes is to protect people from basic truths about themselves, or from the harsh realities of the external world. The ego-defensive function is also called the 'self-esteem maintenance function'. Most people want to protect their self-image from feelings of doubt. By acknowledging this need, adverts for cosmetics and personal hygiene products increase both their relevance to the customer and the likelihood of a favourable attitude by offering reassurance to the customer about their self-concept. For example, Salon Selectives shampoo adverts proclaim that, by using them, you can 'look like you just stepped out of a salon'. This supports and reinforces the potential customers' sense of self-worth.

9.4.3 The value-expressive function

The value-expressive function of attitudes refers to how people express their central values to others. This function allows the customer positively to demonstrate their basic values. For example, a customer can express strong feelings about health by riding a bicycle, eating health foods and giving up smoking. The customer who always buys the least expensive product is exercising the value-expressive function. Value-expressive attitudes give customers an opportunity to show how they feel about the world around them. By knowing their target customers' attitudes, marketers can anticipate their values, lifestyles and outlooks more skilfully, and reflect these characteristics in their adverts.

9.4.4 The knowledge function

Attitudes may also serve as standards that help people to understand their environment, and so give order and meaning to it. For example, customers may develop certain attitudes towards salespeople wearing brightly coloured jackets or towards retail stores that play soft music and have plush interiors. Whenever they come into contact with such a salesperson or store, the customers interpret the encounter according to their established attitudes. Therefore, customers who take a negative view of such salespeople will probably resist these people's selling efforts, without having to think about it. The attitude simplifies the encounter for them, allowing them to focus on matters they think are more important.

9.5 Attitude formation

People are not born with attitudes – they learn them. We now explore the ways in which this happens.

9.5.1 Classical conditioning

Customers often buy new products that are associated with a favourably viewed brand name. Their positive attitude towards the brand name, originally a neutral stimulus, may be the result of repeated satisfaction with other products produced by the same company.[11] Using classical conditioning terms (see Chapter 7), the **brand name** is the unconditioned stimulus that, through repetition and positive reinforcement, results in a favourable attitude – the conditioned response.

The idea of family branding is based on this form of attitude learning. For example, by giving a new blend of coffee the benefit of a well-known and respected family name, the Nestlé company is counting on an extension of the favourable attitudes already associated with the Nestlé brand name to the new product. In other words, they are counting on stimulus generalisation from the brand name to the new product. Similarly, marketers who associate their new products with celebrities are trying to create a positive bond between the celebrity, towards whom many customers may already have a positive attitude, and the 'neutral' new product. The recognition and goodwill (the positive attitude) that the celebrity enjoys is transferred to the product so that potential customers will quickly form positive attitudes towards it.

9.5.2 Instrumental conditioning

Sometimes, attitudes follow the buying and consumption of a product. For example, a customer may buy a brand-name product without already having an attitude towards it because it is the only product of its kind available, for example the last tube of toothpaste in a hotel pharmacy. Customers also make trial purchases of new brands from product categories in which they have little personal involvement. If they find the brand satisfactory, they are likely to develop a favourable attitude towards it.

9.5.3 Cognitive learning theory

In situations where customers seek information about a product in order to solve a problem or satisfy a need, they are likely to form positive or negative attitudes about the product on the basis of an information search and their own cognitions, or knowledge and beliefs. For example, Cathy is a teenager who likes pavlova. She has thought about making one for a party, but is concerned that making a good pavlova is tricky. When Cathy learns that Glad Bake has a product that promises to make 'even the stickiest meringue non-stick', she is likely to form a positive attitude towards the brand Glad Bake.

In general, the more information customers have about a product or service, the more likely they are to form attitudes about it – either positive or negative. However, regardless of available information, customers are not always ready or willing to process product-related information.

9.5.4 Experience[12]

An important way in which our attitudes are formed towards products and services is through our direct experience of trying and evaluating them. Marketers often encourage customers to try new products by offering free trial samples. Their aim is that customers *experience* the new product and then *evaluate* it. If it proves satisfactory, the customer is likely to form a positive attitude and may buy the product when they need it in the future.

9.5.5 External authorities

As we come into contact with others, especially our friends, or individuals such as teachers, parents and other adults whom we admire, we acquire attitudes that influence our lives. The extent to which customers believe one authority over another depends on the feeling of trust and respect that they have for that authority. Customers tend to identify with people who are similar to themselves rather than with movie stars or public figures – a fact used effectively in advertising. This identification is based on the fact that customers trust the opinions of people like themselves because they feel that someone similar can better appreciate their problems and concerns.

9.5.6 Marketing communications[13]

Our attitudes are influenced most strongly when the brand has something unique to offer and its unique benefits are the focus of the advert. The source of a message is important, because customers respond differently to the same message delivered by different sources. It is easier for marketers to influence attitudes when the target market thinks the source of the message is highly credible. Source credibility appears to be composed of two basic dimensions: **trustworthiness** and **expertise**. A source that has no apparent motive other than to provide complete, objective and accurate information would generally be considered trustworthy. For example, most people think that the South African Bureau of Standards' approval of a product is trustworthy, as the bureau makes no money from testing and approving a product.

Many of us would consider our friends trustworthy on various matters. However, our friends might not have the knowledge necessary to be credible in a certain area. While salespeople often have such knowledge, some customers doubt their trustworthiness and also that of advertisers because it might be to their advantage to mislead the customer, since they make their money from selling the product. Frequently, a relatively unknown individual who is similar to the target market can be an effective spokesperson. In a testimonial advert, generally a typical member of the target market recounts their successful use of the product, service or idea. Such advertisements can be fairly effective, for example a soap-powder advert featuring a mother doing her children's clothes washing.

9.6 Attitude change

Because the basic goal of many marketing communications is to influence customers' attitudes toward a product, the ABC model has important implications for marketers. They can identify customers' attitudes and either design products that are consistent with these or try to change the attitudes, which is more difficult to do.

Marketing messages to change attitudes can focus on one of the three components of an attitude. For example, groups against the abuse of animals in experiments have focused on providing hard-hitting information to influence people's attitudes and to discourage them from buying and wearing genuine fur coats. The fur industry has countered with adverts focusing on women's feelings of resentment at being told what to wear. And both groups have emphasised the behaviour component of attitudes – by producing, respectively, an advert depicting a naked women who would 'rather go naked than wear fur' and one in which a woman wears a fur in a wholesome family scene and enjoys a 'very basic luxury'.[14]

We now look at strategies to change attitudes.

9.6.1 Changing the affective component[15]

Increasingly, marketers are trying to influence customers' liking of their brand without directly influencing either their beliefs or their behaviour. If marketers are successful, increased liking will tend to lead to increased positive beliefs, which could lead to the customers buying the product if they need it. We now examine the three basic approaches that marketers use to increase affect.

Classical conditioning
In this approach, marketers consistently link a stimulus that the audience likes, such as music or pictures, with the brand name. Over time, some of the positive affect associated with the stimulus will transfer to the brand.

Producing positive affect toward the advert

Customers' preference for an advert for a product generally increases their tendency to like the product as well. Positive affect toward the advert may increase liking of the brand through classical conditioning. Using humour, celebrities or emotional appeals, marketers also manage to increase affect toward the advert. Adverts that arouse negative affect, or emotions such as fear or guilt, can also enhance attitude change. For example, an advert for a charity that assists refugees could show pictures that cause a variety of unpleasant emotions, such as disgust or anger, and still be effective.

'Mere exposure'

Another method for creating positive feelings in customers is to repeatedly expose them to a stimulus. All else being equal, through mere exposure, people's liking for something may increase simply because they see it over and over again. Thus, the repetition of adverts may well increase liking and cause the customer to buy the product, without altering their initial belief structure. However, if customers perceive the advert negatively, repeated exposures will probably lead to an intense dislike of the advert and the product.

9.6.2 Changing the behavioural component

Buying, or use behaviour, may precede the development of cognition and affect. For example, a customer may dislike the taste of diet soft drinks and believe that artificial sweeteners are unhealthy. However, rather than appear rude, the customer may accept a diet drink when offered one by a friend. Drinking it may alter their perceptions of its taste and lead to them liking it. This in turn may lead to increased learning, which changes the cognitive component. Attitudes formed as a consequence of product trial are usually strongly held.

Behaviour can lead directly to affect, to cognitions or to both simultaneously. Customers often try new brands or types of low-cost items in the absence of prior knowledge or affect. They do so as much to gain information as to satisfy some underlying need such as hunger.

Changing behaviour before changing affect or cognition is based primarily on instrumental conditioning, that is, customers learn through a trial-and-error process in which buying one product results in more favourable outcomes than buying another – they are 'rewarded' for choosing an appropriate behaviour, that is, buying the product they like. Here, the key marketing task is to encourage people to buy or consume the product while ensuring that this will lead to rewards. For this reason, coupons, free samples, point-of-purchase displays and price reductions are often used to encourage trial behaviour. Since behaviour leads to strong positive attitudes toward the consumed brand, it is important to avoid 'stockouts' – situations where the shop runs out of supplies of a product – to prevent customers from trying competing brands.

If they want to establish a customer's brand loyalty, marketers should consider not only behavioural brand loyalty, but also attitudinal brand loyalty. Customers' **behavioural**

brand loyalty can be established easily as it simply shows that customers repurchase the same brand, not whether they actually like the brand more than other brands. It is therefore also necessary to assess customers' attitude toward the brand. Only when the customer attitude to a brand is more favourable than to competing brands should that customer be considered brand loyal to that brand. This way of looking at brand loyalty, that is, a greater liking for the brand, is termed **'attitudinal brand loyalty'**. Marketers measure this by asking customers to rank various brands in terms of how much they like a brand and which brand they like the most.

9.6.3 Changing the cognitive component

To change attitudes, marketers can focus on the cognitive component. To change a customer's attitude towards cigarette smoking, for example, marketers need to present information on the negative health consequences of smoking. By influencing this belief, marketers will change customers' affect and behaviour.

   We now examine the four basic strategies that marketers can use for changing the cognitive structure of a customer's attitude.

Changing beliefs
This strategy involves shifting beliefs about the performance of a brand on one or more attributes. For example, many customers believe that American cars are not as well made as Japanese cars. A lot of advertising for American cars is designed to change this belief, by providing facts or statements about performance.

Shifting performance
Most people consider some product attributes to be more important than others. Marketers often try to convince customers that the attributes on which their brands are relatively strong are the most important. For example, Quaker Oats stresses the fact that consumption of its ingredients has been shown to reduce the risk of heart disease, using the theme 'Thinking about a heart-healthy breakfast' to make this attribute more important to customers.

Adding beliefs
Marketers can also try to add new beliefs to the customer's belief structure, for example by promoting freshness in the form of the 'born on (date)' label as an important attribute for a beer. Before the campaign, few considered the age of a beer to be a relevant attribute.

Changing the ideal
Marketers can change attitude by changing the perceptions of the ideal brand or situation. Many conservation organisations try to influence our beliefs about the ideal product by stressing the advantages to the environment of minimal packaging, non-

polluting manufacturing, extensive use of recycled materials and non-polluting disposal at the end of the product's useful life.

9.6.4 Factors that influence attitude change[16]

Attitudes that are strongly held are more difficult to change than those that are weakly held. For example, few committed smokers read articles on the harmful effects of smoking. If they do experience messages that warn against smoking, they tend to discount these. Because of this, most marketers do not try to capture sales from customers who are committed to competing brands. Rather, they focus on customers who are less committed, as these customers are more willing to attend and respond to their messages.

The source of a message is important, because customers respond differently to the same message delivered by different sources. Celebrity sources, for example, may enhance attitude change for a variety of reasons. They may attract more attention to the advert than non-celebrities would. Or, in many cases, they may be viewed as more credible than non-celebrities. Customers tend to identify with or emulate a celebrity. The effectiveness of using a celebrity to endorse a company's product can generally be improved by matching the image of the celebrity with the personality of the product and the actual or desired self-concept of the target market.

The appeal used in an advert is also a factor in influencing attitudes. Consider the following advertising appeals:

○ **Fear appeals** make use of the threat of negative consequences if attitudes or behaviour are not altered. For example, social fears imply disapproval of our peers for wearing the 'wrong' clothing.
○ **Humorous appeals** are built around the product, for example the Cremora advert, 'It's not inside, it's ON TOP!'
○ **Emotional appeals** are designed to create a positive affective response rather than to provide information or state an argument. Emotional adverts such as those that arouse feelings of warmth trigger a physiological reaction.

Case study

PROTECTING OUR SKIN

South Africa is known as a country with one of the highest rates of skin cancer in the world. A survey commissioned to determine people's attitudes towards protection against the sun's rays discovered several target groups. It found that young people, particularly males, were less likely to consider sun protection and were more likely to spend time outside. It also found that the lack of sun protection among the young was not simply owing to ignorance. This factor suggested that a strategy aimed at making sun protection fashionable might help to change the behaviour of the target audience.

||||▶

The introduction of the Sun Protection campaign represents the continuing efforts to reduce the incidence of skin cancer among South Africans. It not only targeted the whole population, but also developed strategies to target specific sections of the community, such as fair-skinned people, blue-eyed people, children, young men and older adults. Several key areas that could help present Sun Protection education were targeted: the media, sporting events, state and local government authorities, general practitioners and community health centres.

The mass media and public education programmes included adverts and community announcements on TV and radio, promotions, public relations activities and information services. The TV adverts were designed to change attitudes by connecting Sun Protection with a fashionable outdoor lifestyle, and were pitched at a young, particularly male, audience. Sun Protection messages were aired during sports broadcasts and current affairs programmes, and news services were regularly provided with information and research data to support the campaign. The radio campaign was set at a lower level and comprised mainly on-air reminders about Sun Protection.

Schools were a primary target, as childhood exposure to sun has been linked with the development of skin cancer in later life. The establishment of shaded playgrounds encouraged children to wear hats unless playing in the shade. Hairdressers were also encouraged to suggest their customers seek medical advice about any suspicious spots.

By focusing on and using young, attractive people enjoying an outdoor lifestyle, the SunProtection campaign managed to resolve the conflicting attitudes that, although sun protection was sensible, it was not fashionable.

Surveys conducted at regular interviews established that the campaign made a strong impact. About 60% of the respondents have claimed to have taken extra precautions against sun exposure over the summer.

9.7 Summary

In this chapter we focused on customer attitudes, and dealt with the nature of attitudes and their functions. We examined the components of attitudes, using the ABC model. Our discussion of the formation of attitudes involved the ways in which attitudes are formed. We concluded the chapter by looking at ways in which attitudes can be changed.

Questions for self-assessment

To assess your progress, answer these questions:
1. With the aid of practical examples, explain the nature of customer attitudes.
2. Attitudes have three components. What are the implications of these components in terms of the ABC model of attitude?

3. What are the functions that attitudes fulfil in our lives?
4. Explain how attitudes are formed.
5. How can marketers try to change customer attitudes?
6. With reference to the case study, answer the following questions:
   a. What strategies for influencing people's behaviour were adopted in the Sun Protection campaign?
   b. Explain how the concept of a cognitive-oriented strategy was used in the campaign.

Endnote references

1. Botha, J.A.R., Brink, A., Machado, R. and Rudansky, S. 1997. *Consumer-oriented Marketing Communication*. Pretoria: Unisa, p. 94.
2. Ibid., p. 95.
3. Adapted from Hawkins, D.I., Best, R.J. and Coney, K.A. 2001. *Consumer Behavior: Building Marketing Strategy*. Boston: Irwin McGraw-Hill, p. 395.
4. Solomon, M.R. and Stuart, E.W. 1997. *Marketing: Real People, Real Choices*. Upper Saddle River: Prentice-Hall.
5. Botha et al., op. cit., p. 96.
6. Ibid.
7. Ibid., p. 97.
8. Ibid., p. 98.
9. Hawkins et al., op. cit.
10. Botha et al., op. cit., pp. 98–100.
11. Based on Schiffman, L.G., Bednall, D., Watson, J. and Kanuk, L.L. 1997. *Consumer Behaviour*. Sydney: Prentice-Hall, pp. 254–6.
12. Botha et al., op. cit., p. 102.
13. Hawkins et al., op. cit., p. 409.
14. Solomon and Stuart, op. cit., p. 198.
15. Based on Hawkins et al., op. cit., pp. 402–5, and Botha et al., op. cit., pp. 104–5.
16. Hawkins et al., op. cit., pp. 408–15.

Personality and self-concept

After studying this chapter, you should be able to:

○ discuss the nature and characteristics of personality

○ discuss the various personalities theories

○ identify and discuss the influence of personality on lifestyle

○ explain the value of personality to marketers

○ discuss what is meant by self-concept.

10.1 Introduction

Companies seek to maximise sales and profits by appealing to their best customers. These customers spend the most, require the least marketing effort, and spread positive word-of-mouth messages.[1] Organisations must identify and understand these customers in order to satisfy their needs sufficiently. Current assessments of customer behaviour, like satisfaction surveys, often do not deliver a complete picture of target customers. Needs and motives provide the foundation for behaviour, while personality attempts to categorise behaviour systematically. There is therefore a relation between motivation and personality. We seek to fulfil many needs, and research suggests that most people have fundamentally the same needs. However, there are many ways for an individual to meet these needs. Also, people seem to have quite different need strengths. Essentially, the study of personality is aimed at identifying consistent need levels and behaviour patterns that individuals follow in satisfying needs.

Walters and Bergiel[2] contend that the key to understanding a customer lies in personality. They argue that needs, motives, attitudes, learning and perception, taken separately, constitute only bits and pieces of the totality that is a person, and that it is personality that ties all these pieces together. The way in which someone makes a decision in a marketing situation and the resulting behaviour are based on their personality.

Many marketing strategies are closely related to customer characteristics and behaviours, for example strategies which target innovative customers. Customer innovativeness describes 'early adapters' of products who wish to learn about and own the newest product. This coincides with a product's life cycle, where innovators or early adopters play a significant role in the introductory phase of a product.[3] Knowledge about the behaviour and perceptions of these customers is therefore crucial to the sustainable and successful implementation of a marketing strategy. Thus we can say that personality and customer behaviour is intricately linked, and the understanding thereof is vital to marketers.

The majority of segmentation strategies can be grouped into these four categories:[4]

1. **Geographic** and **geodemographic** – region, climate, population density, etc.
2. **Demographic** – age, sex, education, occupation, religion, race, nationality, family size, family life cycle.
3. **Behavioural** – attitudes, knowledge, benefits, user status, usage rate, loyalty status, readiness to buy, occasions.
4. **Psychographic** – personality, lifestyle.

The process of segmenting markets based on customer personality traits can be classified as a psychographic segmentation strategy, which we explore in this chapter. We also discuss customers' self-concept, including the characteristics of personality, the various personality theories, and the influence of personality on lifestyle and self-concept.

10.2 The nature of personality

Psychographics measures the motivations behind a behaviour and tries to explain why some individuals accept or reject a message, act on it, or ignore it. Therefore, using psychographics, marketers can help improve their campaign quality and accountability by zeroing in on the most receptive audience for their message. Psychographic segmentation is thus essentially about the study of attitudes, motivations, personality characteristics and belief systems.[5]

Some theorists, who have examined personality, emphasise the dual influence of heredity and early childhood experiences on personality development. Others have stressed broader social and environmental influences, and the fact that personalities develop continuously over time. Certain theorists prefer to view personality as a unified whole, while others focus on specific traits. The wide variety of views on personality makes it difficult to arrive at a single definition. Perhaps the most simple definition would be: personality comprises 'those inner psychological characteristics that both determine and reflect how a person responds to [their] environment'.[6]

The American Marketing Association endorses a similar definition of personality and state that personality is:[7]

> an individual's consistency in coping with one's environment. Personality is the consistent pattern of responses to the stimuli from both internal and external sources. It is this consistency of response that allows us to type people as aggressive or submissive, as obnoxious or charismatic. The particular theory or philosophy of motivation and personality held by scholars in this field colors their views, research, and even definitions of the term. Nevertheless, "a consistent pattern of responses in coping with perceived reality" is a good working definition.

The emphasis in this definition is on the person's inner characteristics – those specific qualities, attributes, traits and mannerisms that distinguish one individual from another. These deeply ingrained characteristics that we call 'personality' are likely to influence the individual's product and store choices, as well as the way they respond to the marketer's promotional efforts. Therefore, an organisation will find the identification of specific personality characteristics associated with customer behaviour useful in the development of its market segmentation strategies. (For a discussion of market segmentation, see Chapter 11.)

10.3 The characteristics of personality

When studying personality, there are four aspects that we need to take into account. We now consider each one in turn.

10.3.1 Personality reflects individual differences

There are differences in each person's heredity, early childhood experiences, cultural exposure, and personal motivation.[8] The inner characteristics that make up an individual's personality are a unique combination of factors, thus no two individuals are exactly alike.[9] However, many individuals tend to be *similar* in terms of a single personality characteristic. For example, some people can be described as being 'sociable' while others can be described as 'low' in sociability. The value of personality lies in the fact that marketers can categorise people in different groups based on one or a few traits. People are not totally different in all respects. If they were, it would be impossible to group or segment them into similar groups. In that case, there would be no reason to develop products aimed at a specific group or to standardise a promotional campaign. Nevertheless, marketers should always be aware that individual differences in personality account for more variance in customers' behaviour than customer researchers have recognised.[10]

10.3.2 Personality is consistent and enduring

An individual's personality is characterised by stability during change. Consistency gives direction to a person's behaviour and sustains them in the face of experience that changes all the time. Consistency refers to enduring, but not unchanging, qualities of personality. It also gives the behaviour of a person a measure of predictability.

The stable nature of personality suggests that it is unreasonable for marketers to try to change customers' personalities to conform to certain products. At best, they learn which personality characteristics influence particular customer responses, and attempt to appeal to relevant personality traits inherent in their target group of customers. While an individual's personality may be largely stable, specific needs, motives, attitudes and reactions to group pressure may cause a change in their behaviour. Therefore, personality is only one of a combination of factors that influences how a customer behaves, and these factors emphasise the place of learning in individual behaviour.

Marketing segmentation that is based on the assumption that a customer's personality and behaviour changes little over time, and is therefore easy to predict, is called '**tradition-directed behaviour segmentation**' and is a form of psychographic and lifestyle segmentation.[11]

10.3.3 Personality is conceived of as a whole actualising itself in an environment

Just as an individual's separate acts cannot be understood apart from the whole person, so the whole person cannot be fully understood if they are abstracted from their environment. Some of the most important characteristics of the whole individual are derived from their environment, especially from the socio-cultural environment with all its customs. Differences in personality are expressions not only of inherent tendencies but even more of events in the social environment.

10.3.4 Personality can change

Despite the above, personality may change under certain circumstances, even though it tends to be consistent and enduring. On the one hand, this could be owing to major events such as a serious car accident, a hijacking, the death of a loved one or a career promotion. On the other hand, this could be part of a gradual maturing and growth process that all individuals go through.

Based on these rather conflicting characteristics, various personality theories have been developed and subsequently used in marketing and customer behaviour research. These theories provide the structure for a review of a large body of evidence, all of which has implications for the analysis of customer behaviour.

10.4 Personality theories

There are many theories on personality. We have selected the theories that we discuss below because of the prominent role they have played in the study of customer behaviour and personality, and the relationship that exists between them.[12]

10.4.1 Freud's psychoanalytic theory of personality

This theory provides the foundation for the study of motivational research, which operates on the premise that human drives are largely unconscious in nature and serve to motivate many customer actions. As a result, the emphasis in motivational research studies is on discovering the underlying motivations for specific customer behaviour. The motivational researcher tends to focus on what the customer buys, treating the purchases as a reflection and extension of the customer's personality. In other words, the clothes we wear and the images we display often reflect our personality. This view of product personality suggests that using a particular product, such as expensive jewellery, enhances our self-confidence.

10.4.2 Neo-Freudian theory

As the name implies, this is an extension of Freudian theory. It tends to emphasise the fundamental role of social relationships in the formation and development of personality, for example a person's desire to overcome feelings of inferiority, that is, to strive for superiority and to conquer feelings of anxiety. Although neo-Freudian theories of personality have not received wide attention, it is likely that marketers have employed some of these theories intuitively. For example, marketers who position their products as being unique or for non-conformists seem to be guided by the neo-Freudian theory's characterisation of a 'detached individual' – a person seeking independence and individuality.

10.4.3 Trait theory

This theory focuses on the measurement of personality in terms of specific individual psychological characteristics called 'traits'. A **trait** is any distinguishing, relatively enduring way in which one individual differs from another. The theory states that individuals possess innate psychological traits – such as self-confidence, aggression, responsibility, curiosity, etc. – to a greater or lesser degree, and that these traits can be measured by specially designed scales. Trait theorists are concerned with the construction of personality tests that pinpoint individual differences in terms of specific traits. For example, individuals may distinguish other people as being reserved or outgoing. In this way they intuitively evaluate and 'label' them in terms of traits.

10.4.4 Gestalt theory

In marketing, the Gestalt theory is generally used as the basis for evaluating customer personality. This theory views personality as the result of the interaction between the person and the total environment – the two must be considered together as a patterned event.[13] The basic idea is that the whole person is greater than the sum of their parts, and personality cannot be determined by a consideration of separate characteristics. Personality is as much a product of the environment as it is of the individual's mind. Experiments prove that individuals respond to stimuli in relation to their experiences. It is consistent with Gestalt theory that attitudes, perception, aspirations, self-concepts, satisfaction, frustration and motivation are all necessary to explain and understand human personality and, therefore, a customer's behaviour.

Customers try to stabilise their psychological field by providing meaning to the surrounding world. They try to reduce tension and conflict between themselves and their environmental perceptions by the type of market decisions they make. The Gestalt theory sets certain principles for advertising in particular. The use of ordinary people in adverts is consistent with the theory, as the adverts assume that customers can better identify with people like themselves. Personal selling and advertising that emphasise social acceptance, or show people having fun – as in beer adverts, for example – follow Gestalt principles.

Apart from the notions provided by these established theorists, contemporary theories are continually being created to establish the effect of personality on customer behaviour. Harish, for example,[14] argues that there are eight element traits, emerging from genetics and early learning, that are core to the effect of personality on customer behaviour. These traits are:

1. Openness to new experiences.
2. Orderliness or conscientiousness.
3. Extraversion.
4. The need to be agreeable and kind.
5. The tendency to be moody or temperamental.
6. The need to collect and own material things.
7. The desire for excitement.
8. The need to look after the body.

Customers' attitudes towards a brand or adverts, or their satisfaction with service, no longer provide a complete view of customer behaviour and are now seen as passive measures. Therefore, the abovementioned traits form a valuable tool to assess customer behaviour. The tool should preferably be used in conjunction with existing important criteria.[15]

There is no doubt that personality is a major factor in customer behaviour. There is a clear relationship between personality and general behaviour and therefore buying behaviour.

10.5 The influence of personality on lifestyle

Marketers have encountered difficulties in using personality as an easy, reliable and consistent basis for segmentation. Owing to this, in recent years their attention has shifted away from personality to lifestyle, and to the way in which this influences customer demand. Lifestyle has been defined in many ways, but put simply, it is how a person lives and interacts with their environment and is therefore a reflection of a person's way of being and living in the world.[16]

We have seen that a person's personality determines to a large extent how they relate to their environment. This means that their mode of living or lifestyle is an expression of their personality, including their interests, opinions, needs and social activities, as well as demographic characteristics such as age, gender and income.

A person's lifestyle relates to how they spend time and money, and the emphasis and importance they give to certain aspects of life. Lifestyle trends are constantly evolving – a fact that affects what and how marketers sell. For example, in a recent study conducted on a group, the women interviewed announced that they hated cooking. This major change in attitude may have an impact on how adverts are aimed at women as well as on the types of new products developed for them.

Because of the apparent insights offered by lifestyle analysis, a variety of models for categorising consumers has emerged in the last few years. One of these is the Taylor Nelson model based on the UK population, where 'The Monitor' divides people into three main groups, which are again subdivided:[17]

1. **Sustenance driven**. Motivated by material security, they are subdivided into:
   a. the *aimless*, who include young unemployed and elderly drifters
   b. *survivors*, traditionally minded working-class people
   c. *belongers*, who are conservative family-oriented people.
2. **Outer-directed**. Those who are mainly motivated by the desire for status. They are subdivided into:
   a. *belongers,* and
   b. *conspicuous consumers.*
3. **Inner-directed**. This group is subdivided into:
   a. *social resisters*, who are caring and often doctrinaire
   b. *experimentalists*, who are hedonistic and individualistic
   c. *self-explorers*, who are less doctrinaire than social resisters and less materialistic than experimentalists.

Marketers can use these classifications to construct strategic frameworks for marketing campaigns both domestically and internationally. As we have seen, Market Research Africa has developed the Sociomonitor, a method of evaluating customers' lifestyles (see Chapters 4, 8 and 11). Such information helps marketers to segment the market.

Emergence of a wide variety of acronyms and labels

The development of approaches such as those mentioned above has led to the development of a wide variety of acronyms and labels. For example, in grocery markets, we find the following 'slang terms' for customers:[19]

○ 'Yuppies': Young Upwardly Mobile Professionals.
○ 'Bumps': Borrowed-to-the-hilt, Upwardly Mobile Professional Show-offs.
○ 'Jollies': Jet-setting Oldies with Lots of Loot.
○ 'Woopies': Well-Off Older Persons.
○ 'Glams': Greying Leisured Affluent Middle-Aged.
○ 'Kippers': Kids In Parent's Pockets Eroding Retirement Savings.

10.6 The value of personality to marketers

In the past, demographics have governed the way in which marketers have targeted customers. The problem with this is that even though individuals in a specific demographic category share common characteristics like age and race, their values, motivations and beliefs differ significantly. While demographics can render certain objective facts, for example that the customer owns a car, it cannot explain why the customer owns *that* car.[18]

There are common obstacles which marketers encounter when using traditional segmentation strategies:[19]

○ Demographics should not be used to infer an audience's motivations or behaviours, for example the suggestion is made that all mothers believe that it is important for their children to play a musical instrument. These inferences are a 'leap of faith' and are not necessarily based on reality.

○ A multiplicity of attitudes within an audience may exist and a single demographic category may have a wide range of attitudes towards a product or service. Therefore, oversimplifications like 'Resistance to authority is a hallmark of Generation Y' may be incorrect.

○ Messages that are targeted to an average are problematic. The 'average consumer' does not exist, and messages targeted to this 'mythical audience' are simply too general to convince or motivate anyone.

Marketers can remove these obstacles through applying psychographic segmentation – in the use of psychographics, the need to either oversimplify or use averages disappears. Therefore, marketers can select the most effective method for each segment. For one segment, the communicated message may confirm a viewpoint, while for another it may change a mindset. The behaviour of a particular psychographic segment will confirm to marketers whether that segment demonstrating a particular attitude actually follows through with a tangible behaviour.[20]

Although little research has yet been done to relate theory and practice, knowledge of personality and product image is indispensable for marketers, because customers tend to buy products that will reflect, enhance or even defend their personalities. In this way, they attach a certain symbolic meaning to some products, resulting in what is referred to as the **'product image'**.

Knowledge of personality is also valuable in designing appropriate adverts that will appeal to groups with similar personalities. For example, when creating an advertising campaign, marketers should note that highly dogmatic customers, who approach the unfamiliar defensively and with considerable discomfort and uncertainty, may be more willing to accept new products if the marketers present the products in an authoritative manner. This presentation could be done, for example by an admired celebrity or a recognised expert. In contrast, less dogmatic customers, who have the ability to consider unfamiliar or opposing beliefs, seem to be more receptive to messages that stress factual differences and product benefits. Therefore, it would be wise for the marketer to emphasise in the adverts the reasons for a new product being technically as good as competitive products.

'Other directedness' is the term used to describe an individual's attempts to fit in with and adapt to the behaviour of his or her peer group. This is opposed to 'inner directedness', which refers to individuals who are seemingly indifferent to the behaviour of others.[21] Inner-directed people, who use their own values and standards in evaluating products, prefer adverts that stress product features and personal benefits, while other-directed people, who tend to look to others to give direction to their actions, prefer adverts that feature a social environment of social acceptance. Thus, other-directed customers may be more easily influenced because of their natural inclination to go beyond the content of an advert and think in terms of likely social approval of a potential purchase.

The identification of personality variables that appear to be linked logically to product usage is likely to improve marketers' ability to segment markets and enable them to design specific products that will appeal to certain personality types, and to design promotional strategies that will appeal to the personality characteristics of existing target markets.

Table 10.1 provides brief descriptions of five adverts used in a study. It shows that inner-directed individuals tend to prefer inner-directed adverts while other-directed individuals, or extroverts, prefer other-directed adverts.

Table 10.1: Inner- and outer-directed personality appeals[22]

Product	Inner-directed appeal		Outer-directed appeal	
	Slogan	Illustration	Slogan	Illustration
Telephone company	Just dial. It's so easy, fast and dependable	Attractive girl holding telephone and staring into space	The personal touch for every occasion	Five pictures of young women in a variety of situations talking on the telephone
Sea & Ski	For proper sun protection – Sea & Ski	Beach scene with three unrelated couples	For a desirable vacation glow – Sea & Ski	Two men and three women water-skiing from the same boat
Bayer aspirin	Don't spoil your leisure time – Bayer aspirin	Man working in do-it-yourself workshop	Don't spoil your leisure time – Bayer aspirin	Two men holding drinks, talking at a cocktail party
Kodak	For a lasting record	Man photographing London Bridge	Share your experiences with friends at home	Man photographing woman in front of building with European posters in foreground
Fairchild's restaurant	The height of sophistication	Waiter in tuxedo	Good food, reasonable price, festive atmosphere	People being served in a fancy restaurant

10.7 Self and self-concept

Most individuals are aware of how they are differentiated from their surroundings – this awareness is commonly referred to as an individual's 'sense of self'.[25] Moreover, customers have an image of themselves, known as their 'self-concept', which refers to the attitude a person holds about him- or herself. Self-concept can be regarded as the totality of the thoughts and feelings of an individual about him- or herself. Similarly, in the same way that an individual has an attitude toward a car or politics, for example, the self is also a subject of evaluation. An overall self-attitude is frequently positive, but not always; there are certainly parts of the self that are evaluated more positively than others. For example, a man may feel better about himself as a company director than as a ladies man.[23]

The self-concept is a highly complex structure compared to other attitudes. It is composed of many attributes, some of which are given greater emphasis in determining overall self-attitude. Attributes of self-concept can be described in terms of their content, such as attractive appearance versus mental aptitude; a positive or negative attitude to self, that is, self-esteem; intensity; stability over time; and accuracy, that is, the degree to which our self-assessment corresponds to reality. As we will see later in the chapter, customers' self-assessments can be distorted, especially with regard to their physical appearance.[24]

10.7.1 One self or multiple selves?[25]

Historically, individual customers have been thought to have a single self – and to be interested in products and services that satisfy that self. As more research is conducted in the field of customer behaviour, it has become apparent that it is more accurate to think of the customer in terms of a multiple self, or selves. The change in thinking reflects the understanding that a single customer is likely to act differently in different situations, and when they are with different people. For example, a person will behave in one way at a rave club, in another way at a church fête, at work, with parents, and with friends at a rugby game.

The implication of the different selves that a customer embodies is that marketers should target their products and services to customers within the context of a particular self.

10.7.2 The make-up of the self-image[26]

Despite the varying social roles that we play as individuals, we all have an image of ourselves as a certain kind of person, with certain traits, habits, possessions, relationships and ways of behaving. Each individual's self-image is unique, just as with our personalities, as a result of our background and experience. We develop our self-image through interactions with other people: initially our parents, then other individuals or groups with whom we relate over the years, be they friends, peer groups, colleagues at work or others.

Products and brands have symbolic value for us, and we evaluate them on the basis of their consistency, that is, congruence, with our personal picture or image of ourselves. Some products seem to match our self-image, others seem totally alien. It is generally held that customers use products that preserve or enhance their self-image, and avoid products that do not.

A variety of self-image constructs have been identified in the customer behaviour literature. Customers have a number of enduring images of themselves, and these images or perceptions of self are closely associated with personality. People tend to buy products and services and patronise retailers with images or 'personalities' that closely correspond to their own self-image. People have more than one self-concept, and Table 10.2 shows the eight dimensions that researchers have identified.

Table 10.2: Various types of self-concept[27]

Actual self:	This is how a person actually perceives him- or herself
Ideal self:	This is how a person would like to be perceived by others, and therefore how he or she would like to be
Social self:	This is how a person thinks others perceive him or her
Ideal social self:	This is how a person would like others to perceive him or her
Expected self:	This is an image of self between the actual and ideal self
Situational self:	This is a person's self-image in a specific situation
Extended self:	This is a person's self-concept that includes the impact of personal possessions on self-image
Possible self:	This is what a person would like to become, could become, or is afraid of becoming

In different contexts, that is, in different situations and/or with respect to different products, customers might select a different self-image to guide their attitudes or behaviour. For instance, with regard to everyday household products, customers might be guided by their actual self-image, whereas with regard to socially enhancing or socially conspicuous products, they might be guided by their social self-image. When it comes to a so-called 'fantasy product', they might be guided by either their ideal self-image or ideal social self-image.

The concept of self-image has strategic implications for marketers. For example, marketers can segment their markets on the basis of relevant customer self-images, and then position their products or stores as symbols of such self-images. This strategy is fully consistent with the marketing concept, in that marketers first assess the needs of a customer segment, known as **'customer orientation'**, and then proceed to develop and market a product or service that meets the criteria.

10.7.3 The extended self[28]

The relationship between customers' self-images and their possessions, that is, the objects they call their own, is an exciting topic for customer research. Specifically, customers' possessions can be seen to confirm or extend their self-images, for example acquiring a sports car might serve to expand or enrich someone's image or sense of self. The individual might see themselves as being more trendy, more attractive and more successful, because they have added the vehicle to their inventory of self-enhancing possessions. Similarly, if the pen or pocket-knife someone has inherited from their grandfather is stolen or lost, they are likely to feel diminished in some way. In fact, the loss of a prized possession may lead a person to grieve and to experience a variety of emotions such as frustration, loss of control and the feeling of being 'violated'.

The above examples suggest that a great deal of human emotion can be connected to valued possessions. In such cases, possessions can be considered as *extensions* of the self. Schiffman and Kanuk[29] have proposed that possessions can extend the self in a number of ways:

○ **Actually**, by allowing the person to do things that otherwise would be difficult or impossible to accomplish, for example problem-solving using a computer.
○ **Symbolically**, by making the person feel better or 'bigger', for example receiving an employee award for excellence.
○ By conferring **status** or **rank**, for example status among collectors of rare works of art because of the ownership of a particular masterpiece.
○ By conferring feelings of **immortality**, by leaving valued possessions to young family members. This also has the potential of extending the recipients' 'selves'.
○ By conferring **magical powers**, for example a ring inherited from a grandmother might be perceived as a magic amulet bestowing good luck to the wearer.

10.7.4 Altering the self[30]

Customers constantly try to change themselves. To do this, they use a variety of products such as clothing, grooming aids and a range of accessories – cosmetics and/or jewellery – to modify their appearance and so alter their self-image. In using 'self-altering products', customers are trying to express their individualism or uniqueness by creating a new self, maintaining the existing self (or preventing the loss of self) or extending the self (modifying or changing the self). To this end, customers often use self-altering products or services to conform to, or take on, the appearance of a particular type of person such as a stockbroker, lawyer or teacher.

We can alter our self, particularly our appearance or body parts, using cosmetics, hair restyling or colouring, switching from glasses to contact lenses, or the reverse, or undergoing cosmetic surgery. By using these options, it is possible for us to create a 'new' or 'improved' person. Some people also use image consultants to achieve an appropriate and mutually agreed-upon self-image. These consultants provide clients with advice on such personal attributes as clothing, colour, presentation, appearance, posture, speaking and media skills.

Case study

A BILLION HOUSEWIVES EVERY DAY ... POSITIONING BAKED BEANS IN CHINA

At the beginning of 1998, Heinz, the world's leading supplier of baked beans, announced that it was launching them into China, the world's largest consumer market. With a retail price of about 60p a can, the company's strategy was different from that used in the UK and the majority of its sixty or so other markets. Targeted very firmly at China's emerging middle classes and positioned as something of a status symbol, baked beans were positioned to be 'the kind of exotic dish served up to impress the boss when he comes to dinner'.

10.8 Summary

An understanding of the personalities of customers is integral to the success of any marketing campaign. However, marketers should realise that rarely can only one dimension of a customer accurately segment a market effectively.

'In contrast to the theory of segmentation that implies that there is a single best way of segmenting a market, the range and variety of marketing decisions suggest that any attempt to use a singe basis for segmentation (such as psychographic, brand preference, or product usage) for all marketing decisions may result in incorrect marketing decisions as well as a waste of resources.'[31]

Having said this, research on personality and self-concept is extremely useful in the segmenting of markets, developing marketing and promotional strategy, and positioning of products in the market. Although marketers cannot predict from a personality profile the specific brands that a customer will buy, they can use the profile to increase their understanding of the factors that motivate and guide a customer's purchases. Although personality tends to be consistent and enduring, it may change abruptly in response to major life events, as well as gradually over time.

Each individual has a perceived self-image (or multiple self-images) as a certain kind of person with certain traits, habits, possessions, relationships and ways of behaving. Customers often try to preserve, enhance, alter or extend their self-images by buying products or services and shopping at stores believed to be consistent with a particular self-image, and by avoiding products and stores that are not.

Questions for self-assessment

To assess your progress, answer these questions:
1. Although no two individuals have identical personalities, how would you explain the fact that personality is used in customer research to identify distinct and size-able market segments?
2. Contrast the main characteristics of the following personality theories. In your answers, illustrate how each theory is applied to the understanding of customer behaviour:
    a. Freudian theory.
    b. Gestalt theory.
    c. Neo-Freudian theory.
    d. Trait theory.
3. Describe the personality trait theory. Give examples of how personality traits can be used in customer research.
4. Discuss self-concept and its importance to marketers.
5. With regard to the case study, answer the following questions:
    a. Explain how the different types of self-concept need to be taken into account by marketers in advertising messages in particular.
    b. How do you think the case study relates to the influence of personality on buying behaviour?

Endnote references

1. Goldsmith, R.E., Flynn, L.R. and Goldsmith, E.B. 2003. Innovative consumers and market mavens. *Journal of Marketing Theory and Practice*, 11(4). Available on the internet from: http://proquest.umi.com/ (accessed 3 August 2005).
2. Walters, C.G. and Bergiel, B.J. 1989. *Consumer Behavior: A Decision-making Approach*. Cincinnati: South-Western.
3. Wilson, R.M.S. and Gilligan, C. 2005. *Strategic Marketing Management: Planning, Implementation & Control*. 3rd ed. Italy: Elsevier, Butterworth, Heinemann.
4. Morgan, C.M., Levy, D.J. and Fortin, M. 2003. Psycholographic segmentation. *Communication World*, 20(1). Available on the internet from: http://proquest.umi.com/ (accessed 4 August 2005).
5. Schiffman, L.G. and Kanuk, L.L. 1997. *Consumer Behaviour*. 6th ed. London: Prentice-Hall.
6. Botha, J.A.R., Brink, A., Machado, R. and Rudansky, S. 1997. *Consumer-oriented Marketing Communication*. Pretoria: Unisa.
7. American Marketing Association. 2005. *Dictionary of Marketing Terms*. Available on the internet from: www.marketingpower.com// (accessed 3 August 2005).
8. Harish, S. 2001. The 3M model of motivation and personality: Theory and empirical applications to consumer behaviour. *Journal of Marketing Research*, 38(3). Available on the internet from: http://proquest.umi.com/ (accessed 3 August 2005).
9. Schiffman and Kanuk, op. cit., p. 118.
10. Harish, S. 2001. The 3M model of motivation and personality: Theory and empirical applications to consumer behaviour. *Journal of Marketing Research*, 38(3). Available on the internet from: http://proquest.umi.com/ (accessed 3 August 2005).

11. Wilson, R.M.S. and Gilligan, C. 2005. *Strategic Marketing Management: Planning, Implementation & Control*. 3rd ed. Italy: Elsevier, Butterworth, Heinemann.

12. Ibid., pp. 119–27.

13. Walters and Bergiel, op. cit., p. 411.

14. Harish, S. 2001. The 3M model of motivation and personality: Theory and empirical applications to consumer behaviour. *Journal of Marketing Research*, 38(3). Available on the internet from: http://proquest.umi.com/ (accessed 3 August 2005).

15. Harish, S. 2001. The 3M model of motivation and personality: Theory and empirical applications to consumer behaviour. *Journal of Marketing Research*, 38(3). Available on the internet from: http://proquest.umi.com/ (accessed 3 August 3005).

16. Wilson, R.M.S. and Gilligan, C. 2005. *Strategic Marketing Management: Planning, Implementation & Control*. 3rd ed. Italy: Elsevier, Butterworth, Heinemann.

17. Wilson, R.M.S. and Gilligan, C. 2005. *Strategic Marketing Management: Planning, Implementation & Control*. 3rd ed. Italy: Elsevier, Butterworth, Heinemann.

18. Wilson, R.M.S. and Gilligan, C. 2005. *Strategic Marketing Management: Planning, Implementation & Control*. 3rd ed. Italy: Elsevier, Butterworth, Heinemann.

19. Morgan, C.M., Levy, D.J. and Fortin, M. 2003. Psychographic segmentation. *Communication World*, 20(1). Available on the internet from: http://proquest.umi.com/ (accessed 4 August 2005).

20. Morgan, C.M., Levy, D.J. and Fortin, M. 2003. Psychographic segmentation. *Communication World*, 20(1). Available on the internet from: http://proquest.umi.com/ (accessed 4 August 2005).

21. Morgan, C.M., Levy, D.J. and Fortin, M. 2003. Psychographic segmentation. *Communication World*, 20(1). Available on the internet from: http://proquest.umi.com/ (accessed 4 August 2005).

22. Based on Botha, J.A.R., Brink, A., Machado, R. and Rudansky, S. 1997. *Consumer-orientated Marketing Communication*. Pretoria: UNISA.

23. Wilson, R.M.S. and Gilligan, C. 2005. *Strategic Marketing Management: Planning, Implementation & Control*. 3rd ed. Italy: Elsevier, Butterworth, Heinemann.

24. Reed, A. 2002. Social identity as a useful perspective for self-concept-based consumer research. *Psychology & Marketing*, 19(3). Available on the internet from: http://proquest.umi.com/ (accessed 4 August 2005).

25. Solomon, M.R. 1999. *Consumer Behavior: Buying, Having and Being*. Upper Saddle River: Prentice-Hall, p. 289.

26. Ibid.

27. Based on Mowen, J.C. and Minor, M. 1998. *Consumer Behaviour*. 5th ed. Upper Saddle River: Prentice-Hall, p. 212; and Botha, J.A.R., Brink, A., Machado, R. and Rudansky, S. 1997. *Consumer-orientated Marketing Communication*. Pretoria: UNISA.

28. Ibid.

29. Schiffman and Kanuk, op. cit., p. 135.

30. Ibid.

31. Ibid., p. 136.

11 Market segmentation

Learning Outcomes

After studying this chapter, you should be able to:

○ explain and illustrate how a market can be segmented with the aid of the bases for market segmentation

○ define targeting and explain the criteria that need to be met to choose a target market

○ explain which targeting strategies can be utilised in selecting a target market

○ explain the meaning and implications of positioning.

11.1 Introduction

The market consists of people who differ in their tastes, needs, attitudes, motivations and lifestyles. As organisations cannot satisfy all the consumers in the world, marketers must determine who should be part of their consumer base. The most effective method they can use to help them make this decision is to divide the market into segments or target markets. In order to define consumer needs more precisely, marketers therefore use this process known as 'market segmentation'.

Market segmentation helps marketers to know where and how consumers shop and how much they are willing to pay for a product. A profile of the intended target market will also help to determine the methods of communication that marketers will use to reach a particular market. In a country with a diverse population consisting of many racial and social groups, as in South Africa, marketers should study their consumers more closely to serve the needs and preferences of each distinct group. Marketers should tailor the marketing mix instruments into a marketing strategy that suits the target market. These instruments are commonly known as the '4 Ps' – for physical products (product, price, place and promotion) – and/or the '7 Ps' – for services (product, price, place, promotion, people, processes and physical evidence). In this chapter we consider the STP process, which stands for segmentation, targeting and positioning.

11.2 The STP process

To compete more effectively, many companies are embracing the STP approach to marketing.[1] This means that instead of scattering marketing efforts in a 'shotgun' approach, marketers need to focus on the consumers that they have the greatest chance of satisfying – a 'rifle' approach. The STP process requires from marketers to do the following:[2]

○ They should **segment** the market, which means that they identify and profile distinct groups of buyers who differ in their needs and preferences. In other words, segmentation deals with an aggregated process that clusters people with similar needs into a market segment, thereby allowing marketers to focus their resources more effectively. Segmentation also guides the redesign, the repositioning or the extension of product, brand or service targeting to a new consumer segment.[3]

○ **Targeting** involves selecting one or more of the identified market segments to enter. During this process the marketing mix is tailored to fit the specific target consumers' needs.

○ **Positioning** enables marketers to establish and communicate the distinctive benefits of the company's market offering. Positioning deals with the way consumers perceive proposed or present products and/or services and/or brands in a market in relation to those offerings of competitors.

We now discuss each of the above steps in more detail.

11.3 Market segmentation

Market segmentation is the process of dividing a market into subsets or segments of consumers so that the members of each segment share characteristics, and are distinct from members of other segments.[4] Each market segment shares one or more similar characteristic that causes them to have relatively similar product needs. Note that segmentation always refers to *aspects of the consumer* and not to the product or service itself.

It is important to remember that each market segment requires its own marketing strategy. Each element of the marketing mix should be examined to determine if changes are required from one segment to another. At times, each segment will require a completely different marketing mix. The marketing mix can differentiate based on the product offering, the advertising message or even the retail outlets where products are available.[5] Think, for example, about 'Pay-as-you go' cellular vouchers. Various amounts are available at various outlets, and the message being conveyed will be focusing on the specific market segment within that area. We can compare, for example, vouchers sold at a spaza shop, at a school kiosk or even at an ATM. How do they differ?

But why do marketers need to segment the markets? Some of the advantages of segmentation are as follows:[6]

○ It provides the ability to define and thus satisfy consumer needs more accurately.
○ It enables better utilisation of scarce resources.

○ It provides more opportunities to build long-term relationships with consumers.
○ It sets more accurate or detailed goals and objectives, and thus enhances performance assessment.

11.3.1 Steps of market segmentation

To be viable, a segment must be large enough to be served profitably. To some extent,
each individual or household has unique needs for most products. The smaller the
segment, the closer the total product can be to that segment's desires. Historically, the
smaller the segment, the more it costs to serve the segment. Thus, a tailor-made suit
costs more than a mass produced suit. However, flexible manufacturing and customisation makes it increasingly cost-effective to develop products and communications for
small segments or even individual consumers.[7] As such, the BMW plant in Rosslyn,
Pretoria enables all its consumers to customise their BMW 3-series. No two cars are
exactly the same. Every BMW is produced according to the consumer's needs and
wants, thereby allowing mass customisation.

Market segmentation involves the following four steps:[8]
1. Identifying product-related need sets.
2. Grouping consumers with similar need sets.
3. Describing each group.
4. Selecting an attractive segment to serve.

We now briefly discuss each of them.

Identifying product-related need sets

The first task of the firm is to identify need sets that the organisation is capable of
meeting. The term 'need sets' is used to reflect the fact that most products satisfy more
than one need. Thus, a car can meet more needs than simply basic transportation.
Some consumers purchase cars to meet transportation and status needs, while others
purchase them to meet transportation and entertainment needs. Still others purchase
cars to meet status, entertainment and transportation needs. Thus, depending on the
needs, advertising material will differ because the firms are pursuing different market
segments with distinct need sets.

Consumer needs are not restricted to product features. They also include types and
sources of information about the product, outlets where the product is available, the price
of the product, services associated with the product, the image of the product or firm, and
even where and how the product is produced.

Identifying the various need sets that the firm's current or potential product might
satisfy typically involves consumer research, particularly focus groups and depth interviews as well as logic and intuition. These needs sets are often associated with other
variables such as age, stage in the household life cycle, gender, social class, ethnic group,
or lifestyle. Many firms start the segmentation process focusing first on one or more of

the groups defined by one of these variables. The variables allow marketers to identify the base to be used for segmentation and target market selection.

Marketers can use one or a combination of the following bases to segment the market:

○ **Usage or behavioural segmentation**: Most companies in South Africa are able to segment consumers by usage criteria because a great deal of marketing research data on product and media consumption is available.[9] It is therefore possible to divide current users of a product or service, or brand into categories of light, medium and heavy users. For example, assume that research has indicated that 25% of beer drinkers account for more than 70% of all beer consumed. For this reason, most marketers prefer to target their campaigns to the heavy users, rather than spend a lot more money trying to attract light users. Marketers of many other products have found that a relatively small group of heavy users account for a disproportionately large percentage of product usage, and targeting these users has become the basis of their marketing strategies. Non-users are a particular challenge. Marketers have to decide whether non-users are a potentially worthwhile segment, or whether the resources needed to turn them into users cannot be better spent in trying to lure users away from competitive products.

Sometimes, brand loyalty is used as the basis for segmentation. Marketers often try to identify the characteristics of their brand-loyal consumers so that they can direct their promotional efforts to people with similar characteristics in the larger population. Other marketers target consumers who show no brand loyalty, in the belief that such people represent greater market potential than loyal consumers. Marketers should attempt to encourage brand loyalty, as it has been found that brand-loyal consumers are also heavy users and pay less attention to competing marketing messages.

On its own, usage or behavioural segmentation lacks sufficient depth for it to be applied effectively when developing marketing strategies.[10] Therefore, this segmentation base can be used along with one and/or a combination of the other segmentation bases.

○ **Demographic segmentation**: This is based on aspects such as age, gender, marital status, family life cycle, income, occupation and education. Marketers rely on these demographic characteristics firstly because they are often closely linked to a consumer's product needs and buying behaviour, and secondly because they can be measured easily. Potential users of a product, service or brand can be divided into categories consisting of different age groups, gender and basic income levels. Perhaps the demographic characteristic most used to segment household markets is gender. Clothing, cosmetics, hair-care products, toiletries, and so on are all marketed differently to men than they are to women.

Income has long been one of the most important variables for distinguishing market segments. However, marketers often combine other demographical variables to define their target markets more accurately, for example they tend to

closely correlate education, occupation and income. Marketers are usually interested in affluent consumers, and for good reason. High-level occupations, that is,
those that produce high incomes, usually require advanced educational training.
Individuals with little education rarely qualify for high-level jobs. Because of the
close correlation, these variables are often combined into an index of social class.
Life cycle can also be used to segment the market for housing and home furnishings, for example start-up families would need smaller houses compared to those
needed by full-nest families.

The LSM, which we discussed in Chapters 3, 5 and 6, is a South African model
that allows marketers to segment the market based on aspects such as monthly
household income, urbanisation, access to services and ownership of cars and
major appliances.

○ **Lifestyle and psychographic segmentation**: Psychographic segmentation involves
the breaking up of the market in terms of attributes such as social class, lifestyle
and personality. It refers to the analysis of consumers on the basis of their activities, interests and opinions (AIO). To establish the different lifestyle categories,
marketers collect information concerning consumers' activities, interests, opinions
and lifestyles and subject it to factor analysis in order to identify separate groups.

The clearest example of lifestyle segmentation, according to Sheth et al.,[11] is
the values and lifestyle segmentation scheme (VALS), used in the USA and Japan.
Consumers in these two countries are classified according to their motivations,
activities, interests and opinions.

In South Africa, as we have seen in Chapters 4, 8 and 10, the Sociomonitor
Value Groups Survey is a comprehensive lifestyle and psychographic study of
the population groups conducted by MRA. It has been a household name to
South African marketers since its inception in 1975.[12] In order to create the value
groups, respondents answered an extensive battery of psychographic statements.
Their answers were then grouped and scored, giving every single respondent
a different score and position on the 'social map', depending on their answers.
These scores were analysed statistically and the value groups – broad groups of
consumers with similar values, attitudes and motivations (psychographics) – were
the result. These value groups help marketers to understand their consumers'
behaviour, and hence how best to appeal to them. It also provides information on
brand and media usage.

Psychographic segmentation based on lifestyle has become increasingly popular,
as it goes beyond demographic, geographic and social class measurements in
predicting consumer behaviour.

○ **Geographic segmentation**: With geographic segmentation, the market is divided
according to geographical location, such as countries and regions. Variations such
as the size of a city or town, or population density may also be appropriate bases.
Geographic segmentation is most often performed in conjunction with other
types of measurement and is mostly useful when differences in product consump-

tion correspond closely with demographic or lifestyle 'types' who live in different areas and suburbs. Today, two aspects that play an increasingly important role in geographic segmentation are the use of local advertising media – community newspapers such as the *Rekord* – and the allocation of sales representatives to different areas. The sales representatives are allowed to operate only within the specified area.

Rural and urban markets may also be distinguished, and other territorial subdivisions within larger geographic areas are also possible. For example, in a geographic area such as Johannesburg, marketers realise that there are diverse markets, such as the central, southern, northern, western and eastern areas of the city, which can be treated as separate market segments with different needs.

○ **Needs/benefit segmentation**: A market can be effectively segmented by classifying consumers into groups according to the specific benefits they want from a product. Different benefit segments want different benefits.[13] Products and services are bundles of multiple attributes, and marketers use benefit segmentation to find out the relative importance of one benefit over others, for example toothpaste cleans the teeth and freshens breath. Thus, with regard to benefit segmentation, marketers should find out what criteria consumers use to evaluate brands, how important each of these criteria are and also which brands will be able to satisfy each of these criteria.

Users of benefit segmentation claim that the benefits people are seeking are the basic reason for buying a product, and therefore the proper basis for market segmentation.[14] There is no doubt that benefit segmentation is a powerful and important basis for market segmentation.

Table 11.1 summarises the various bases of market segmentation.

Table 11.1: A summary of the bases of market segmentation[15]

Segmentation base	Variables included
Usage/Behavioural segmentation	Usage-rate, occasions, brand familiarity
Demographic segmentation	Age, gender, income, ethnic, family life cycle
Lifestyle/Psychographic segmentation	Personality, motives, lifestyles, geodemographics
Geographic segmentation	Region, city or metro size, density, climate
Needs/Benefits segmentation	Benefits sought

Grouping consumers with similar need sets

Using the bases discussed above, the next step is to group consumers with similar need sets. For example, the need for moderately priced, fun, sporty cars appears to exist in many young single individuals, young couples with no children, and middle-aged couples whose children have left home. These consumers can be grouped into one segment as far as product features, and perhaps even product image, are concerned, despite sharply different demographics. This step generally involves consumer research, including focus group interviews, surveys and product concept tests. It could also entail an analysis of current consumption patterns.

Description of each group

Once consumers with similar need sets are identified, they should be described in terms of their demographics, lifestyles and media usage. In order to design an effective marketing programme, it is necessary to have a complete understanding of the potential consumers. It is only with such an understanding that marketers can be sure they have correctly identified the need set. In addition, they cannot communicate effectively with consumers if they do not understand the context in which the product is purchased and consumed, how it is perceived by the consumers, and the language they use to describe it. Thus, while many young single individuals, young couples with no children, and middle-aged couples whose children have left home may want the same features in a car, the media required to reach each group and the appropriate language and themes to use with each group would likely differ.

Selecting attractive segment(s) to serve

Once they have a thorough understanding of each segment, marketers must select the target market – the segment of the larger market on which they will focus the marketing effort.

We now address targeting in more detail.

11.4 Targeting

Once the firm has identified its market segment opportunities, it needs to decide how many and which segments to target. A **target market** is a group of people for whom the firm designs, implements and maintains a marketing mix intended to meet the needs of the group. During targeting, marketers link the needs and wants of consumers with the resources and objectives of the organisation and select those segments that offer the greatest potential return on investment (ROI).[16]

11.4.1 Evaluating market segments

Before marketers select a specific market segment as a target market, they must first realise that not all segmentation schemes are useful. Therefore, they need to evaluate each segment according to certain significant evaluation criteria. To be a useful market segment, segments must rate favourably on these five key criteria:[17]

○ **Measurability**: Marketers must be able to measure the size of the market, purchasing power and characteristics of the segments.
○ **Substance**: Marketers must identify segments that are large and profitable enough to serve. An organisation must identify the largest possible homogeneous group

for which it is worth spending time and effort in tailoring a specific marketing programme.

○ **Accessibility**: Marketers must be able to reach the segment effectively so that the segment can be served cost-effectively.

○ **Differentiability**: The identified segments must be distinguishable from one another, and each segment must respond differently to different marketing-mix strategies and programmes. For example, if married and unmarried women respond similarly to an advertisement, then they do not justify being split into two segments.

○ **Actionable**: Effective programmes must enable the organisation to attract and serve these segments. The development of unique marketing programmes for target segments cannot be justified if the segments fail to respond to the efforts.

11.4.2 Strategies for selecting target markets APPROACHES?

Once they have evaluated the various segments, marketers need to employ a strategy to target a specific market. We now briefly consider the three strategies that can be used for selecting target markets.[18]

Undifferentiated targeting

With this strategy, the organisation views the market as one big market with no individual segments. The firm uses one marketing mix for the entire market. When using undifferentiated targeting, the organisation assumes that all individual consumers have similar needs that can be met with a common marketing mix. An organisation entering a new industry often makes use of undifferentiated targeting, since no competition exists and it does not need to tailor marketing mixes to the preferences of individual market segments. Henry Ford is probably the perfect example of a marketer following an undifferentiated targeting strategy. He was the first man to manufacture a car, introducing the Ford in black, and in black alone. As he commented: 'They can purchase the Ford in any colour, as long as it is black.'

Concentrated targeting – NICHE MARKETING

With this strategy, organisations are appealing to a single segment. They focus on understanding the needs, motives and satisfactions of that segment's members, and on developing and maintaining a highly specialised marketing mix. Firms frequently use the concentrated targeting strategy, as at times they have found that concentrating resources and doing a better job of meeting the needs of a narrowly defined market segment is more profitable than spreading resources over several different segments. Concentrated targeting is popular among smaller firms as it allows them to compete more effectively with the bigger role-players in the industry. For example, the First for Women car and household insurance company targets women only and advertises this in all relevant woman's magazines, which allows the company to introduce its discounted insurance packages catering specifically for the woman of today.

Multi-segment targeting

When a firm chooses to serve two or more well-defined market segments and develops a distinct marketing mix for each, the organisation engages in multi-segment targeting. With this strategy, organisations frequently use differing promotional appeals, rather than different marketing mixes, as their basis. The basic marketing strategy remains the same, but some of the names and product attributes are designed to meet different wants.

Following target market selection, marketers need to position the product, service or brand in the minds of the target market.

11.5 Positioning

A product's positioning is an image of the product or brand in the consumer's mind relative to competing products and brands. This image consists of a set of beliefs, pictorial representations and feelings about the product or brand. It is determined by communications about the brand from the firm and other sources, as well as by direct experience with it. Most marketing firms specify the product position they want their brands to have and measure these positions on an ongoing basis. This is because a brand whose position matches the desired position of a target market is likely to be purchased when a need for that product arises.[19]

Through product positioning, marketers influence how consumers perceive a brand's characteristics relative to those of competing products. The goal of product positioning is therefore to influence demand by creating a product with specific characteristics and a clear image that differentiates it from competitors. Positioning assumes that consumers compare the important features of products.[20] If they perceived a product or a service to be exactly like another product or service on the market, consumers would have no reason to buy it instead of the other product.[21] Furthermore, positioning allows marketers to differentiate their products or services or brands from those of competitors and to create a sustainable competitive advantage. According to Lamb et al.,[22] this competitive advantage forms the basis of a positioning strategy.

There are no fixed rules, and few guidelines, for the positioning of a product, service or brand. But marketers should pose these types of questions: 'How do consumers perceive our product or service?', 'Which attributes are important for differentiating purposes?' and 'How are competitive products or services being perceived?'.[23]

11.5.1 Developing a positioning strategy

To develop a positioning strategy, marketers need to analyse competitors' positions and then identify their own competitive advantage. Thereafter, it is possible for them to determine where their organisation wants to be and to develop a marketing mix that will achieve this.[24]

Marketers can use the following seven-step approach when positioning products or services.

Step 1: Identify a relevant set of competitive products or services

Marketers must understand the current 'lie of the land', in other words, the competitors that exist, and how they are perceived by the target market. It is vital that an organisation identifies all the relevant competing products or services and identifies the strengths and weaknesses of their own offering. This involves doing research, but also looking at the bigger picture. Marketers should consider whether, apart from direct competitors in the product category, there are other goods or services that could provide the same benefits that people are seeking. For example, when a company such as Coca-Cola develops a new product like Fruitopia, it must consider the drink's attractiveness compared to colas, fruit drinks and even bottled water.

Step 2: Identify differentiation variables

The next task is to offer a product with a competitive advantage, that is, the ability to deliver whatever it promises better than the competition can do. Marketers must select the variables that play a major role in helping consumers to differentiate between alternative products or services in the market.

Effective positioning requires an assessment of the positions that are currently being occupied by competing products, determining the important dimensions underlying these positions and choosing a position in the market where the organisation's marketing effort will have the greatest impact. Clearly, differentiation is key. Most profitable strategies are based on differentiation – the process of identifying 'something' different that is not offered by competitors.[25]

The differentiating variable used is not necessarily a competitive advantage and thus, as with targeting, marketers need to evaluate whether a factor serves as a competitive advantage. The criteria against which marketers should evaluate the factor include the following:[26]

○ Do consumers desire the differentiating factor/variable?
○ Can we sustain the advantage over an extended period of time?
○ Can we manufacture and market the product at a price consumers are willing to pay?
○ Is it profitable?

If the answers to these questions are yes, the differentiating variable can be described as a competitive advantage and it can form the basis of the subsequent positioning strategy.

But how do marketers differentiate? There are various ways in which they can differentiate their products from competitors. The typical bases available for differentiation are related to the following:

○ **Product differentiation**: This is a positioning strategy used to distinguish products from those of the competitors. The distinctions can either be real or perceived, and either standardised or highly differentiated. There are major characteristics that can be utilised for product differentiation. These relate to the product's features, performance standards, durability and reliability, reparability, style, reseller brand and available range. For example, Levi's 501 jeans stand out because of their distinctive buttoned fly, which makes this style hard to copy.

○ **Differentiation based on services accompanying the product**: With regard to products that cannot be differentiated by physical means or that have to compete in a fiercely competitive market, marketers are likely to use differentiation by means of accompanying services. Consider, for example, car rental companies. If not for the accompanying services, they would not be able to differentiate, because they offer exactly the same vehicles at more or less the same rates. They therefore need to differentiate in terms of superior service delivery. Service variables influencing differentiation based on accompanying service include delivery services, installation, consumer training, consulting services, repairs and other, miscellaneous services.

○ **Personnel differentiation**: It often happens that firms gain a competitive advantage by carefully selecting and training people to become more competent than the personnel of competitor firms. Better trained personnel exhibit competence, courtesy, credibility and reliability; they are more responsive and they have the ability to communicate effectively. Many organisations today regard their people as the key success factor and the most valued asset.

○ **Image differentiation**: Consumers may often perceive a difference between organisations, products, brands or brand images. Images convey a single message in a distinctive way that establishes a brand's major characteristic and positioning. A good image sets a brand or organisation apart from competitor's images and further delivers an emotional power that appeals to consumers. The images and impressions that consumers have about the organisation, whether true or false, guide and shape consumer behaviour. Because images are seen as one of the most powerful tools in attracting and satisfying consumers, it is imperative that a marketer actively manage and adapt in the long run owing to the fact that markets and consumers' perceptions change over time. Organisations are constantly crafting distinctive 'brand personalities' through the clever use of symbols, package design, celebrity endorsers, etc. For example, many product names, whether Calvin Klein or Harley Davidson, are licensed by other manufacturers to provide their own brands with 'instant status'.

Step 3: Determine consumers' perceptions
After determining the differentiation variables, the marketer must establish how consumers perceive the various products or services in terms of the variables selected. This is usually done through research.

Step 4: Analyse the intensity of a product or service's current position
When a consumer is aware of a product or service, the intensity of the awareness may vary. In many markets the awareness set for a particular product or service offering

may be as little as three or four products or services, although there might be more than twenty products or services in the product or service class. In these markets, the marketers of the lesser known product or service must attempt to increase the intensity of awareness by developing a strong relationship between the product or service and a limited number of variables.

Step 5: Analyse the product or service's current position

Marketers then establish how strongly a particular product or service is associated with a variety of determinant variables. To do this, a positioning map or perceptual map is developed. This map graphically displays, in two dimensions, the location of products, brands or groups of products in consumers' minds. It displays the psychological distances between products or brands and is an extremely useful tool in developing a positioning strategy. The products and services lying close to one another on the positioning map can be expected to be rivals.

Figure 11.1 is an example of a positioning map illustrating the electricity carriers in South Africa.

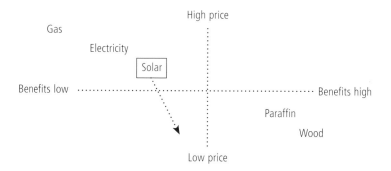

Figure 11.1: The positioning of energy carriers from a South African household perspective

Step 6: Determine the most preferred combination of attributes

The question that now arises relates to the position of a product or service that appeals most to consumers. Marketers need to ask themselves: 'Where do we as an organisation want to be in terms of our product's position in relation to competitors' products?' Usually, they can answer this with the help of research in which respondents are asked to rate their ideal product or service. The determinant variables that lie closest to the ideal point are more important to consumers, while those that lie further away are considered less important.

Step 7: Select a positioning strategy

Deciding where to position a new product or service or an existing one depends on the market targeting analysis, which we discussed earlier in this chapter, as well as on the market positioning analysis. The position must reflect consumer preferences and the positions of competitive products or services. The decision must also reflect the expected attractiveness of the target market, the relative strengths and weaknesses of competitors, and the organisation's own capabilities. There are various positioning methods that can be used:[27]

○ **Attribute positioning**: Here, a product is usually associated with an attribute or product feature. For example, Benson & Hedges has chosen to position its cigarettes in terms of their lightness and taste.

○ **Benefit positioning**: This highlights consumer benefits that can be gained because of a specific product attribute or feature. For example, Gillette Contour blades promise an even closer shave.

○ **Price and quality positioning**: This positioning base focuses on high price as a signal of quality or emphasises low price as an indication of value. While Woolworths is known for its high quality clothing, Mr Price is known for its reasonable prices.

○ **Use or application positioning**: Focusing on use or application can be an effective means of positioning a brand. Graca wine is positioned as a wine that makes all kinds of occasions enjoyable.

○ **Product user positioning**: This positioning base focuses on a personality or type of user. Marketers of bungy-jumping can position their market offering to appeal to thrill seekers.

○ **Product class positioning**: The objective here is to position a product as being associated with a particular category of products, thereby expanding its business opportunities. A museum or planetarium that is traditionally regarded as an educational institution may elect to position itself as a tourist attraction.

○ **Competitor positioning**: This is positioning against competitors. BMW could find it useful to position its cars directly against those of Mercedes Benz, its closest rival in South Africa.

○ **Origin positioning**: Some organisations want to be associated with a certain geographical region or origin, for example BMW positioning themselves as 'German engineered'.

Once marketers have gone through these steps, they may realise that it is necessary to reposition the current image of the product or service offering. We now address repositioning.

11.5.2 Repositioning

Repositioning is the process whereby a brand's original 'personality' is altered to appeal to a different segment.[28] It happens fairly often.

The following factors can serve as reasons for conducting repositioning:[29]

○ **The original positioning strategy was inappropriate**: Organisations sometimes overestimate their competitive advantage or the size of the sub-segment for whom the positioning was intended and they could be forced to re-evaluate their positioning strategy.

○ **Consumers' demands have changed**: Change in the external environment can change consumer needs as well as their demand for certain products or services.

○ **The service provider wants to build on its strengths**: The service provider wants to use its strength to position itself more profitably in various subsegments.

○ **Own brand competition**: Marketers may also decide that a brand is competing too closely with another of their own products and sales are being cannibalised, that is, the two brands are taking sales away from each other, rather than from competing companies.

○ **Overemphasis on attributes**: Too many competitors may stress the same attributes. For example, nearly all promotional strategies in the airline industry focused on price advantages over the last few years, but now several airlines are stressing comfort instead.

We can see that repositioning refers to marketers' deliberate decision to alter significantly the way the market views a product. This could involve its level of performance, the feelings it evokes, the situation in which it should be used, or even which consumers use it. Here are some examples of repositioning:

○ Kentucky Fried Chicken is trying to reposition itself in consumers' eyes in the hope of attracting more careful eaters to its 5 000 restaurants. To change the perception among more health conscious consumers that its food contains too much cholesterol, sodium and fat, KFC has started to offer non-fried items like broiled chicken and chicken salad. Focus is also shifting from using the words 'Kentucky Fried Chicken' to 'KFC', thereby reducing the emphasis on the word 'fried'.

○ The Gap clothing store has repositioned itself to attract an older consumer base. The firm changed its image from a maker of jeans for teenagers to a purveyor of casual and active sportswear for middle-aged men and women.

○ Pages decided in 1997 that it was imperative for the company to reposition itself within the core market. Its management noted that most retailers were concentrated on the ends of the core spectrum, with only a few paying attention to the critical core. Pages successfully transformed from a branded and traditional retailer to a value-driven, home-branded (in-house) retailer known as Exact!

Case study

MARKET SEGMENTATION AND PRODUCT POSITIONING

A large food processing company gets the idea of producing a powder to add to milk to increase its nutritional value and taste. This company needs answers to the following questions:

O Who will use this product – infants, children, teenagers, young or middle-aged adults?
O What primary benefits should be built into this product – taste, nutrition, refreshment, energy?
O What is the primary occasion for this product – breakfast, mid-morning break, lunch, mid-afternoon break, dinner, late evening snack?

By answering the questions above, the company developed three product concepts:
O **Concept 1**: An instant breakfast drink for adults who want a quick nutritious meal without having to prepare a full breakfast.
O **Concept 2**: A tasty snack drink for children to drink at mid-day.
O **Concept 3**: A health supplement for older adults to drink in the late evening before going to bed.

11.6 Summary

Organisations need to identify groups of individuals, households or firms with similar needs. These market segments are described in terms of demographics, media preferences, geographic location, and so on. Management selects one or more of these segments as target markets based on the firm's capabilities relative to those of its competition, and thereafter creates an image within consumers' minds in relation to competitors. This plays out the STP process – segmentation, targeting and positioning are essential steps taken by marketers before developing the marketing mix into a suitable marketing strategy to ensure that the right product blend is offered, at the right price and in the right place, and that it is promoted through the right communication medium/media.

Questions for self-assessment

To assess your progress, answer these questions:
1. What is market segmentation?
2. Explain how market segmentation, targeting and positioning interrelate.
3. Refer to the case study above, and do the following activities:
    a. Select a market segment for one of the three product concepts listed in the study.
    b. Discuss the steps that you would follow in segmenting the market.
    c. What targeting strategy would you use to reach this market?
    d. What process will you follow in positioning the product concept?
    e. Draw a positioning map for your selected product concept.
    f. Develop a marketing strategy for your selected product concept.
    g. Visit the website of the South African Advertising Research Foundation (www. saarf.co.za) and select an LSM group to which you would market the product you have selected.

Endnote references

1. Kotler, P. 2000. *Marketing Management: Analysis, Planning, Implementation and Control*. London: Prentice-Hall.
2. Kotler, P. and Keller, K.L. 2005. *Marketing Management*. 12th ed. USA: Pearson Prentice-Hall.
3. Schiffman, L.G. and Kanuk, L.L. 1997. *Consumer Behaviour*. 6th ed. London: Prentice-Hall.
4. Kotler, op. cit.
5. Lamb, C.W., Hair, J.F., McDaniel, C., Boshoff, C. and Terblanché, N.S. 2004. *Marketing*. 2nd ed. Cape Town: Oxford University Press.
6. Lamb et al., op. cit.
7. Hawkins, D.I., Best, R.J. and Coney, A. 2004. *Consumer Behaviour: Building Marketing Strategy*. 9th ed. New York: McGraw-Hill/Irwin.
8. Hawkins et al., op. cit.
9. Du Plessis, P.J. and Rousseau, G.G. 1999. *Buyer Behaviour: A Multi-cultural Approach*. 2nd ed. Johannesburg: International Thomson Publishing.
10. Ibid.
11. Sheth, N.J., Mittal, B. and Newman, B.I. 1999. *Consumer Behavior: Consumer Behavior and Beyond*. Orlando: Dryden.
12. Du Plessis and Rousseau, op. cit.
13. Sheth et al., op. cit.
14. Du Plessis and Rousseau, op. cit.
15. Lamb et al., op. cit.
16. Du Plessis, P.J., Jooste, C.J. and Strydom, J.W. 2001. *Applied Strategic Marketing*. Johannesburg: Heinemann.
17. Kotler et al., op. cit.
18. Lamb et al, op. cit.
19. Hawkins et al., op. cit.
20. Lamb, C.W., Hair, J.F., McDaniel, C., Boshoff, C. and Terblanché, N.S. 2000. *Marketing*. Cape Town: Oxford University Press.
21. Kotler, P., Armstrong, G., Saunders, J. and Wong, V. 1996. *Principles of Marketing*. Hertfordshire: Prentice-Hall.
22. Lamb et al., op. cit.
23. Available on the internet from: www.saarf.co.za.
24. 2004. Certificate in Marketing and Customer Centricity. Study Manual. Johannesburg: University of Johannesburg.
25. Lamb et al., op. cit.
26. Lamb et al., op. cit.
27. 2004, op. cit.
28. Lamb et al., op. cit.
29. 2004. Certificate in Marketing and Customer Centricity. Study Manual. Johannesburg: University of Johannesburg.

12 The consumer decision-making process

After studying this chapter, you should be able to:

- ○ explain the process that consumers undergo when engaging in decision-making
- ○ explain why consumers engage in decision-making
- ○ illustrate the five stages in the consumer decision-making process
- ○ describe the impact of the level of consumer involvement on the decision-making process
- ○ illustrate and explain the influence of information search, and individual and environmental influences on the consumer's final decision
- ○ distinguish between four types of individuals involved in decision-making
- ○ distinguish between habitual, limited and extended decision-making
- ○ explain the importance of post-buying evaluation
- ○ explain the differences between satisfaction, dissatisfaction and cognitive dissonance
- ○ explain the marketing implications of the consumer decision-making process.

12.1 Introduction

The success of any business depends on the development of effective marketing strategies. Since marketing focuses on target markets, it is necessary to analyse and understand the complex activities, both physical and mental, that consumers engage in if we want to design effective marketing strategies.

Consumer analysis includes an evaluation of four interrelated dimensions, namely, cognition, behaviour, environment and marketing strategies, in order for marketers to obtain a profile of the target market. While **cognition** refers to the psychological processes that consumers experience, **behaviour** is the overt actions that they perform. For example, if you feel hungry on campus you may evaluate whether to buy a sandwich, a burger or a doughnut, considering the cost or nutritional value of each. This action of assessment is referred to as 'cognition'. After evaluating which type of food has the greatest potential to fulfil your need, you would go to the cafeteria and buy the one you have decided on. This act is your behaviour. The stimuli external to consumers that influence their cognitions and behaviours are referred to as the **'environment'**. In the same example, the external stimuli may be the price of the item or the nutritional value. **Marketing strategy** is made up of the processes by which marketers create marketing stimuli, such as adverts, price, products and stores, and locate them in consumer environments. For example, you may take into consideration the promotion that the cafeteria is offering – if you buy a sandwich you will get a soft drink for only R2.00.

The analysis process is illustrated in Figure 12.1.

Need	Cognition (search for alternatives)	Cognition (evaluation)	Purchase	Post-buying evaluation
Hungry ?	Buy a sandwich? Buy a burger? Buy a doughnut?	**External stimuli** eg. Cost Nutritional value **Internal stimuli** eg. I enjoyed the sandwich the last time I bought it **Marketing strategy** Advertising eg. Promotion on sand- Price wich that offers a cold Products drink for only R2.00	**BUY A SANDWICH**	**Need/Problem solved** No longer hungry-sandwich was good

Figure 12.1: Consumer analysis

Figure 12.1 indicates that stimuli, together with limited disposable income, force consumers to weigh the pros and cons of available alternatives in order to obtain maximum utility from scarce resources.

Therefore, behaviour can be seen as a decision-making process that takes the form of problem-solving actions. This process is not a single activity or step. Rather, consumers need to identify and evaluate choices, explore the results of particular actions and analyse the consequences of their behaviour once they have bought something. This means that consumers do not just buy objects, but also solutions to problems. Furthermore, consumer decision-making is influenced by a large number of individual and environmental variables. The former encompasses variables that control internal thought processes while the latter involves influences that are external to consumers. An understanding of consumer behaviour and the decision-making process is therefore a critical element that enables marketers to know, serve and influence consumers.

12.2 The consumer decision-making process

Consumers are continuously making decisions about what products and services to consume. There are two fundamental reasons why individuals must make decisions:
1. They have to satisfy their needs and desires.
2. Frequently, more than one choice or alternative will satisfy their needs.

For whichever reason, consumers have to make decisions, and consumer decision-making determines what goods and services people will want, buy, own and use.

Consumer behaviour is triggered by needs. Consumer decision-making directs needs by assessing and selecting the actions that will fulfil them. However, the process of consumer decision-making, unlike consumer actions, cannot be observed. Consumer decision-making is a cognitive process that consists of those mental activities that determine what activities are undertaken to remove a tension state caused by a need.

Consumer decision-making is very similar to problem-solving. A problem arises when someone seeks a goal or particular end-state, but is uncertain as to the best solution to the problem. In consumer decision-making, the unsatisfied want is the problem and the solution is the act of buying something to satisfy the want. Therefore, a decision or a solution is a course of action that provides a desired result to a perceived state of need. This implies that problem-solving is associated with the perceptual state of a particular consumer.

Perception is the whole process by which an individual becomes aware of the environment and interprets it so that it will be congruent with their own frame of reference.[1] A problem occurs only when consumers perceive a difference between their present situation and what they want. For example, a matriculant realises that a matric is not enough to get her a good job, perhaps in middle management. She recognises a problem of inadequate qualifications, and so the need for further education arises. This unfulfilled need creates a tension state that must be eliminated by the fulfilment of the need. Thus, the student evaluates possible courses of action by speaking to others and seeking information. She learns that possible courses of action are to register for a degree at a South African university, a diploma at a technikon or a short course at a private college. After evaluating these alternatives, the student will choose a course of action that will achieve what she wants. This may sound like a simple cause-and-effect process, but in reality it can become rather complex.

The consumer decision-making process is a sequential and repetitive set of psychological and physical activities ranging from problem recognition to post-buying behaviour. Since the stages in the process do not necessarily follow each other in strict order, consumers can launch into any stage in the process and follow any order, or even skip certain activities. However, the consumers' final decision depends upon certain influential variables that can affect any of the stages.

When focusing on the decision-making process of individual consumers, it is obvious that the basic decision made by the individual is whether to spend or not to spend, thereby saving. As we have seen, the outcome of the individual's decision will depend on many influencing variables, which can be divided into internal or individual influencing variables (see Chapters 7, 8, 9 and 10) and external influencing variables (see Chapters 3, 4 and 5). Needs or motives, personality, perception, learning, attitudes and lifestyle are **individual influencing variables** that control internal thought processes. *External* influences that direct internal thought processes include culture, social influences, reference groups and family. Other factors influencing decision-making are personal characteristics (see Chapter 6), environment (Chapter 3) and marketing (Chapters 15, 16 and 17).

12.3 Buying situations

Consumers do not function in isolation – they are influenced by many individual and environmental factors that can collectively be referred to as the 'psychological domain' or field. These variables constantly and simultaneously interact, and play a significant role in the final outcome of consumers' choices.

In any buying situation, individuals absorb information from their external environment and integrate or combine it with their inner needs, motives, perceptions and attitudes. The choice they make may also be influenced by the past, the act of recalling and personality factors. The past may operate through experience or learned patterns of behaviour and patterns of thinking, many of which are unconscious. For example, while planning a holiday you might recall that a travel agent at Flight Centre, who planned your holiday, offered you a good package and gave efficient service. In addition to past product experiences, anticipating future consequences of behaviour may also influence the choice someone makes when buying something now. Thus, you may expect – that is, anticipate – that you would have a problem-free holiday if you arrange the vacation with the same travel agent.

People are also profoundly influenced by their surrounding environment, including family and cultural influences, peer group pressure, reference groups, economic demands and advertising. For example, while planning your holiday you may:

○ choose places to visit – for example, the Drakensberg, Table Mountain, Kruger National Park – based on positive feedback from family and friends (or reference groups)
○ choose to visit Dubai, for example, because Flight Centre is offering an excellent holiday package (advertising)
○ choose a destination that will not be too expensive, because of the need to distribute limited resources, that is, money, across unlimited needs, while facing constant price increases (economic demand factors)
○ choose a destination where you can visit art galleries that display the kinds of paintings you like (cultural influences).

However, despite these pressures, the decision whether to buy or not in the final buying situation is an individual one.

12.4 The stages in the decision-making process

We now explore the five stages in the consumer decision-making process, as illustrated in Figure 12.2.

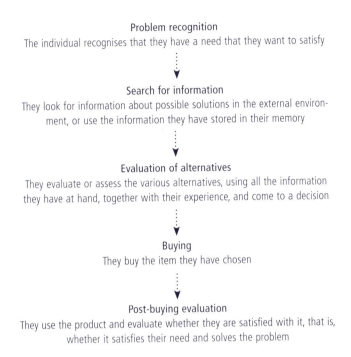

Figure 12.2: The stages in the decision-making process[2]

12.4.1 Problem recognition

The first stage entails the recognition of a problem. A problem arises when consumers recognise a difference between what they perceive as the current or actual state of affairs and the state of affairs that they want. Problem recognition is an awareness of the need to change the existing state to conform to the desired or ideal state. For example, a stressed chief executive officer (CEO) of a major South African company may recognise that she has not taken a holiday for a long time, and therefore needs a vacation. Problem recognition is predominantly a perceptual phenomenon. The difference between the existing and desired state of affairs triggers a state of motivated behaviour. The result is the development of a spectrum of mental activities and attitudinal reactions which we call **'cognitive processes'**. The CEO evaluates places that she likes and can visit. She obtains information on various holiday packages and offerings from brochures, travel agents, resorts, family, friends and reference groups.

The process of problem recognition may vary widely, depending on the effect of the various influencing factors. Three factors that affect need or problem recognition are information stored in memory, individual differences and environmental influences. In addition, social influences are important for consumers who value the response of others. Need or problem recognition, especially in complex decision-making, is likely to be multi-faceted and complex.

Problem recognition can take place at every stage of the decision-making process:
○ Problems associated with whether a product is **needed** – the most basic level of problem recognition.
○ Problems concerning **what product** to buy or which brand to select – resulting from the information search and processing.
○ Problems concerned with whether to buy for **cash or on credit**, or how to postpone the act of buying – resulting from the buying response.
○ Problems concerning whether consumers are **satisfied** with what they have bought – resulting from post-buying behaviour.

This is depicted in Figure 12.3.

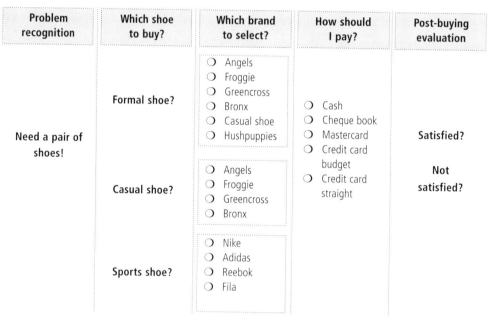

Problem recognition	Which shoe to buy?	Which brand to select?	How should I pay?	Post-buying evaluation
Need a pair of shoes!	Formal shoe?	○ Angels ○ Froggie ○ Greencross ○ Bronx ○ Casual shoe ○ Hushpuppies	○ Cash ○ Cheque book ○ Mastercard ○ Credit card budget ○ Credit card straight	Satisfied? Not satisfied?
	Casual shoe?	○ Angels ○ Froggie ○ Greencross ○ Bronx		
	Sports shoe?	○ Nike ○ Adidas ○ Reebok ○ Fila		

Figure 12.3: Problem recognition in the stages of decision-making

Most consumer problems arise as a result of internal and external barriers. **Internal barriers** include distorted perceptions and negative attitudes. **External barriers** include lack of funds and credit facilities, the unavailability of a product, the need for more information, uncertainty about the expected outcome because of unforeseen circumstances, the inability to make a decision and the lack of criteria on which to base post-buying assessment.

Most consumer problems arise as a result of the following:

○ **Assortment inadequacies**: This situation comes about when consumers' supplies of a particular item are running out, for example when we reach the end of a tube of toothpaste.
○ **New information**: This creates states of awareness that make consumers feel the need for products and services and view them as solutions to their problems, for example when a fitness fanatic sees an advert for a new home exercising machine that is easy to use and highly effective.
○ **Expanded desires**: People are continuously driven by their desire to improve their standard of living, which results in a desire for new goods and services, for example people who own a small car usually want a bigger car. These expanded desires can be caused by consumers' constantly changing roles, lifestyles, views and images.
○ **Expanded or reduced means**: These will cause consumer problems. An increase in income will almost always mean an increase in consumer spending, for example someone who gets a job promotion and therefore a pay increase might decide they need to build a swimming pool in their garden. A financial loss or loss of employment can have the opposite effect, for example someone who has just been retrenched may feel the need to move into a smaller house, and accept that they cannot have a swimming pool. In other words, consumers' financial resources are a major factor in determining how much and what goods and services they will consume.

12.4.2 The search for, and processing of, information

The second stage is the search for and processing of information. In many buying situations, once the consumer has recognised the problem, they begin to look for information. **Consumer search** is the mental and physical activities undertaken by consumers to obtain information on identified problems. It is a learning process by which consumers become aware of alternative products or brands, specific stores, specific trading centres, prices of products, terms of sale and consumer services. The process provides information that is necessary to the consumer when they are evaluating alternatives in order to arrive at the choice that produces the best benefits at the lowest cost. It is selective, since consumers choose information that is most in keeping with their wants and which is most likely to correspond with their views, beliefs, personality and attitudes.

The search consumers engage in may be internal or external. An **internal search** concerns information in consumers' memories, and they will use this to shorten an otherwise lengthy process. The information comes from their learning processes in the past. Someone wanting to buy a car, for example, might remember that other members of his family always bought Toyotas because they believed the cars were reliable and economical, and had good resale value. As well as such experiences with a product, internal searches based on the process of learning include such things as interaction with a salesperson and consumer advisory services, parking facilities, store layout, availability of items and prices paid for items. The consumer buying the car might also remember that his father said that he always received good after-sales service from the local Toyota dealership.

Consumers also get information from outside their experience to help their decision-making. This is an **external search**. This type of search is affected by individual differences and environmental influences. **Individual differences** include consumer resources, motivation and involvement, knowledge, attitudes, personality, lifestyle and demographics. **Environmental influences** include personal information sources; the business and marketing forces of advertising, in-store promotions and personal selling; neutral sources such as booklets, brochures and pamphlets; human sources such as financial consultants; and social and cultural influences. For example, the car buyer may speak to salespeople at various dealerships, talk to family and friends, read car magazines and test-drive different makes and models of cars.

Figure 12.4 depicts the influence of internal and external factors in the search for, and processing of, information.

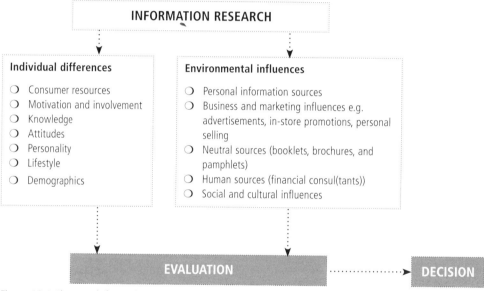

Figure 12.4: The search for and processing of information

From this we can see that one of the main challenges facing marketers is to present consumers with information on which to base their decisions. Ariely[3] found that controlling the information flow can help consumers to better match their preferences, have better memory and knowledge about the domain they are examining, and be more confident in their judgements.

Consumer involvement in decision-making

The process of consumer decision-making will depend on the individual consumer's level of involvement in that process. The extent of the involvement is determined by the extent to which a consumer feels a product or brand will lead to results that they value. Consumer involvement is therefore a motivational state of arousal that a person experiences about a purchase, and includes both feelings and thoughts.[4] Product involvement implies that the product is important to a consumer's self-identity, and it can bring strong attitudes and preferences to the surface. The more important and central the results are to the consumer, the higher is the level of personal involvement in a purchase.

Assael[5] categorises the distinction between high and low levels of involvement in terms of beliefs, preferences and attitudes. A low involvement purchase has taken place when consumers do not consider the product to be sufficiently important to their belief systems and do not significantly identify with the product. Low involvement decision-making implies that consumers may act without thinking and may not even be concerned about brand or product differences. Conversely, high involvement decision-making suggests that consumers may think carefully about the process of buying something.

It is evident that a relationship exists between the level of involvement and the degree of decision-making. The higher the level of purchase involvement, the more intensive or the greater the degree of decision-making.

The primary ingredients for enduring involvement are the product's importance to the self-image of a consumer, an ongoing interest in the product, the product's emotional appeal and its badge value to the consumer's reference groups.[6] The basic conditions for situational involvement in a product are perceived risk and badge value to the reference group. **Perceived risk** is the amount of risk the consumer perceives in the buying decision as a result of uncertainty about the decision and/or the potential consequences of a poor decision. **Badge value** means that a person becomes involved with a purchase because it is socially desirable. For example, you may want to buy a pair of Soviet jeans because your friends think they are 'cool'. Both types of involvement lead to higher levels of information processing, which means greater information search and an evaluation of brand options on a wider set of evaluative criteria. McColl-Kennedy and Fetter[7] found that involvement influences consumers' propensity to search externally. Such information processing reflects complex decision-making.

Types of consumer decision-making

Although there are many different levels of consumer decision-making, three distinct types can be recognised, that is, habitual, limited and extended decision-making. As consumers move from an extremely low level of purchase involvement to a higher level, the decision-making process becomes increasingly complex, moving from habitual decision-making to limited decision-making to extended decision-making. However, these types of decision processes cannot be clearly separated from one another, but instead blend into one another, and the buying process changes as buying involvement increases.

We now briefly explore the three types of decision-making:

1. **Habitual decision-making**: Consumer satisfaction with a product or service may lead to repeat buying and, gradually, to buying based on habit. Habitual buyer

behaviour is based on experience and is a way of simplifying the process of decision-making by decreasing the need for information search and evaluation of
brands, for example with regard to toothpaste or soap. Habitual decision-making
exists when there is low involvement with the buying process, and it results in
repeat buying behaviour. Habitual decisions can be categorised into brand loyalty
and repeat buying behaviour.

a. *Brand loyalty*: At first consumers may be deeply involved in choosing a
   product. Having selected a brand through a complex decision-making process,
   consumers buy it again and again without thinking about it further. They
   become committed to the brand they have chosen, because they feel that it
   meets their overall needs. For a true state of brand loyalty to exist, there must
   be some degree of psychological commitment to the brand.[8]
b. *Repeat buying behaviour*: This is often misinterpreted as brand loyalty. However,
   while the latter implies a psychological commitment to the brand, the former
   simply means that consumers buy the same brand over and over again. In
   other words, repeat buying behaviour refers to the pattern of brand choice over
   time, with or without psychological commitment.

2. **Limited decision-making**: This fills the gap between habitual decision-making
   and extended decision-making. In its simplest form, limited decision-making is
   closely related to habitual decision-making. This is because in limited decision-
   making consumers are not highly involved with the alternatives. The available
   alternatives are similar in essential features and there is less need for high involvement and evaluative buying.
3. **Extended decision-making**: This is the response to a high level of buying
   involvement, where internal and external information searches are followed by a
   complex evaluation of many alternatives. After buying a product, consumers will
   evaluate it carefully. Relatively few consumer decisions reach such an extreme level
   of complexity, where extensive problem-solving takes place. However, extended
   decision-making usually happens when a consumer buys a house, a personal
   computer, a car or a complex recreational item, and in other high involvement
   buying situations that require the decision-maker to progress relatively slowly and
   cautiously through all the stages of the decision-making process. Extended or real
   decision-making is characterised by conscious planning, and occurs:
   a. when durable products are bought
   b. when something is expensive, or extremely important to the consumer
   c. when experience in a similar situation resulted in disappointment
   d. when the consumer becomes aware that their behaviour patterns differ drasti-
      cally from those that are generally acceptable.[9]

Habitual, limited and extended decision-making are respectively associated with
minimal, limited and extensive search effort.

12.4.3 The evaluation of alternatives

The evaluation of alternative resolutions to a problem is the third step in the consumer decision-making process. Consumer evaluation is the act of identifying alternative solutions to a problem and assessing the relative merits and demerits of each. When evaluating alternatives, consumers compare product features and assess them according to pre-established criteria. For example, a car buyer may choose between a VW, a Toyota and an Opel. Evaluation criteria are the limits which consumers decide are acceptable when searching for a solution to their problems. The criteria for evaluation are the standards, characteristics or specifications used by consumers to compare products and brands. Consumers use different evaluation criteria when evaluating products and stores, and change the criteria in response to the situation or particular environment. The criteria for buying a car, for example, may include safety features, durability, economy, price, appearance, performance and resale value.

Evaluative criteria are moulded and influenced by individual and environmental variables. Individual influences, such as personality and attitudes, have an impact on expected outcomes. This is because consumers buy the products towards which they hold favourable and positive attitudes and which are in keeping with their personalities. Schiffman and Kanuk[10] identify four types of individuals involved in decision-making:

1. The **economic individual** takes a calculated, rational decision based on complete information, for example a car buyer who carefully considers issues of economy such as cost, fuel consumption and resale value when choosing a car.
2. The **passive individual** is not knowledgeable and can be manipulated by the marketer. They react impulsively and irrationally, for example the car buyer who is easily influenced by an advert claiming that the buyer's social status will improve if they buy the advertised make of car.
3. The **emotional individual** takes consumer decisions based entirely on personal and irrational needs, for example a car buyer who buys a car only because their family always owned that make.
4. The **cognitive individual** bases consumer decisions on information from the environment, on social influences, on personal needs, attitudes and perception, and on experience, for example the car buyer who carefully considers all the evaluative criteria and actively seeks information from various sources before making a decision.

It is obvious that individuals get involved in varying degrees of evaluation, based on their personal orientations. Ideally, the cognitive individual best represents consumer behaviour, since the theory of consumer decision-making focuses on the behaviour of cognitive consumers that actively and rationally evaluate a range of products in order to arrive at the decision that provides optimum utility and satisfaction.

To sum up, evaluation brings a consumer to the point of making a decision on a specific course of action.

12.4.4 The response/buying decision

The fourth step is the consumer's response or decision. Consumer decision is the outcome of evaluation, and involves the mental process of selecting the most desirable alternative from a set of options that a consumer has generated. The most suitable choice is the one that comes closest to the evaluation criteria formulated by the consumer. It is the data obtained as a result of search activity and effort that lays the foundation for the evaluation and decision. The appropriate decision is dependent upon adequate information.

12.4.5 Post-buying evaluation or response

Post-buying response is the final stage in the consumer decision-making process. The reason for someone entering the consumer decision-making process in the first place is the perception of a difference between what they have and what they need. Consumers therefore buy things in order to fulfil needs and seek greater satisfaction. Hence, a crucial question from a marketing point of view is whether consumers are satisfied once they have bought a particular product.

Thus, **post-buying assessment** involves a consumer's evaluation of the performance of the product or service, in relation to the criteria, once it has been bought, that is, it is the consumer's perception of the outcome of the consumption process. The post-buying phase involves different forms of psychological processes that consumers can experience after buying something.

Post-buying learning means that after buying a product or service, the consumer discovers something about it, stores this new knowledge in their long-term memory, modifies relevant attitudes and is ready for the next decision process with an improved base of knowledge.[11] Some researchers[12] maintain that the result of buying can either be satisfaction or dissatisfaction, which refers to an *emotional* response to an evaluation of a product or service. Du Plessis et al.[13] include another possible outcome – in the form of a *neutral* assessment.

Figure 12.5 on the next page presents the process of post-buying evaluation and response tendencies, which we now examine.

Post-buying satisfaction

A positive assessment of the purchase decision results in post-buying satisfaction. Satisfaction occurs when the outcome, which may be a product, brand or store, and the conditions surrounding its purchase, are matched with the consumer's expectations. Lee et al.[14] found that perceived service quality determines satisfaction, rather than vice versa. During shopping, consumers reach their final choices with quite different decision goals in mind. Shiv and Huber[15] believe that while some consumers' goals could be choice-oriented – deciding on which alternative to buy from a set of choices, the goal of others may be value-oriented – evaluating each alternative with the aim of obtaining 'good value for money', and the goal of others still may be anticipated satisfaction

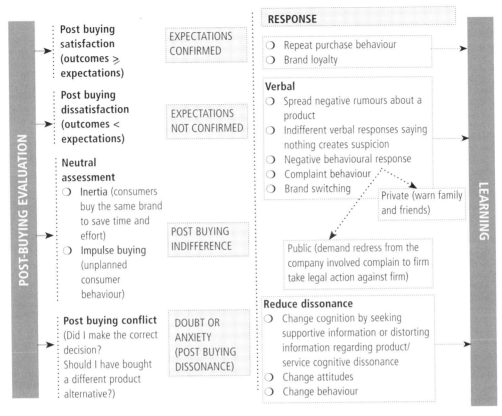

Figure 12.5: Post-buying evaluation

– where consumers assess the likely satisfaction with each alternative before making the final choice.

Post-buying dissatisfaction

Conversely, a negative assessment results in post-buying dissatisfaction. Consumers experience dissatisfaction when the outcome does not match their expectations or when they feel that the product they bought falls short in significant ways. Performance of the bought product/brand is found to be the most important determinant of satisfaction. When people realise that an alternative would have been more attractive and fulfilling, they tend to be more dissatisfied with the product they chose.[16] Hence, satisfaction or dissatisfaction with the product attributes determine the consumers' overall satisfaction or dissatisfaction with the product they have bought. Therefore, satisfaction or dissatisfaction stems respectively from the confirmation or disconfirmation of the consumers' expectations.[17] A neutral assessment results in post-buying indifference (see below).[18]

Consumer responses to a dissatisfying purchase may be verbal or behavioural, that is, consumers may talk about or act out their dissatisfaction in some way:

○ **Verbal response**: While a positive verbal response may cognitively reinforce the buying decision, a negative one may result in a consumer effectively spreading negative rumours about a product. Equally dangerous to the product's reputation is indifferent verbal responses – where consumers say neither negative nor positive things about the product – or responses that can cause other potential consumers to be suspicious about the product. Cognitively, satisfaction is part of the dynamic buying process and influences repeat buying intentions.[19] Positive behavioural responses usually involve repeat buying behaviour or brand loyalty in the case of satisfaction.

○ **Behavioural response**: A negative behavioural response may involve complaint behaviour or brand switching in the case of dissatisfaction:
  – *Complaint behaviour* can be private, such as warning friends or switching products. Also, consumers may take public actions, such as demanding redress from the company involved, complaining to the firm or taking legal action against it.
  – *Brand switching* is one of the ways in which consumers having problems with a product or service may express their dissatisfaction.[20] Dissatisfaction with products is one of the reasons for consumers switching brands, so as to avoid more dissatisfaction in the future.[21] Brand switching can also be caused by some inner desire for novelty or variety. While the former is called 'instrumental brand switching' the latter refers to 'exploratory brand switching'.[22]

A neutral or indifferent behavioural response

This type of response can include inertia or impulse buying:

○ **Inertia** exists when consumers buy the same brand because they feel it is not worth the time and effort to search for an alternative.

○ **Impulse buying** is an unplanned consumer buying pattern. There is no thought before buying a product, and virtually no external search activity.

Post-buying conflict

At times, consumers undergo post-buying conflict, and question whether they made the correct decision or should have bought a different product. Consumers may experience doubt or anxiety, especially after making a difficult, important and long-lasting decision. This type of anxiety is called '**post-buying dissonance**'. Dissonance occurs because making a relatively permanent commitment to a particular choice of product requires us to give up the attractive features of the alternatives that we did not choose.[23]

In some cases, consumers may try to reduce this dissonance by changes in cognition and attitudes: 'They will find a balance in their psychological field by seeking supportive information or distorting information regarding the product or service.'[24] This response is termed 'cognitive dissonance'. **Cognitive dissonance** belongs to the family of cognitive consistency theories. Each consumer has many cognitions about themselves or other people and the decisions they make. If these elements follow logically from one another, consonant cognitions exist, but if there is logical inconsistency, dissonant cognitions arise. Since dissonance produces unpleasant feelings, the individual will try to reduce the amount of dissonance experienced.

It is vital for marketers to know whether consumer attitudes towards their product or service change *negatively* or *positively*. Undoubtedly, positive responses prove that marketing strategies have been successful. Marketers can use negative responses as guidelines for corrective action.

Although post-buying assessment is the final stage in the consumer decision-making process, it is not necessarily the *end* of the process. The information gained as a result of buying and post-buying evaluation is stored in individuals' memories as part of their experience. Consumers remember this information when starting another buying decision-making process. In other words, 'regardless of the outcome, postpurchase evaluation is a learning process that provides feedback to the consumer and is stored as information for future reference'.[25]

12.5 Marketing implications

Understanding how consumers engage in analysis and decision-making when undertaking purchases will enable marketers to take advantage of market opportunities, to target markets appropriately and to design effective marketing strategies. Such knowledge will assist in market segmentation and product positioning, and will enable marketers to know, service and influence consumers.

By analysing the internal thought process of consumers as they undergo the process of decision-making, marketers can discover the criteria that consumers use in buying decisions and the variables that influence the decisions. Having such insight will enable marketers to effectively manipulate external influences to attract consumers and enhance market share. It will also enable them to predict future consumer behaviour.

Assessing consumers' product involvement and level of decision-making will enable marketers to provide consumers with the right kind and amount of information on which to base their decisions. This will enable marketers to guard against information overload, to provide relevant information and to develop suitable communication campaigns. Furthermore, the occurrence of consumer dissatisfaction and dissonance emphasises that information provided must be correct and should not exaggerate product performance. To encourage purchases and to reduce perceived risk, product samples may be strategically distributed.

Evidently, consumers engage in post-buying evaluation, which impacts on future consumption behaviour, brand preference and loyalty, and positive word-of-mouth communication, thereby indicating that consumers are rational beings. Hence, it is imperative for marketers to devise strategies for enhancing post-buying satisfaction. While effective service or product quality delivery is the ultimate goal, complaint behaviour will exist. The implication is that marketing management should not discourage or suppress complaints as this often results in increasing levels of consumer complaints.[26]

Furthermore, irate consumers may engage in negative word-of-mouth communication, the consequences of which can be detrimental. Such communication also signifies one external source of information that marketers have no control over. However, a mechanism at their disposal is to engage in effective complaint management, which is imperative as it influences repeat buying behaviour.[27]

While it is crucial for marketers to be responsive to complaints, they need to investigate the underlying source or reason for the unhappiness. This will equip them to take corrective action. Moreover, they should adopt strategies to provide easy access to dissonance-reduction information. Likewise, it is important that they maintain the segment of satisfied consumers, sustain sales, and instil and harness loyal behavioural patterns in consumers. Marketers will also be able to extend their market by designing effective in-store and advertising appeals and strategies to capture the impulsive buyer's attention.

Despite the internal and external influences on the consumer engaging in decision-making, the final decision of whether to buy or not rests with the consumer. Securing a significant market segment would therefore signal to the marketer that the strategy adopted is effective. Failing to capture a suitable market or to reach the target market effectively would also provide valuable feedback to marketing strategists to redesign the marketing approach, taking cognisance of consumer needs, information search and processing behaviour and decision-making patterns. This will enable marketers to capitalise on market trends and to gain competitive advantage or secure a substantial market segment. Undoubtedly, living in an age of continuous improvement and technological advancement, market share can be enhanced by service/product development and innovation.

Case study

Instead of the usual case study, we ask you to examine your own buying behaviour:
1. Identify a product that you or your household buy every month, such as toothpaste. Explain the process you follow in making the decision on which brand of toothpaste to buy and which store to buy it from. Identify the extent to which you engage in each step in the decision-making process.
2. Explain the process that you have followed when buying a cell phone/TV set/car/expensive item of clothing. Identify the extent to which you engaged in each step of the decision-making process.
3. How did your decision-making process in 1 differ from that of 2?

12.6 Summary

Consumers engage in decision-making because they have unlimited wants and limited resources to satisfy these wants. To make sure that their most important needs are fulfilled first and that they derive maximum utility from their purchases, consumers undergo the process of decision-making. Sometimes a consumer can go through the entire decision-making process without even realising it, while at other times consumer decision-making may be complex, deliberate and time-consuming. The level of decision-making that the consumer engages in depends on the extent of their involvement in a particular purchase. The greater the degree of satisfaction derived from buying a product or service, the greater the chances are of repeat buying behaviour. Consumers experiencing dissatisfaction with what they have bought may experience cognitive dissonance or post-buying regret.

Our analysis of the various stages of the consumer decision-making process showed that the buying of consumer goods and major durable products are much alike. Irrespective of the situation, consumer buying behaviour is the outcome of rational considerations in selecting goods and services that fulfil consumption goals. The only variation is in the emphasis or value that the individual places on the various stages in the decision-making process.

Questions for self-assessment

To assess your progress, answer these questions:
1. Explain the nature of, and need for, consumer decision-making.
2. Illustrate and explain the five stages in the consumer decision-making process.
3. Illustrate and explain the search for, and processing of, information when engaging in consumer decision-making.
4. Explain the importance of post-buying evaluation in marketing management.
5. Explain the interrelationships between consumer involvement, search effort and consumer decision-making.
6. Distinguish between habitual, limited and extended decision-making, using examples.
7. Identify situations in which a consumer engages in habitual, limited and extended decision-making, giving examples of these situations.
8. Distinguish between satisfaction, dissatisfaction, post-buying indifference and cognitive dissonance with the aid of a flow chart or illustration.

Endnote references

1. Walters, C.G. and Bergiel, B.J. 1989. *Consumer Behavior: A Decision-Making Approach*. Cincinnati: South-Western College.
2. Adapted from Peter, J.P. and Olson, J.C. 2005. *Consumer Behavior & Marketing Strategy*. 7th ed. Boston: McGraw-Hill Irwin, p. 169.
3. Ariely, D. 2000. Controlling the information flow: Effects on consumers' decision making and preferences. *Journal of Consumer Research*, 27, 233–48.
4. Wilkie, W.L. 1990. *Consumer Behavior*. 2nd ed. New York: Wiley.
5. Assael, H. 1987. *Consumer Behavior and Marketing Action*. 3rd ed. Boston: Kent.
6. Assael, H. 1995. *Consumer Behavior and Marketing Action*. 4th ed. Cincinnati: South-Western College.

7. McColl-Kennedy, J.R. and Fetter, R.E. 2001. An empirical examination of the involvement of external search relationship in services marketing. *Journal of Services Marketing*, 15(2), 82–98.
8. Horton, R.L. 1984. *Buyer Behavior: A Decision-Making Approach*. Columbus: Merrill.
9. Van der Walt, A., Strydom, J.W., Marx, S. and Jooste, C.J. 1996. *Marketing Management*. 3rd ed. Cape Town: Juta.
10. Schiffman, L.G. and Kanuk, L.L. 2004. *Consumer Behaviour*. 8th ed. Upper Saddle River: Pearson Prentice-Hall.
11. Wilkie, op. cit.
12. Walters and Bergiel, op. cit.; and Engel, J.F., Blackwell, R.D. and Miniard, P.W. 1995. *Consumer Behavior*. 8th ed. Chicago: Dryden.
13. Du Plessis, P.J. and Rousseau, G.G. 2003. *Buyer Behaviour: A Multi-cultural Approach*. 3rd ed. Cape Town: Oxford University Press.
14. Lee, H., Lee, Y. and Yoo, D. 2000. The determinants of perceived service quality and its relationship with satisfaction. *Journal of Services Marketing*, 14(3), 217–31.
15. Shiv, B. and Huber, J. 2000. The impact of anticipating satisfaction on consumer choice. *Journal of Consumer Research*, 27, 202–16.
16. Tsiros, M. and Mittal, V. 2000. Regret: A model of its antecedents and consequences in consumer decision making. *Journal of Consumer Research*, 26, 401–17.
17. Sheth, J.N., Mittal, B. and Newman, B.I. 1999. *Customer Behavior: Consumer Behavior and Beyond*. Orlando: Dryden.
18. Du Plessis et al., op. cit.
19. LaBarbera, P.A. and Mazursky, D. 1983. A longitudinal assessment of consumer satisfaction/dissatisfaction: The dynamic aspect of the cognitive process. *Journal of Marketing Research*, 20(4), 393–405.
20. Kasper, H. 1988. On problem perception, dissatisfaction and brand loyalty. *Journal of Economic Psychology*, 9(3), 387–97.
21. Raju, P.S. 1984. Exploratory brand switching: An empirical examination of its determinants. *Journal of Economic Psychology*, 5(3), 201–21.
22. Ibid.
23. Hawkins, D.I., Best, R.J. and Coney, K.A. 2004. *Consumer Behavior: Building Marketing Strategy*. 9th ed. Boston: McGraw-Hill, Irwin.
24. Du Plessis et al., op. cit., pp. 53–4.
25. Assael, 1987, p. 29.
26. Hawkins et al., op. cit.
27. Cohen, J.B. and Chakravarti, D. 1990. Consumer psychology. *Annual Review of Psychology*, 41, 243–88.

13 Family decision-making

13.1 Introduction

As consumers, we interact with other people every day, especially with members of our families. The family, therefore, is possibly the most important reference group for consumer decision-making.

We begin this chapter with an examination of some basic consumer unit concepts. We discuss family decision-making and consumer behaviour, and explore the marketing implications of the family life cycle. We also consider the various roles of family members and their influence on decision-making.

There are at least three reasons for analysing families from a marketing strategy perspective:

1. An individual may not perform all the buying/consumption tasks for even a single product.
2. There is a long-term influence of family buying patterns on children's behaviour.
3. Children influence the family budget allocation and buying consumption behaviour.

13.2 The family as primary reference group

The family is a basic concept in society, but it is not easy to define because family composition and structure, as well as the roles played by the members, are almost always in transition.

Bearden and Etzel[1] define a reference group as any person or group of people that significantly influences an individual's behaviour. If an individual is not a member of such a group, he or she would aspire to membership. A primary reference group is a social aggregation that is sufficiently intimate and facilitates unrestricted face-to-face interaction.[2] The family is the most obvious example of a strongly influential primary reference group.

Traditionally, the family is defined as two or more persons related by blood, marriage or adoption, who reside together. The term 'household' is becoming a more important unit of analysis for marketers, because of the rapid growth in non-traditional families and non-family households. Martins[3] suggests two types of households:

1. A **multiple household** consists of one or more families, or a group of two or more persons, dependent on common or pooled income, and usually living in the same house. Its members need not be related by blood or marriage. People who usually sleep and eat under the same roof and, generally speaking, are bound by domestic and economic ties comprise a household unit.
2. A **single household** consists of one person who is financially independent of any person or household group, although he or she may be supporting people elsewhere.

Table 13.1 on the next page shows the estimated number of households in South Africa by province for 2004.

Marketers frequently use information on household numbers in estimating expenditure patterns on main expenditure items. Table 13.1 clearly shows that households in certain provinces are financially better off than those in other provinces. Gauteng, KwaZulu-Natal and the Western Province account for two thirds of total household expenditure in South Africa, while 50% of households reside in these provinces. Marketers can use the analysis on household expenditure patterns by expenditure items for calculating market potentials for individual items by demographic variable – province, population group, language group, income group, gender, etc. – or lifestyle measure. Marketers and other business organisations, as well as government structures, can take note of differences in expenditure patterns in different areas and compare the results to other countries to enable them to take strategic decisions.

Marketers can avoid the problem of whether to study families or households by using the term '**consumer unit**' (CU). The role of the family or CU in consumer decision-making is important for two reasons:

1. A CU buys many products.
2. Other CU members may heavily influence an individuals' buying decisions.

Table 13.1: Households in South Africa, 2004

Province	Households	Total expenditure (R billion)	Annual expenditure per household (R'000)
Gauteng	2 590 828	243	94
Western Cape	1 205 912	104	87
Northern Cape	257 851	12	48
Free State	862 846	41	47
KwaZulu-Natal	2 264 645	106	47
Mpumalanga	801 098	36	45
North West	1 037 668	42	41
Eastern Cape	1 681 769	56	33
Limpopo	1 274 279	33	26
South Africa	11 976 900	673	56

In most societies, three types of families dominate:
1. The **married couple**, a husband and wife, is the simplest structure.
2. The **nuclear family** consists of a husband and wife and a child or children. This is still common.
3. The **extended family** consists of the nuclear family plus other relatives, such as grandparents, uncles and aunts, cousins and parents-in-law.
4. The **single-parent family**, consisting of one parent and at least one child, is growing because of divorce, separation and out-of-wedlock births.

The predominant form of CU is largely influenced by the culture within which families exist. Khoza[5] found that the extended family was the norm among the majority of South Africa's population. However, these families are diminishing and becoming an exception, particularly in urban areas. The nuclear family is considered to stand a greater chance of a better quality of life and economic prosperity.

13.3 The functions of the family

The family as CU facilitates the socialisation of family members, contributes to their economic well-being, provides emotional support and shapes their lifestyles.

13.3.1 The socialisation of family members

Blackwell et al.[6] define **socialisation** as the process by which people develop their values, motivations and habitual activity. In other words, it is the process of absorbing a culture. Although many studies focus on how young people learn consumer skills, it is recognised as a lifelong process.[7]

The socialisation of family members from young children to adults is a central family function. In the case of young children, the process entails teaching children the basic values and types of behaviour consistent with their culture. These generally include moral and religious principles, interpersonal skills, dress and grooming standards, appropriate manners and speech, and the selection of suitable educational and occupational or career goals.

Marketers often target parents who are looking for help in the task of socialising their children. To this end, marketers are sensitive to the fact that the socialisation of young children provides an opportunity to establish a foundation on which later experiences continue to build throughout life.

Various studies[8] have focused on how children develop consumer skills. Many pre-adolescent children acquire their consumer behaviour norms by watching their parents and older siblings, who function as role models and sources of cues. In contrast, adolescents and teenagers are likely to look to their friends for models of acceptable consumer behaviour. Shared shopping experiences, that is, co-shopping, when mother and child shop together, also give children the opportunity to acquire in-store shopping skills. Co-shopping is a way for the parent to spend time with the children while also carrying out a necessary task.

Consumer-related socialisation also serves as a tool by which parents influence other aspects of the socialisation process. For instance, parents often promise to buy something for the child as a way to modify or control his or her behaviour.

'Intergenerational socialisation' refers to product or brand loyalty, or preference, passed from one generation to another, sometimes across three or four generations.

13.3.2 Economic well-being

Providing financial means, that is, money, to dependants is unquestionably a basic family function. However, the way in which the family divides its responsibilities for providing economic well-being has changed considerably during the past 25 years. The traditional roles of husband as economic provider and wife as homemaker and child-rearer are no longer valid. It is common for married women with children in urban areas of South Africa to be employed outside the home and for their husbands to share household responsibilities.

The economic role of children has also changed. Today, while many teenage children work, they rarely assist the family financially. Teenagers are expected to pay for their own amusements; others contribute to the costs of their formal education and prepare themselves to be financially independent.

13.3.3 Emotional support

Providing emotional support – love, affection and intimacy – to its members is an important core function of the contemporary family. The family provides support and encouragement, and helps its members to cope with decision-making and personal or social problems. If the family cannot help, it may turn to a counsellor, psychologist or other professional for assistance.

13.3.4 Suitable family lifestyles

Another important family function in terms of consumer behaviour is the establishment of a suitable lifestyle for the family. Upbringing, experience and the personal and jointly held goals of the parents determine the importance placed on education or career, on reading, on television viewing, on the learning of computer skills, on the frequency and quality of eating out, and on the selection of other entertainment and recreational activities. Family lifestyle commitments, including the allocation of time, greatly influence consumption patterns.

13.4 Family decision-making

The major focus of consumer and marketing research is on the individual as the unit of analysis. The research findings are concerned with describing, understanding and trying to predict how individuals buy products and how marketing strategies can be developed to more effectively influence this process. The area of family research is an exception: it views the family as a decision-making unit. **Family research** attempts to describe, understand and predict how family members interact and influence one another in terms of individual, family or household buying.

Marketers most often examine the attitudes and behaviour of the family member who they believe is the major decision-maker. Sometimes they also examine the attitudes and behaviour of the person most likely to be the primary user of a particular product or service.

13.4.1 Role behaviour

For a family to function as a cohesive unit, one or more family members must carry out various tasks. Different people may therefore carry out different tasks in the buying process. For this reason, family decision-making and buying processes are highly complex and difficult to study. Even with the individual as the unit of analysis, marketers find it difficult to try to understand consumer behaviour. However, with the family as the unit of analysis, the thinking, behaviours and environments of several people have to be taken into account, as do the interactions among them.

In a dynamic society, family-related duties are constantly changing. Schiffman and Kanuk[9] identify eight distinct roles in the family decision-making process. The number and identity of the family members who play these roles vary from family to family, and from product to product.

1. **Influencers** provide information to other members about a product or service.
2. **Gatekeepers** control the flow of information about a product or service into the family.
3. **Deciders** decide by themselves or with others whether to shop for, buy, use, consume or dispose of a specific product or service.
4. **Buyers** do the actual buying of a particular product or service.
5. **Preparers** transform the product, for example raw meat, into a form suitable for consumption by other family members, for example a cooked meat dish.
6. **Users** use or consume a particular product or service.
7. **Maintainers** service or repair products so that they will provide continued satisfaction.
8. **Disposers** decide on or carry out the disposal or discontinuation of a particular product or service.

Marketers need to communicate with the consumers assuming each of these roles, remembering that family members will assume different roles depending on the situation and product.

13.4.2 Husband-and-wife decision-making

Many studies investigating consumer decision-making have implicitly assumed that one individual in a family, most often the wife, makes all of the consumption choices for the family. This is puzzling, as research has clearly shown that when husbands and wives are polled independently of each other, their responses regarding consumer choices often vary significantly.[10] Krampf et al.[11] found more evidence of joint decision-making for the products that involve higher levels of involvement.

Marketers are interested in the relative amount of influence that a husband and a wife have when it comes to family consumer choices. Their relative influence on a particular consumer decision depends in part on the product and service category. It changes over time. Husband-and-wife decision-making also appears to be related to cultural influence.

Lucas[12] found that younger, urbanised, more educated families make more joint consumer decisions.

13.4.3 Influences on the decision-making process

According to Davis and Rigaux,[13] spouses exert different degrees of influence, depending on the decision stage, on the employment status and on gender:

○ **Influence of decision stage**: The information search stage tends to be carried out more by one spouse than jointly, particularly when compared to final decisions. This movement may be minimal in the case of many low involvement goods but more pronounced for goods that are risky or have high involvement for the family.

○ **Influence of employment**: The increasing number of urban women working outside the home, coupled with changing spouse roles, has affected the way in which couples divide their buying responsibilities.

○ **Influence of gender**: As the gender gap narrows, decisions are increasingly made jointly.

13.5 The family life cycle

Sociologists and consumer researchers have long been attracted to the concept of the family life cycle (FLC) as a means of depicting what was once a rather steady and predictable series of stages that most families progressed through. The current decline in the percentage of families that progress through a traditional FLC seems to be caused by these societal factors:

○ The increasing divorce rate.
○ The increase in out-of-wedlock births.
○ The decline in the number of extended families, as many young families move away to advance their job and career opportunities.

FLC analysis enables marketers to segment families in terms of a series of stages spanning the life course of a family unit. The FLC is a composite variable created by systematically combining such commonly used demographic variables as marital status, the size of the family, the age of family members – focusing on the age of the oldest or youngest child – and the employment status of the head of the household.

The ages of the parents and the relative amount of disposable income usually are inferred from the stage in the family life cycle.

13.5.1 The traditional family life cycle

We now explore the five basic stages of traditional FLC models.

Stage 1: Bachelorhood
The first FLC stage consists of young single men and women who have established households apart from their parents. Most members are fully employed; many are college or graduate students who have left their parents' homes.

Young single adults are apt to spend their incomes on rent, basic home furnishings, cars, travel, entertainment, clothing and accessories. It is relatively easy to reach this market segment, because many special interest publications target singles.

Marriage marks the transition from the bachelorhood stage to the honeymooner stage.

Stage 2: Honeymooners
The honeymoon stage starts immediately after the marriage vows are taken and generally continues until the arrival of the couple's first child. This FLC stage serves as a

period of adjustment to married life. The couples have available a combined income that often allows them to buy what they want or to save or invest their extra income. Honeymooners have considerable start-up expenses when establishing a new home – major and minor appliances, bedroom and living-room furniture, carpeting, curtaining, crockery and cutlery, and a host of utensils and accessory items. So-called 'homemaker' magazines are an important source of product information at this stage.

Stage 3: Parenthood

When a couple has its first child, the honeymoon is considered over. Sometimes also called the 'full nest stage', the parenthood stage usually lasts longer than 20 years. Because of its long duration, this stage can be divided into shorter phases: the pre-school phase, the elementary school phase, the high school phase and the tertiary education phase.

Throughout these phases, the interrelationships of family members and the structure of the family gradually change, while the financial resources of the family change significantly. Many magazines cater to the information and entertainment needs of parents and children.

Stage 4: Post-parenthood

Post-parenthood, when all the children have left home, is traumatic for some parents and liberating for others. For many parents, this so-called 'empty nest stage' signifies a kind of 'rebirth', a time for doing all the things they could not do while the children were at home and they had to worry about soaring educational expenses. The mother can now further her education, enter or re-enter the job market and seek new interests. The father can now indulge in existing hobbies or pursue new ones. For both, it is a time to travel, to entertain, and perhaps to refurnish their home or sell it and buy a smaller home.

Married couples tend to be most comfortable financially, and many 'empty nesters' retire while they are still in good health. Older consumers usually use TV as an important source of information and entertainment, preferring programmes that help them to 'keep up with what's happening', especially news and public affairs programmes.

Stage 5: Dissolution

Dissolution of the basic family unit occurs with the death of a spouse. The surviving spouse, usually the wife, tends to follow a more economical lifestyle. Some surviving spouses seek each other out for companionship; others enter into second, third or even fourth marriages.

13.5.2 Modifications to the FLC

The traditional FLC model has lost some of its ability to represent the stages that a family passes through, and has thus been modified. The underlying socio-demographic forces that drive the modified model include divorce and later marriages, with and without the presence of children. Marketers in South Africa often use the SAARF life-stage groups to segment consumer markets.[14]

The nine life-stage groups are as follows:

1. **At-home singles**:   *Up to 34 years old*
Live with parents
Not married/not living together
No children of their own/no dependants

2. **Starting-out singles**: *Up to 34 years old*
Not living with parents
Not married/not living together
No children of their own/no dependants

3. **Mature singles**:   *35–49 years old*
Not married/not living together
No children of their own/no dependants

4. **Young couples**:   *Up to 49 years old*
Married/living together
No children of their own/no dependants

5. **New parents**:   *Married/living together*
With children up to 12 years old
No children 13+ years old
Children dependent on them

6. **Mature parents**:   *Married/living together*
With children – at least one 13+ years old
Children dependent on them

7. **Single parents**:   *Not married/not living together*
With children of their own *and* children
dependent on them

8. **Golden nests**:   *50+ years old*
Married/living together
No children dependent on them *or* no children

9. **Left-alones**:   *50+ years old*
Not married/not living together
No children dependent on them *or* no children

The modified FLC model is more realistic as it recognises other forms of families than simply the nuclear family, like single-parent households. Figure 13.1 shows the percentage profile of the 9.8 million households in South Africa.

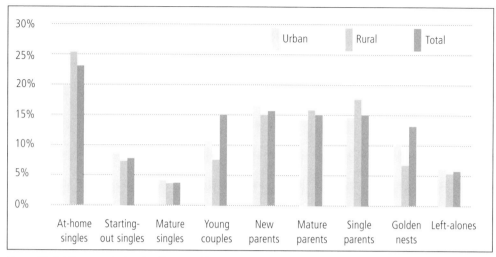

Figure 13.1: Life stages in South Africa 2004[15]

Non-traditional stages include non-family households, as well as family households, that is, those consisting of a single individual and of two or more unrelated individuals. Approximately 33% of all households comprise men and women living alone, or non-family households – starting-out singles, mature singles, single parents and left-alones. Approximately 41% of all households have children dependent on parents.

Figure 13.1 also illustrates the differences between *urban*, that is, living in closed settlements of at least 250 000 people, and *rural*, that is, those living in areas containing less than 500 people per square kilometre in South Africa.

13.5.3 Consumption in non-traditional families

When the status of households changes, the households become attractive targets for many marketers. In another sphere, the substantial increase in dual-income households, that is, working wives and the subset of working mothers, has also tended to confuse the assumptions about lifestyle implicit in family life cycle segmentation. The side-by-side existence of traditional and non-traditional FLC stages is another example of our opinion, which we express in this book frequently, that today's marketplace is complex in its diversity, and is a challenge for marketers to segment and serve.

13.6 Summary

Consumer reference groups serve as a frame of reference for individuals in their buying decisions. For many consumers, the family is the primary reference group for various attitudes and behaviours. The family is the prime target market for most products and product categories.

Socialisation is a core function of the family. Other functions are the provision of economic and emotional support and the pursuit of a suitable lifestyle for its members. The members of a family assume specific roles in their everyday functioning; such roles or tasks extend to the realm of consumer buying decisions. A family's decision-making style is often influenced by its lifestyle, roles and cultural factors.

The majority of consumer studies classify family consumer decisions as husband-dominated, wife-dominated, joint or autonomic decisions. The extent and nature of husband-and-wife influence in family decisions depends, in part, on the specific product or service being bought and selected cultural influences.

Classification of families by stage in the FLC model provides valuable insights into family consumer-related behaviour. Dynamic socio-demographic changes in society have resulted in many non-traditional stages that a family or non-family household might pass through, thus necessitating a modification of the traditional model. These non-traditional stages are becoming increasingly important to marketers, as they provide specific market niches.

Questions for self-assessment

To assess your progress, answer these questions:

1. How would you use the knowledge you have gained in this chapter in evaluating a new promotional campaign for a large gym chain? The campaign is aimed at increasing how often families visit gyms. What recommendations would you make?

2. How does the family influence the socialisation of children? What role does TV play in the socialisation of children?

3. Design a study investigating how families make holiday decisions. Which family member(s) would you interview? What kinds of questions would you ask? How would you assess the relative role of each family member in making holiday-related decisions?

4. Which of the family life cycle stages constitute the most lucrative segment(s) for the following products and services:
    a. McDonald's burgers
    b. pay-as-you-go cell phone contracts
    c. life assurance policies
    d. timeshare membership
    e. long-life milk?

Endnote references

1. Bearden, W.O. and Etzel, M.J. 1982. Reference group influences on product and brand purchase decisions. *Journal of Consumer Research*, 9, September, 184.
2. Witt, R.E. and Bruce, G.D. 1972. Group influence and brand choice. *Journal of Marketing Research*, 9, November, 440–3.
3. Martins, J.H. 2004. Household Expenditure in South Africa by Province, Population Group and Product. Report no. 322. Pretoria: Bureau of Market Research.
4. Ibid.
5. Cited in Brink, A. 1998. The marketing perception of grocery store retailers belonging to black business associations in Gauteng. Unpublished DCom thesis. Pretoria: Universiy of South Africa.
6. Blackwell, R.D., Miniard, P.W. and Engel, J.F. 2001. *Consumer Behavior*. 9th ed. Orlando: Harcourt, pp. 187–97.
7. Moschis, G.P. 1978. *Consumer Socialization*. Lexington: Lexington Books.
8. Moschis, G.P. 1985. The role of family communication in consumer socialization of children and adolescents. *Journal of Consumer Research*, 11, March, 898–913; Carlson, L. and Grossbart, S. 1988. Parental style and consumer socialization of children. *Journal of Consumer Research*, 15, June, 77–94; and Ward, S. 1974. Consumer socialization. *Journal of Consumer Research*, 1, September, 9.
9. Schiffman, L.G. and Kanuk, L.L. 2000. *Consumer Behaviour*. 7th ed. Upper Saddle River: Prentice-Hall.
10. Davis, H.L. 1970. Dimensions of marital roles in consumer decision-making. *Journal of Marketing Research*, 7, 168–77; and Hopper, J.S., Burns, A.C. and Sherrel, D.L. 1989. An assessment of the reliability of husband and wife self-report purchase decision-making measures. *Journal of the Academy of Marketing Science*, 17, 227–34.
11. Krampf, R.F., Burns, D.J. and Rayman, D.M. 1993. Consumer decision-making and the nature of the product: A comparison of husband and wife adoption process location. *Psychology and Marketing*, 10(2), 95–109.
12. Lucas, G.H.G. 1989. *The Task of Marketing Management*. Pretoria: Van Schaik.
13. Davis, H.L. and Rigaux, B.R. 1974. Perception of marital roles in decision processes. *Journal of Consumer Research*, 1, June, 5–14.
14. South African Advertising Research Foundation. 2004. All Media and Products Survey 2005. Johannesburg: SAARF.
15. Ibid.

14 Organisational buying behaviour

Learning Outcomes

After studying this chapter, you should be able to:

○ differentiate between the different types of buying decisions and highlight the marketing implications of each type of decision

○ explain the different forces that influence organisational buying behaviour

○ explain the concept of a buying centre

○ identify the role-players in a buying centre and explain their respective roles

○ identify the different stages in the buying process and discuss how marketers can influence decision-making in each of the stages

○ identify the criteria industrial buyers take into account when they choose suppliers

○ identify and explain some of the new developments in buying practice

○ discuss how marketers can build relationships with organisational buyers.

14.1 Introduction

Organisational buying concerns the buying of products and services for use in an organisation's activities. Organisational buyers buy goods and services for one of the following purposes:[1]

○ To manufacture other products and services – raw materials, equipment, tools.

○ To resell to other organisational buyers or to customers – retailers, wholesalers.

○ To carry out the organisation's operations – office equipment, stationery, cleaning materials.

The stereotype of organisational buying behaviour is one of a cold, efficient, economically rational process, but little could be further from the truth. Organisational buying behaviour is as human and individual as household buying behaviour.[2] Organisations pay price premiums for well-known brands, they avoid risk and sometimes fail to properly evaluate products both before and after buying them.

However, organisational buying decisions take place in situations with varying degrees of time pressure, importance and newness. They typically involve more people and criteria than do individual customer decisions. Products are normally bought according to planned and structured procedures by trained and well-informed buyers employed by the organisations concerned.

In this chapter, we discuss the following issues regarding organisational buying behaviour:

○ Types of buying decisions.
○ Forces shaping organisational buying behaviour.
○ The buying centre.
○ Stages in the buying process.
○ New developments in buying practice.

14.2 Types of buying decisions

The organisational buyer faces a wide range of decisions when buying a product or service. The number and nature of the decisions depend on the buying situation. We now explore the types of buying situations.

14.2.1 New task buying

In this situation, which comes into being when customers are buying something they have never bought before, the problem or need is totally different from previous buying experiences. Decision-makers will therefore need a significant amount of information to enable them to explore alternative ways of solving the problem and to search for other suppliers. This is the most complex and difficult buying situation and normally involves several people. The risk can be great and the information needs are high. The buying decision-makers lack well-defined criteria for comparing alternative products and suppliers, but they also do not have strong predispositions toward a particular solution.

Marketing implications
Marketers trying to sell a product or service to an organisation can gain a differential advantage in such a situation by participating actively in the initial stages of the procurement, or buying, process. They should gather information on the problems facing the buying organisation, determine the organisation's specific requirements and offer proposals, or solutions, to meet those requirements. Marketers who are presently supplying other items to the organisation, which makes them so-called 'in' suppliers, have an edge over competitors because they are more familiar with the nature, culture and behaviour patterns of the buying organisation.[3]

14.2.2 Straight rebuy

This is a situation in which an organisation is buying more of the products that it has bought before. This is routine, low involvement buying with minimal information needs and no great consideration of alternatives. The straight rebuy represents a routine problem-solving process where organisational buyers have well-developed choice criteria. The criteria have been refined over time, as the buyers have developed a preference for the goods of one or a few carefully selected suppliers.

For straight rebuys, organisations are using the internet to streamline the buying process. To this end, buyers are adopting electronic procurement systems or are turning to electronic marketplaces that have been designed specifically for their industry.

Marketing implications

The buying department handles straight rebuy situations by routinely selecting a supplier from a list of approved suppliers and then placing an order. As organisations shift to electronic procurement systems, individual employees are allowed to buy directly online from approved suppliers. Therefore, it is important that marketers direct their marketing communications not only to buying managers but also to individual employees who have the power to choose the products they prefer.

The marketing task appropriate for the straight rebuy situation will be influenced by whether a marketer is an 'in' supplier, that is, on the list of approved suppliers, or an 'out' supplier, that is, not on the list of selected suppliers. An 'in' supplier must concentrate on:

○ building and reinforcing the buyer–seller relationship
○ meeting the buyers' expectations
○ adapting to the changing needs and new needs of the buying organisation.

The 'out' supplier faces a number of obstacles, and must convince the buyer organisation of the significant benefits that it can get from changing to this supplier. The aim of the marketing efforts should be to persuade decision-makers to re-examine alternative solutions and to revise their list of preferred suppliers to include the new supplier.[4]

14.2.3 Modified rebuy

This buying situation differs from the abovementioned two in terms of the time and people involved, the information needed and the alternatives considered. In a modified rebuy, the buyer wants to modify product specifications, prices, terms or suppliers, and re-evaluate suppliers from time to time.

Marketing implications

Again, the marketing effort of a supplier depends on whether it is an 'in' or 'out' supplier. An 'in' supplier should make every effort to understand and satisfy the needs of the buyer and to move decision-makers into a straight rebuy decision. The 'out' supplier should try to hold the buyer organisation in the modified rebuy situation long enough for the buyer to evaluate alternative offerings. Knowing the factors that led decision-makers to re-examine alternatives could be extremely helpful to 'out' suppliers.[5]

14.3 The forces shaping organisational buying behaviour

Organisational buying behaviour is influenced by a variety of forces, each of which we now briefly examine. Figure 14.1 summarises the factors.

Environmental	Organisational	Group	Individual	
○ Level of demand	○ Objectives	○ Interests	○ Age	
○ Economic outlook	○ Policies	○ Authority	○ Education	
○ Interest rates	○ Procedures	○ Status	○ Job positions	
○ Exchange rates	○ Organisational structures	○ Empathy	○ Personality	Organisational buyer
○ Technological change	○ Systems	○ Persuasiveness	○ Risk orientation	
○ Regulations			○ Culture	
○ Competitors				
○ Cultural values				
○ Environmental issues				
○ Social responsibility				

Figure 14.1: Major influences on organisational buying behaviour[6]

14.3.1 Environmental forces

Business buyers actively monitor economic, technological, political, regulatory and competitive developments. The economic factors that they observe are the level of production, investment and customer spending, as well as interest rate and exchange rate movements. For example, if they expect a worsening of the rand's value against foreign currencies, they can develop a buying policy to establish long-term price agreements with foreign suppliers. Environmental concerns can also lead to a situation in which a buyer switches to suppliers who are offering environmentally friendly products.

14.3.2 Organisational forces

Like any other business function, buying is affected by the organisation's general policies, objectives and strategies. Although many of an organisation's major policies and objectives may be broad, they will still affect the buying task and decisions. For example, an organisations' emphasis on cost-effectiveness will influence its buying approaches and decisions.

Marketers of products and services directed to organisational buyers need to be aware of certain trends and the influences thereof on buying behaviour. The trends are as follows:[7]

○ **Upgrading of buying departments**: Buying departments play a more important role in modern business, and marketers have to upgrade their sales personnel to match the high calibre of business buyers.

○ **Centralised buying**: Some organisations have started to centralise their buying activities in order to gain more buying clout and to save money. For business marketers, this trend means dealing with fewer and higher level buyers.

○ **Buying on the internet**: The move to internet buying has far reaching implications for suppliers and will change the landscape of buying in years to come.

○ **Long-term contracts**: Business buyers are increasingly trying to negotiate and establish long-term contracts with reliable suppliers.

○ **Buying-performance evaluation**: Many organisations are setting up incentive systems to reward buying managers for good buying performance, in much the same way that salespeople receive bonuses for sales performance. This leads to buyers putting pressure on sellers for the best deals.

○ **Lean production**: Manufacturers are trying to produce a greater variety of high quality products at lower cost, in less time and using less labour. Just-in-time production, stricter quality control, frequent and reliable delivery from suppliers, suppliers relocating to be closer to major customers, computerised buying systems, stable production schedules made available to suppliers and single sourcing with early supplier involvement are all elements of the leaner approach that pose challenges to the marketers of industrial products.

An internet website offering a full tourism package with personalised service is causing jitters among traditional travel agents. eTravel was the first South African travel website to offer reservations online. The company is connected to over 540 airlines, 50 car rental companies and 50 000 major hotels throughout the world. eTravel was launched in 1999 and today is rated as one of the largest privately owned retail travel agencies in South Africa, with monthly sales of more than R10 million.

eTravel fills a gap formed by internet travel booking services that bypass travel agencies. Most travel arrangements need professional assistance, and eTravel offers a solution in combining the best of the internet – the 'clicks' – with the best of South African travel consultants – the 'bricks'. Visitors to eTravel can make travel arrangements for any destination in the world and then have a travel consultant handle the deskwork. This allows customers to access products directly through the internet and make a booking online.

Over 80% of eTravel's business comes from corporate clients. South African corporate companies with unique members or users have also contracted with eTravel to use the booking engine. Keith Kirsten's 20 000 subscribers use www.greenclubtravel, *Business Day's* 30 000 site users use www.bday.co.za and Standard Bank's online bankers use www.bluebean.com, to mention a few. Any visitors to the Standard Bank or *Business Day* websites can connect on them to eTravel's booking engine.[8]

14.3.3 Group forces

Multiple buying influences and group forces are critical in organisational buying decisions. The organisational buying process typically involves a complex set of smaller decisions made or influenced by several individuals. The degree of involvement of group members in the procurement process varies from routine rebuys, where the buyer simply takes into account the preferences of others, to complex new-task buying situations, where the group plays an active role throughout the decision-making process.[9]

The concept of a buying centre provides insights into the role of group forces in organisational buying behaviour. We discuss buying centres in more detail in section 14.4 below.

14.3.4 Individual factors

Individuals, not organisations, make the buying decisions. Each member of a buying centre has a unique personality, a particular set of learned experiences, a specific position and role in the organisation, and a personal perception of how best to achieve both personal and organisational goals.

To understand this factor in organisational buying, marketers have to be aware of the following:[10]

○ **The individuals' evaluative criteria**: An engineer will use different evaluative criteria than will production managers or accountants.
○ **How an individual buyer processes information**: What an individual buyer chooses to pay attention to, comprehend and retain has an important influence on buying decisions.
○ **The individuals' risk-reduction strategies**: Individuals differ in their approaches to reduce the level of risk in buying decisions (see section 14.5.5 for a brief discussion of perceived risk).

> The Mount Nelson Hotel, one of Cape Town's leading hotels, identified corporate clients as one of its prime target markets. There are various ways in which the hotel has managed to attract corporate clients: it has opened a special wing for businesspeople; each room in the Business Wing offers a mini business centre, including modem access, a printer, fax-copier and stationery; and specially trained IT staff are available to respond to technical queries.[11]

14.4 The buying centre

Whether or not an organisation has a separate buying department, to a greater or lesser extent buying will be a group activity, that is, the focus of many decision influences from a number of individuals within different parts of the organisation. Although buyers may be involved in most purchases, they will be influenced and sometimes guided by shared decision-making among members of the buying centre.

A buying centre consists of the people who participate in the buying decision and who share the goals and risks arising from that decision. The size and make-up of the buying centre varies for different purchases and buying situations. The people concerned also differ in terms of the authority they possess, the status of their positions, their credibility and their degree of empathy.

The members of the buying centre can play any of the following roles:

○ **Users of the product or service**: This category includes the people who usually initiate the act of buying and who play an important role in defining the various buying specifications. Users can influence the buyer's actions – *negatively*, for example by refusing to use a particular supplier's product, or *positively*, for example by using a new product that is more cost-effective.

○ **Influencers**: These can be any people who have a direct or indirect influence on the buying decision, such as engineers involved in the design of product specifications or the evaluation of alternatives.

○ **Buyers**: They have the authority to select suppliers and sign contracts.

○ **Decision-makers concerned with the approval of transactions**: With routine purchases, the buyer usually makes the decision, but with unique and important purchases, members of senior management usually approve the transactions.

○ **Gatekeepers**: These are the individuals in the business who control the flow of information from one person/department to another person/department, for example restricting sales personnel from making direct contact with users or influencers.

In analysing a buying centre, marketers should answer the following questions:

○ Who are the individuals that form the buying centre?
○ What is each member's power base?
○ What is each member's relative influence in the decision?
○ What are each member's evaluation criteria, and how does he or she rate each prospective supplier on these criteria?[12]

14.5 Stages in the buying process[13]

Figure 14.2 on the next page shows the decision-making process that an organisation follows when buying a product. The exact nature of the process will depend on the buying situation. In general, the more complex the decision and the more expensive the product, the more likely it is that each stage will be passed through and that the process will take more time.

14.5.1 Recognition of the problem/need

A firm may recognise a need or problem through either internal or external factors. An example of an **internal factor** is the realisation that production capacity has to be

Recognition of a problem/need

Determination of specification and quantity needed of item

Search for and qualification of potential suppliers

Acquisition and analysis of proposals

Evaluation of proposals and selection of suppliers

Selection of an order routine

Performance feedback and evaluation

Figure 14.2: Phases in the organisational decision-making process[14]

increased, which leads to the need for new machinery. Examples of **external factors** are indications of a need by salespeople, adverts, direct mail or new product developments. For instance, a salesperson can encourage an organisation to recognise a problem by showing it how a new product can save money through lower maintenance costs.

14.5.2 Determining the specification and quantity of the needed item

At this stage of the decision-making process, the firm will draw up a description of what is required and in what quantity. The ability of marketers to influence this specification can give the company an advantage at later stages of the decision-making process. By persuading the buying organisation to specify features that only their product possesses or that fit their product's features and advantages, marketers ensure that the sale is virtually closed at this stage.

14.5.3 The search for and qualification of potential suppliers

The buyer now tries to identify the most appropriate suppliers. A great deal of variation in the degree of search takes place in industrial buying. Generally speaking, the cheaper and less important the item and the more information the buyer possesses, the less of a search takes place.

14.5.4 The acquisition and analysis of proposals

The buyer will now invite qualified suppliers to submit proposals. Where the item is complex and/or expensive, the buyer will require a detailed written proposal from each supplier. Suppliers can even be invited to make formal presentations. Marketers of business products must therefore be skilled in preparing and presenting proposals. The written proposals should be marketing documents, not just technical documents. The presentations should inspire confidence and should position the company's capabilities and resources in such a way that they are differentiated from, that is, they stand out from, the competition.

14.5.5 The evaluation of proposals and selection of supplier(s)

Before selecting a supplier, the buying centre will specify the qualities they want in a supplier and their relative importance. Suppliers will then be rated on these attributes and the most attractive will be identified.

Marketers of industrial products try to identify and understand the attributes or motives that role-players in buying organisations use to evaluate and compare suppliers and the products they offer. These can vary from technical, economic and organisational consider-ations to personal considerations. Examples of such considerations are as follows:

○ **Quality**: Buyers look for consistency of product and service quality in order to ensure that end products are reliable and production processes run smoothly.
○ **Price**: For materials and components of similar specifications and quality, price becomes a key consideration.
○ **Life cycle costs**: Increasingly, buyers take life cycle costs into account. These may include productivity savings, maintenance costs and residual values as well as initial price.
○ **Continuity of supply**: Suppliers must be able to guarantee reliable supply of components, raw materials, etc.
○ **Perceived risk**: This type of risk comes in two forms:
   – *Functional risk*, such as uncertainty regarding product performance.
   – *Psychological risk*, such as fear of upsetting the boss, losing status, being ridi-culed by others, etc.
○ **Office politics**: Factors such as interdepartmental conflict can affect the supply process.
○ **Personal likes and dislikes**: Buyers may personally like or dislike one sales-person, brand or supplier more than another. These personal likes or dislikes may influence supplier choice, particularly when competing products are similar.

14.5.6 Selecting an ordering routine

Next, details of payment and delivery and/or installation are drawn up. Usually, this is part of the procurement department's responsibilities.

A leading manufacturer of electronic components determined, through marketing research, the following
key buying criteria that buyers value in the selection of suppliers:
○ consistency of product
○ reliability of delivery
○ technical performance
○ continuity of supply
○ speed of delivery
○ speed of response
○ willingness to solve problems
○ technical advice
○ competitive pricing.

14.5.7 Performance feedback and evaluation

After-buying evaluations of products are typically more formal for organisational buying
than are evaluations for customer products. They may be **formal**, such as completing
an evaluation form or writing a formal report, or **informal**, such as through everyday
conversations.

The performance review may lead the buyer to continue, modify or end the relationship with the supplier. It is therefore important for the supplier to monitor the same
variables that are monitored by the buyers and end users.

14.6 New developments in buying practice[15]

Several new trends have become evident within the buying function, which has
marketing implications for supplier firms.

14.6.1 Just-in-time buying

The just-in-time concept aims to minimise how much stock companies hold by organising the supply system so that it provides materials and components as they are
needed. The costs of holding large amounts of stock are significantly reduced or eliminated, resulting in improved profits. Suppliers are therefore evaluated on their ability to
provide high quality products, streamlined delivery, reduced production down-times,
quality certification, and so on.

14.6.2 Reverse marketing

Traditionally, suppliers tried to meet buyers' requirements better than the competitors
were able to do. Thus, the initiative rested with suppliers, and buyers assumed a more
passive role by relying on suppliers' sensitivity to their needs. Recently, by contrast,
buyers are taking on a more proactive, aggressive stance in acquiring products and

services needed to compete. This process, whereby the buyer attempts to persuade the supplier to provide exactly what the organisation wants, is called 'reverse marketing'. The essence of **reverse marketing** is that buyers take the initiative in approaching existing or new suppliers and persuading them to meet their supply requirements.

The implications of reverse marketing are that it may pose serious threats to non-cooperative 'in' suppliers but enormous opportunities to responsive 'in' and 'out' suppliers. Suppliers who are willing to be responsive to the buyers' requirements have the opportunity to develop stronger and longer lasting relationships with the buyers.

14.6.3 Relationship building

Establishing and managing buyer–seller relationships is becoming a key ingredient in successful organisational marketing. Relationship marketing concerns the shifting from activities concerned with attracting buyers to activities concerned with retaining current customers. Relationships can be built by:

○ **technical support** – cooperation in research and development, after sales service, the training of a customer's staff, etc.
○ **expertise** – suppliers providing expertise to their customers in the form of offering design and engineering assistance, financial support, management and marketing consultations, etc.
○ **resource support** – extended credit facilities, low interest loans, co operative advertising, reciprocal buying practices, etc.
○ **service level agreements** – on delivery speed, product specifications, reorders, maintenance, etc.
○ **risk reduction** – for example the offer of products for trial, product and delivery guarantees, preventative maintenance contracts, fast complaint handling, etc.

Nashua, the market leader in the office automation industry, believes that understanding the importance of buyer behaviour plays a significant part in securing the company's success in the marketplace. At the heart of Nashua's marketing strategy is a company-wide commitment that begins with a comprehensive analysis of every customer's needs and ends with the right product being offered to each customer. Once this has been accomplished, the company utilises its extensive after-sales and support resources to ensure that customers stay with Nashua 'for life'.

Nashua undertakes an annual customer survey with the aim of identifying and determining customer needs and perceptions. This exercise rates not only key customer buying criteria, but also how Nashua performs as a supplier, relative to its key competitors.

From its close association with customers, Nashua has learned that the most important buying criteria focus on the buyer's relationship with the supplier. Nashua values direct contact with its clients as the most important part of its marketing communication strategy. Nashua focuses strongly on the building of relationships. Sponsorships of events are used as a platform for customer entertainment and as a means of getting closer to customers.

Furthermore, Nashua focuses its attention on customer service as a way of gaining and sustaining a competitive advantage. This service culture not only includes the engineers who respond quickly and efficiently to a service call, but also extends to everyone else in the organisation – to ensure that all external and internal customers are served well. The concept of the lifetime value of a customer is implemented by Nashua nation-wide and is summed up by its mission statement: 'We are committed to strengthening our leadership position in office automation through total quality service by saving you time, saving you money and putting you first'.[16]

Case study

BELL EQUIPMENT[17]

Founded in 1954, Bell Equipment has grown from a small engineering and equipment repair service company into an equipment designer, manufacturer and distributor operating in all parts of the world. The company expanded from northern KwaZulu-Natal to the whole of South Africa and from there to various countries in Africa, North America, Europe, Australia, New Zealand and the Asian Pacific region.

Bell Equipment's product range comprises more than 50 different models of articulated dump-trucks, front-end loaders, haulers and tri-wheel rough-terrain material handlers. These products fulfil haulage and materials-handling needs across many industries such as construction, mining timber and sugar-growing. In South Africa and Africa, Bell has established a comprehensive network of Bell-operated customer support centres and independent dealers. Globally, Bell operates through a network of independent dealers supported by regional offices in Europe, Singapore and Australia. A strategic alliance with John Deere gives Deere's Construction Equipment Division responsibility for sales and support in the Americas.

Every machine in Bell's product range, which includes more than 15 000 Bell machines in operation worldwide, is backed by strong, reliable after-sales support. Through this operation, Bell seeks to reduce customer operating costs and to contribute to the customer's bottom line. It is important for Bell to know their customers' requirements, to go beyond customer's current wants and needs, and to look for new ways to exceed expectations and be the lowest cost-per-ton solution for customers.

Innovative thinking is seen as the key to progress, and forms the core of Bell's research and development efforts. To this end, Bell invests some 5% of its revenue in research and development. Every major machine component is selected on the criterion of fitness-for-purpose from the best the world has to offer. Engineers spend a lot of time at customer sites, gaining insight into what can be done to develop the next generation of machines.

> The slogan of the company is: 'Strong reliable machines, strong reliable support'. When marketing against big companies, such as Caterpillar and Hitachi, Bell has to find ways to outpace and outmanoeuvre the big players. This is done in two ways:
> 1. It empowers employees in the field to make decisions regarding pricing, product support and customer relationship building.
> 2. It ensures that product-support personnel quickly respond when a client's machine breaks down. Engineers have even learned to fly so that they can reach construction sites quickly. Bell's customer-support teams have cultivated long-term relationships with their customers, meeting – and in many instances exceeding – their expectations in terms of machine up-time and cost per ton.

14.7 Summary

Understanding organisational buying behaviour is a prerequisite for choosing a marketing strategy to target a specific segment or buying organisation. Organisational buying decisions take place in situations with varying degrees of time pressure, importance and newness. They typically involve more people and criteria than do individual customer decisions. Products are normally bought according to planned and structured procedures by trained and well-informed buyers.

Marketers should know the following about organisational buying behaviour:

○ The type of buying decisions, which can vary from a straight rebuy to an extensive buying decision process.
○ The variety of forces that influence organisational buying behaviour.
○ The composition, power bases and roles of the members of a buying centre.
○ The influence that can be exerted in each of the phases of the buying process.
○ The latest developments in the buying process, such as just-in-time buying, reverse marketing and relationship building.

Questions for self-assessment

To assess your progress, answer these questions:
1. You are a buyer employed at Toyota's factory, and you are responsible for buying major components, machinery and tools. Discuss the factors that will influence your buyer behaviour.
2. Explain the composition of a buying centre. What preparations are necessary before a salesperson approaches a buying centre with a presentation and proposal?
3. Identify several evaluation criteria that buyers may use in choosing a particular brand of notebook computer for an organisation. In your view, which criteria would be the most decisive in the buying process?
4. A supplier of computer software programs wants to establish long-term relation-

ships with industrial buyers. Which methods can be used to establish and build these relationships?

5. Refer to the case study, and answer the following questions:
   a. Discuss the forces that will influence the buying behaviour of a coalmine that is considering buying earth-moving equipment.
   b. A road construction firm wants to buy several articulated dump-trucks. Who will be members of the buying centre, which factors will influence their behaviour and what should Bell's salespeople do to influence each member's choice?
   c. Assume you are employed as a salesperson by Bell Equipment. Which issues will you emphasise in your sales presentation in order to ensure that Bell becomes the preferred supplier of a construction company that operates globally?
   d. How does Bell Equipment build relationships with its most important customers?

Endnote references

1. Strydom, J.W., Jooste, C.J. and Cant, M. 2000. *Marketing Management.* Cape Town: Juta.
2. Hawkins, D.I., Best, R.J. and Coney, K.A. 1998. *Consumer Behavior: Building Marketing Strategy.* Boston: McGraw-Hill.
3. Hutt, M.D. and Speh, T.W. 2001. *Business Marketing Management.* New York: Harcourt College.
4. Ibid., pp. 59–63.
5. Ibid., pp. 63–6.
6. Adapted from Kotler, P. 2000. *Marketing Management: Analysis, Planning, Implementation and Control.* Upper Saddle River: Prentice-Hall, p. 197.
7. Ibid., pp. 198–9.
8. Based on Simpson, J. and Dore, B. 2002. *Marketing in South Africa: Cases and Concepts.* Pretoria: Van Schaik.
9. Hutt and Speh, op. cit.
10. Ibid., pp. 77–80.
11. Based on Simpson and Dore, op. cit., p. 147.
12. Strydom et al., op. cit.
13. This section is mainly based on Kotler, op. cit., pp. 203–8; and Jobber, D. 1998. *Principles and Practice of Marketing.* London: McGraw-Hill, pp. 84–9.
14. Adapted from Jobber, op. cit., p. 84.
15. This section is based on ibid., pp. 91–100.
16. Based on Dorian, P. 1998. *Marketing Magic.* Halfway House: Zebra Press, pp. 203–8.
17. Based on Welcome to the World of Bell Equipment, an internal document published by Bell Equipment. Available on the internet from: www.bellequipment.com (accessed 17 August 2003); and Du Plessis, P.J., Jooste, C.J. and Strydom, J.W. 2001. *Applied Strategic Marketing.* Johannesburg: Heinemann, pp. 382–3.

15 Consumer loyalty

15.1 Introduction

The long-term success of a particular brand is based not on the number of consumers who buy it once, but on those who become repeat buyers and are loyal to it. The objectives of marketing management are to:

○ encourage occasional buyers to become repeat buyers
○ increase the amount consumed by the repeat buyers of its brand
○ attract buyers from competing brands
○ maintain high levels of repeat buying for its brand by discouraging repeat buyers from brand-switching behaviours.

The overall aim of marketing is to increase market share by adopting strategies that will ensure brand loyalty and store loyalty.

15.2 Brand loyalty

Branding is seen as a form of security that adds value and profitability to the overall marketing effort. All marketers aim to satisfy the needs, wants and desires of consumers. While specific products satisfy basic needs, well-positioned brands fulfil consumers' deeper needs, wants and urges. There is a relationship between the consumers' attitude toward the brand and their buying behaviour.

The repeat buying of a brand does not imply loyalty towards it. Instead, for brand loyalty to exist, there must be psychological commitment to the brand. Brand loyalty is the opposite of variety-seeking behaviour. Consumers engage in variety seeking when they buy different brands because of their urge to try different things, curiosity, novelty or the desire to overcome boredom with the original choice.[1] Consumers typically seek variety among products such as restaurants, music or leisure activities. Research shows that to get variety, individuals often switch to less-preferred options even though they enjoy those items less than they would have enjoyed repeating a preferred option.[2]

Branding serves to distinguish products from other similar ones so that they can be marketed separately. Kotler and Armstrong[3] define a **brand** as a name, term, sign, symbol or design, or a combination of these characteristics, intended to identify the goods or services of one seller or groups of sellers and to differentiate them from those of competitors. For example, its brand distinguishes Colgate toothpaste from Aquafresh and Mentadent P. Brands are given added value when advertisers associate them with prominent social groups, style and excitement. For example, Edblo beds were advertised by the ten-times Comrades Marathon winner Bruce Fordyce, implying that Edblo supplies the rest needed by a top athlete to perform at his best. Hence, brands are a necessary prerequisite for effective marketing. Kellogg's is a well-known, extensively advertised and established brand of cereal, to the extent that children often refer to cereal as 'Kellogg's'. A brand name may serve as 'shorthand' for quality by giving consumers a bundle of information about the product, and may be a stronger cue than price for evaluating overall quality.[4] Similarly, Janiszewski and Van Osselaer[5] maintain that brand names can help consumers recall important product information and also serve as predictive cues about product performance.

15.2.1 The influence of brand names on product preference

Brands offer consumers convenience in shopping. They make it easier for the consumer to identify particular items from a multitude of goods and assure them that it will always be the same product. For example, Kellogg's cereal is easily identified by its colourful package, with the picture of a cock crowing to signify that it's time for the morning meal. Brands provide consumers with consistent quality. Once they have established a preference for a specific brand, they can be assured of the same quality every time they buy it. A health conscious individual, for example, will continually buy a light margarine if they believe that the product will benefit their health.

Brands simplify the buying of replacement parts, service and accessories, and often assure consumers that they will get a proper replacement part or their money back if the product does not work properly. Perceived risk can be reduced substantially when consumers buy established brands that are known to satisfy a need optimally. For example, a family may choose to buy a Defy washing machine because of the company's good reputation.

Consumers can also express their self-concepts through branding. Moreover, as a result of sophisticated buyers and marketers, brands have acquired an emotional dimension that reflects buyers' moods, personalities and the messages they wish to convey to others.[6] Individuals may buy brands that maintain or enhance their self-concepts in a non-verbal manner. For example, consumers may buy a brand of jeans, which they feel are trendy, to improve their self-image. The brand also meets needs such as affiliation and the desire for dominance. Undoubtedly, consumers prefer the brands that they view as highly satisfying. Table 15.1 summarises these advantages.

Table 15.1: The definition and benefits of brands

Definition	Benefits/advantages
○ Name, term, symbol or design or a combination of traits that help to identify the product or service ○ Product with a personality ○ Unique character and appeal	○ Convenience in shopping through easy identification and easy recognition of product ○ Facilitates the consumer decission-making process. ○ Provides consumers with consistent quality ○ Simplifies the buying of replacement parts, service and accessories ○ Reduces perceived risk when established brands are purchased ○ Enables consumers to express their self-concepts eg. buying Soviet jeans

15.2.2 Brand image

The many advantages of branding suggest that consumers have strong feelings about brands. A brand is a product with a personality. While a product is something physical created by a manufacturer, a brand consists of all the living impressions a consumer has of a product or service.[7] These impressions combine to give the brand a unique character and appeal. For example, the deodorant called 'Impulse' is associated with the fragrance of flowers, which inspires ideas of femininity, beauty, appeal and attraction.

Brand image is the sum total of a consumer's attitudes to, and knowledge about, a brand. Experience and social and marketing influences affect brand image. Consumers' experiences with brands are recorded in their consciousness and form a substantial part of the image they have of the brand. Social influence is a major factor in the development and modification of brand images. For example, Glen tea is associated with togetherness with neighbours/community, and its advertising presents images of the fulfilment of the need for belonging and affiliation. Hence, brands are symbols of social relationships, and their images can be influenced by groups that consumers feel are important, such as peer groups, family, celebrities and friends.

Marketers are building an image when they launch a new product, and engage in an extensive amount of decision-making about its profile. This image is communicated to individuals through the promotion mix of advertising, selling and packaging. Brand image is as much a part of the process of buying a product as is the product itself. It can add value to a product and play a critical role in brand preference. Brand image is illustrated in Figure 15.1.

Figure 15.1: Brand image

15.2.3 Brand preference

Brand preference is the consumers' tendency to select a brand or product from among a set of known available brands. This is shown in Figure 15.2 on the next page.

When confronted with a choice of brands, consumers are more positive towards one brand than towards others. Brand preference behaviour, as depicted in Figure 15.2, reflects the knowledge-attitude-behaviour (KAB) model of consumer behaviour. This model maintains that consumers have knowledge of several brands and hold positive attitudes towards a few of them, which will elicit behaviour, indicated by the act of buying their most favoured brand. As knowledge changes over time, so too do attitudes and behaviour.

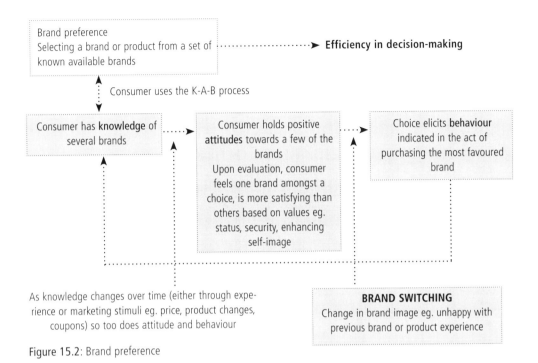

Figure 15.2: Brand preference

Brand preference exists for two major reasons:
1. In a choice of brands, consumers feel one is more satisfying than others and there-fore favour it. According to Foster and Tindale,[8] consumers buy values other than the purely physical features of the product – they also buy intrinsic, psychological values that add things like status, security and self-image to their satisfaction.
2. Brand preference occurs as a result of efficiency in decision-making. Consumers would struggle if, on each shopping trip, they had to logically select among brands for every item on their grocery list. Habits that develop as a result of past experiences and reinforcement of purchases provide efficiency to consumer shopping.

Brand preference may change as a result of marketing efforts such as price, product changes and coupons. For example, a consumer who generally buys Rama margarine may buy Rondo margarine if it is offered at a cheaper promotional price.

Brand switching is one of the ways in which consumers having problems or expe-riencing dissatisfaction with a product or service may express their unhappiness. The purpose of switching is to get rid of the problems with the purchase. However, a change in brand image must occur before a change in brand preference takes place.

15.2.4 The formation of brand loyalty

'Brand loyalty' refers to a situation where a consumer strongly prefers one brand to others. Consumers become brand loyal in different ways. Some individuals try different brands and may even buy a different brand every time they go shopping. Becoming brand loyal is essentially a learning process, which takes place over a period of time.

There are three factors that appear to be vital in its development:
1. Exposure to information concerning the brand.
2. Favourable experience in buying and using the brand.
3. The extent of its use by peers and social reference groups.

There are a number of factors that can influence the degree of brand loyalty that develops within a target market. Brand loyalty is lower when:
- more brands are available for consumers to choose from
- more products of greater value are bought
- prices are relatively active among competing brands
- consumers use a number of brands at the same time.

15.2.5 Brand loyalty and repeat buying behaviour

While repeat buying involves buying the same brand frequently, possibly because it is the only one or the cheapest one available, for brand loyalty to occur there must be some level of psychological commitment to the brand. This is presented in Figure 15.3.

Figure 15.3: Repeat purchase behaviour and brand loyalty

Repeat buying behaviour refers to consumers buying the same brand over time, while brand loyalty includes psychological and evaluative processes. These processes need not be elaborate or extensive, but they should show that a person has reasons for acting and develops a commitment – a psychological attachment – to one or more brands. Brand loyal consumers, by contrast, tend to be consistent buyers of the brands they buy; they hold strong beliefs about their quality, feel considerable devotion towards the brands and often resist competitors' efforts to persuade them of the quality of other brands.[9] Therefore, they are not vulnerable.

15.2.6 Complex decision-making and brand loyalty

Brand loyalty is often measured by how involved consumers are in the decisions to buy particular products, as shown in Figure 15.4.

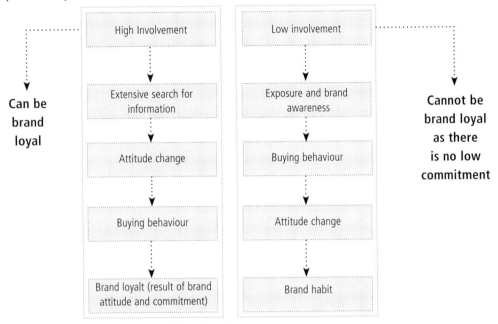

Figure 15.4: Level of involvement and brand loyalty

As depicted in Figure 15.4, high involvement leads to extensive search for information, attitude change, buying behaviour and then brand *loyalty*, while low involvement creates exposure and brand awareness, buying behaviour, perhaps attitude change and then brand *habit*. Since brand loyalty is defined as a commitment, the low involvement consumer cannot be considered to be brand loyal. Brand commitment is the result of consumer attitude. The greater the brand commitment, the more rooted the brand is in the consumer's mind as the only choice within the product class. If a shop does not have the brand in stock, this will be a serious problem for the consumer, who will then look for the brand in another shop. Hence, brand commitment implies brand loyalty, but brand loyalty does not imply brand commitment. Consumers who are not brand loyal may be persuaded to buy a competitor's brand.

15.2.7 Brand loyalty and vulnerability

Different patterns of brand loyalty exist. Furthermore, different brands of the same product are able to command varying degrees of loyalty. While the marketing objective with loyal consumers is to maintain and extend their loyalty, the aim with non-loyal consumers is to encourage them to try the firm's brand and to develop loyalty. The more a firm's market share is built upon a base of loyal consumers, the more stable is that share of the total market. Management therefore needs to pay attention to the degree and distribution of loyalty in the market.

The term **'vulnerability'** may be used to distinguish loyal consumers, that is, those who both buy and like the brand, from those consumers who buy a brand but like other brands equally well, or better, and therefore are vulnerable to these other products, that is, they may buy them. Brand loyalty and vulnerability are based on the interrelationship between two dimensions, namely, the buying pattern of a particular brand and the attitude toward that brand.[10] This vulnerability matrix provides the marketing manager with useful information. Many consumers have varying levels of attitudinal loyalty towards a brand and have different degrees of vulnerability. The matrix is useful because it recognises differences in the magnitude and the nature of vulnerability. It identifies loyal consumers as well as those who are unlikely to become loyal – it is not worth the effort to try to develop the latter's loyalty.

15.2.8 The stages of brand loyalty

A consumer progresses through various stages before becoming truly brand loyal. Figure 15.5 on the next page depicts these phases in chronological order.

Stage 1 Brand awareness
Consumers cannot buy a brand unless they are aware of its existence. Hence, brand awareness is a general communication aim of all promotional strategies. By creating brand awareness, marketers hope that whenever the need for the product arises, the consumer will remember the brand and include it among the choice alternatives during decision-making. Salespeople within a store, attractive price discount signs, end-of-aisle displays, shelf-positioning, billboards, mobile advertising on buses and car windows, and adverts can all create brand awareness. A high level of brand awareness is vital to influence brand choice.

Stage 2 Brand trial
Consumers will know a brand only if they try it. Thus, most promotion strategies are aimed at increasing the probability of consumers trying out the brand. Marketers encourage this by providing free samples, or coupons or attractive reductions on prices as compared to competitors' prices.

Stage 3 Brand image
As we have seen, this is the consumer's impression of the brand created by brand messages and experiences, and assimilated or evaluated into a perception through the processing of information.[11]

Stage 4 Brand preference

This is the tendency to select a brand or product from among a set of known available brands. When confronted with a choice of brands, the consumer will have a more positive feeling about one brand than about competitor brands.

Stage 5 Brand habit

A consumer who prefers a particular brand of product will habitually buy it without thinking about or evaluating it. Such a consumer may display repeat buying behaviour. However, they may consider another brand if their preferred brand is out of stock or becomes too expensive in comparison with other brands.

Stage 6 Brand loyalty

As we have seen, brand loyalty indicates that a person has a psychological commitment or attachment to a brand. They will visit another store if their preferred brand is unavailable or out of stock, and may even do without it until they are able to get the brand from another store. Loyalty is a true measure of brand preference.[12]

Figure 15.5: The stages of brand loyalty

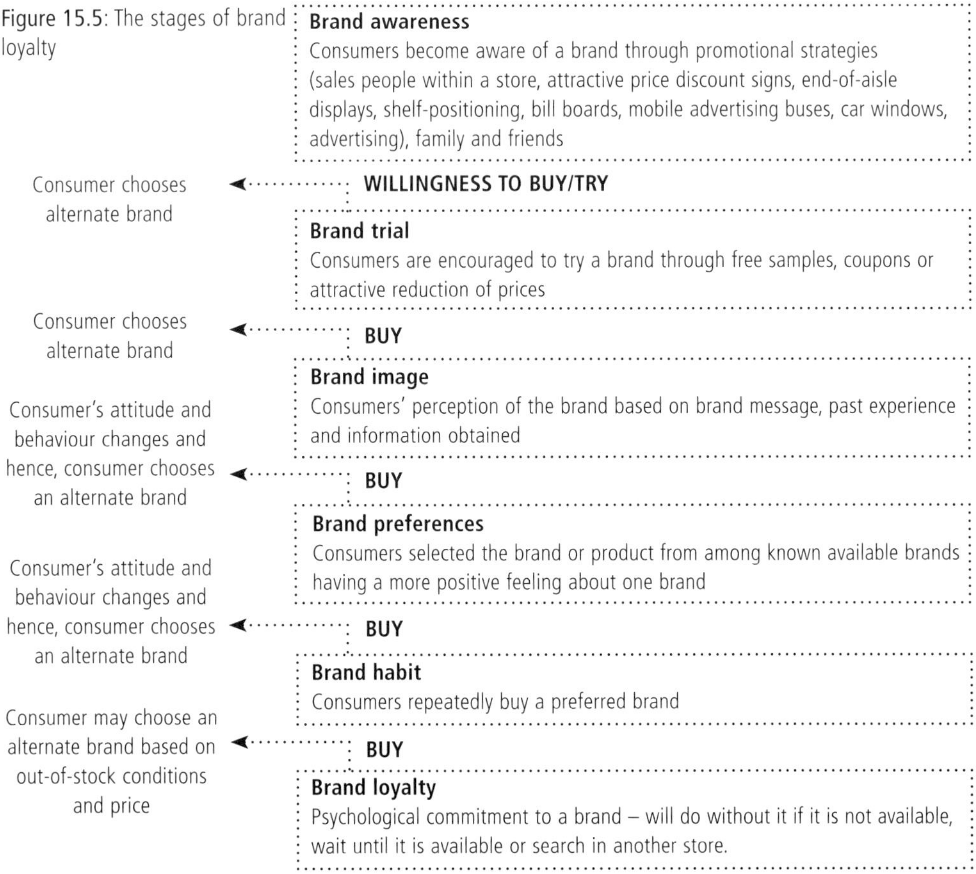

Brand awareness
Consumers become aware of a brand through promotional strategies (sales people within a store, attractive price discount signs, end-of-aisle displays, shelf-positioning, bill boards, mobile advertising buses, car windows, advertising), family and friends

Consumer chooses alternate brand ◄ **WILLINGNESS TO BUY/TRY**

Brand trial
Consumers are encouraged to try a brand through free samples, coupons or attractive reduction of prices

Consumer chooses alternate brand ◄ **BUY**

Brand image
Consumers' perception of the brand based on brand message, past experience and information obtained

Consumer's attitude and behaviour changes and hence, consumer chooses an alternate brand ◄ **BUY**

Brand preferences
Consumers selected the brand or product from among known available brands having a more positive feeling about one brand

Consumer's attitude and behaviour changes and hence, consumer chooses an alternate brand ◄ **BUY**

Brand habit
Consumers repeatedly buy a preferred brand

Consumer may choose an alternate brand based on out-of-stock conditions and price ◄ **BUY**

Brand loyalty
Psychological commitment to a brand – will do without it if it is not available, wait until it is available or search in another store.

15.2.9 Brand loyalty and brand segmentation

A firm can find out essential information by analysing loyalty patterns in its market and carrying out segmentation analysis. Segmentation analysis is the process of identifying consumers who are more likely to be influenced by an effort to market a specific product, service or brand than the rest of the market population. For marketers, the aim of segmentation analysis is to reduce risk in deciding where, when, how and to whom they will market a new product, service or brand. Their aim is to increase marketing effectiveness by directing their efforts towards the designated segment in a way that will fit that segment's characteristics and hence appeal to them.

A market can be segmented by consumer loyalty to brands, stores and companies. Buyers can be divided into groups according to their degree of loyalty. A brand loyal market is one with a high proportion of consumers showing strong brand loyalty. Segmentation analysis informs marketers about:

○ their products' and brands' positioning in the market in relation to possible substitutes, as perceived by consumers
○ the way in which consumers distinguish their product or service from others
○ the importance of various product attributes to consumers' evaluations of the products and brands
○ the psychological aspects of consumers that lead them to buy or not to buy in a specific product class.

This kind of information guides marketers in deciding on the strategy and tactics with which to achieve their goals and secure their market share.

15.2.10 Determining the brand loyal segment

A loyal consumer has a commitment toward a brand and is willing to pay a premium price for it, to exert more effort to buy the brand if it is out of stock in a specific store and is less subject to competitors' actions, especially product promotions.

Researchers have tried to find out why brand loyalty varies across consumers and products. Consumer shopping patterns and market structure characteristics are associated with varying degrees of brand loyalty. Researchers have adopted the behavioural and attitudinal or cognitive approaches to understanding brand loyalty in order to understand the buying patterns of consumers. Brand loyalty depends on the following:

○ The number of consecutive times that an individual buys a brand. For example a consumer who buys a brand five times in a row (behaviour) may be considered to be brand loyal.
○ Consumer's knowledge of the brand (cognition), liking for the brand (feeling/attitude) and the act of buying the brand (behaviour).

The behavioural approach to brand loyalty

Followers of the behavioural school of thought define brand loyalty in behavioural terms by the sequence and/or the proportion of purchases, as we can see in Figure 15.6.

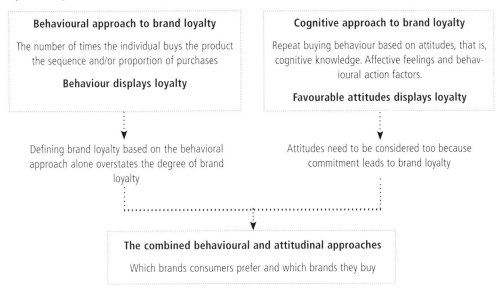

Figure 15.6: Approaches to brand loyalty

Brown[13] defines loyalty as buying the same brand five times in a row, Tucker[14] three times in a row and Lawrence[15] four times in a row. Blattberg and Sen[16] used proportion of purchases rather than sequence as the behavioural measure of loyalty. For example, a person who buys Dove soap six times in a row is brand loyal, as is a consumer who buys Dove soap 70% of the time.

Behaviourists argue that what consumers think or believe is unimportant, but that the consumers' behaviour is the full statement of what brand loyalty is. This approach is rather limited – it views brand loyalty simply as a function of past behaviour. Nevertheless, it is a multi-dimensional concept that must include a consumer's commitment to a brand.

The cognitive approach to brand loyalty

Many of the shortfalls of a purely behavioural approach to measuring brand loyalty are overcome when both attitudes and behaviour are included. Since attitude is recognised as a crucial element in the buying process, the cognitive approach states that brand loyalty implies repeat buying behaviour based on cognitive, affective and behavioural factors – the basic components of attitude, as shown in Figure 15.6. In order to be truly loyal, a consumer must have a favourable attitude toward the brand in addition to buying it repeatedly. For example, a consumer is said to be brand loyal to Tastic rice if they like it and buy it on every, or almost every, occasion. The brand that the individual likes the most will be the one having the highest probability of selection in the market (brand choice) and the brand least favoured will have the lowest probability of selection.

The cognitive approach offers marketing researchers the advantage of enabling them to gather valuable information about the strengths and weaknesses of their brands on relevant attributes, which can help to alter an existing marketing strategy to influence the cognitive-attitudinal-behavioural hierarchy.

The combined behavioural and attitudinal approach

Research indicates that measures of brand loyalty that use both attitudinal and behavioural approaches provide a more powerful definition of the concept.[17] Researchers need to determine which brands consumers prefer as well as which ones they buy (see Figure 15.6). Day[18] found that the predictive power of the model using both attitude and behaviour measures was almost twice as good as using only the latter. Also, if the behaviour measure alone was used, over 70% of the sample would have reflected brand loyalty, but when the attitudinal component was considered, the proportion of brand loyal consumers was reduced to under 50%.[19] The implication is that defining brand loyalty based only on repeat buying overstates the degree of loyalty. The misclassification of individuals as brand loyal misleads marketers to believe that consumers are responding more favourably to the brand than they actually are.

15.2.11 Brand loyalty correlates

Studies on brand loyalty, based on the behavioural and attitudinal measure, have found that it has a particular relationship to consumer buying behaviour, patterns of shopping and various features of market structure. Figure 15.7 on the next page makes this evident.

Consumer buying habits

Brand loyal consumers are more likely to be influenced by reference groups because of lack of information and the desire to conform and be accepted. A consumer may be encouraged by a personal or non-personal source to buy a particular brand without acquiring product-specific information. This often happens when the consumer is short of time or believes the referrer to be particularly knowledgeable and reliable. Brand-loyal consumers also tend to be more self-confident in their choice. Furthermore, they are more likely to see and use repeat buying of a single brand as a means of reducing risk. Some socio-economic, demographic and psychological variables, including personality, are related to brand loyalty.

Shopping pattern characteristics

Studies have produced findings indicating the relationships between brand loyalty and various shopping pattern characteristics. Carman[20] and Rao[21] have shown the importance of store loyalty in determining brand loyalty. Shopping proneness has been related to brands. Consumers who are not prone to shopping go to only a few stores.

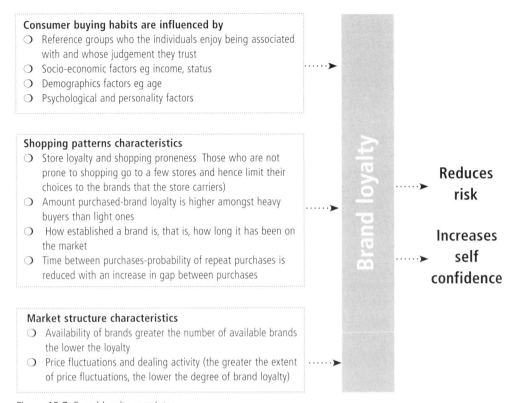

Consumer buying habits are influenced by
- ○ Reference groups who the individuals enjoy being associated with and whose judgement they trust
- ○ Socio-economic factors eg income, status
- ○ Demographics factors eg age
- ○ Psychological and personality factors

Shopping patterns characteristics
- ○ Store loyalty and shopping proneness Those who are not prone to shopping go to a few stores and hence limit their choices to the brands that the store carriers)
- ○ Amount purchased-brand loyalty is higher amongst heavy buyers than light ones
- ○ How established a brand is, that is, how long it has been on the market
- ○ Time between purchases-probability of repeat purchases is reduced with an increase in gap between purchases

Market structure characteristics
- ○ Availability of brands greater the number of available brands the lower the loyalty
- ○ Price fluctuations and dealing activity (the greater the extent of price fluctuations, the lower the degree of brand loyalty)

Brand loyalty

Reduces risk

Increases self confidence

Figure 15.7: Brand loyalty correlates

Within these stores, they tend to remain loyal to a small number of brands rather than make careful choices among the values being offered by these stores.

A relationship has also been observed between amount purchased and brand loyalty. Kuehn[22] found that brand loyalty was higher for heavy buyers, that is, people who buy a lot, than for light ones. In addition, brand loyalty is related to the length of time the product has been on the market. Kuehn[23] also observed the relationship of the time between purchases and brand loyalty, finding that the probability of a consumer buying the same brand twice in a row decreased exponentially with an increase in time between these purchases. In other words, the more time has passed, the greater the decay in loyalty.

Market-structure characteristics
Sometimes the difference between products in some important aspects of brand choice can be the result of the structure of the markets in which the products are sold, and does not depend on the specific features of the products or on consumer attitudes to these products. Engel and Blackwell have studied the relationship between brand loyalty and certain market structures – the availability of brands, price fluctuations and dealing activity – and found that:

consumers tend to be less loyal towards products with many available brands, where number of products and [rand] expenditures per buyer are high, where prices are relatively active, and where consumers might be expected to simultaneously use a number of brands of the product.[24]

Consumers tend to be loyal in markets where a wider distribution of brands exists and where market share is represented by the leading brand. Therefore, market structure influences brand loyalty.

15.2.12 Models of brand loyalty

Many mathematical models have been developed in an attempt to understand brand loyalty behaviour over time. We now explore the two models that seem to predominate.

Deterministic models
These models have been designed to explain the processes through which buyers make their brand choices, decide to engage in repeat buying behaviour or become brand loyal. Deterministic models are an attempt to predict behaviour in exact or non-probabilistic terms. They contain no random, probabilistic or stochastic elements and are therefore different from a stochastic model, with its built-in probability component.

Stochastic models
These models allow for many variables that are not or cannot be measured and are a simplification of reality. There are two basic philosophies of stochastic models. In the first, variables that are internal and external to the individual determine the outcome of behaviour, even though many of these factors are not measured or included in the model of market response. The second philosophy is based on the premise that the model of market response and the actual consumption process are both stochastic, and not just the model.

However, we cannot prove conclusively whether behaviour is primarily stochastic or deterministic, because many variables influence consumer choice.

15.2.13 Consumer behaviour and brand type

Branding is central to marketing, since a brand name makes product identification possible, commands a particular price, implies distribution decisions and dictates the promotional strategy. Consumers tend to recognise the following types of brand and consider them when they decide to buy a product.

Manufacturer brands
These are products produced and merchandised under a brand name identified with a specific manufacturer. They are developed and owned by their producer, who is usually involved with their distribution, promotion and, to some extent, pricing decisions.[25] Since these brands are widely marketed and dominate advertising, they are frequently

called 'national brands'. They comprise the major share of consumer purchases because there are many more manufacturer brands than store or generic brands. Consumers may trust manufacturer brands more than other brand types because of the extensive information available about them.

Store brands

These are brands of products whose distribution is controlled by retailers and wholesalers. These brands are often sold by one chain of stores. They are called 'private brands' because the producers are unknown to the consumers. Store brands tend to be less expensive than manufacturer brands, except those sold in elite stores where consumers buy brands for their distinctiveness. Weiss[26] identifies the major trends supporting the rise of store brands to be:

- the drop in consumer loyalty to many manufacturer brands
- the better value for money often offered by store-controlled brands
- the growing similarity of brands within given merchandise categories
- the growing knowledge among consumers that store brands are often the 'Siamese twins' of manufacturer brands – frequently offered at lower prices[27]
- the ongoing move towards impulse shopping and self-service
- the increasing willingness of retailers to support their brands by providing satisfaction guarantees and warranties, thus reducing perceived risk in the minds of consumers
- the increasing ability of giant retailers to promote their own brands.

Corstjens and Lal[28] deduced that store brands and national brands play complementary roles. Store brands create store differentiation and loyalty, whereas national brands enable the retailer to raise prices and increase store profitability.

Generic brands

These are a phenomenon found mainly in supermarkets. The basic marketing strategy used for generic brand products is to reduce or eliminate traditional marketing frills, such as packaging and advertising, and to offer the product at a much lower price.[29] Generic brands are packed and distributed by major supermarket chains, which have also been selling their own store brands for many years. The supermarket decides which generic products it will carry in competition with national and store brands as well as their price levels and location in the store. Generics have enjoyed a much higher rate of sales growth than national and store brands.

It is clear that South African shoppers can choose among national, store or generic brands for many grocery products. The brands differ in price, grade, packaging, advertising information and availability of supply, of which generics are more limited. These three types of brands compete directly with each other, at least within a particular store.

15.3 Store loyalty

Consumer loyalty is the tendency of a person to act in the same way in a similar situation in order to secure satisfaction. Store loyalty is the customer's intention to repeatedly patronise a given store and is based on the consumer's feelings towards the store (affect) and knowledge and beliefs (cognition) about the store. Hence, the consumer's store patronage (behaviour) depends on feelings (affect) and knowledge (cognition). This is depicted in Figure 15.8.

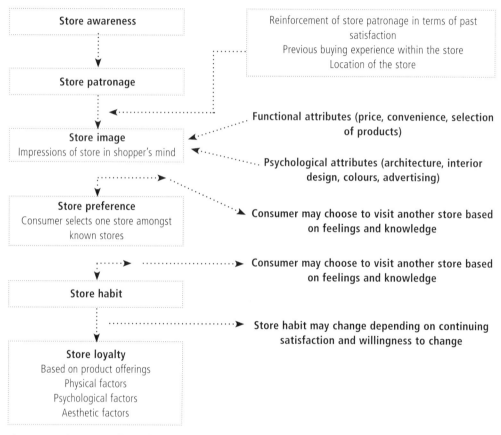

Figure 15.8: The stages of store loyalty

The consumer mentally establishes certain evaluative store criteria and compares their perceptions of the store's characteristics with these criteria, as shown in Figure 15.9 on the next page. If the store fulfils these set criteria, the consumer will patronise the store, perhaps repeatedly. If it does not, the consumer will visit the store that comes closest to meeting their expectations. Repeated satisfaction results in repeated patronage and store loyalty.

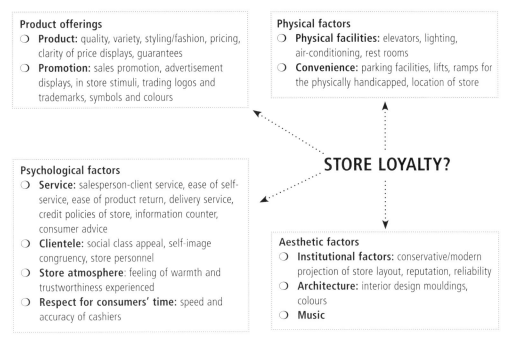

Figure 15.9: Evaluative criteria used in determining store patronage and store loyalty

Retailers want consumers to patronise their stores all the time. However, consumers' attitudes towards the store, that is, the consumers' affect, cognition and behaviour, is largely influenced by the store image and store environment. The **store environment** comprises the in-store stimuli; the speed, accuracy and friendliness of cashiers; the quality of products; store layout; lighting; the clarity with which prices of products are displayed; promotional strategies and overall store atmosphere. Therefore, it is impor-tant for marketers to strongly influence consumers' behaviour towards their business and its products and to create a positive store image. The store image reflects a mixture of meanings and relationships that characterise the store for consumers, that is, what consumers think about a particular store.

A **store image** is the definition of the store in the shopper's mind, composed partly by its functional qualities and partly by an aura of psychological attributes. In other words, consumers gain a perception of the store not only from the functional attributes of price, convenience and selection of merchandise, but also from the influence of variables such as architecture, interior design, colours and advertising (see Figure 15.8). Store choice determinants are intimately related to a store's image, and they influence its power to attract consumers.[30] Consumers react to the store's characteristics. They may be drawn to it if they feel a sense of trustworthiness and warmth, and they may be repelled if they view the store as deceitful, exploitative, unpleasant and antagonistic.

In essence, store loyalty is based on product offerings, physical factors, psychological factors and aesthetic factors (see Figure 15.9). Loyalty towards products and stores reduces ambiguity, it reduces risk in store choice and it makes decision-making easier and more efficient. Store patronage habits develop as a result of experience, reinforcement and previous buying responses. It minimises time and effort in store selection. For example, a consumer who enjoys shopping at a particular store because of its location, service, credit facilities or convenience will go to this store as soon as they need something, without stopping to think which store to visit. In other words, visiting the store becomes a habit when they need something.

However, product and store loyalty can change, and depend on the consumer's propensity or willingness to change, which in turn depends on the satisfaction consumers got from present and past brands as well as how easy it is to change. Assael[31] reports that store loyal consumers engage in less pre-purchase searches, know about fewer stores, and are less likely to shop even in a store known to them, and associates this shopping style with low income consumers who are constrained in their ability to shop.

In accordance with their different images, stores tend to attract different types of clients. In fact, individuals patronise stores whose image they feel matches their own, which then forms the basis of store loyalty.

15.4 Marketing implications

For an organisation to secure the long-term success of its brand, it must base its market share on its brand loyal consumers. Marketers should therefore engage in segmentation analysis to gain insight into their product's and brand's positioning as compared to perceived alternatives, the perceptions of consumers of their brands and the evaluative criteria or salient features that consumers use and consider to be important. Such knowledge will not only enable marketers to obtain a better understanding of their segment profile and loyalty patterns, but will also guide them in engaging in strategic marketing so as to secure a significant market share. Undoubtedly, brands that are well managed can become like trusted friends to consumers.[32] Managing brands effectively means shifting towards targeting more intangible, psychological and emotional wants in order to influence consumer demands. Marketers can thereby strategically leverage their brands towards brand profitability.

Brand loyalty differs across product categories. Hence, marketers need to assess consumer consumption patterns. This provides insight into the various categories of consumers in the marketplace, that is, truly loyal consumers with a strong brand commitment, current customers who may engage in brand switching, occasional users of the brand and non-users of the brand. While attracting consumers who are brand loyal to a competitor's brand may not be cost-effective, it would be profitable to sustain loyal consumers and to stimulate the usage of occasional users. Undoubtedly, usage rate and loyalty will assist marketers in developing appropriate strategies for maintaining their loyal customers and increasing their usage rate, as well as adopting strategies to prevent brand switching and to entice impulsive and variety-seeking shoppers to engage in brand trial and habit.

Since there is a relationship between consumers' attitude towards the brand and their purchasing behaviours, assessing and influencing attitudes in favour of the brand will result in increased sales. Therefore, marketers need to aim to develop consumer loyalty through changing attitudes by means of ensuring that the product's or brand's performance equals, or exceeds, consumer expectations, and that its performance is consistently good. This is particularly important at a time when there is a growing number of brands in the market that intercepts the potential for brand loyalty. Hence, the need for product development and innovation becomes increasingly imperative. Product improvements may be tactfully advertised to also attract those consumers who engage in variety-seeking behaviour. Brand awareness is critical to enlarging the current base of buyers; it is also the start to building a loyal consumer, and numerous promotional strategies, as we discussed above, may be used in this regard. Coupled with brand awareness is brand trial, which may be enhanced through free samples, coupons or significant price reductions.

Marketers gain leverage by ensuring that their brand has a distinct image or 'personality', that it provides added values and that it is unique yet easily identifiable. This must be effectively communicated through a coherent marketing approach that skilfully integrates all elements of the marketing mix and the promotion mix of advertising, selling and packaging. The image of the brand should be linked to the self-concept and personality of the target market. Ideally, the brand should possess the trait of superiority, which differentiates it from its competitors. Undoubtedly, brand image, product or brand quality and sales promotions are success ingredients or mechanisms for enhancing brand equity in the marketplace.

Marketers must aim to maintain the bond between the customer and the brand. The break in the bond can result in brand failure, which may be owing to a distorted perception of the brand, the competition or the market.[33] According to Haig, this may be due to one or more of the following 'seven deadly sins' of branding:

1. **Brand amnesia** – when a brand forgets what it is supposed to stand for.
2. **Brand ego** – when a brand overestimates its own importance and capability.
3. **Brand megalomania** – egotism can lead to megalomania, when the brand wants to expand into every conceivable product category.
4. **Brand deception** – the act of covering up the reality of the product/brand.
5. **Brand fatigue** – when companies get bored with their brand and the brand starts to lack creativity.
6. **Brand paranoia** – the opposite to brand ego, which generally occurs when the brand faces increasing competition.
7. **Brand irrelevance** – when a market evolves drastically, the brand faces the risk of becoming irrelevant and obsolete.[34]

The overall marketing implication is to adopt an integrated branding programme. This entails assessing *within* the organisation to understand how culture, competencies and staff alignment mould a brand's promise, and assessing *outside* the organisation to determine how the brand's promise has been delivered and received.[35] It is therefore important to become brand-driven through company-wide action. Hence, **integrated branding** 'is [a] way of operating, an overall way of doing business and a way to make certain a company's products are based on the right answers to two mutually reinforcing questions:

○ What do customers value? and
○ What does the company do best in relation to what customers want?'[36]

Therefore, marketers need to engage in holistic brand building processes from strategy to marketing tactics to effective implementation thereof, using effective tools or drivers.

Similarly, store loyalty may be enhanced by assuring effective store design and a store image that appeals to the target market. This means that marketers need to assess what evaluative criteria consumers use in store choice, how salient these features are and how their store's image compares to that of competitors. Reinforcing tactics such as in-store unadvertised specials may be used to attract repeat patronage.[37] Marketers need to recognise that the increasing level of unemployment and tight financial circumstances forces consumers to place greater emphasis on economy rather than conveniences and luxuries. Therefore, marketers need to consider using pricing strategies effectively in their appeals.

Case study

Organisation A decided to find out how many customers buy its brands. Its market research department conducted research to assess this. Market research teams approached various households and asked them to collect the packaging of the products they used for five months. In return for doing this, each household received a shopping voucher for R200 and a large utility bin.

They were given five large plastic bags marked January, February, March, April and May. The research teams collected the bags at the end of the five months and assessed the extent to which the organisation's brands were bought, in what quantities and how often. They tried to link purchases to price promotions and stock-out conditions. They labelled their product A, and other organisations' products B, C, and so on.

Having analysed the results, the market research team noticed these patterns:

○ Thirty-five per cent of the subjects, that is, the customer taking part in the survey (Group 1), bought the products in this sequence: AAAAAA.
○ Forty per cent of the subjects (Group 2) bought the products in this sequence: ABABABA.
○ Fifteen per cent of the subjects (Group 3) bought the products in this sequence: AAABBB.
○ Ten per cent of the subjects (Group 4) bought the products in this sequence: ABCDEF.

Cognisance must be given to the product offering, and to physical, psychological and aesthetic factors as the strategic combination of these factors can enhance a store's image and, hence, patronage and loyalty to a store. Furthermore, due to the increasing levels of competition, relationship marketing may play a pivotal role in securing both brand and store loyalty.

15.5 Summary

The gradual and continuous decline in the leverage of manufacturers has increased the need to differentiate products through the marketing activities of packaging and branding. The essence of successful branding involves the totality of the brand and the creation of a brand personality – the 'who' of the brand. The brand image is a perceptual phenomenon and the brand personality comes from product quality, packaging, important characteristics to consumers and the importance of the marketer's mark.

To create a successful and enduring brand, a combination of energies and strategies is needed. The brand concept must be developed by addressing consumers' needs and should be a promise of consistent quality. The success of the marketing effort is equal to the escalating value of the brand. Therefore, marketers must understand consumers, their needs and their concept of quality, as well as how they relate to brands. Marketers should also study the causal relationship between a consumer's brand attitude and buying behaviour.

Brand loyal consumers and brand loyalty allow marketers to develop highly effective market segmentation and promotion strategies. The development of brand loyalty depends on marketers acknowledging better ways to develop and identify better advertising, to guide the successful development of new products and to improve the overall effectiveness of the marketing mix.

Questions for self-assessment

To assess your progress, answer these questions:
1. Define brand loyalty.
2. Explain the influence of brand names on product preference.
3. Explain what we mean by brand image.
4. Explain what we mean by brand preference, brand loyalty and brand switching, and illustrate the influence of knowledge, attitudes and behaviour in determining brand preference.
5. Explain the relationship between brand loyalty and vulnerability.
6. Illustrate and explain the stages of brand loyalty.
7. Explain how loyalty patterns may be used for segmentation analysis.
8. Explain the behavioural, attitudinal and combined behavioural and attitudinal approaches to brand loyalty.
9. Distinguish between stochastic and deterministic models of brand loyalty.

10. Explain the difference between manufacturer brands, store brands and generic brands, using examples.
11. Explain the marketing implications of brand loyalty.
12. Draw up a model of store loyalty and explain the importance of store loyalty to marketing.
13. Illustrate the evaluative criteria used in determining store patronage and store loyalty.
14. Refer to the case study, and answer the following questions:
    a. Assess the patterns of brand loyalty to Organisation A in terms of the percentage of subjects/households that displayed unstable, divided and undivided loyalty.
    b. Which group is likely to engage in brand switching when the price of a competitor brand falls?
    c. Which group is likely to search for Organisation A's brand in another store when the store its members are in is out of stock?
    d. Which group displays variety-seeking behaviour?
    e. Which group displays brand loyalty and brand preference?
    f. What kind of message would you direct to each of the market segments if you were aiming to optimise market share?
    g. How would a marketing manager use this kind of information to develop a strategy to optimise market share?

Endnote references

1. Peter, J.P. and Olson, J.C. 2005. *Consumer Behavior and Marketing Strategy*. 7th ed. Boston: Irwin McGraw-Hill, Irwin.
2. Ratner, R.K., Kahn, B.E. and Kahneman, D. 1999. Choosing less-preferred experiences for the sake of variety. *Journal of Consumer Research*, 26, June, 1–15.
3. Kotler, P. and Armstrong, G. 2001. *Principles of Marketing*. 9th ed. Upper Saddle River:: Prentice-Hall.
4. Brucks, M., Zeithaml, V.A. and Naylor, G. 2000. Price and brand name as indicators of quality dimensions for consumer durables. *Journal of the Academy of Marketing Science*, 28(3), 359–74.
5. Janiszewski, C. and Van Osselaer, S.M.J. 2000. A connectionist model of brand-quality associations. *Journal of Marketing Research*, 37, August, 331–50.
6. Chernatony de, L. and McDonald, M. 2000. *Creating Powerful Brands in Consumer, Service and Industrial Markets*. Boston: Butterworth Heinemann.
7. Foster, J. and Tindale, K. 1984. Stretching the brand – the low-risk, high yield strategy. Brandtastic. *Marketing Mix*, 3(10), 25–8.
8. Ibid.
9. Hoyer, W.D. and MacInnis, D.J. 1997. *Consumer Behavior*. Boston: Houghton-Mifflin.
10. Horton, R.L. 1984. *Buyer Behavior: A Decision-making Approach*. Columbus: Merrill.
11. Duncan, T. 2002. *IMC: Using Advertising & Promotion to Build Brands*. Boston: McGraw-Hill, Irwin.
12. Heilman, C.M., Bowman, D. and Wright, G.P. 2000. The evolution of brand preferences and choice behaviours of consumers new to a market. *Journal of Marketing Research*, 37, May, 139–55.

13. Brown, G. 1952. Brand loyalty – fact or fiction? *Advertising Age*, 19, June, 53–5.
14. Tucker, W.T. 1964. The development of brand loyalty. *Journal of Marketing Research*, 3, August, 32–5.
15. Lawrence, R.J. 1969. Patterns of buyer behaviour: Time for a new approach? *Journal of Marketing Research*, 6, May, 137–44.
16. Blattberg, R.C. and Sen, S.K. 1976. Market segments and stochastic brand choice models. *Journal of Marketing Research*, 13, February, 34–45.
17. Day, G.S. 1969. A two-dimensional concept of brand loyalty. *Journal of Advertising Research*, 9, September, 29–36.
18. Ibid.
19. Assael, H. 1995. *Consumer Behavior and Marketing Action*. 5th ed. Ohio: South-Western College.
20. Carman, J.M. 1970. Correlates of brand loyalty: Some positive results. *Journal of Marketing Research*, 7, February, 67–76.
21. Rao, T.R. 1969. Consumers' purchase decision process: Stochastic models. *Journal of Marketing Research*, 6, August, 321–9.
22. Kuehn, A.A. 1962. Consumer brand choice as a learning process. *Journal of Advertising Research*, 20(4), 393–405.
23. Ibid.
24. Engel, J.F. and Blackwell, R.D. 1982. *Consumer Behavior*. 4th ed. Chicago: Dryden.
25. Skinner, S.J. 1990. *Marketing*. Boston: Houghton-Mifflin.
26. Weiss, E.B., cited in Patti, C.H. and Fisk, R.P. 1982. National advertising, brands and channel control: An historical perspective with contemporary options. *Academy of Marketing Science Journal*, 10(1), 90–108.
27. Patti and Fisk, op. cit.
28. Corstjens, M. and Lal, R. 2000. Building store loyalty through store brands. *Journal of Marketing Research*, 37, August, 281–91.
29. Cunningham, I.C.M., Hardy, A.P. and Imperia, G. 1982. Generic brands versus national brands and store brands. *Journal of Advertising Research*, 22(5), 25–32.
30. Loudon, D.L. and Della Bitta, A.J. 1993. *Consumer Behaviour: Concepts and Applications*. 4th ed. New York: McGraw-Hill.
31. Assael, op. cit.
32. Drawbaugh, K. 2001. *Brands in the Balance: Meeting the Challenges to Commercial Identity*. London: Reuters.
33. Haig, M. 2003. *Brand Failures*. London: Kogan Page.
34. Ibid.
35. Chernatony de, L. 2001. *From Brand Vision to Brand Evaluation: Strategically Building and Sustaining Brands*. Boston: Butterworth Heinemann.
36. Joseph LePla, F. and Parker, L.M. 2002. *Integrated Branding: Becoming Brand-driven through Company-wide Action*. London: Kogan Page, back blurb.
37. Loudon and Della Bitta, op. cit.

16 Building relationships with customers

16.1 Introduction

In the past, the marketing process was seen as ending when the sale occurred. This was known as 'transaction marketing' – the sale was the objective and the end result of the marketing effort. In **transaction marketing**, the main focus of marketing programmes has been to make customers buy, regardless of whether they are existing or new customers. According to this approach, the organisation was interested only in a single sale and the features of the product, with little emphasis on customer service. Furthermore, there was limited customer commitment and only moderate customer contact, and it was accepted by management and staff that quality is the concern of production.

Relationship marketing,[1] the new approach, is the opposite of transaction marketing. In **relationship marketing**, the focus has shifted from one-time transactions to ongoing relationships. The sale is not considered the end of the marketing process, but the *beginning* of a relationship in which buyers and sellers become interdependent. Ongoing relationships imply a new focus on customer retention, high customer commitment, high customer contact and a long-term perspective.

Relationship marketing can thus be seen as the shift from a transaction approach to a relationship approach, with the organisation growing interested in long-term commitments to maintaining and enhancing relationships with all customers. The purpose of these relationships is to create customer loyalty, and customer loyalty is a major factor in maximising profitability, the primary objective of all profit-seeking organisations. In this whole process, technology plays a crucial role; in fact, technology is seen as the facilitator of relationship marketing. If it had not been for technological advances in recent years, the entire concept of relationship marketing would not have been possible.

In this chapter we look at the changes in the practice of marketing and the solutions offered by relationship marketing. We stress the impact of technology on virtually every aspect of marketing and the organisation, and discuss how technology enables the business to focus on individual customers. We begin by considering the traditional approach to marketing.

16.2 The traditional marketing approach

16.2.1 Traditional marketing framework

It is generally recognised that marketing is central to an organisation because it defines what customers want and need, and because it directs the resources of the business to meet these needs.[2] Marketing is about people – marketers and customers – and about the ways in which marketers try to create a product or service that will satisfy the customers and generate sufficient profit. Finding and keeping the right customers is no simple task in today's business environment where the competition is tougher than ever. The central aim of marketing, therefore, is to satisfy needs. The marketer begins to fulfil this aim by identifying those needs.

Traditionally, marketing has been seen as a process of perceiving, understanding, stimulating and satisfying the needs of specially selected target markets by channelling an organisation's resources to meet those needs. If consumer needs are neglected, or if consumers are exploited, success can be achieved only in the short term and long-term relationships cannot be established. The main objective of any business is to achieve long-term profitability.

The traditional marketing framework comprises the following:[3]

○ The marketing mix, made up of the 4 Ps, which are the important elements or ingredients that make up a marketing programme.

○ Market forces, that is, the opportunities and threats that have an influence on the marketing operation of an organisation.
○ A matching process, that is, the strategic managerial process of ensuring that the marketing mix and internal policies are appropriate to the market forces.

On examining the traditional view of the marketing mix, we see that the marketing mix has been used to describe the important elements or ingredients that make up a marketing programme. Over time, the marketing mix decisions have been simplified under four headings, which became known as the '**4 Ps**'. This fixed list of categories has now become 'enshrined' in marketing theory, but perhaps less so in marketing practice. The 4 Ps consist of the following:

1. **Product** – the product or service being produced.
2. **Price** – the price charged for the product and terms associated with its sale.
3. **Promotion** – promotion and communications activities associated with marketing the product.
4. **Place (or distribution)** – the distribution that needs to be considered in making the product or service available.

The 4 Ps of traditional marketing are depicted in Figure 16.1.

Product	Price	Promotion	Place/Distribution

Figure 16.1: The 4 Ps of marketing

This traditional model has been reviewed frequently throughout the 1980s and there seems to be increasing doubt about its relevance to international, industrial and services marketing. Critics believe that the model does not suit relationship marketing where relationships with customers are ongoing and of critical importance.

The traditional marketing mix is based on the philosophy of the marketing concept.

16.2.2 The marketing concept

Traditional marketing, based on the marketing concept, was conceptualised in the 1950s by marketing scholars such as Theodore Levitt and Peter Drucker. As Drucker comments, 'Marketing ... is the whole business seen from the point of view of its final result, that is, from the customer's point of view.'[4] The essence of the marketing concept is in understanding customer needs and wants, thus the focus is on the customer. If a company offers goods and services that satisfy needs and create value for the customer – providing customer satisfaction and the right customer-perceived quality – it stands the best chance of maximising profitability.

This customer focus has become a widespread slogan, although it was understood and implemented only by a few of those who expressed it. Although rational in principle, it was flawed in practice. The actual needs, wants and expectations of the customer, in fact, were not perceived in reality as being of paramount importance. Thus, while lip service was paid to customer supremacy in principle, in practice, marketers ignored it.[5]

We can therefore say that the marketing concept has failed in its implementation over the last 20 years or more. Moreover, the entire traditional marketing approach is flawed, in particular, aspects such as the 4 Ps of marketing, transactional marketing and market segmentation.

16.2.3 Marketing in crisis

During the 1980s, many organisations began to question the large expenditure on marketing without a measurable return on investment that had been assumed in past decades. Most brands showed little growth, and markets became dominated by oligopolies, the few competing producers and sellers. It also became obvious that strategic competitive advantage could no longer be delivered on the basis of product and service characteristics alone since there was little difference between products. Because of this, customers were bombarded with advertising messages in the companies' attempts to increase their profitability.

It was suggested that the marketing mix and other aspects of traditional marketing were dying.[6] Some authors went so far as to propose that 'marketing is dead because the old rules of identifying and satisfying customer demand no longer apply. Technology has seen to that and, in the process, created entirely new opportunities for marketers. The world is changing but marketing appears stuck in a rut'.[7]

As marketing entered the 1990s, relationship marketing – a new paradigm and a shift in business thinking – was regarded as the biggest change in 50 years, in effect taking marketing back to its roots.

The relationship marketing concept evolved from the marketing concept.

16.3 Relationship marketing

16.3.1 New marketing paradigm

As we have seen, relationship marketing was the 'battle cry' of the 1990s. Not a wholly independent philosophy, it draws on traditional marketing principles. This suggests that the basic focus on customer needs still applies, but that it is the way marketing is practised that required fundamental alteration.[8]

Relationship marketing can be defined as follows:

> The objectives of relationship marketing are to identify and establish, maintain and enhance, and, when necessary, terminate relationships with customers and other stakeholders, at a profit so that the objectives of all parties involved are met. This is done by mutual exchange and fulfilment of promises.[9]

While recognising that customer acquisition was, and would remain, part of a marketer's responsibilities, this viewpoint emphasised that a relationship view of marketing implied that retention and development were more important to the company, in the longer term, than customer acquisition.

The implementation of the new philosophy usually takes place in the well-known process of **customer relationship management** (CRM). However, while today many companies realise the importance of CRM, most companies continue to operate using a mixture of the transactional marketing and relationship marketing approaches.[10]

Walking the extra mile for customers

Joe is a car salesman. He has sold more new cars and trucks, each year, for 11 years running, than any other salesperson. In fact, in a typical year, Joe always sells more than twice as many cars as whoever is in second place. What is Joe's magic formula? It is simply service, overpowering service, especially after-sales service. Joe says: 'There's one thing that I do that a lot of salesmen don't – I believe the sale really begins after the sale, not before. The customer is not out of the door, and I'm already writing a thank-you note.' Joe always intercedes personally, a year later, with the service manager on behalf of his customers. Meanwhile he keeps the communications flowing.

Joe seems genuinely to care and says: 'The great restaurants have more than just good food coming out of their kitchens ... and when I sell a car, my customer is going to leave with the same feeling that he'll get when he walks out of a great restaurant.' Joe's sense of caring continues to shine through after the sale: 'When the customer comes back for service, I fight for him all the way to get him the best ... You've got to be like a doctor. Something is wrong with his car, so feel hurt for him.' Joe emphasises: 'My customers are not an interruption or a pain in the neck – they are my bread and butter.'[11]

Joe's story is a good illustration of the marketer being close to the customer. We can say that Joe believes, and behaves as if, the customer really does count. This is in line with the best companies in the world, which are obsessed about quality, reliability and service. This is also in line with CRM – the act of establishing lasting relationship with customers. However, CRM encompasses much more, as we shall see.

We now look at how the marketing mix of the traditional marketing approach should be adapted to fit in with CRM.[12]

16.3.2 Adapting the 4 Ps of traditional marketing

The traditional 4 Ps of marketing – namely, product, price, promotion and place/distribution – need to be approached differently according to the new focus on customer relationships. Technology can assist in combining the 4 Ps in numerous variations, thereby offering the customers many choices so that they can obtain precisely what they want (product), when and how they want it (distribution), and at a cost that represents the value they wish to receive (price). Moreover, technology enables the company to engage individual customers when and how they wish to communicate (promotion).

We now consider how each of these should change in CRM terms.

Product

Traditionally, the marketer devised product concepts, researched the customers and then developed the product that would yield the desired profit margin to the business. This did not take into account the fact that customers want different things at different times and are not interested in one standard product or service.

By contrast, relationship marketing involves real-time interaction between the company and its priority, that is, the most profitable customers, as the company seeks to move more rapidly to meet customer requirements. The customer participates in the development of the product. The product resulting from the collaboration may be unique or highly tailored to the requirements of the customers, with much more of their knowledge content incorporated into the product than was previously the case. Thus, for products and services, where the lifetime and volume and margin warrant it, individual customers can and should be considered in every aspect of the business, including the processes that drive new product and service design. This act recognises that customers are not equal, they want different things in different amounts at different times, and the profit derived from each will vary.

Car manufacturers could consider offering customers the following:

- O They should allow customers to specify what types of wheels they prefer.
- O Instead of telling a customer that a particular car is available in only a certain range of colours, they could allow them to choose the colour.
- O They could consider customising the steering wheel to suit the particular needs of customers.

It is interesting to note that some of the American car manufacturers, such as General Motors, are offering customers the opportunity of ordering cars, that have been customised exactly to their particular specifications, on the internet!

The key challenge for the marketer is to identify the core strategic value that will be delivered to the customer and the elements that the customer can change, allowing the latter to be firmly in charge, assembling the value they want. For most organisations, mass customisation requires a material shift in current practice – and the marketer can lead the charge.

Price

Traditional marketing sets a price for a product and offers the product at that price in the market. In this way, traditional marketers seek to secure a fair return on the investment that the company has made in its more-or-less static product. By contrast, with regard to relationship marketing, the product varies according to the preferences and dictates of the customers, and the value varies along with it. Thus, when customers specify features that a product should have and expect certain services to be delivered before, during and after the sale, they naturally want to pay for each component of the value bundle separately. Just as the product and services are set in a process of collaboration, so too will the price need to reflect the choices made and the value created from these choices.

Customers want to participate in decisions regarding the value they receive and the prices they pay. Give them a standard offering and they will expect to pay a single price. But offer them options in the product and they will want some more than others, and will pay more for these. Give them a chance to have an even more tailored solution and they might pay more again. Give them options they do not want and they will expect these to be removed, and the price reduced accordingly.

Especially in the case of industrial marketing, relationship marketing therefore invites customers into the pricing process and all other value-related processes, giving them an opportunity to make any trade-offs and to further develop trust in the relationship.

Marketing communication (or promotion)

Traditional marketing uses one-way mass advertising to communicate with customers. This communication comprises promotional offers, manuals, price lists and warranty response cards. It must be replaced with two-way communications to involve the customers much earlier in all matters that affect their future purchase behaviour. Technology can turn promotion into *communication* because it can engage individual customers when and how they wish to respond. Relationship marketing gives individual customers an opportunity to decide how they wish to communicate with the business.

Marketers can serve customers as individuals by using technology appropriately. With technology, individual end-customers can be interactively and uniquely engaged. With the internet, computer telephony integration (CTI) at all centres, intelligence at point-of-sale, smart cards and interactive voice response, companies can give customers a host of options for interactive communication, and have information on hand to engage, inform and direct each customer with complete knowledge as to their preferences.

Distribution (place)

Traditional marketing sees distribution as the channel that takes the product from the producer to the consumer. For example, in the case of the computer industry, Dell sees distribution as a direct sales approach, primarily using telephone sales and other placement, while IBM uses many approaches to distribution, including its own stores, a direct sales force and retailers that resell its personal computers.

Relationship marketing instead considers distribution from the perspective of the customer, who decides where, how and when to buy the combination of products and services that comprise the supplier's total offering. Seen this way, distribution is not a channel, but a *process*. The process allows customers to choose where and from whom they will obtain the value they want.

> **Buying a computer the relationship marketing way**
>
> The customer can choose whether to buy a computer off the shelf from a reseller and take it home immediately, or order one that is built to individual preferences at the factory and shipped within a week or so, or have one configured in-store and made available within a few days.

It is thus more accurate to think of distribution as a 'placement,' giving the customers choice with regard to location at which they will specify, purchase, receive, install, repair and return individual components of the products and services. While traditional marketing considers a product as a bundled package of benefits, relationship marketing unbundles the product and service and allows the customer to initiate a placement decision for each element.

The relationship marketing concept offers many solutions to the dilemma of traditional marketing. Relationship marketing provides an opportunity for the company and the marketer to break out of existing frameworks such as the traditional 4 Ps, and to fix the firm in its customers' minds, and wallets. It offers marketers a chance to help the company to grow in a competitively challenging environment. Enabled by new technologies, relationship marketing provides the marketer with the tools needed to serve individuals as they wish to be served, throughout their purchasing and consumption lifetimes. Companies that are first to adopt relationship marketing principles in their industries, and to apply the concepts with vigour, have the potential to gain a first-mover advantage, which is difficult for competitors to emulate. Importantly, this means that companies have the potential to gain a pre-emptive position with the best customers and to ensure that the needs of these customers are well addressed long before competitors try to copy and target these individuals or companies.

No organisation can simply decide to use CRM, without making sure it has all the prerequisites in place.

16.4 Prerequisites for implementing CRM

Before CRM can be implemented in any organisation, the organisation needs to be transformed entirely. Processes need to focus on the customer, thus teamwork becomes a major factor.

16.4.1 Teamwork and processes

According to relationship marketing, teamwork is particularly important and assumes precedence over the importance of the individual employee. Relationship marketing requires that teams be more formal than informal and that they include the customer. Teamwork is one of the new capabilities that any organisation should enhance among its employees. This means that, for example, processes in the organisation need to change from the traditional 'silo approach' to the integration of all the functional areas.[13]

Processes should be changed to focus on the customer. **Processes** are the fundamental tasks, or 'the way things are done'. Thus, **process management** involves the procedures, tasks, schedules, mechanisms, activities and routines by which a product or service is delivered to the customer.

Relationship marketing takes the view that the company should be organised around the customers it has chosen to serve, and that all technologies and processes should help the company to foster the customer relationship. According to this view, management should focus on incorporating customers into the main processes and customers should collaborate with management in all the processes that are geared to creating value. For example, marketers should develop products by consulting the customer, and decision-making should be decentralised to the point of relationship contact. It also means shifting from a focus on individual effort to team-based processes.

However, process is only one of the new capabilities needed for CRM. The others are equally important and include support at top management level, excellent customer service and technology to gain customer knowledge.[14]

Chrysler: The value of teamwork

In the early nineties, Chrysler, the American motor manufacturing company, realised that it would eventually lose millions of dollars and over 25 percent of its workforce, and of course many of its customers, to mainly Japanese competition. The company had no choice but to go back to the basics and build cars that would lure customers to Chrysler showrooms and keep them coming back for more.

Chrysler's goal in 1991 was to build America's first small car that could compete with Toyota's and Honda's quality and sell at a profit. The company subsequently developed the Neon, a sub-compact car. The car had to be developed quickly and it also had to be made cheaply. This car is also available in South Africa.

These goals were achieved. Teamwork was the key – teams of marketers, purchasing agents, design engineers and manufacturing engineers created the car. Chysler's new focus on long-term customer satisfaction and excellent quality and above all teamwork, has allowed the company to come back from the verge of bankruptcy as it builds relationships with a whole new generation of drivers.

16.4.2 Support at executive level

It is top management's task to direct the activities of the organisation. Without its support in all its forms, a CRM strategy will not succeed because the implementation of this strategy has far-reaching effects throughout the organisation. Changes need to be made in each part of the organisation and the leadership must show the way.

Management must recognise the fact that the relationship with customers needs to be managed. A relationship manager should work with customers to ensure that they receive the value they seek. Each person within the organisation communicates and creates value with its customer counterpart, while the relationship manager guides the overall process. In this process, it is necessary to integrate all communications with the customer using technology, as well as people and process.

16.4.3 Excellent customer service

There is a saying that 'the customer is always right'. It is necessary to give customers satisfaction when they complain. Marketers should engage them positively and offer restitution. When customers complain it is a signal of a breakdown in the process somewhere in the business. Perhaps the breakdowns have to do with understanding and shaping customer expectations or delivering on these expectations. Hence, an organisation that works collaboratively with customers throughout the value chain should have a limited need for a customer service department.

Today, the customer service department is at the frontline, where it engages the irate, the disappointed or the ill-informed. But this role is miscast, as it provides service after the customer has had an unpleasant experience. In terms of relationship marketing, the customer service centre should be changed into a customer information centre geared to anticipating customer issues so that the service role assumes greater significance. The customer information centre could proactively engage customers, ensure lifetime customer satisfaction and be at the cutting edge of the marketing communication changes required for relationship marketing.

16.4.4 Technology to gain customer knowledge and insight

Relationship marketing is simply not possible without the enabling effects of technology to store, retrieve, process, communicate and analyse data, including customer data. If used effectively, technology has enormous potential for relationship building. Developments in information technology (IT) allow a relationship-oriented management to store and manipulate information about their customers, and ultimately to provide those customers with a better service. In CRM terms, perhaps the biggest danger is for marketers to assume that technology can always effectively replace personal contact.

In the relationship marketing era, customer knowledge and insight come from data on customer interactions, transactions and manifested behaviours, including purchase, service and return activity. This means that the capability of knowledge development is closely tied into the underlying technologies that can help to develop customer knowledge and, in particular, the data warehousing, data mining and predictive modelling that allows you to forecast customer behaviour and ask 'what if?' questions at the customer level.

Learning about each and every customer may be the single most powerful capability a CEO can put in place, and customers can help an organisation to populate a data warehouse. However, knowledge should also be created about the business environment of the customers, including those that the organisation serves and the competitors and regulators that it faces. It pays to invest in customer knowledge and insight.

It is worth emphasising again that all these capabilities should be in place before an organisation can even contemplate implementing CRM. If top management does not support the process of implementation, CRM is doomed to fail. Processes should be adjusted so that the customers can be served in the way they prefer to be served, that

---

More customer knowledge than competitors

Amcan Castings, a supplier of engineered aluminium castings to the motorcar industry, bids on contract opportunities according to a well-defined set of specifications from the car companies. But Amcan has improved its chances of winning each contract by having more customer knowledge than its competitors. It places staff in the customers' premises and collaborates with them on product conceptualisation, design and planning, blurring the line between where Amcan ends and the car company begins. Amcan has grown rapidly in this competitive industry, one contract at a time, through improved customer knowledge and mutual learning.

---

is, individually. It is also no good if an organisation first implements CRM, or CRM software, and then attempts to improve its customer service. Technology is only the *enabler* of CRM; it enables the organisation to serve customers as individuals, giving them what they want, where they want it and at a price they are willing to pay, and to communicate with the customer on a one-to-one basis. However, it does not solve any problems that the organisation might already have.

16.5 Technology: The facilitator of CRM[15]

While technology cannot solve any problems that an organisation may be experiencing, it facilitates the implementation of CRM. Without technology, CRM would not be possible.

16.5.1 Crucial role of technology

Imagine the way business was conducted 20 years ago in comparison to the way we do business now. Then, communication was by telex or telegram, typing was done on manual typewriters, and copies were made on Roneo machines. Today, we use e-mail or telefax, type on a personal computer or laptop, and use a copy machine to make copies. The rate of change in technology is one of the environmental variables that has the most effect on businesses today.

More than any other change in the marketing environment, technology enables the successful implementation of relationship marketing. Its power can put **custom** back into the word 'customer'. However, if it is applied inappropriately, it can serve to alienate the customer. Used appropriately, it can help the company to learn from every customer interaction, to deepen the relationship by advancing ideas and solutions likely to suit the customer, and to ask questions so that it can serve the customer even better the next time. Technology drives the mega-processes needed to provide value for customers.

Why do some companies persist in thinking that technology is the answer to tackling customer care issues? When will it dawn on marketers everywhere that technology only improves customer service if it helps to solve customers' problems?

Thus, we can see that it is dangerous to assume that technology can effectively replace personal contact. Technology-supported developments, such as call centres and telephone menus, aimed at increasing the efficiency of the organisation do not necessarily increase value or convenience for the customer.

Today's 'interactive age' customers are used to having their needs met immediately, conveniently and inexpensively. For many people, this is why contacting customer service representatives can be an uncomfortable experience. Between navigating lengthy menus of push-button options, waiting on hold for what seems an eternity, never receiving a reply to an e-mail, and not having our problems remembered the next time we call, it is no wonder many of us as customers think that 'customer service' is a cruel joke.

Technology no substitute[16]

Alfa Romeo in Britain is said to have spent over £1 million building and staffing a call centre. But all it has got for its money is a mechanism by which to antagonise even the mildest customer who needs anything more than a brochure. Alfa has fallen into the trap of assuming that investment in technology is a substitute for developing processes that lead to good customer care experiences. It seems to find it easier to spend money than commit the time to think about how to deal effectively with the genuine concerns of its customers.

16.5.2 Technology for building relationships

The changes in technology and, more importantly, the performance of technology have led to tremendous opportunities for companies to tie technology in with the implementation and use of relationship marketing. Now organisations can communicate with consumers and serve them in real time – thus, they need never ask the consumer a question more than once. The potential exists for the company to have an information system that gives a complete, current and intelligent profile of the customer to the customer interface, be it a call centre, a website or sales automation.

We now look at ways in which technology contributes to building relationships with customers.

Enhancing customer care and service

As we have seen, technology plays a major role in providing customers with the care they want. The internet can be particularly cost-effective in shifting cost structures away from human operators with regard to enquiries to which the customer needs basic, standard format or repetitive information-type answers. For example, a person who needs specific information on paying the instalments for a new car can automatically be given the following response: 'You can calculate your car repayments by entering the total amount to be borrowed, the interest rate and the loan terms'.

In a number of vertical markets today, technology is being applied to facilitate and add value to customer relationships. For example, look at a major hotel chain and see the power of its reservation systems at work – they are becoming increasingly sophisticated, with guest history records and customer profiles that enable a much more personal and useful dialogue.

Technology facilitates superior service

Jenny Brown is on her third business trip this month. She takes a taxi from Boston's Logan Airport to the Ritz-Carlton, her favourite hotel. The doorman opens the car door for her and greets her, 'Welcome back to the Ritz-Carlton, Mrs Brown'. When she goes to the registration desk, the receptionist gives her the room key and asks if she would like to have her stay charged to her American Express card. Then she goes to her room and finds just what she likes – a room with a view of the Boston Commons, a queen-sized bed, an extra pillow and blanket, a fax machine connected to her telephone, and a basket with her favourite fruit and snacks.

By contrast, customer care in South Africa is particularly poor. Consider the following observation.

Training in customer care is wasted

Although South African companies spend millions a year on customer service training, with only a few exceptions customer service levels have remained low. Emphasising the role of customer loyalty and retention would help to stem the leak of customers, for many customer defections are caused by rude or poorly selected employees and a lack of service recovery skills. By understanding the worth of each customer and their own importance in the organisation, the employees could come to understand the value of customer service better.

Identifying the best customers[17]

A key role of the CRM marketer is to define which customers will be served, that is, the most profitable customer, the bonding and other objectives to be achieved, and the strategies to be followed in working with chosen customers to create more value for the customer to be satisfied and for the business to be more profitable.

With technology, the specific customers with which the company wishes to do business can be identified and further evaluated for their amenability and suitability for a long-term relationship. If the data warehouse is built appropriately, the marketer should be able to 'slice and dice' the data in an infinite number of ways, so that the people not trained in the technology can still find it easy to use.

Technology thus helps to decide which customers to focus on and what is needed to deliver customer value. Without technology, marketers would still be thinking in terms of serving the mass market or segments. They would still be using one-way communication and long production runs of standardised products, with one size fitting all.

Establishing the product/service to provide

Technology helps to establish the types of products or services that should be provided to customers, as well as whether the business should produce these itself or outsource the production. For example, if a company makes home furniture, should it offer financing to its retailers for them to package financing terms to customers?

Consider the case of a customer who is buying furniture. The product comprises 'hard' features and benefits, such as the style, fabric and construction. It may also comprise 'softer', intangible features such as attractiveness and function.

Enhancing capabilities

Another important effect of technology, especially for implementing CRM, is that it substantially enhances the capabilities of the business. Technology implementations themselves comprise the heart of the company's capabilities, by providing, for example, computing and data warehousing content such as a website or interactive voice response (IVR) to the customer, and communications linkages within the business and with customers.

Managing costs and value of relationships

Technology can help the company to manage the costs of securing, serving and retaining customers by allowing marketers to understand, in 'real time', the revenues and costs associated with each customer. This can clearly help the CRM manager to control and focus the relationship. Moreover, technology can intercede and help to manage the costs and value of the relationship, drawing upon previously developed 'business rules'. These rules incorporate decisions that management makes to guide the administration of its business and interaction with customers.

Technology to engage patrons interactively

Administration responsible for the management of local libraries may decide that any books that are more than three days later than has been the historical return practice of borrowers should result in a phone call being placed to remind the borrower the books are overdue. The call is placed by an automated dialler with a recorded message. When the borrower returns the books, late charges can be applied automatically after the books have been logged. Frequent borrowers might be allowed a longer period of time than infrequent borrowers, and different messages might be employed. Software companies offer libraries some aspects of these features in their software, and could extend their offering to learn from the behaviours of individual borrowers, before helping librarians to engage their patrons interactively: 'I see you like books by Author X. Did you know we have this new one on our shelves?'[18]

Performing a control function

Technology performs a control function to ensure that value is indeed created for customers and for the company, and that invoices are sent and payment is received on time. Technology assists in tactical and strategic control functions. **Tactical controls** ensure that the business processes actually perform as planned. **Strategic controls** track not only product profitability but all costs associated with the product and the customer, for example account management, servicing, support and communications. This assessment can help with the management of the customer mix. For example, in the case of a customer retention problem, technology will operate in the background, gathering and evaluating data, and providing the relationship marketer with exception reports.

Overdue telephone and electricity accounts

Technology, combined with a more caring attitude, helps to build better customer relationships, thereby increasing the value of these relationships:

○ Telkom offers us the service of informing us if our telephone account becomes overdue. When we pick up the receiver to dial, a pre-recorded message tells us that our account has not been paid. By warning us before the service may be discontinued, Telkom enhances its relationship with us.

○ By contrast, if our electricity account is in arrears, the municipality simply cuts off the electricity and requires us to pay a large amount to be reconnected. The municipality should follow Telkom's example and warn those of us who have overdue accounts.

Customising products

Technology can help customers to work together with their suppliers so that there is a joint effort to continuously create and improve value. Technology allows the customer to become integrated into the processes so that customisation is reasonable. This means that the business collaborates with the customer to design a product that the customer wants. In effect, customers can order exactly what they want and have it made so as to best meet their needs.

Customising communication and interaction

Marketers can serve customers as individuals by using technology appropriately. A data-driven approach enables companies to assess each customer's needs and potential profitability, and to tailor sales offers and service accordingly. This entails using multiple channels – including the internet, direct mail, telesales and field sales – as a means of improving effectiveness and efficiency. The challenge for the marketer is to work with IT managers to design processes and incorporate technologies to engage the customer collaboratively at appropriate times, for the benefit of the customer *and* the organisation.

Thus, technology can help businesses to adapt their communication efforts to include business-to-individual customer conversations, that is, the all-important two-way communication. In this way, customers can make their needs clear to the business and the business can make itself more transparent to the customers.

Furthermore, technology can help the company to converse with individuals at a cost that reflects the value of the communications, and can discriminate among the purposes of different communications, assigning the appropriate media to fulfil each task. For example, if the purpose of the communication is not to add customised value to the customer, then mass media can be used. If interaction is required, the company may choose to deploy web casting or call centres for outbound calling. If the intention is to deliver considerable, customised information, then it is more appropriate for the company to use its sales force. More commonly, a combination of these is required, and it becomes appropriate for the company to allocate the lowest cost technology or approach to achieve each communications objective.

Technology provides the knowledge and insight to let the company contact the customer at the right time – when they are ready to buy – and use the media each customer prefers to make this communication.

We now look at some major changes that have elevated the role of technology as a strategic capability.

16.5.3 Developments in technology[19]

We now examine the relevant technological developments.

The internet

The internet provides opportunities for marketers to engage interactively with the customer using processes that are standardised, but which afford customers the opportunity to assemble the value they want in a customised product. The internet offers two main types of virtual experiences for customers, using so-called 'pull' and 'push' technologies.

Pull technology comes into play when a customer visits a website and makes a product or information selection decision during the course of the visit, not unlike traditional shopping. **Push technology** resembles a standing order that a customer has set up with the retailers. For example, historically, a fashion conscious customer may tell the store owner to notify them when a new collection from a specific designer comes in. Similarly, with push technology, customers specify what it is they wish to be informed about and under what conditions, and then they receive this information when it becomes available. Push technology makes the computer seem more like TV, in that the consumer's experience can become more passive, but the information will still have been tailored to individual preferences.

Many people are familiar with the potential inherent in using pull technology, which is the basis of most internet store-fronts and websites. Using this approach, customers enter terms in a search engine at sites such as Yahoo or Alta Vista. The engine goes out on the Web and locates sites that may meet the parameters entered. Push technology, by contrast, may offer much more opportunity to the CRM marketer as it makes more use of technology to learn of individual preference and then acts on it.

Data warehouses

The engine that enables customer relationship management is the database. Customer data warehouses can be defined as large repositories of information about the customer gathered from sources internal to the company, and from the customer, and from externals such as the government, a credit bureau and market research companies. Data can include behaviour, preferences, lifestyle information, transactional data and data about communications with the company before, during and after the sale. It may also include information about customer profitability, satisfaction, retention, loyalty and referrals.

More generally, data warehouses can be described in terms of the processes and layers needed to automate and add value to communications with the customer and to facilitate mass customisation. Data warehousing enables companies to extract information from the underlying data to develop a better understanding of, for example, the most profitable relationships.

Data mining

Data mining is the process that employs IT – both hardware and software – to uncover previously unknown patterns of behaviour, trends and issues arising from the assessment of warehoused data.

Using data mining, companies may employ massively parallel computers and task-appropriate software to search through large volumes of data. Often, the data is about customers and their purchasing behaviour. Companies are looking for patterns that describe the behaviours and permit them to segment their markets in new ways, to retain customers and to become more relevant. They can do this by designing products and services to meet the needs of customer 'clusters', communicate with them more effectively and earn their loyalty.

Data reveals patterns of behaviour

A mass merchandiser discovered through data mining and clustering that one segment of their customer base comprises female consumers who buy cosmetics and sweets. This led them to place the cosmetics and sweets sections of their stores closer together to accommodate such purchases.

Convenience stores have found that many of their nappies are bought by men, who often buy beer at the same time. Using this information, some stores have placed these products closer together on their shelves.

Database queries are enabled by front-end tools such as FastStats and Rapidus to speed intelligent data review and response to enquiry. Data mining differs from database queries. **Queries** answer specific requests for information – either simple requests, or ones that need multi-dimensional analysis or online analytical processing to provide the required answers. For example, if you want to know the names of customers that bought two red Fords in Gauteng in 2002, the database could be queried for the information.

Data mining, by contrast, employs tools that look for meaning, find patterns in the data and infer rules that may be causal, predictive or descriptive. This can lead to better management decision-making in areas such as planning, matching inventory to customer requirements, customer targeting and improving marketing and operating processes more generally.

Technologies used by call centres

One of the technologies used by call centre operations in South Africa is CTI, which involves a high degree of human–data interaction. Another is IVR, whereby pre-recorded data can be played to callers in response to touch-tone telephone input.

Technology is advancing rapidly to help marketers to mine the gold in the slurry of data they have in their warehouses, and firms are adapting the technology in ever-increasing scale and complexity to build their capability for CRM. Many companies are building large data warehouses, believing that these provide a competitive edge and 'information *beyond* the product', allowing a lifetime of value creation with customers.

Large data warehouse

Johnson & Johnson's finance department employs a data warehouse to enable managers in 50 countries to slice, dice and analyse information from computers all over the company on many financial matters – from accounts receivable to inventories. J&J is considering dropping one product line that this process suggested. The company may use data warehousing for value engineering, developing a real time 'virtual financial statement' to help make capital allocation decisions earlier and cut the number of hours required to do this and related work.

The purpose of establishing and maintaining customer relationships through technology is to retain customers so that they will become loyal. We now deal with relationship loyalty.

16.6 Relationship loyalty

To understand relationship loyalty, we need to explore customer loyalty, customer retention and the lifetime value of customers.

16.6.1 Customer loyalty

As the objective of CRM, customer loyalty means more than customers making repeat purchases, and being satisfied with their experiences and the products or services they purchased. It means that customers are committed to purchasing products and services from a specific organisation, and will resist the activities of competitors attempting to attract their patronage. They have a bond with the organisation, and the bond is based on more than a positive feeling about the organisation.

The objective of relationship marketing is therefore to turn new customers into regularly purchasing customers, and then to move them through being strong supporters of the company and its product to being active advocates for the company, thus playing an important role as a referral source. Customer service plays a pivotal role in this process.

Loyalty towards a retailer[20]

Loyal customers have an emotional connection with the retailer. Their reasons for continuing to patronize the retailer go beyond the convenience of the retailer's store or the low prices and specific brands offered by the retailer. They feel such goodwill toward the retailer that they will encourage their friends and family to buy from it.

16.6.2 Customer retention

Many companies spend a great deal of effort, time and money wooing new customers, yet surprisingly few take equal trouble to retain existing customers. Also, few companies go to the trouble of regularly measuring customer satisfaction in any systematic way, partly because they are obsessed by a perceived need to win new business and partly because they fail to understand the real and demonstrable relationship between customer retention and profitability.

Customer bonding at banks[21]

Most banks probably devote most of their resources and energy to attracting new customers, but few take the trouble to retain existing ones. This of course is changing, but one wonders whether South African banks will truly adopt the strategies of CRM or whether they will merely pay lip service to the theory. In the last decade, the emphasis was on quality and quality service and, while banks certainly attempted to focus on these issues in training and other strategies, little impact in terms of excellent customer service has been felt by the average banking customer.

Customer retention has a profound influence on the profitability of an organisation:
- Acquiring a new customer costs more than retaining an existing one.
- Normally, 80% of the profits are derived from 20% of the clients, according to the Pareto Principle. It thus makes sense to concentrate on the clients that produce profits; in other words, the existing clients.
- Regular customers tend to place frequent and consistent orders, thereby decreasing the costs of servicing those customers.
- Efforts to retain customers make it difficult for competitors to enter the market or to increase their share of the market.
- Improved customer retention can lead to an increased level of employee satisfaction which in turn leads to increased employee retention and which feeds back into an even greater customer longevity.
- Long-time customers tend to be less price sensitive, permitting the charging of

higher prices – they will not move for the 5% difference in banking charges, for example.

○ Long-time customers are likely to provide free word-of-mouth advertising and referrals.

16.6.3 Lifetime value[22]

Customer lifetime value (CLV) describes the present value of the stream of future profits that the company expects to make from the customer's lifetime purchases. Marketers estimate lifetime value (LTV) using past behaviours to forecast the future purchases, the gross margin from these purchases and the costs associated with servicing the customers.

Marketers base their assessments of LTV on the assumption that the customer's future purchase behaviours will be the same as they have been in the past. Sophisticated statistical methods are typically used to estimate the future contributions. For example, these methods might consider how recent purchases have been made. The expected LTV of a customer at a grocery store who purchased products to the value of R2 000 in one visit, for instance, is probably less than the LTV of a customer who has been purchasing products to the value of R500 every month for the last six months.

Customers have different values to the organisation, and they need different things from the organisation. What do the customers want and what is the customer worth? The value of a customer relative to other customers allows the business to prioritise its efforts, allocating more resources to ensuring that the more valuable customers remain loyal and grow in value. Catering to the needs and demands of a specific customer forms the basis for creating a relationship and winning the customer's loyalty.

One other critical element of the customer's LTV is their growth potential or strategic value. **Strategic value** is the additional value a customer could yield if marketers had a strategy to obtain it.

A customer's growth potential or strategic value[23]

A banking customer has both a cheque and a savings account. Every month the customer provides a certain profit to the bank, and the net present value of this continuing profit stream represents the customer's actual value to you. But the home mortgage that same customer has at a competitive bank represents strategic value – potential value you could realize if you had a proactive strategy to obtain it.

When an organisation has determined the LTV of its customers, it should have a well-informed financial view of its customer base. In particular, it will know that a relatively small number of customers accounts for the majority of the profits. As most companies attempt to establish relationships with their customers, they should bear in mind that in some cases there are reasons that make the attempt to develop a relationship a fruitless pursuit – certain some relationships are simply unrealistic.

16.7 Limitations of implementing CRM

Some companies may find it difficult to implement the principles of relationship marketing. We now explore the various reasons for this.

16.7.1 Little value to be created

In some industries there may be little value to be created between the company and its customers, and the customers may not be amenable to what value creation there could be. Consumers buying soap, for example, may consider this a low-involvement purchase decision that requires little input from the supplier. This is at the lower end of the market. At the higher end there is more value, for example as in the case of Dove soap.

16.7.2 Insufficient lifetime value

In some situations, although potential mutual value exists, there may be insufficient LTV to warrant value creation. While the LTV of the average purchaser of motorcars may be R300 000, the average LTV for the purchase of specific consumer non-durables, such as food and beverages, may be a fraction of this. Clearly, the Ford company can afford to spend more on attracting and retaining appropriately profiled customers than, for example, could a processor of cheese, if this was the only product promoted. Lever Brothers can indeed try to attract and retain the most valuable customers (as done by Ford) because these customers buy so many of Lever Brothers products on a shopping trip.

16.7.3 Large investments in product design and development

For companies that have recently spent major sums on the design and development of products, and for those firms that have also invested heavily in infrastructure or business processes, adopting a relationship marketing approach may result in a portion of their investments being severely depreciated, or even wasted.

16.7.4 No capability for relationship marketing

Not every company has the capability of applying relationship marketing principles with more than basic commitment. It will not have the financial depth, technological capabilities or relationship marketing sophistication to do justice to the principles. And if a company is struggling to survive, it is essential that it pays attention to the short-term issues that it faces, in order to ensure that there is a long term.

The extent to which a company adopts CRM principles should depend upon careful consideration of strategic issues and economics. But one thing is indisputable: the trend towards individualised, customised and personalised marketing is now in full force.

If a company is to adopt relationship marketing in its entirely, the company will need convincing evidence that the destination will be worth the journey. If change is required, it must be demonstrated that relationship marketing can deliver the goods.

As we have seen, focusing on the most profitable individual customers and investing in these customers is one of the key factors of relationship marketing. We now discuss this aspect of the issue.

16.8 The individual customer approach[24]

One of the key tenets of relationship marketing is that, ideally, an organisation should focus on its most profitable customers. Profitability of a customer goes hand in hand with his or her LTV. Marketers should confine high-intensity relationships to the customers with the highest profit potential who actively seek customised products. The customers with lower profit potential, who offer less opportunity or need for customisation, should be served through low-cost, 'transactional' marketing strategies.

As we have seen, traditional marketing advocates that the marketer should focus on a specific segment, or a few segments, of the market. According to the philosophy of relationship marketing, the marketer should focus on recognising the importance of establishing relationships with individual customers. Three important changes have occurred that render segment-based marketing not only inappropriate, but also potentially damaging for a business:
1. Customers have become more sophisticated and knowledgeable.
2. There have been dramatic advances in technology.
3. Competing suppliers and products are cluttering the market.

Customer expectations are rising and competitors – often incorporating new technologies in aspects of their communications, internal and customer-facing processes, and production – have not only been meeting these expectations but also shaping them with yet higher standards of performance and value. Thus the cycle repeats itself, as customers ask for more and receive it.

Marketers need to recognise that the rules of competition have now been changed forever. They must accept that they have to decide the customer mix and the level of resources to be committed to each customer. They should know the so-called 'cost-to-serve' of each customer, and be able to produce an integrated view of customer profitability. All costs should be allocated to customers, including sales and marketing, finance, customer service and support, advertising, and so on. Customer profitability, including the LTV of customers, should then determine from which customers the company makes its money. Based on this, strategies need to be developed to treat each customer differently, for example for the company to invest more in the most profitable customers and less in the unprofitable ones.

Relationship marketing means that businesses should focus on customers who are appropriate for their strategy and reject others that do not fit. For this reason, companies should analyse their customer base, identify the levels of service necessary for each customer and implement a framework to balance resources so that customers receive exactly what they need. It requires strong leadership to reject unprofitable customers.

> **Customer rejection**
>
> An accounting/consulting firm, having been through an account review, decided to focus on a limited subset of companies, narrowing its worldwide priority focus customer list from several thousand firms to under 200. Although the move initially met stiff opposition among the firm's partners, it is now achieving record sales and profits.

16.9 Developing CRM strategies

Once an organisation has identified its most profitable customers, it can start segmenting the customer base according to various differentiators, such as profitability, potential value and its own organisational values. It has been proven that customer profitability increases as a result of differentiated and more personalised treatment.[25]

As we have seen, in order to decide the customer mix and the level of resources to be committed to each customer, an organisation should know the 'cost-to-serve' of each customer and be able to produce an integrated view of customer profitability. This includes allocating revenues, cost of goods sold, advertising, selling time, time for service, product returns, and so on. Not only is it important for marketers to understand which customers are profitable today, they also need to know which customers will be profitable tomorrow.

To treat each customer differently, it is necessary to group them into value-based tiers, that is, groups of customers with similar values to the organisation. In this way, the most valuable customers, the ones that have the most potential to grow and the unprofitable ones can be identified. It is necessary to look at each group more closely, and profile them by their needs and preferences.

Next, a specific set of strategies for retaining and growing the best customer must be defined. The organisation should recognise that these customers are the key to its success. But cost-reduction strategies should also be devised for the least profitable ones, or for those who cost the organisation more than they contribute to it.

After analysing the customers' LTV or future profitability, and the projected duration of their relationships, the organisation can place each of them into one of four categories, as shown in Figure 16.2 on the next page.

We now examine each quadrant in Figure 16.2.

16.9.1 Butterflies

These customers are profitable but 'un-loyal'. They could become less profitable or even unprofitable in the future. The challenge in managing these customers is for marketers to get as much benefit from them as possible in the short time that they are buying from the company. It is usually a mistake to manage these accounts by continuing to invest in them once their activity has ended. Research shows that attempts to convert butterflies into loyal customers are seldom successful.[26] Instead, marketers should devise ways to benefit from them and find the right moment to cease investing in them. In practice, this usually means a short-term hard sell through promotions and mailing blitzes that include special offers on other products, an approach that might well irritate loyal customers. If this and all other communications prove fruitless, the company should stop the contact altogether.

However, some of these customers may be made profitable and should not be ignored. Marketers should give them strategic attention, and ongoing opportunities to create mutual value that will enhance prospects for the organisation and the customers, so that the relationship will remain profitable and perhaps even merit reward in the future.

Figure 16.2: Selecting CRM strategies[27]

16.9.2 Strangers

These customers are not loyal and do not contribute to profits. Marketers should identify them as soon as possible, and should not invest anything in them. Customers who are currently unprofitable will be unprofitable in the future, and do not merit further attention. Thus, marketers can encourage them to go to competitors.

16.9.3 True friends

These are the ideal customers. They are profitable now and are likely to be profitable in the future. They are also loyal and tend to be satisfied with the existing arrangements with a company.

In managing true friends the risk is overkill. For example, if a mail-order company intensifies the level of contact through increased mailing, the loyal and profitable customer may be put off and sales may not be increased. People who receive a great deal of mail tend to throw it all away without looking at it. If they receive less mail, however, they are more likely to look at it. The mail-order company may find that its profitable, loyal customers are not among those who receive the most mail.

What is more important than constant contact is for companies to concentrate on finding ways to bring to the fore their true friends' feelings of loyalty, because 'true' believers are the most valuable customers of all.

16.9.4 Barnacles

Between 30 and 40% of an organisation's revenue base is generated by customers who, on a stand-alone basis, are not profitable because the size and volume of their transactions is too low. Like barnacles on the hull of a ship, they create additional 'drag'.

Properly managed, though, they can sometimes be turned into profitable customers. The first step is to determine whether the problem is a 'small wallet', that is, the customers are not valuable to begin with and are not worth chasing, or a 'small share of the wallet', that is, they could spend more and should be chased. Some grocery chains do this rather well. By looking closely at data on the type and number of products that individuals purchase, such as baby or pet food, the company derives reliable estimates of the size and share of the individual customers' wallets that it has already captured in each product category. It can easily distinguish which loyal customers are potentially profitable, and then offer them products associated with the ones already purchased, as well as certain other items in related categories.

There is no correct way to make loyalty profitable. A certain approach will be more suited to a business than others, depending on the profiles of the customers and the complexity of their distribution channels. Whatever the context, a company should never take for granted the idea that managing customers for loyalty is the same as managing them for profits. The only way to strengthen the link between profits and loyalty is to manage both at the same time. Fortunately, technology is making this task easier every day, allowing companies to record and analyse the often complex and sometimes even perverse behaviour of their customers.

16.10 Relationship with all stakeholders

Thus far we have looked at building relationships with end-customers only. We need to bear in mind that an organisation should also build relationships with other stakeholders, such as:
- employees
- suppliers
- intermediaries
- co-venture partners and strategic alliances
- investors
- the community.

The principles used to build relationships with end-customers apply also to building relationships with all other stakeholders, albeit with a somewhat different focus.

Building relationships with employees is probably one of the most important factors in the CRM process.

16.10.1 Building relationships with employees[28]

As we have seen, the employees of an organisation are central to building relationships with customers, given the link between employee satisfaction and customer satisfaction. It has been proven that the companies with the best profitability are those that are customer focused and that motivate and reward their employees. It was also found that the best organisations attract the best people by targeting specific traits that often include passion for their product or service. They focus on keeping their employees for longer, which in turn allows the employees to cultivate and develop insights about long-term relationships with customers.

Proceeding on the basis of mutual trust, the employee should be prepared to knowledgeably and happily entrust their future to the organisation, and the organisation should treat the gesture as sacred. A way to foster trust is to encourage self-managed work teams for key processes, thereby empowering employees to some extent to make decisions.

16.10.2 Enhancing employee relationships through internal marketing

The employees of a business may be viewed as an internal market, and they form part of an organisation's stakeholders. In CRM terms, we also refer to the employees as 'internal customers'. The objective of internal marketing within relationship marketing is to create relationships between management and employees, and between functions. Management has a responsibility to train and motivate employees, but should also persuade them to actively support marketing strategies. For this purpose, there should be open and free communication. The most successful companies are those that create channels allowing feedback to flow both upward and downward. Employees feel they have a stake in the organisation when they are listened to.

Internal marketing emerged from services marketing. The purpose of services marketing was to ensure that the frontline personnel – who have interactive relationships with external customers – handle the service encounter better and with greater independence. It is essential not only that the employees who are in contact with the customers are well informed about the organisation's offering, but also that they understand the business mission, goals, strategies and organisational processes. It is equally important for support staff to be knowledgeable in these areas in order to be able to handle the internal customer relationships successfully.

To a large extent, internal marketing must be interactive. Traditional methods of internal mass marketing, such as the distribution of formal memos and internal magazines, are inadequate. An intranet may help, but social gatherings are also important. As an introduction to the sales season, for example, large groups could gather to learn, be entertained and mix socially for a day or two.

16.10.3 Training and motivating employees

Training is an important part of building relationships with employees.

Training employees

Disneyland has its own university for training employees. McDonald's has the Hamburger University, which trains employees and franchisees. Taco Bell, one of the world's largest fast-food chains, uses the Muzak system to communicate with staff in all their restaurants. In South Africa, Telkom is planning to open its own university for training staff.

An organisation committed to building relationships with its customers needs to broaden its employees' scope of knowledge. The type of employee required has a broad understanding of how everything the company does lives up to customers' expectations. Employees today therefore need to increase their skills in processes and technologies, and have a greater understanding of the customers they serve.

Employees to master more processes

A customer calling to enquire about the operation of a new product should be met by someone who has the necessary information. This information will come either directly from the company employee, or indirectly from data warehouses or experts who have the knowledge required. This means that the employee should be able to engage new processes to access, assess and communicate the information.

Before starting a learning process, it is necessary for marketers to establish the identity of the target audience, its expectations, the knowledge it needs, the skills it needs and the way in which the learning process can be monitored. The following guidelines for training will help marketers to correctly plan the process of building relationships with employees:

○ **Identify** the relationship marketing skills required from the employees who are to participate in all the processes that deliver customer value.

○ **Assess** the performance of employees in respect of these skills, and **determine** any knowledge gaps by working through an assessment process with employees and communicating effectively in real time, not simply in a questionnaire or other impersonal manner.

○ **Develop** training programmes and technology support to re-skill and/or de-skill processes where employees require additional knowledge or context.

Employees are best motivated to demonstrate service spirit and customer orientation if they are well trained and informed. Motivating and rewarding employees appropriately does not necessarily involve money.

Rewards that do not involve money

○ Sprint PCS rewards strong sales performance with rotating assignments to coveted special projects.

○ Intel augments its stock options, profit sharing and performance bonuses with various achievement awards and eight-week paid sabbaticals for employees who spend seven years with the company.

○ Charles Schwab pays customer teams salaries as well as bonuses, based on customers' service experience and overall asset growth rather than commissions.

We will now examine the database – the component at the centre of an employee relationship.

16.10.4 Employee-centric database

Typically, relationships with customers will not be enduring or committed until the relationships with employees deepen. To ensure that new value will be created with employees, the best employees should be identified. Particular attention should be paid to those who can create the most value for the company.

This implies the need for an employee-centric database, which captures the full value of the employee by describing and seeking to qualify the value that each one creates for the company in relation to their total cost to the business. The database facilitates profiling the person, understanding the meaning they seek, knowing the barriers they face and the level and nature of bonding with the enterprise, and learning more about them as they make their personal journey.

The suitability of the person to do the job and their appropriateness to the customer personality, industry and other typology may be assisted by a human resource information system geared to achieve this. This entails populating the system with data crucial to the individual's development in terms that they find relevant, according to the meaning they want. The system could become a key organisational capability, matching people to processes and functions, and, most importantly, to customers. End-customer relationships often depend on people to go beyond standard policies and procedures to make a difference in problem resolution and to the attachment a customer experiences with the organisation. The policies in support of the system may sometimes need to change, for example employees may need to be given access to their files.

Just as the organisation will pay particular attention to the needs of its best customers, so too should it focus on its best employees. It should provide mass customised development for each, both in the functional nature of the job and in terms of their intellectual and interpersonal development. Some of the current employees may not be suitable for relationship marketing and may need to be trained and upgraded, or may have to be referred to companies that remain focused on mass marketing.

Case study[29]

TOYOTA: CONTINUOUS IMPROVEMENT AND MASS CUSTOMISATION

For three decades Toyota enlisted its employees in a relentless drive to find faster, more efficient methods to develop and make low-cost, defect-free cars. The results were stupendous. Toyota became the benchmark in the car industry for quality and low cost.

However, the same cannot be said for mass customisation, one of Toyota's pioneering efforts. With US companies finally catching up, Toyota's top managers set out in the late 1980s to use their highly skilled, flexible workforce to make varied and often individually customised products at the low cost of standardised, mass-produced goods. They saw this approach as a more advanced stage of continuous improvement.

By 1992, Toyota seemed to be well on its way to achieving its goals of lowering its new product development time to 18 months, offering customers a wide range of options for each model, and manufacturing and delivering a made-to-order car within three days.

However, Toyota ran into trouble and had to retreat, at least temporarily, from its goal of becoming a 'mass-customiser'. As production costs soared, top managers widened product development and model life cycles, and asked dealers to carry more inventory. After Toyota's investigations revealed that 20% of the product varieties accounted for 80% of the sales, it reduced its range of offerings by one-fifth.

What happened? Many answers to this question have been put forward, but according to Toyota's top managers, they had learned the hard way that mass customisation is not simply continuous improvement plus. Continuous improvement is a prerequisite for mass-customisation. However, continuous improvement and mass customisation require very different organisation structures, values, management roles and systems, learning methods, and ways of relating to customers.

One of the main causes of the problems was that while Toyota had been pursuing mass customisation, it had retained the structures and systems of continuous improvement organisations. Also, like mindless continuous improvers, engineers created technically elegant features, regardless of whether customers wanted the additional choices. In mass customisation, customer demand drives model varieties.

16.11 Summary

One business rule from the past has remained constant: the customer reigns supreme. Successful companies never lose sight of their customers' demands, and are careful to keep track of their needs as these evolve and change.

A company can attract and retain customers by knowing and delivering what they want, when they want it and how they want it, and by making it easy for customers to interact with it. Thus, CRM solutions have become strategic requirements in a customer-focused economy. These solutions can help organisations to attract and retain customers in highly competitive markets.

Questions for self-assessment

To assess your progress, answer these questions:
1. Explain how relationship marketing has evolved from the marketing concept.
2. Explain and illustrate why traditional marketing practices are no longer as relevant today as they used to be.
3. How does relationship marketing, and in particular CRM, solve the problems that are encountered with the traditional approach to marketing?
4. Explain the prerequisites for implementing CRM to determine if a company has the ability to adopt the CRM approach.
5. How does technology contribute to building relationships with customers?
6. Give an overview of the developments in technology which assist the implementation of CRM.
7. Explain relationship loyalty by referring to customer loyalty, customer retention and LTV of customers, and indicate the implications for any business of your choice.
8. How would you be able to find out whether a company is in a position to implement the principles of relationship marketing? In other words, what are the limitations of implementing CRM?
9. What are the principles involved in the individual customer approach in terms of CRM?
10. 'In order to decide the customer mix and the level of resources to be committed to each customer, an organisation can group customers into four categories in a matrix, based on profitability and the projected duration of their relationship.' In light of this statement, explain to a bank of your choice how it could develop CRM loyalty strategies based on the four categories in the matrix.
11. Explain to the bank the most important factors involved in building relationships with employees, and illustrate to the bank how they should implement these principles.
12. Refer to the case study, and answer the following questions:
    a. Identify all the mistakes that Toyota made in their pioneering effort with regard to mass customisation, and make suggestions on how to rectify them.
    b. Explain to Toyota the ways in which the company should have changed in order to implement mass customisation, or simply CRM.

Endnote references

1. Brink, A., Machado, R., Strydom, J.W. and Cant, M.C. 2001. *Customer Relationship Management Principles*. Unisa: Centre for Business Management, pp. 10–11.
2. Brink et al., op. cit., pp. 5–6.
3 Based on Brink, A. and Berndt, A. 2004. *Customer Relationship Management and Customer Service*. Lansdowne: Juta, pp. 3–6.
4. Drucker, P. 1954. *The Practice of Management*. New York: Harper & Row, p. 36.
5. Gummesson, E. 2002. *Total Relationship Marketing*. Oxford: Butterworth-Heinemann.
6. Mattsson, L.G. 1997. *Relationships in a Network Perspective*. Oxford: Elsevier.
7. Gordon, I.H. 1998. *Relationship Marketing*. Toronto: Wiley.
8. Christopher, M. 1996. From brand values to customer values. *Journal of Marketing Practice*, 2(1), 55–66.
9. Gronroos, C. 1994. From marketing mix to relationship marketing: Towards a paradigm shift in marketing. *Management Decisions*, 32(2), 4.
10. Hollensen, S. 2003. *Marketing Management: A Relationship Approach*. Harlow: Financial Times/ Prentice-Hall.
11. Brink et al., op. cit., p. 7.
12. Based on Brink, A. 2005a. *Customer Relationship Management Principles*. Unisa: Centre for Business Management, pp. 8–12.
13. Brink, A. 2005b. *Relationship Marketing*. Pretoria: Unisa, pp. 20–25.
14. Based on Brink and Berndt, op. cit., pp. 8–13.
15. Brink, A. 2005c. *Customer Relationship Management: Applied Strategy*. Pretoria: Unisa, pp. 8–15.
16. Egan, J. 2001. *Relationship Marketing*. Harlow: Pearson Education, p. 192.
17. Brink, 2005a, op. cit.
18. Gordon, op. cit., p. 173.
19. Based on Gordon, op. cit., pp. 186–94; and Egan, op. cit., pp. 189–201.
20. Levy, M and Weitz, B.A. 2004. *Retailing Management*. 5th ed. New York: McGraw-Hill, pp. 338–9.
21. Brink et al., op. cit., p. 4.
22. Based on Brink and Berndt, op. cit., pp. 36–7.
23. Brink and Berndt, op. cit., p. 37.
24. Based on Brink and Berndt, op. cit., pp. 17–19.
25. Du Plessis, P.J., Jooste, C.J. and Strydom, J.W. 2001. *Applied Strategic Marketing*. Sandown: Heinemann.
26. Reinartz, W. and Kumar, V. 2002. The mismanagement of customer loyalty. *Harvard Business Review*, 93.
27. Brink and Berndt, op. cit., p. 172.
28. Based on Gordon, op. cit., pp. 273–77; and Brink, 2005a, op. cit., pp. 30–34.
29. Gilmore, J.H. and Pine, B.J. 2000. *Markets of One*. Boston: Harvard Business School, pp. 149–50.

E-commerce and its value for customer behaviour

Learning Outcomes

After studying this chapter, you should be able to:

○ discuss the unique nature and benefits of new technologies such as the internet, the Web and e-commerce

○ explain the role of e-commerce in facilitating customer behaviour

○ describe the new e-commerce paradigms affecting customer behaviour

○ describe the factors that an organisation should consider when embracing technology

○ demonstrate how technology can be used in support of customer decision-making

○ identify some of the unique features of online customer behaviour.

17.1 Introduction

Bursting onto the scene in the early 1990s, the internet has had a significant impact on our business and social lives. With over 676 million users already on the internet at time of writing (2005),[1] the global value of business-to-customer e-commerce is expected to reach $12.8 trillion (R84 trillion) in 2006, which is up from approximately $40 billion (R280 billion) in 1999.[2,3] The internet clearly represents both a massive market environment and a powerful marketing channel that organisations simply cannot afford to ignore.

In this chapter, we look at the significance of these developments from a marketer's point of view, with particular focus on customer behaviour.

17.2 The three main features of the internet

The figures we provide above underline the growing importance of the internet as a channel for business-to-customer transactions. But what *is* the internet and why has it become so popular? The internet is essentially a global network of computer networks,[4] and the value of linking together these networks around the world is embodied in the three main functions of the internet, namely, a communications channel, an information source and a business environment.

17.2.1 A communications channel

The internet enables cheaper, faster and more effective communication between organisations and their customers. In this regard, the internet puts powerful tools such as e-mail, auto-response facilities, discussion forums, online chat services, interactive voice response, video conferencing and internet telephony in the hands of marketers.

17.2.2 An information source

The internet enables organisations to gather information about customers, including their profiles, online behaviour, and wants and needs. At the same time, the internet makes it possible to share vast amounts of information with customers, especially marketing information. Such information is invaluable in the customers' decision-making processes and helps in the relationship-building process between organisations and customers.

17.2.3 A business environment

The internet can be used as a marketing tool in order to advertise products, transact sales and brand a company, as well as to collect information about customers and markets. At the same time, the internet can be used just as effectively as a business tool. It can provide customer support, integrate suppliers and customers into the supply chain, improve customer relationships, enable electronic procurement, facilitate electronic billing and payments, and much more. It can also bring about cost savings through automation and integration with legacy systems. Legacy systems generally refer to older types of IT systems and applications that are mainframe-based and written in Cobol or other first-generation languages. They also sometimes refer to more recent server-based technologies and applications that may already have been displaced by newer systems.

17.3 The internet, the Web and e-commerce

The terms 'internet' and 'World Wide Web' (or 'Web', as we now call it) are often used as if they mean the same thing. However, they are essentially different. The **internet** includes the networking infrastructure and protocols that allow computers to communicate with each other, while the **Web** represents a user-friendly, point-and-click environment that serves as an interface with the internet. The Web provides us with a graphic way of organising and viewing the information that we find on the internet.

17.3.1 Advantages of the Web as a business tool

With the Web serving as a 'window' to the world of the internet, it is useful to consider the advantages of using the Web as a tool in business, particularly in customer behaviour. The advantages are as follows:

○ It is a **multimedia environment**. It can display video, sound, text, graphics and animations on the Web. This translates into a powerful business presentation tool, as well as an easy-to-use tool from the customer's point of view.

○ It is a **computer environment**. It can integrate the Web with other information technology (IT) infrastructure, such as software applications, databases and networks. This enables an organisation to tightly integrate and share information gathered about a customer among various applications. For example, the information supplied through an online registration form can immediately be entered into customer management applications such as GoldMine.

○ It is a **hyper-mediated environment**. It can bring or link together information from other sources spread across the globe, thereby helping to influence customer decision-making. For example, an astute car manufacturer may offer links on their website to an independent report about the great after-sales service it provides or perhaps to an article that highlights the fact that it won the Car of the Year award in Europe. In so doing, this hyper-mediated information helps to convince customers to buy the car.

○ Large amounts of **information** can easily be **stored and updated** on the internet, and this information is available to anyone with access to the internet. This is another powerful feature, as product details and other marketing information – useful in the decision-making process, but normally too much to include in a television, radio or print advertisement – can now be shared with customers through the internet.

○ Any information disseminated on the Web by a firm is **immediately available** to a **global audience**. Customers are no longer only local.

○ The information is **interactive**, which is an important component in building customer relationships. Customers can complete a reply or order form, access frequently asked questions, supply information through an online survey form, or send e-mail messages to the company concerned.

○ The Web is an **'always on' environment** – available 24 hours a day, every day of the year. This makes it possible to deliver customer value all the time.

○ The internet is a **flexible environment**. It can add or change information at the last moment, which is often extremely difficult to do using other marketing media. Again, this makes the internet a valuable tool for keeping customers informed of changing circumstances.

○ Many Web-based services can be **automated**, which saves an organisation money yet enables it to continually serve its customers. Automation is also an important component of customisation and personalisation, allowing the organisation to serve customers as individuals.

- If websites are well designed, the Web can be an **intuitive and easy-to-use channel** that facilitates interaction between customers and the organisation.
- The Web allows us to **reach the masses**. Currently the global market comprises over 500 million users, a figure which is expected to rise to one billion in the next few years.
- Organisations can **transact sales directly** on the Web, making it possible for income to be generated through this channel. This is a powerful feature, as an organisation can close a deal immediately with a satisfied customer – an important element of the decision-making process.

17.3.2 The internet and e-commerce

Conducting business on the internet and the Web – in particular, transacting sales – is more commonly referred to as 'electronic commerce' or 'e-commerce', which is a widely used term today. Sometimes we also use the term 'e-business', which refers to a more integrated view of online business pervading the entire organisation. E-commerce is about online marketing and transaction of sales – essentially the 'front-end', with which customers commonly interact. See Figure 17.1 on the next page for some examples.

There are many definitions of e-commerce, and the range bears testimony to the difficulty that organisations have in getting to grips with doing business in the virtual world. One of the more accurate definitions is proposed by the Gartner Group, which states that e-commerce is a 'dynamic set of technologies, applications and management systems that enable and manage relationships between an enterprise, its functions and processes and those of its customers, suppliers, value chain, community and/or industry'.[5]

It is clear that this definition links e-commerce not only with the internet or the Web. If we consider the full meaning of the term – namely, electronic commerce – then it is logical that we view e-commerce as the conducting of business *electronically*. Thus, interactive kiosks, call centres, interactive CDs, the short messaging service (SMS) available on cell phones, smart cards, interactive voice response (iVR), internet-based telephony systems and other similar technologies all fall within the broader definition of the term and should be considered in the context of facilitating customer service.

17.4 E-commerce and customer behaviour

In the new millennium, organisations are entering an era of customer-centred service and value creation in order to remain competitive. Indeed, customer care is no longer a differentiator, but a minimum requirement. To this end, market-intelligent organisations are:[6]

- viewing each and every transaction as an investment in a long-term customer relationship, that is, lifetime customers
- improving two-way, any-time, any-place communication with customers
- involving customers in improving their service levels by asking for constant feedback from them

Figure 17.1: Examples of typical South African e-commerce websites

○ collecting and sharing this customer interaction data across the value chain
○ segmenting customers into different value and profile groups
○ operationalising the use of customer information, that is, putting it to work
○ creating alternative channels or 'touch-points', such as websites, kiosks and call centres, for customers to reach and do business with them
○ enabling customers to take control of and personalise the channel of choice

○ ensuring that customers receive consistent service
○ creating communities of like-minded customers
○ using technology to support and enhance the interaction between customers, themselves and other participants in the value chain
○ reducing the prospect-to-sale cycle time by enabling immediate online buying.

This move to customer-centred organisations and customer relationship management (CRM) (see Chapter 16) is being accelerated by e-commerce technologies that now make it possible to facilitate and automate customer interaction and two-way communication at any time and place. E-commerce-driven CRM (eCRM) systems are able to track customers and their preferences, habits and buying patterns, and to remember them when they return. This information is made actionable and repeatable, which means that organisations can *proactively* react to the behaviour of customers by *personalising* their online experiences.

New eCRM systems should be flexible enough to constantly and regularly adjust to changing business rules. The firm then builds a predictive model to address alternative future scenarios, before putting the changes into place. These new changes, or 'adjustments', re-start the process. In this way, the firm creates a self-sustaining closed loop to optimise its relationship with customers, as shown in Figure 17.2.

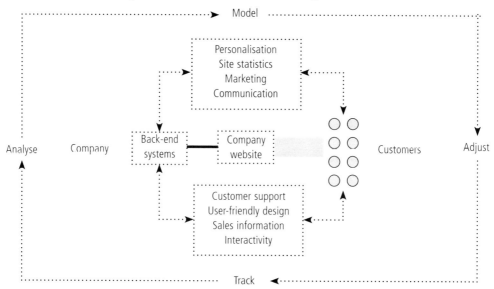

Figure 17.2: An online model for an eCRM system[7]

We need to stress that eCRM efforts represent **multi-channel strategies**. The Web alone is seldom the best solution. Indeed, organisations are increasingly turning to web-enabled call centres as a more encompassing solution. Other technologies such as iVR and interactive kiosks are also being considered as part of a total eCRM solution.

Research undertaken by PricewaterhouseCoopers, however, has shown that the more channels that are used, the lower the rate of success.[8] It is essential, therefore, for an organisation to identify two or three of the most appropriate technologies and channels that it can use to support customers and build relationships.

Finally, **community building** is an important component in the eCRM drive. Communities generate a sense of belonging for customers and provide a familiar environment where they can exchange ideas and information, share interests, build relationships, solve common problems and obtain support from other community members. As such, they serve as a powerful tool to help connect customers with the organisation. See Figure 17.3 for an example of an online buying/shopping community.

Figure 17.3: An example of an online buying/shopping community

17.4.1 The threat of the 'invisible customer'

Yet, almost paradoxically, the use of technologies such as the internet, call centres and interactive kiosks to facilitate customer interaction with organisations is creating a situation where customers rarely have face-to-face contact with these organisations – inevitably, we are moving into an era of the so-called 'invisible customer'.[9]

This situation is a serious threat to organisations, as customers may be treated more casually and indifferently than before. Clearly, this negates the very purpose of the use of technology, which is to bring customers closer to organisations. It is therefore essential that organisations consider three important factors when embracing technology:

1. Organisations must take care not to use technology for technology's sake. The implementation of a customer-orientated technology must serve a clearly understood, and specified, purpose.
2. The technology must be tried and tested to ensure that it fulfils its purpose. To begin with, it should always be available – there must be no engaged signals or websites that are down. Once connected, the technology should represent a positive first contact, stressing interest and concern. It should also facilitate the exploration of solutions to problems that exist either on a self-service basis or through the efforts of an agent. The experience should instil a 'positive glow' in customers. To this end, the interaction needs to be speedy, and all the relevant content must be made easily available to customers. In addition, the system should put the opportunity to transact a sale within easy reach of customers, and there must always be follow-up.

   The organisation must make the effort to keep the personal touch, especially for its more valued customers. Organisations with physical infrastructure, such as retail stores, have an advantage in this regard – the stores represent touch-points where customers can enjoy human contact and assistance.
3. Customer segmentation into different buying categories in order to establish personal contact with more important and lucrative customers will be an essential task of larger organisations. Technology will also then be used to address the masses and to support physical interactions in order to reduce the drag of time and place on the consumption process.

17.4.2 Dealing with e-commerce paradigm shifts

As organisations become familiar with the nature and functioning of the virtual world and the technologies associated with it, Sheth et al.[10] suggest that there are certain paradigms that they need to deal with. We now focus on these paradigms.

Disintermediation and reintermediation

In the pre-internet environment, customers relied heavily on intermediaries, such as retailers and wholesalers, in the consumption process. These intermediaries provided customers with broader and more convenient access to products and information about products, and thereby added the utility of time, place and information – including 'expert advice' – to the functional utility that the product inherently offered. At the same time, these intermediaries served as the producer's eyes and ears in the marketplace. They represented an essential channel of information about customer wants and needs. Therefore, building an effective distribution channel – one that can fulfil the above roles – has always been an essential element in the success of any producer.

   The internet is changing this. By using the internet as a transaction tool, it is now possible for organisations to put the ability to buy inside the customer's home or office. What is more, this facility is available 24 hours a day, 365 days a year. The utility of time and place has thus been extended to its maximum benefit. The internet brings the producer into direct contact with the final customer and in this way **disintermediates** its previous intermediary partners. Dislocations occur among producers, wholesalers and retailers as a result of disintermediation. This leads to another trend, namely, **reintermediation**, as new categories of online intermediaries – also referred to as 'cybermediaries' or 'infomediaries' – are created. Cybermediaries will bring value to customers by creating new ways of facilitating the interaction between producers and their customers.

Personalisation and customisation

Providing customers with value is about meeting their individual needs. This is where customisation and personalisation come into the picture. **Customisation** is the adaptation of a product or service by the supplier or producer to meet the individual needs of a customer. **Personalisation** exists where customers are in control and choose for themselves what they prefer to have from a range of options. The internet has the power to deliver both services.

Consider a car manufacturer that allows customers to create a personalised car from a range of component options – all available on a website. This is a genuine opportunity for the manufacturer to provide value to customers. The next logical step would be to integrate this service with the production systems located in the manufacturing plant, so that customers can order and have manufactured for themselves the car they have just created in 'cyberspace'. There are car manufacturers in the USA and Japan that are already doing this. Customers can even view snapshots of their cars at various stages in the production process – an effective way of 'bonding' the customer with the car, and with the organisation. In South Africa, BMW offers its customers the opportunity to create a 'virtual car', but if a customer wants to order that car, they must deal with a real salesperson.[11]

Shopping on demand

Customer behaviour in the future will increasingly be aimed at shopping and consuming on demand, without having to be restricted by time and place. Samsung, for example, is already advertising a fridge that will automatically detect when a homeowner has run out of things like milk, butter, cheese and eggs, and which then orders these items on the internet from an online supplier. Shopping on demand will include any-time, any-place procurement and consumption. As yet, this is not an easy matter to deal with from a supplier's point of view, but one that will nevertheless drive the production and distribution strategies of future organisations.

Customers as co-producers

Customers can be expected to become involved in designing and customising the products they buy. In the future, customer-centred organisations will open a direct channel between themselves, their production processes and customers. Customer complaints and requirements will be fed directly to the product designers and production engineers. This information will drive their activities and thinking, resulting in products that more closely match customers' needs.

Blurring between customer and business markets

As technology enables an increasing number of people to work from home, or at least conduct some of their business tasks at home, and as a growing number of workers undertake some of their personal tasks at the office, there will be a blurring between customer and business market boundaries. Already we can see a movement of home-based services and technologies to businesses, and vice versa. Many larger corporations, for example, provide laundry collection services and gyms at the office.

A power shift to customers (customer pull)

Although the saying 'The customer is king' has been used for a long time, organisations have not always practised the idea in their dealings with customers. However, there is now a *genuine* move towards putting power in the hands of customers – it is one of the few competitive advantages left.

Until now, the marketer has largely been in charge. The thinking was that if a company 'pushes out' a strong enough marketing message, it will draw customers. This is often referred to as 'push marketing', as the message is *pushed* to the customer. Traditional advertising media such as TV, radio and the print media are examples of typical push media, which give customers little choice about the message they receive.

New technologies are changing this paradigm, and customers now have the power to choose whether or not to receive the message marketers are putting out. There has consequently been a move from supplier-push to **customer-pull** marketing, and organisations are using interactive media such as the internet, interactive kiosks and interactive TV to this end.[12]

The automation of consumption

The power of technology to automate regular and standard activities, combined with the general shortage of time that an increasing number of customers have available, is likely to lead to the automation of consumption.

Online grocery shopping is one such example. As a customer uses an online shopping service more and more, so the service learns what they usually buy. Soon the program begins to function proactively, identifying commonly bought goods and asking the customer whether they want to repeat the purchases. The program could also learn to track the average time it takes for a customer to consume typical items of groceries and could proactively suggest that certain items be bought at given times. As this system grows more 'intelligent', the time-scarce customer may leave the entire shopping process to the program, especially if this can be combined with the abovementioned shopping-on-demand service that could 'fill any gaps'.

17.4.3 Facilitating customer decision-making through e-commerce

We discuss the decision-making process in Chapter 12. To review, the process includes problem recognition, information search, the evaluation of alternatives, the buying of goods and the post-buying experience. E-commerce puts powerful tools in the hands of marketers to facilitate each of these activities, as shown in Figure 17.4.

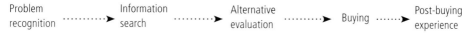

Problem recognition ·········➤ Information search ·········➤ Alternative evaluation ·········➤ Buying ·······➤ Post-buying experience

Figure 17.4: Facilitating the customer decision-making process[13]

We now explore each of the activities.

Problem recognition

While customers usually know when they have a problem, this is not always the case. Either they may be completely unaware of a problem, or they may sense a problem but not know what it is or what they should do about it. For example, an individual is experiencing problems with her computer. She is typing a text document and her word-processing package appears to be randomly inserting spaces in the middle of words. As a novice to word processors, the typist may assume that this is normal practice. She does not realise that the program's auto-spacing feature is turned on and that that is the cause of the problem. Imagine that there exists an astute website – The Typist's Friend – aimed at helping typists to improve their word processing capabilities. It offers an in-depth, online help-desk that the frustrated typist can search through and, simply by entering 'spacing problem' as a search term, she is directed to information that helps to solve her problem.

This is a simple example, but the idea could just as easily be applied to, for example, an injection-moulding company experiencing the irregular rejection of moulded plastic containers from its plant, because of the use of a molten plastic raw material with a higher-than-normal viscosity. In the e-commerce era, the supplier of the injection-moulding plant would run a website and call centre that its customers could access in order to help them with problem-solving.

Using collaborative and interactive methodologies, such as collaborative browsing and remote video cameras, organisations can provide a higher level of remote assistance to identify and solve problems. For example, The Typist's Friend could offer a daytime expert advisory service using collaborative browsing technology. This would allow an expert at the site to 'take control' of the typist's browser via the internet and experiment with the word-processing package to work out what is wrong with it. Once the expert has identified the problem, he can explain to the typist how to fix it herself in the future – she simply watches her screen as he moves the cursor around on her computer, showing her where to go and what options to select to correct the problem. He would generally use the telephone to explain to the customer what he is doing on the screen.

Information search

E-commerce technologies put huge amounts of interactive multimedia information at the disposal of decision-makers. Modern search algorithms and artificial intelligence make it easy to find the specific information required for problem-solving. Indeed, there are probably few managers today that have not at some stage used the internet in the workplace to find information.

Imagine that an insurance salesperson is advising a client about a particular life assurance product. The customer says he does not know what life assurance policies he currently has. The broker enters an identification code, the customer's surname and a short query into her cell phone's SMS facility and sends this message to the insurance company. The message is automatically recognised and handled by the insurance organisation's IT system, a query is generated and submitted to the database, the relevant information is obtained from the database and converted into an SMS format and a reply is sent to the broker's cell phone, listing the customer's life policies and their respective values. This service is also available online for customers to access for themselves. In this way, an information search – 'What life policies do I have at present?' – can assist in problem identification – 'What life policies do I still need, if any?'.

Evaluation of alternatives

Here again, technology has a role to play. The internet, for example, is a useful environment in which we can comparison-shop. More and more websites offer a service that allows us to choose a particular set of specifications for a product and obtain comparative prices for it from different suppliers. Besides pricing information, these comparisons provide detailed product information, reviews, ratings and a host of other value-added services. CD-ROMs and interactive kiosks are alternative technologies that we can use for comparison-shopping.

Of course, the customer could instead simply visit the corporate websites of competing product suppliers to learn more about what each organisation has to offer, assuming that they know who the competing suppliers are. The information may not be available within a single, easy-to-compare table or webpage, but it is probably with this method that most customers compare products online. Indeed, although online shopping is still in its infancy, many customers do their product comparisons online and then go to the store that offers the best deal in order actually to buy the product.

Furthermore, online shoppers are increasingly using intelligent agents to do the shopping for them. These agents are software programs that search the Web automatically for certain product specifications and price parameters that the customer has provided. The results that they produce are usually presented in a table containing a list of alternative websites that offer the product in question. The table also contains the prices of these products for comparison purposes, and any other relevant information that might help the customer to make a buying decision. As the number of webpages and online stores increases and the amount of 'clutter' that makes browsing the Web so difficult multiplies, so we can expect an increase in the number of shopping agents.

For example, in the case of the typist we imagined above, while she is interacting with the website, the site will auto-detect her word-processing package and suggest to her that she is using an old version of the particular package. It could advise her that a newer version is now available and is on special offer as an upgrade. Moreover, she is invited to subscribe to the site's e-newsletter, which is sent out each week.

This auto-detection is generally possible only in the case of software. However, many websites will track a user's movements to determine what the customer is interested in. Or the website may require the customer to complete a registration form that directly asks the customer what they are interested in. Based on the information provided by the customer on the registration form, or on the apparent interest detected through the tracking program, the site sends the customer appropriate product news and special offer information. It is considered proper to first ask the customer's permission before sending them this product information – this is referred to as **'permission marketing'**. However, some organisations send the customer the information first, and give them the option of indicating that they do not want to receive any further information in the future – often referred to as 'unsubscribing'.

Buying

Once customers have had the opportunity to evaluate the alternatives, the next stage in the decision-making process is the actual decision to buy something. Here again the internet makes it easy by enabling customers to buy online. The typist can immediately buy the latest version of the software she requires online. Indeed, in the case of 'bits and bytes' products such as software, the product can even be delivered immediately, directly to the customer.

Although many online shoppers are still reluctant to actually buy something online, mainly because of the concern about security and online payments using credit cards, this situation is changing. An increasing number of customers are choosing to shop and buy online.

It is important in the online environment for organisations to give customers as much information as possible about the buying process and its security, including warranties, to put to rest any fears that customers might have.

The post-buying experience

The final stage in the decision-making process is the post-buying experience, and here again the Web serves as a powerful tool to deal with any dissatisfaction the customer might have with the product. An **online help-desk**, for example, to deal with frequently asked questions or to provide any other information that would help the customer to use the product better is an extremely useful tool to ensure post-buying customer satisfaction.

An **online complaint form** is also helpful in this regard, and customers should be encouraged to submit their complaints about a product. It is essential, however, that such submissions be acknowledged and feedback provided as to what the organisation plans to do about them. This two-way communication can be effective in giving customers a positive image of the company and in building relationships between the two.

A similar tool is an **online survey**, which asks customers to provide feedback about certain aspects of an organisation's products and customer service. Recent research undertaken in the USA has revealed that just the process of surveying customers results in much higher brand awareness and a positive product image among customers.[14] Essentially, the organisation should make customers feel that they and their opinions are important to the organisation, thereby encouraging a sense of 'belonging'.

17.4.4 Habitual decision-making

The Web can also play a valuable role when the customers' decision-making becomes routine, such as when a customer always buys the same cleaning products. The ability of software to detect regular or routine purchases and to automate this task is a major advantage in facilitating habitual decision-making. For instance, online grocery stores regularly track what their customers buy, and if the software detects that a customer is buying the same product again and again, the software can do one of two things:

1. It can pre-select these items into the customer's shopping basket, with the option that the customer simply agrees to all of the selected items using a single check box. The customer can deselect any particular item if necessary.
2. If the customer grows confident with this type of habitual buying, the entire process can be automated, with the selected products being delivered to the customer on a pre-determined day without the customer doing anything.

What is more, the program can indicate to customers when:
○ a product is on special offer – in order to encourage customers to buy more of the product
○ a substitute product is on special offer – even providing an easy comparison of the two products
○ changes to a product have occurred – for example, a new package size
○ newer or better products are available – to encourage so-called 'up-selling'
○ complementary products are available – to encourage 'cross-selling'.

All of these features add value for customers, especially in an environment where time, effort, money and space are at a premium. The Web is also a particularly valuable tool for the retailer to use to encourage increased sales, in addition to the abovementioned up-selling and cross-selling.

17.4.5 Getting to know individual customers

Before value can be delivered to customers and even before any effort can be made to help customers in their decision-making, it is essential that an organisation clearly understands what values drive each customer. To this end, the internet can be used to gather information about customers.

By using 'cookies', organisations can track and record the online activities of customers. This can prove valuable in understanding an individual customer's mindset. **Cookies** are little data files containing information about the recorded actions of a visitor to a website. In other words, when a customer visits an organisation's website, the organisation uses special software to track how the customer navigates through the site, the pages that they visit, whether they buy anything and any other relevant information. These files are then stored on the customer's own computer.

The next time the customer visits the website, the organisation's server first checks the customer's computer for cookies that the server might have left there on the customer's previous visit. If a cookie is found, the server checks to see what information is in the cookie and then can react to the information by customising the website in the light of the profile that has been built up on the customer. Besides personalising the online experience for customers, these cookies can also be used to build up a profile on the customer over time – a valuable resource for any marketer.

The organisation can also use online surveys to learn more about a customer. These can be comprehensive surveys with many questions, or they can be narrow surveys that focus only on certain pieces of information, for example 'How do you rate our response time to your e-mail queries?'. There is also a move towards using the virtual discussion facilities of the internet to run virtual focus groups in order to better understand what drives customers. The advantage of these surveys and focus groups is speed and cost – they can be launched quickly and are much less expensive than a normal survey or focus group.

The move towards a more integrated organisational information system, combining both front-end and back-end IT systems, and incorporating data-mining and data-warehousing technologies, makes it possible for organisations to unlock a far greater amount of information about customers than was possible before.

17.5 Online customer behaviour

The online world is different from the physical world. We now consider some of the factors unique to customer behaviour on the internet.[15]

17.5.1 Online shopping behaviour

We need to further our understanding of online shopping behaviour. The Web is a fairly new environment that is rather different from the physical marketplace. Shopping catalogues are always easily at hand, there is no need for us to wait for a salesperson and there are no queues.

The shy shopper can remain anonymous, yet be aggressive – there are no face-to-face confrontations or unpleasant disagreements. For extroverts, the internet may not be exactly what they want, as they generally prefer face-to-face contact, yet there is still the opportunity to interact with others using discussion and chat forums, instant messaging and e-mail.

The virtual world is particular popular among the youth – referred to as Generation Y (which we discussed in Chapter 6) – and recent findings reveal that the electronic community never sleeps and knows no physical boundaries. The young people who 'live' there are building an entirely new set of values regarding what constitutes a community and what their social and political responsibilities are.[16]

17.5.2 Isolation and integration

It is argued that the internet not only removes the restriction of geography, but also the constraint of isolation for whatever reason, be it sickness, a physical handicap, a busy schedule, bad weather or social shyness. The internet also makes it possible for like-minded people to come together as a community and share their interests or concerns. Physical or social isolation can easily be overcome in this way.

17.5.3 An abbreviated attention span

For some individuals, the time spent online and in front of a computer can be tiring and frustrating, leading to aborted online interactions and even a rejection of this technology. For others, the long wait between the loading of webpages or the verbose, vague or complicated navigation structures often found online can translate into frustration with the organisation in question and/or brand rejection.

17.5.4 Instant gratification

The more time customers spend online, the more they will demand faster download times and instant gratification with regard to the information, product or service they are looking for. In the USA, organisations are already finding it difficult to put together the logistics that will deliver a product ordered online as quickly as possible.

17.5.5 Your world in a monitor

Customers are increasingly turning to the computer monitor as their preferred shopping environment. There may well be a world of people, infrastructure and services that lies behind the glare of the screen, but it is nevertheless the physical monitor with which users will interact. This has serious implications for an organisation. It is a focused world where organisational weaknesses are quickly highlighted and where it is easy for customers to move on to the next supplier – hence the saying that 'A competitor is only a click away'.

In a sense, it is also a rather limiting world, constrained by pixels, screen size, software version, processor speed and connection speed. Organisations will need to become adept at reaching out and 'touching' customers – **web usability**, which is the measure of the effectiveness of websites, is certain to become an important weapon for the online marketer.

17.5.6 Dependence on shopping agents

Referring to the abovementioned shopping agents, we can expect an increase in the use of such programs in future and that the programs themselves will improve in their ease of use, function and effectiveness. Therefore, while organisations are hard at work digitising and automating many of their customer services and interactions, customers are doing the same. They are instructing their software 'robots' to do the shopping for them, such as request information, fill in forms, make certain payments and much more. Soon a time may come when organisations need to consider not how to attract and keep their online customers, but instead how to engage the customers' shopping agents.

17.5.7 Too much information

Information overload is a problem that many people face. The increase in e-mail alone is becoming a serious issue. In 2004, almost 17 billion e-mails were exchanged every day. Fifteen billion of these were automatically generated, much of it '**spam**', or electronic junk mail.[17] Given this deluge of e-mail and an equally large number of webpages (already exceeding ten billion), online customers are finding it increasingly difficult to deal with the information overload, and companies that do not quickly and clearly demonstrate to their online customers the value that they offer will find that customers soon desert them.

Case study

FORD – AN EXAMPLE OF A CUSTOMER-CENTRED CAR PRODUCER?[18]

Motor vehicle producers such as Ford, BMW, Toyota and others are all highly concerned with customer relationship management. It makes good business sense, after all. A motor vehicle is a big and expensive item that most customers buy only occasionally, and there is fierce competition for this business. A satisfied customer, committed to a brand, is likely to be a repeat customer, giving the car producer concerned a major advantage over its competitors. Most of the car producers have therefore turned to the internet and e-commerce to build customer-oriented features into their websites.

In the case of the Ford website, this includes:
- A **showroom**, where customers can see detailed information about the cars in the Ford range, including colours, a picture gallery, specifications, accessories, interior and engine – customers can even download e-mercials of specific vehicles
- A **gallery** of glitzy pictures of the various models in the Ford range, which customers can download as screensavers..

⑈➡

- O A comprehensive list of Ford **dealers** in the country, browsable by province or postal code.
- O A link to the **Ford Credit website**, which includes a range of financial options, budgeting advice, financial calculators and an online finance application facility.
- O A **contact page**, where customers will find a telephone number for the Ford call centre, as well as an online form that they can complete in order to ask for more information about a particular car, or ask for a salesperson to call on them at some later stage.
- O A **brochure page**, where customers can ask for a car brochure to be posted to them.
- O A **news page**, listing news about Ford and its products.
- O A **test-drive page**, which enables a customer to arrange a test drive of a particular Ford model.
- O A **calculator page**, which enables a customer to work out what a particular model would cost in terms of financing.
- O A **links page**, which offers links to other Ford websites around the world.

See Figure 17.5 for the Ford homepage.

Figure 17.5: The Ford homepage

17.6 Summary

In this chapter, we addressed some of the issues that play a role in an organisation's use of technology to enhance customers' interaction with them. We recognised the fact that e-commerce refers not only to the internet and the Web, but also to all other forms of electronic technologies. We examined some of the benefits that the Web offers managers in facilitating customer behaviour.

We discussed the characteristics of market-intelligent organisations, including customer-centredness, a focus on value creation and use of technology to enhance customers' interaction. We explored some of the emerging trends in customer behaviour, and examined e-commerce in the context of customer decision-making, using the model showing the various stages of the buying process as a framework. Using the premise that online customer behaviour is different from customer behaviour in the traditional market-place, we looked at the unique features affecting the former.

Questions for self-assessment

To assess your progress, answer these questions:
1. Identify the primary benefits of the World Wide Web as a tool for facilitating and shaping customer behaviour.
2. Explain what market-intelligent organisations do.
3. Discuss the emerging trends in customer behaviour.
4. Explain how e-commerce can be used to support customer decision-making.
5. Discuss how e-commerce can be used to facilitate habitual decision-making.
6. Identify some of the unique features of online customer behaviour.
7. Referring to the case study, answer the following questions:
   a. Do you think the Ford website is customer-oriented? Explain your reasoning.
   b. Discuss how each of the features on the website might enhance the customer experience.
   c. What other features or services could Ford add to their website?

Endnote references

1. 2002. E-Commerce and Development Report. UNCTAD, p. 37. Available on the internet from: www.unctad.org/ (accessed 12 October 2005).
2. 2002. NUA Internet Surveys. How many online? Available on the internet from: www.nua.ie/surveys/how_many_online/index.html (accessed 12 October 2005).
3. OECD. 2001. Consumers in the online market place: Business-to-consumer statistics. Addendum to a presentation delivered by the OECD Directorate for Science, Technology and Industry, Berlin. Available on the internet from: www.oecd.org/pdf/M00000000/M00000261.pdf (accessed 18 February 2005).
4. Bothma, C.H. 2000. E-commerce for South African Managers. Pretoria: Interactive Reality.
5. ACL Services Ltd. 2002. Auditing e-business: Challenges and opportunities. E-commerce White Paper. ACL. Available on the internet from: www.continuousauditing.org/Papers/bouwer.pdf (accessed 7 August 2002).
6. Gordon, H. and Roth, S. 2000. The need for a market-intelligent enterprise (MIE). In S.A. Brown (ed.). Customer Relationship Management: A Strategic Imperative in the World of Business. Toronto: Wiley, pp. 23–4.
7. Adapted from Morris, H. 1999. Closing the loop to optimize – Customer relationships. Available on the internet from: www.cio.com/sponsors/091599_sequent.html (accessed 12 October 2005).
8. Collart, D. 2000. Foreword. In Brown, op. cit., p. xvii.
9. Clegg, B. 2000. The Invisible Customer: Strategies for Successful Customer Service down the Wire. London: Kogan Page, p. 7.
10. Sheth, J.N., Eshghi, A. and Krishnan, B. 2001. Internet Marketing. Orlando: Harcourt, pp. 79–85.
11. BMW SA. Available on the internet from: www.bmw.co.za (accessed 12 October 2005).

12. Seddon, J. 2000. From push to pull: Changing the paradigm for customer relationship management. *Journal of Interactive Marketing*, 2(1), pp. 19–28.
13. Adapted from Sheth, J.N., Mittal, B. and Newman, B.I. 1999. *Customer Behavior: Consumer Behavior and Beyond*. Orlando: Dryden, p. 520.
14. Dholakia, P.M. and Morwitz, V.G. 2002. How surveys influence customers. Preview of research published in the *Harvard Business Review*. Available on the internet from: www.informative.com/news/newsArticles/HBRArticle.pdf (accessed 12 October 2005).
15. Based on Tiernan, B. 2000. *e-Tailing*. Chicago: Dearborn, pp. 52–6.
16. Omelia, J. 1998. Understanding Generation Y: A look at the next wave of US consumers. *Global Cosmetic Industry*, 163(6), pp. 90–92.
17. Schwarz, K.D. 1998. Improving customer service through e-mail. Available on the internet from: www.datamation.com/PlugIn/workbench/ecom/11serv.html (accessed 12 October 2005).
18. Available on the internet from: www.ford.co.za.

Index

Note: Entries in **bold type** refer to tables, diagrams and figures.